Using PageMaker® on the IBM®

Diane Burns
S. Venit

Que™ Corporation
Indianapolis, Indiana

Library of Congress Catalog No.: 86-063978
ISBN 0-88022-285-9

91 90 89 88 87   8 7 6 5 4 3 2

Interpretation of the printing code: the rightmost double-digit number is the year of the book's printing; the rightmost single-digit number, the number of the book's printing. For example, a printing code of 87-1 shows that the first printing of the book occurred in 1987.

Using PageMaker on the IBM is based on PageMaker Version 1.0a and includes instructions for the IBM Personal System/2.

About the Authors

Diane Burns
Sharyn Venit

Diane Burns and Sharyn Venit own and operate TechArt, a graphic design and production shop in San Francisco, where they use PageMaker as one of their primary tools. At TechArt they designed and developed *The PageMaker Classroom*, training material for Aldus Corporation.

Burns and Venit have coauthored 5 books and over 50 articles about microcomputer applications in the business environment and have trained hundreds of users in hands-on computer classes for business applications. Their articles have appeared in national magazines, including *PC Magazine*, *PC Week*, and *Publish!* Their articles include reviews of laser typesetters, page composition systems, and desktop publishers. Both are experienced in training the staffs of large corporations in the use of microcomputers and in developing the written training materials used. Their books integrate text and graphics to provide practical applications for new users.

Product Director
David Paul Ewing

Editorial Director
David F. Noble, Ph.D.

Managing Editor
Gregory Croy

Editors
Jeannine Freudenberger, M.A.
Pamela Fullerton
Ann Campbell Holcombe, M.S.Ed.

Technical Editor
Karen Rose

Production Foreman
Dennis Sheehan

Production
Jennifer Matthews
Joe Ramon
Peter Tocco
Lynne Tone
Carrie L. Torres

Composed in Times Roman and Que Digital
by Que Corporation

Cover designed by
Listenberger Design Associates

Book designed by
Ellen J Sickle

Table of Contents

Part II   Designing and Producing Different Types of Publications 249

8   Typography.................................... 251

11   Designing and Producing Newsletters and Similar Publications   359

12   Creating Overhead Transparencies, Slides, and Handouts   391

13   Creating Brochures, Price Lists, and Directories........................... 421

14 Creating Fliers and Display Ads............. 459

Acknowledgments

This book would not have been possible without the help of the following individuals and corporations: Aldus Corporation; American Electronics Association; Ben Bowermeister, Aldus Corporation; Chris Chenard; Laurie Deutsch, McCutchen, Doyle, and Brown and Enerson; Leticia Gueverra, TechArt San Francisco; Ike Computer Company; Judy Jacobson, Aldus Corporation; Know How, Inc.; Sam Louie, TechArt San Francisco; Grace Moore, TechArt San Francisco; National Association of Professional Women (NAPW); Barry Owen; Pacific Heights; Shana Penn, stylist; Emily Rosenberg, Venture Development Service; Mike Sherwood, Aldus Corporation; Robert Sheridan; David Smith, designer; TechArt San Francisco; Thompson and Company; and Zablocki Printing Company.

Trademark Acknowledgments

Que Corporation has made every effort to supply trademark information about company names, products, and services mentioned in this book. Trademarks indicated below were derived from various sources. Que Corporation cannot attest to the accuracy of this information.

1-2-3, Symphony, and Freelance Plus are registered trademarks and Lotus Manuscript is a trademark of Lotus Development Corporation.

Apple, LaserWriter, and LaserWriter Plus are registered trademarks and Macintosh is a trademark of Apple Computer, Inc.

AST TurboLaser is a registered trademark of AST Research, Inc.

AutoCAD is a registered trademark of Autodesk, Incorporated.

Bitstream is a registered trademark of Bitstream Inc. of Cambridge.

COMPAQ Deskpro 286 and 386 are registered trademarks of COMPAQ Computer Corporation.

Canon is a registered trademark of Canon, Inc.

ConoVision 2800 is a trademark of Conographic Corporation.

Epson FX-80 is a trademark of EPSON America, Inc.

HALO DPE is a trademark of Media Cybernetics, Inc.

Hercules Graphics Card is a trademark of Hercules Computer Technology.

Hewlett-Packard, LaserJet, LaserJet Plus, and Vectra are registered trademarks and ScanJet is a trademark of Hewlett-Packard Co.

IBM is a registered trademark and IBM Proprinter, IBM Personal System/2, IBM DisplayWriter, and IBM DisplayWrite 3 are trademarks of International Business Machines Corporation.

In*a*Vision and Windows Draw are trademarks and Micrografx is a registered trademark of Micrografx, Inc.

Instinct is a registered trademark of Cadlogic Systems Corporation.

LaserView is a trademark of Sigma Designs, Inc.

Linotronic is a trademark of Allied Linotype.

LogiMouse is a registered trademark of Logitech, Inc.

Manager Mouse is a registered trademark of The Torrington Company.

Moniterm Viking I is a registered trademark of Moniterm Corporation.

Microsoft, Microsoft Mouse, Microsoft Windows, Windows Paint, Windows Print, Windows Draw, Windows Write, Microsoft Word, and MS-DOS are registered trademarks of Microsoft Corporation.

Conventions Used in This Book

The conventions used in this book have been established to help you learn to use the program quickly and easily. As much as possible, the conventions correspond with those used in the PageMaker documentation.

Names of PageMaker menus are written as they appear on the screen, with an initial capital letter: File menu.

PageMaker commands, options, menu choices, and dialog boxes are written as they appear on the screen and are enclosed by quotation marks: "Actual size". Commands followed by three periods always display a dialog box, where you supply more information: "New...".

Names of files and directories are written in all capital letters: WINDOWS, NEWS.TXT.

PageMaker tools and icons are written in all lowercase letters: text tool, pencil icon.

Keys are referred to as they appear on the keyboard of an IBM PC.

Any words or letters that the user types are written in boldface letters: **INSTALL PM**.

This book contains a large number of illustrations. Reproductions of screens are enclosed by rounded-corner marks; reproductions of printouts are enclosed by square corner marks.

Introduction

PageMaker®, by Aldus Corporation, is one of the most sophisticated page-layout programs for microcomputers on the market today. First released for the Macintosh™ computer in July, 1985, and now available for IBM® PCs, Personal System/2™, and compatibles (including WANG® systems), PageMaker is credited with starting the desktop publishing revolution.

Briefly, desktop publishing uses personal computers to produce typeset-quality text and clean graphic images, merge the text and graphics on the same page, and then print the merged product on a high-resolution laser printer or typesetter. With desktop publishing, you eliminate the need for rulers, ink pens, blue lines, boards, wax, tape, screens, and X-ACTO® knives as you produce final camera-ready pages for offset printing or photocopier reproduction.

PageMaker is an especially easy-to-use desktop publishing program. With it, you perform all the production tasks on a screen that displays an exact image of your page as it will be printed. Because of the program's power and sophistication, almost any user can produce professional publications with a minimum investment in equipment and software.

Why a Book about PageMaker?

Although PageMaker basics are easy to learn, developing efficient operating techniques can take months. Moreover, the fact that the *program* is capable of producing beautiful publications does not guarantee that every *user* will be capable of producing beautiful documents without getting advice from professional designers or studying graphic design.

Using PageMaker on the IBM helps solve the problems of the less experienced user. This book offers tips to help you both design and produce a wide variety of documents. The types included range from short brochures and fliers to full-length books and reports.

This book is not intended as a substitute for Aldus' excellent documentation. Instead, *Using PageMaker on the IBM* is a practical guide that goes beyond the basics of the manual and provides practical examples and hints for using the program in a production environment.

Who Should Use This Book?

No matter what your background and experience, you will need to learn new methods and terms when you enter the world of desktop publishing. This book brings together the special vocabularies of the typesetter, designer, word processor, and computer operator to explain clearly the concepts from these disciplines, which are merged in desktop publishing applications.

This book is intended for professional designers, typesetters, publishers, people in corporate publishing departments, and independent publishers who are already using or considering using PageMaker. The numerous examples demonstrate the wide range of possibilities with PageMaker. By studying these examples and tips, users can improve the appearance of their documents, as well as reduce the overall production time.

Although this book is addressed specifically to PC users, those using PageMaker on the Macintosh or WANG systems also will find these examples and suggestions useful.

What Is in This Book?

Part I of the book (Chapters 1-7) addresses PageMaker's basic features and describes the steps involved in producing a publication. Part II (Chapter 8-9) offers specific advice about defining the type specifications and designing and producing different types of publications. Part III (Chapters 10-14) presents examples of publications produced by PageMaker and highlights specific design and production tips. If you already are using PageMaker on the PC (or version 2.0 on the Macintosh), you may want to skim Part I, looking for the Tips; read Part II; and use Part III as a reference source when you have a specific production problem.

Part I

The information in Part I lays a foundation. Chapter 1 defines desktop publishing and describes PageMaker's basic functions. After a comparison of PageMaker with word-processing and graphics programs, the material describes the final form of a page created in PageMaker and gives an overview of the production process.

Chapter 2 discusses the equipment required to run PageMaker and provides a list of optional equipment and compatible software programs. Then comes a discussion of the steps for installing and starting the program for the first time, with descriptions of the opening screens and menu commands. This chapter also offers a quick summary of the steps necessary to produce a complete PageMaker document.

Chapter 3 discusses the three methods of placing text on a PageMaker page (typing, placing, or pasting) and distinguishes between formatting in a word-processing program and formatting in PageMaker. Chapter 4 demonstrates the techniques you use to edit and format text once it is in PageMaker, including changing paragraph formats (alignment and spacing) and character formats (font, leading, and kerning).

Chapter 5 describes PageMaker's built-in graphics tools and tells how to bring in graphics created in other programs. You learn how to scale and crop graphics and how to position graphics on a page. You also see the differences between object-oriented and bit-mapped graphics.

Chapter 6 presents detailed instructions and tips for laying out a document page-by-page and step-by-step, after you have prepared your text and graphics files in other programs. This chapter illustrates how to use PageMaker's ruler line, master page grid, and automatic page numbering capability. The chapter also offers specific tips about creating layouts that call for mixed formats, such as different numbers of columns, and unusual formats such as text wrapped around graphics.

Chapter 7 takes you through the steps involved in printing with different printers, including Apple®'s LaserWriter®, Hewlett-Packard®'s LaserJet™, and Allied's Linotronic™ typesetters. You learn how to work with multiple printers and how to print thumbnails and tabloid-size newspapers.

Part II

In Part II, the discussion focuses on design decisions. Chapter 8 begins with a discussion from the typographer's view of a document—specifically, how to select fonts for a document. The chapter also tells which fonts are available for each printer, how you install the fonts, and how you create new fonts. As a result, you learn what fonts, font sizes, and font styles are available for your printer before you start the design process. You also learn how to work with a limited font selection. The chapter contains definitions and illustrations of leading and kerning and gives special tips on copy fitting.

Chapter 9 explores the process of designing with PageMaker, including the development of a series of different design alternatives for a single document and the use of master pages and templates to standardize a series of documents. This chapter offers special tips for creating design specifications for files from different sources, including word processors and graphics programs. In this chapter, you also find tips about preparing pages for the offset printer, including photographs and color separations.

Part III

Part III, Chapters 10 through 14, offers several examples of different types of documents. These examples illustrate specific design principles and production tips that were given in Part II. The examples also demonstrate the range of fonts available with different printers.

Appendix and Glossary

The Appendix provides a list of hardware and software manufacturers who offer products compatible with PageMaker.

The Glossary includes terms used on PageMaker's menus and dialog boxes as well as traditional terms used in typesetting, design, and printing.

We hope that you enjoy *Using PageMaker on the IBM* and that you profit from the many useful tips offered in this book.

I

The Production Process with PageMaker

Part I introduces PageMaker's outstanding features and the basic steps of the production process. You'll learn about the equipment needed for an installation of PageMaker, the advantages of creating text in a word processor, and the methods of bringing text and graphics into PageMaker. Part I also teaches you how to edit and format text and graphics in PageMaker itself. In short, Part I gets you started in PageMaker.

Part I at a Glance

Overview of PageMaker and Desktop Publishing

1

PageMaker is a page-layout program with which you can compose a complete document—both text and graphics—and preview full pages on-screen before printing the document on a high-resolution printer or typesetter. When combined with text and graphics from other software programs, PageMaker's commands can perform the functions of the layout artist's tools and materials: typeset galleys of type, photographic reproductions of line art, halftones of photographs, pens, pressure-sensitive tapes, knives, wax, blue lines, boards, and acetate overlays.

Created by Aldus Corporation for the Macintosh computer and LaserWriter printer, PageMaker helped launch the revolution called desktop publishing. This book tells you how to use PageMaker for desktop publishing on your IBM PC and its compatibles. You also will find tips and suggestions for using PageMaker on Macintosh and WANG computers.

In this chapter, you see how desktop publishing has evolved from technological breakthroughs in a number of different fields and how desktop publishing is changing the way printed pages are produced in many different communication areas. You learn about PageMaker's basic capabilities by examining a page that was produced using PageMaker and several other programs, and you get an overview of the production process itself.

Development of Desktop Publishing

The term *desktop publishing* did not exist just a few years ago. It was originally coined by one of the designers of the PageMaker program, Paul Brainerd, the president of Aldus Corporation. The term itself quickly caught on as a way of describing the combined results of changes in the technologies. First, the cost of microcomputer equipment for on-screen graphics processing dropped noticeably. New breakthroughs in laser technology also reduced drastically the price of high-resolution printers and typesetters. To take advantage of the new laser printers, manufacturers of type started designing new typefaces or adapting traditional typeface designs for these printers. Software developers then realized that these factors had opened the way for the creation of programs, like PageMaker, that merge text and graphics directly on-screen. These factors formed the basis of complete "publishing" systems assembled for revolutionary new low prices (see fig. 1.1).

Fig. 1.1. Elements of desktop publishing.

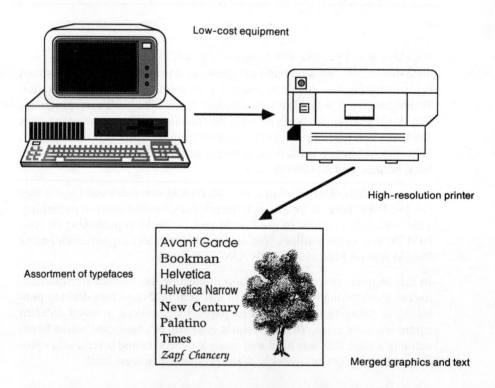

Low-cost equipment

High-resolution printer

Assortment of typefaces

Avant Garde
Bookman
Helvetica
Helvetica Narrow
New Century
Palatino
Times
Zapf Chancery

Merged graphics and text

This combination of capabilities, now embodied in PageMaker, has a tremendous impact on typesetters, designers, professional publishers, corporate publications departments, and small businesses (as well as those of us who dream of producing our own great novels). To understand the significance of these capabilities, you need to understand something about these factors, which are the roots of desktop publishing.

Using Low-Cost Equipment

The cost of the computer itself has fallen significantly during the past few years. Owning a personal computer once meant a $5,000 investment in a simple computer with no software and little memory. Nowadays, many PCs that are priced under $2,000 already include the extra memory and graphics capabilities required for desktop publishing functions.

Using High-Resolution Printers

With the introduction of laser printers into the market, high-resolution printers and typesetters became more widely available. *Resolution* is a measure of the sharpness of the edges of printed characters and graphics. The resolution is commonly measured by the number of dots, or spots, per inch. For example, dot-matrix printers print both text and graphics by pushing pins onto the ribbon that strikes the paper. The resolution of the image is limited by the number of thin metal rods the manufacturer puts in the printing head. The common resolution for dot-matrix printers is 120 dots per inch (see the example shown in fig. 1.2). This resolution is considered coarse compared to the resolution of typesetting equipment, which uses a different technology to print images at 1,200 or 2,400 dots per inch (see fig. 1.2). Typesetting equipment, however, can cost from $20,000 to $100,000.

This revolution in printing came when Canon introduced the 300-dots-per-inch laser engine that is used in many printers now available for less than $5,000, such as Apple's LaserWriter (used to print the example shown in fig. 1.2) and Hewlett-Packard's LaserJet. Other manufacturers also have made laser printers that print 400 or 600 dots per inch. Allied's Linotronic typesetters use the same laser technology to phototypeset images at 1,200 or 2,400 dots per inch. PageMaker was designed to take full advantage of these printers' capabilities.

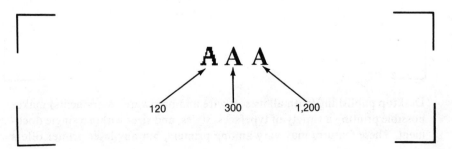

Fig. 1.2. Characters printed at 120, 300, and 1,200, dots per inch.

To the untrained eye, documents printed at 300, 1,200, and 2,400 dots per inch appear the same. The text looks typeset at all three of these settings. As a result, desktop publishers can achieve—with PageMaker and a $5,000 printer—the same results that previously required an investment of more than $20,000.

Professional typesetters and others in the graphics industry, however, can see the difference between 300 and 1,200, and this difference can affect the appearance of the final document when it is reproduced with offset printing. These professionals can get the best results from PageMaker with $30,000 typesetting equipment, and many typesetting service bureaus offer printing services for PageMaker publications.

Using Different Typefaces

The changes in printers naturally led to changes in typefaces for these printers. A typeface formats a character. For example, Courier and Helvetica are two different typefaces. Desktop publishing introduces a broader range of typefaces than was ever possible in most office environments. Not so long ago, a typewriter had only one typeface—either pica or elite. More recently, you could change the typeface in your typewriter or printer, by changing the daisy wheel or type element; but each document usually showed only one typeface throughout—Courier, for example. You could mix boldface and normal characters on a page, but you couldn't mix normal characters and italic. Dot-matrix printers made possible mixing normal, boldface, and italic and printing different sizes of letters; but the jaggedness of the output was considered inferior to the output of letter-quality printers (see fig. 1.3).

Fig. 1.3. Typefaces from a daisy-wheel printer, a dot-matrix printer, and a laser printer.

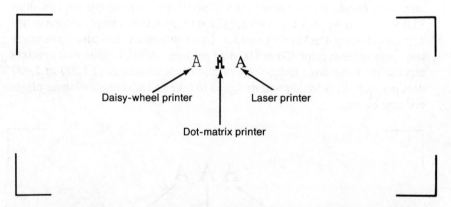

Desktop publishing (with all its software and hardware components) makes possible printing a variety of typefaces, styles, and sizes within a single document. These features may vary among printers, but any laser printer offers more than two options—the limit for most letter-quality printers. Desktop publishing still does not offer as many typefaces as professional typesetting, but new typefaces are being added to the list daily. And PageMaker supports many of the new typefaces as downloadable fonts.

Merging Text and Graphics

The end result of these changes was the development of software programs to merge text and graphics. Merging text and graphics on a screen is not new. Professional page-composition systems have been doing this for years. *TIME* magazine, for example, started composing pages on a computer more than 15 years ago. Time, Inc., however, paid more than $250,000 for that system. Most publishers continued to use X-ACTO knives and wax to paste up printed text and line art on boards—usually slow and tedious work (see fig. 1.4).

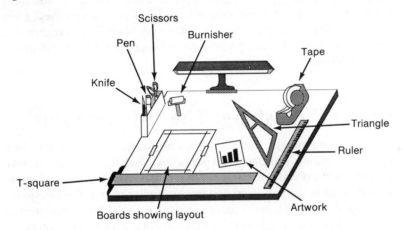

Fig. 1.4. Tools of manual pasteup.

Meanwhile, microcomputer users were able to produce text with word-processing programs and graphics with their spreadsheets or drawing programs, but the output from these various programs rarely was merged on-screen or on paper. Instead, reports were assembled with all the graphics in an appendix, for instance; or the graphics were printed on pages without text and merged with the text pages later. A few adventurous departments, using scissors and glue, left spaces in the text and inserted the graphics later.

PageMaker is one of the first page-composition packages that actually eliminates pasteup. With PageMaker, microcomputer users can merge text from a word processor with graphics from a drawing program and print fully composed documents in one step. The basic tools of on-screen pasteup are the computer with its various programs and a high-resolution printer. Page-

Maker incorporates the text and graphics from other programs. The graphics then can be copied and scaled directly on the screen. After the layout of all the pages is finished, any changes made on one page cause linked text on following pages to shift automatically.

With PageMaker, you actually can see on the screen exactly what the page will look like; PageMaker is a *WYSIWYG* system (pronounced "wizzy-wig"). WYSIWYG means that "what you see is what you get." In other words, you actually can see the graphics and the text on the screen exactly as they will appear on the printed page (with slight variations due to the difference in resolution between the screen and the printer). Only two such packages were available for the IBM PC before 1984, and both were priced at more than $5,000.

As you can see, desktop publishing has emerged as a result of technological breakthroughs in several fields. The fact that desktop publishing programs are personal computer applications means that many individuals and businesses already have desktop publishing facilities. Even though these users might not consider themselves publishers, they are beginning to realize that these new capabilities have the potential of making *all* printed communications more effective.

Desktop Publishing: The "Melting Pot"

Desktop publishing merges traditions from four different disciplines: typesetting, graphic design, printing, and computing. Each discipline has its own set of technical terms and standards. Professionals from all these fields find that they need to add a few terms to their vocabularies in order to "speak" desktop publishing. Users are discovering, for example, that terms such as *spot*, *dot*, and *pixel* can mean the same thing and that each area of experience has something to teach the others.

Typesetting Traditions

Typesetters work with codes: one code sets the typeface, another sets the style, another the size, and so on. The disadvantage of the code-based systems is that they are difficult to learn. Furthermore, many typesetting machines lack the capability of previewing exactly how the text will look when it is printed; the typesetters have to print the text through the photochemical typesetting device in order to find any errors in the coding.

The advantage of traditional typesetting is precision. Most typesetting systems let you set the spacing between lines and letters in finer increments than are possible with PageMaker, for instance. Furthermore, typesetters can set the width or depth of text precisely in code rather than using a less precise ruler line. Typesetters, therefore, may need to adapt their demands and expectations to match the capabilities of desktop publishing systems.

Although menu-driven systems like PageMaker can be slower than typesetting machines, some typesetters welcome desktop publishing's low-cost WYSIWYG screens, short learning curve, and economical printing options. At the same time, desktop publishers can learn something from typesetting. The typesetter can tell you how many words or characters of a certain typeface and size will fit in a given space, for instance. You'll learn some of the tricks of the typesetter's trade later in this book.

Design Traditions

Professional designers take pride in their ability to take a client's tastes and ideas and translate them into beautiful finished products. The process of putting design ideas down on paper has been painstaking and time-consuming in the past, as is reflected in the fees charged for design services.

In the beginning, some professional designers may balk at the idea of using a computer for such creative tasks, not to mention the lower billing amounts. These economies, however, can result in increased demand for design services at all levels.

With PageMaker, you can rough out design ideas quickly and deliver what looks like finished work rather than the traditional penciled sketches in the preliminary stages. In many cases, the efforts of producing a design idea with PageMaker are not lost because the same files can be fine-tuned for final production. Furthermore, the same files can be duplicated and modified for other documents in the same series or for similar documents in another series. In the long run, therefore, the economies of designing with desktop publishing techniques will pass through to clients as lower design fees.

The fact that even amateurs can produce nice-looking designs with Page-Maker seems a bit frightening to the professionals, but good design will always require the knowledge and skills of the designer trade. You will learn some of these principles in this book, as well as production methods that will help you match the designer's tradition of excellence with the business community's demand for expedience.

Printing Traditions

Not so long ago, to make multiple copies of a document, you had to take your masters to an offset printer to get the best results. More recently, some copying equipment has been improved to the point of producing good-quality reproductions. In either case, the final result depended on the condition of the original page. You needed clean, clear, black images on white paper.

Now, laser printers print the entire image, including gray scales, directly on any color paper you choose. You can print hundreds of "originals" for immediate distribution. If you take the same image to an offset printer, however, you may find that the camera which makes plates does not see the image the same way you do. In later chapters in this book, you learn how to prepare your master for offset printing. You also learn the vocabulary you need in order to communicate with the printer, who is accustomed to dealing with graphics professionals. You will also discover that PageMaker pages can be sent directly to a plate-making output device.

Computing Traditions

The final elements in the "melting pot" come directly from the computer industry. *Pixels* and *screen fonts*, *ports* and *baud rates*, *icons* and *menus* are all terms that you will become familiar with as you are moving into desktop publishing from these other trades.

Throughout this book, you will find production tips for getting the most out of your computer, for using PageMaker's commands, for using DOS commands, and for implementing other procedures unique to computer operation. You will see the importance of developing good "housekeeping" habits for your disk files, just as many designers practice good housekeeping with the papers and tools in their studios.

PageMaker

We have talked about desktop publishing in general, using PageMaker as an example. What about PageMaker itself? How is it similar to and different from some other programs you may be using on your computer?

PageMaker is a page-composition program. It enables you to compose pages using elements created in other programs, as well as elements created in PageMaker. Figure 1.5 shows some examples of the types of publications that you can produce using PageMaker.

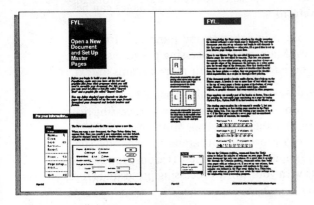

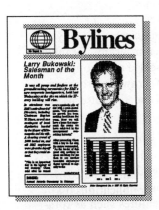

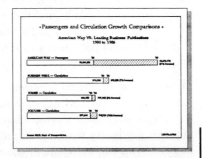

Fig. 1.5. Publications produced using PageMaker.

You can type text directly into PageMaker, or you can type text using your word processor and then bring that text onto a PageMaker page. You can create simple graphics directly in PageMaker, and you can bring in graphics that were created using a graphics program such as Windows Draw™ or PC Paintbrush®. Once the graphics are in PageMaker, you can easily move them around on the page, change their size and shape, duplicate them, or delete them.

PageMaker and Word Processors

You can type text in PageMaker much the way that you type text with your word processor. On the PageMaker screen, though, the text looks very nearly as it will when you print the page. For example, you can see the difference between 12-point Times italic and 14-point Helvetica boldface. Most word processors do not let you make or mix type selections this way, let alone display different typefaces on the screen.

PageMaker also lets you arrange text in columns and jump text from one page to other nonsequential pages. Many word-processing programs do not handle multiple columns or let you interweave two or more streams of text.

On the other hand, because PageMaker is a graphics-oriented program, it tends to be much slower for word processing than a true word-processing program, which is designed for speed. Furthermore, PageMaker does not have some of the functions that most word-processing programs incorporate, such as global searches and mail-merge capabilities. For these reasons, you should prepare and edit long documents with your word-processing program before bringing the text into PageMaker.

PageMaker and Graphics Programs

You can draw simple graphics, such as lines, boxes, and circles, directly in PageMaker; or you can bring in graphics created by other programs. Graphic images that have been brought into PageMaker can be scaled and cropped to fit the space allowed on individual pages. Like most drawing programs, PageMaker also has menus of different types of lines and fill patterns for graphic objects.

Most drawing programs accommodate some form of text entry, but they do not handle text formatting, such as columnar layouts and tabular data, the way Pagemaker does. Furthermore, most graphics programs do not handle multiple pages. By working directly with a drawing or painting program, however, you can use some of the more sophisticated features such as rotation, airbrush effects, and pixel-by-pixel image manipulation. You also can use a paint program to clean up images that have been digitized through a scanner.

The Final PageMaker Document

A completed PageMaker publication may be composed of text and graphics created in PageMaker and brought in from other programs. Figure 1.6 shows a typical page created using PageMaker. The text was typed in a word-processing program, Microsoft® Word®. Then the text was moved into PageMaker with the program's "Place..." command. The bar graph was created in 1-2-3®. Detailed graphics were created in a drawing program, Windows Draw. A scanned image was modified using PC Paintbrush before the image was placed on the page in PageMaker. Some of the short text elements, such as the banner text across the top of the page, were typed directly into PageMaker. Hairline rules and boxes were added with PageMaker's graphics tools. Running feet and automatic page numbering were set up on the publication's master page, the page that holds the basic grid and other elements appearing on every page of the publication.

Fig. 1.6. A page created using PageMaker.

Figure 1.6 shows you what's possible with PageMaker. The rest of the book shows you how to create such a document.

PageMaker and the Publishing Cycle

PageMaker brings together functions that were once divided among different people at different locations. For example, before desktop publishing, a typist might have typed the text of a newsletter and sent the file, either on paper or on disk, to the typesetter for formatting and typesetting. Meanwhile, the graphics department might have used a computer or pens and ink to create the graphic images for an outside service to photostat to the correct size. Eventually, the galleys of type and the reproductions of the figures would land on a drafting table, where the layout artist would use X-ACTO knives and wax to trim the paper and paste it down on boards into final pages.

With PageMaker, the same person can type the text, draw the graphics, and compose the pages on-screen. Just because one person is performing all the steps does not mean that the steps themselves are much different. However, the one person responsible for the entire production may be strong in some areas and weak in others. Many desktop publishing departments, therefore, still divide the tasks of desktop publishing among different people. Nevertheless, when the production team is small (as is common in desktop environments), weak spots still can develop in the production cycle—areas in which no one on the team has experience. This book provides tips in areas of expertise where you and your team may be lacking.

Division of Responsibilities

Even if only one person produces the document, the responsibilities can still be divided conceptually among different publishing roles: production manager, author, editor, copy editor, designer, illustrator, and production crew.

The production manager oversees the entire project, makes sure that everyone else involved meets the schedule, or adjusts the schedule as needed.

The author delivers complete, accurate text, probably on a disk. An author also can format the text if the author knows the final design specifications.

An editor then reviews the text and graphics to be sure that the document is clear and complete. The copy editor reads the text and graphics for grammatical, typographical, and formatting errors and makes sure that all references to figures or other sections or pages of the document are accurate. The editors also may be responsible for tone and content.

The designer determines the overall appearance of the pages: paper size and orientation, margins, and basic grid structure. The designer also specifies the typefaces, sizes, and styles to be used in the document and also may specify fill patterns or treatments for all illustrations. The illustrator produces the graphics files that will be placed on the page. In some cases, the illustrator may be the author or the designer.

Finally, the production crew refers loosely to anyone who actually sits down at the computer and uses PageMaker to assemble the pages. The production crew also may format the text with a word processor if the formatting has not been done by the author.

As stated previously, these responsibilities may be performed by one person or divided among several, depending on the situation. A knowledge of these different functions will help you more easily produce high-quality work with PageMaker.

Steps in the Production Process

Whether you produce a document from start to finish on your own or work with a team, you can set up an efficient production schedule if you recognize the steps involved in a typical production cycle. Some of these steps can take place at the same time, and some projects may drop some steps or call for a slightly different sequence. A typical production schedule showing relationships among the following steps is shown in a GANNT chart in figure 1.7. (A GANNT chart shows the length of time allowed for each task in a project, as well as the *period* of time during which it must be completed in order to meet the schedule—that is, the earliest start and latest finish dates.)

1. Gather the team, identify the division of responsibilities, and prepare the production schedule. In this case, the team may include the client ordering the work as well as the production group; or a "team" may be simply the talents of one individual who sketches a single timetable.

2. Write the text with a word processor. Even if the authors are not using the same type of computer that you will be using with PageMaker, almost any text can be converted or telecommunicated before the final PageMaker stage.

3. Sketch or list illustration ideas.

4. Determine the design specifications, including

   - Typefaces, sizes, and styles for different elements within the text

   - Basic text format

     Will the paragraphs have a first line indentation? What space will be left between paragraphs? Will the text be justified? Will headings be flush left or centered?

   - Basic page layout or grid

     Include page size, margins, orientation, number of columns, and positions of other nonprinting guides. Some of this information is required before you start a new PageMaker document.

- Final (maximum) size of illustrations as well as typefaces, sizes, and styles to be used within the illustrations and in the captions

- Final page count or the range of pages expected to be filled

  This count will help you decide whether to divide a long publication into smaller documents or sections, determine how to divide the publication, and estimate the printing costs. The page count has traditionally been performed after the text is written because the design itself may be affected by the content and structure of the text. If, however, the authors know the design specifications (including page count) before writing the text, the authors can participate in the production by setting tabs and other format requirements.

5. Let one or more editors read the text:

   - One reading for accuracy and completeness of the content

   - One reading for grammar and consistency of usage

   - One reading to mark the text according to the design specifications

     Most professionals find that one person cannot read on all these levels in one round. If you have only one reader, these readings should be done separately.

6. Edit and format the text with the word processor. Do as much of the editing as possible in the word-processing program before you place the text in PageMaker.

7. Create the illustrations using the graphics program best suited for each:

   - Scanners can digitize photographs and line drawings that would be difficult to reproduce otherwise.

   - Paint-type programs are best suited for working with digitized images and for "fine art" illustrations—original artwork that is never modified or edited.

   - Drafting-type packages are best suited for line art and technical illustrations.

   - Spreadsheets or charting programs are most efficient for charts that are derived from tables of numbers.

   - Some illustrations or graphic elements can be added directly in PageMaker.

8. Set up a single directory on the hard disk for this document or publication; move all the text and graphics files into that directory.

9. Use PageMaker to create a master template for the entire publication (if the publication requires more than one document file). The document always includes the master page elements and can include elements on the numbered pages as well.

10. Use PageMaker to build each document. Use the PageMaker tools to insert the text and graphics files created in other programs and add elements.

11. Print the publication. (This step will occur many times during the production cycle.)

12. When the project is finished, copy all the files related to that publication onto one or more floppy disks.

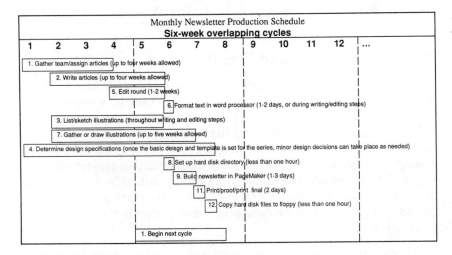

Fig. 1.7. A typical production schedule.

Some of these steps are essential for any PageMaker production; but other steps, such as designing a publication from scratch, are considered advanced. If you are new to design, you should probably start with small projects that mimic other document designs. After you have learned how to use Page-Maker's basic features (described in Chapters 3 to 7) and tried building a few pages, you can tackle the advanced topics covered in Chapters 8 and 9. Table 1.1 gives the levels of the steps and lists the chapters that provide information about each step.

Table 1.1
Where To Find More Information

Step	Level	Chapter
1	Basic	Chapter 1 (this section)
2	Basic	Chapter 3
3	Advanced	Chapter 9
4	Advanced	Chapters 8 and 9
5	(not covered in this book)	
6	Basic	Chapter 3
	Advanced	Chapters 8 and 9
7	Basic	Chapter 5
8	Basic	Chapter 2
9	Basic	Chapter 6
	Advanced	Chapter 9
10	Basic	Chapters 3, 4, 5, 6
11	Basic	Chapter 7
12	Basic	Chapter 2

Quality, Economy, and Deadline

More than almost any other business or activity, publishing is ruled by deadlines. You can't send June's news out in July, for example. When the published document is part of a larger product package, the marketing or distribution group will probably want the documents finished as soon as the product itself is ready for shipment, although you can't write the text until the product is complete. One way or another, the publication department is always pushed to complete everything as quickly as possible. Therefore, professionals must struggle to maintain the highest quality in their productions. In the end, you will find that no document is ever perfect in the eyes of those who worked on it.

When you produced your business reports with a word processor and a letter-quality printer, you probably spent more time editing the content of the document than you spent formatting the pages. With desktop publishing, you may find that the reverse is true; you will spend more time formatting than editing.

This reversal of formatting and editing will be especially true if your production group includes professional designers or typesetters, who will not tolerate inconsistencies and misalignments. During the final stages, you will discover that what you see on a 72-dots-per-inch screen is not exactly what you get when you print with a 300-dots-per-inch laser printer. You may then have to make fine adjustments to the file to get exactly what you want.

You will probably need to print your document more than once during the final production stages, so plan for several printings as part of the production schedule. Remember that printing time can be significant when you are producing a 400-page book with graphics.

Summary

The process of putting text and graphics on a page is changing drastically and quickly, thanks to the revolution called desktop publishing. PageMaker holds a central position in this new field and is quickly transforming the appearance of a wide range of printed communications. Some people believe that desktop publishing with personal computers will revolutionize our communications as significantly as Gutenberg's press did in the fifteenth century. In the end, of course, the real impact of this revolution will not be on the production methods alone, but on the readers who will benefit from the clearly formatted and illustrated publications.

Getting Started 2

PageMaker runs in the Microsoft Windows environment on a PC AT or compatible system. PageMaker's 3-1/2-inch version runs on the IBM Personal System/2 and the Toshiba 3100 portable. The PC AT-compatible system must run under MS-DOS® and have a minimum of 512K of memory (640K is preferable), a graphics card, and a hard disk for storage. Microsoft Windows is a graphic front end for MS-DOS. If you do not already have Microsoft Windows, you still may be able run PageMaker. Beginning with Version 1.0a, specially marked PageMaker packages come with the so-called "run time" version of Windows. During the PageMaker installation process, you specify which version of Windows you are using.

This chapter takes you through the basic steps from installing PageMaker to starting the program. You see how DOS and Windows work, and you are given enough detail to use PageMaker efficiently. You learn how to manage your files on a hard disk and copy files to floppy disks. You also learn how to create directories for your own publications, as well as the directories used by Windows and PageMaker.

The last part of the chapter presents a quick run-through of the steps involved in producing a document, from verifying that you have all the necessary disk files, to printing the final copy. Later chapters provide more details and tips on how to execute the steps in this chapter. Beginners may need to refer to users' manuals for DOS and the Windows operating environment to find information not presented in this book.

If you already know how to use PageMaker on the Macintosh, you should review the first part of this chapter to learn how DOS and Windows work. If you are familiar with DOS and Windows, you can skip ahead to the section on installing PageMaker. If someone else has installed PageMaker on your system, find out whether you need to change to a particular directory and then read the section called "Starting PageMaker." If you are new to both Windows and PageMaker, you probably should read this entire chapter before starting the installation process.

Equipment Configuration

Along with PageMaker, a full desktop-publishing system may include a computer, a draft-quality dot-matrix printer, a high-resolution printer for final copies, and a scanning device. Before installing PageMaker on your system, be sure that your equipment meets PageMaker's minimum requirements. Generally, a system equipped to run Microsoft Windows also runs PageMaker.

Hardware Requirements

PageMaker runs on Apple's Macintosh computer, IBM® ATs and equivalents (including Hewlett-Packard's Vectra® Systems), the IBM Personal System/2 series, and some models of WANG systems. By definition, the term *IBM AT* indicates that the system includes a hard disk and some of the other elements shown in figure 2.1. Compatible PC systems that can run PageMaker must have a hard disk and include all the elements listed in figure 2.1.

Fig. 2.1. Elements required for running PageMaker on a PC AT.

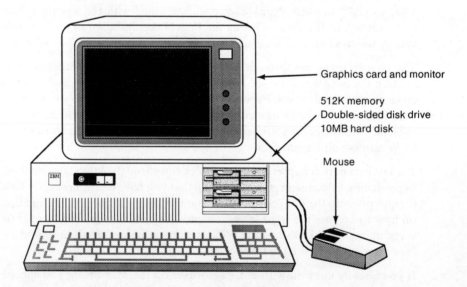

Graphics card and monitor

512K memory
Double-sided disk drive
10MB hard disk

Mouse

PC systems require at least a 10-megabyte hard disk and a double-sided disk drive. Be sure that your hard disk has at least 2 megabytes of free space before you install PageMaker. Microsoft Windows requires a half megabyte of hard-disk storage, and the PageMaker program requires an additional 1.5 megabytes.

PageMaker requires at least 512K of memory in RAM, but the program tends to run faster with more memory. You should have at least 640K of memory to use PageMaker on a network or with other memory-resident programs. With the retail version of Microsoft Windows and sufficient memory, you can run more than one program at a time.

The PC also requires a graphics card, such as an Enhanced Graphics Adapter (EGA) or Hercules Graphics Card™, and a monochrome or color monitor that can display graphics. The better the screen resolution of your monitor, the more accurately your screen displays text and graphics. Finally, to work with Windows and PageMaker, you need a pointing device, such as a mouse.

Before trying to install PageMaker, you should already have on your system both DOS and the Windows program (if you have it). If you do not have the complete separately packaged Windows program, you can run PageMaker under the run-time version that comes on the installation disk (described in this chapter). Microsoft Windows V1.04 and 2.0 provide seven drivers to support the IBM Personal System/2 series.

Printers

PageMaker documents can be printed on some dot-matrix printers, but the final printer usually is a laser printer or typesetter. At this writing, the printers supported by the program include

    Hewlett-Packard LaserJet and LaserJet Plus®
    Apple LaserWriter
    Allied Linotronic 100 or 300
    Any PostScript® printer
    Any PCL printer that is fully HP LaserJet compatible

Your choice of a printer affects your options for selecting fonts on the menu. Chapter 7 explains how to install printer drivers and fonts and how to choose different printers on a multiprinter network. For specific instructions on installing a particular printer, refer to the documentation provided with your equipment.

Scanners

Artwork that is already on paper can be *digitized* (converted to a disk file PageMaker can use) with a scanning device. Digitized images are saved in one of the paint-type formats supported by PageMaker or in Microsoft's Tag Image File Format (TIFF). Canon, Datacopy Corporation, DEST Corporation, Microtek Lab, Inc., Hewlett-Packard, and Ricoh Systems, Inc. also make software programs that create scanned images which can be saved in one of these formats.

PageMaker Installation

Before actually installing PageMaker on your system, you should read through this description of the installation process. The installation program asks you what kind of equipment you are using (keyboard, graphics adapter, pointing device, or monitor) and what names to use for the Windows and PageMaker directories. You should decide the answers to these questions before you start the installation process. (As you will see, though, the installation program lets you stop the process if you come to a question that you cannot answer.) If you change your equipment configuration after installation, you must reinstall Windows and PageMaker.

The PageMaker package includes five disks that are required for installation. These PageMaker disks are labeled INSTALL, PROGRAM, DICTIONARY, TUTORIAL, and DRIVERS.

Begin the installation process by inserting the INSTALL program disk into drive A and typing **INSTALL** at the A prompt. The installation program begins telling you what to do. The following steps explain when and how you can change the settings made during the installation process.

On a hard disk system, the normal prompt shown on the screen is

    C>

To begin the PageMaker installation process, turn on your computer and wait until the prompt is displayed. Insert the INSTALL disk into drive A and change to drive A by typing

    A:

Then press the Enter key. (Pressing Enter activates your responses to all prompts and commands.)

Starting the INSTALL Program

With the INSTALL disk in drive A, type

    INSTALL

Press the Enter key. The first screen display explains that the INSTALL program will copy the PageMaker programs, copy tutorial files to a separate subdirectory, and set up Microsoft Windows if that program is not already set up. INSTALL then gives you step-by-step installation instructions.

At any point during the installation process, you can press the Q key to leave the process and cancel the installation. Normally, you press the letter C to continue the installation process and view the next screen. In this case, the next screen lists the five PageMaker disks you need in order to install the program. Again, you can press Q to stop the procedure if you do not have all these disks, or you can press C to continue.

Naming the PageMaker Directory

The next screen prompts you to select the directory you want to use for the PageMaker program and related files. A hard disk is normally divided into a number of directories. A directory is a named portion of the disk that is reserved for a set of files. This method of organizing files is often called a *hierarchical* filing system because each directory can have subdirectories. You can create a new directory or use one already on your hard disk. If you use an established directory, be sure to specify the full path name of the directory.

If you do not know how to create directories and copy files into them, you should read the section "Managing Files and Directories" in this chapter. Make sure that you do not already have on your hard disk a directory named PM allocated for other uses. If such a directory exists, use a different name for the PageMaker directory. If you decide to stop installing the program, just press Enter and leave the installation process from the next screen display. This screen gives you a chance to change the directory name, quit, or continue the installation process.

Assume that you've chosen the C:\PM directory. If this is what you want, press C to continue. If not, press D to change the directory.

Once you select a directory for the PageMaker files, the installation program begins copying files from the five disks into the directory, prompting you for each disk as needed. To respond, you must insert the requested disk and press C to continue or Q to stop the installation process.

Installing Run-Time Windows

After the PageMaker disks have been copied, the next screen offers you the options of using your own previously installed complete Windows program, installing a full version of Windows, or installing the abbreviated run-time version supplied on the PageMaker installation disk. The run-time version provides all the features of the Windows environment that you need for PageMaker but omits MS-DOS Executive and other Windows applications. If you have Windows on your system, press C.

To install the run-time version of Windows, press W. INSTALL determines whether you are installing a full version of Windows or the run-time version, by the disk you have inserted in the disk drive.

If you press W when you are installing the run-time version, the installation process prompts you to identify your keyboard, mouse type and port, and graphics adapter and screen, and to provide other information about your system. You also are asked to install selected printer drivers (see the following sections). If you have already installed the full Windows program on your system, be sure to press C to bypass installation of the run-time version of Windows.

Installing Aldus Printer Drivers

The Windows program comes with drivers for a wide range of printers that PageMaker can use to print publications. Aldus also supplies its own drivers for some printers, usually to improve the quality and reduce printing time. The PageMaker installation program lets you use the drivers you already have installed for Windows or replace those drivers with those supplied by Aldus. You should always use the latest drivers on the PageMaker disks because these drivers are usually the most recent. Windows V1.04 has V1.04 drivers; PageMaker V1.0a is shipped with V1.05 PCC and PostScript drivers.

Unless you know that your version of Windows is newer than your version of PageMaker, you should probably install the drivers supplied by Aldus. If you choose not to replace the printer drivers at this time, you can do so later, using the Windows Control Panel or DOS commands for copying files from one directory to another (see "Naming and Copying Files," in this chapter).

Finally, if you already have installed Windows, you should specify the name of the Windows directory where the active drivers are stored. The installation program displays the appropriate prompts:

```
Since Microsoft Windows was not set up during this process,
INSTALL needs to know the directory where Windows resides.

To accept C:\WINDOWS as the directory:

    -press the Enter key
```

To specify a different directory:

            –Use the BACKSPACE key to delete characters.
            –Type the new directory name
            –Press the Enter key

[C:\WINDOWS

After you name the Windows directory, the next screen lists printer drivers supplied by Aldus. These drivers can be moved into the Windows directory. You can install as many drivers as you like. If you know that you will be using only one printer model for all your jobs, install only the driver for that printer. If some of your publications may use other printer models or if you use different printers for draft copies and final copies, install the driver for each printer you will use, even if the printers are on separate networks. Your default printer will be the first one installed.

The next screen lists the Aldus drivers that supplement or replace drivers that may have been installed with the full Windows system. You choose the printer driver you need by selecting one of the options. After you select one printer, the installation program gives you a chance to choose as many as four more printers. Be sure to install drivers for every type of printer that your publications will use, even if the printers are not hooked up to your own system.

Customizing Confirmation

Finally, the installation program tells you how to start PageMaker, given the directory names you have specified. If you accepted all the default names during the installation process, your hard disk directory map may look like the one pictured in figure 2.2. In this case, the installation program appends the following commands to your AUTOEXEC.BAT file so that it will work correctly the next time you restart the computer:

    PATH C:\PM;\DOS
    SET TEMP=C:\PM

If you do not have a path created, PageMaker creates the path C:\PM and appends it to your batch file.

The installation program also changes your CONFIG.SYS file in order to enhance the performance of PageMaker. After installing the program, you should reboot your machine; then start PageMaker by typing

    CD C:\PM
    WIN PM

The PATH command causes DOS to search all the listed directories whenever you enter a command that is not found in the current directory. In this case, enter the command WIN PM from any directory in order to start PageMaker.

To see the contents of your AUTOEXEC.BAT file, change to the directory where that file is stored—the root directory—and type

    TYPE AUTOEXEC.BAT

You can edit this file directly with any word-processing program, saving the file as text-only. Information about the commands listed in the AUTOEXEC.BAT file is available in the DOS operating system manual. The command or statement of special interest here, the PATH command, should list all the directories that contain frequently used programs.

Directory and File Management

As you know, PageMaker requires a hard disk system in order to run on an IBM PC or a compatible system. You should use a hierarchical system of directories. For instance, in the typical PageMaker setup (see fig. 2.2), the directory named PM has two subdirectories named DRIVERS and PMTUTOR. The root directory contains the primary directory list. Most programs and data files are stored in subdirectories below the root directory. The DOS directory contains most of the MS-DOS utilities; these programs can be activated through Windows menu commands. The WINDOWS directory includes the special programs that come with the full Windows program—including Windows Write® and Windows Paint® and the printer drivers and fonts. The PM directory holds the PageMaker program and its support files. The PageMaker directory itself includes one subdirectory: PMTUTOR (where tutorial files are stored). You also need to create another subdirectory: DRIVERS (where the printer drivers supplied by Aldus are stored). Remember that the Aldus drivers must be copied from C:\PM\DRIVERS into C:\WINDOWS in order to be active.

The PageMaker installation program automatically sets up these directories on the hard disk for you. As you see in the installation steps, you can accept all PageMaker's defaults for naming the directories or define your own standards. Before you install the program, be sure that the directory names used by PageMaker are not already in use on your system. Any directory already on your system and named PM or WINDOWS is affected by installation unless you select alternative names before you begin.

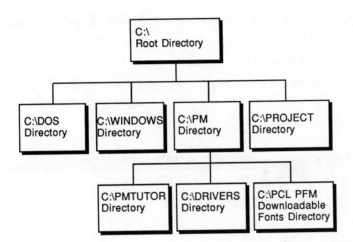

Fig. 2.2. Typical hard disk directory for PageMaker.

The following paragraphs show you how to create, rename, and delete files and directories. You can learn more about the intricacies of these commands directly from your DOS and Windows manuals.

Creating a New Directory

To create a new directory, you begin in DOS. From the C prompt, type

MKDIR*directoryname*

or

MD*directoryname*

For example, to create a new directory for an in-house newsletter, you can type

MD\\NEWSLTTR

In other words, you make a directory and give it the name that is typed after the backslash (\\). The directory name must consist of no more than eight characters with no spaces. You can use hyphens in the directory name, but none of the following characters:

. " / \\ [ ] : | < > + = ; ,

To create a subdirectory, type the MD command followed by the names of the full *path* to the new directory, starting with the highest directory level. For example, to make a subdirectory named NEWSLTTR under the directory named PM, you type

MD\PM\NEWSLTTR

If you are using the full Windows program, you also can make new directories using the Special menu "Create Directory..." command (see fig. 2.3).

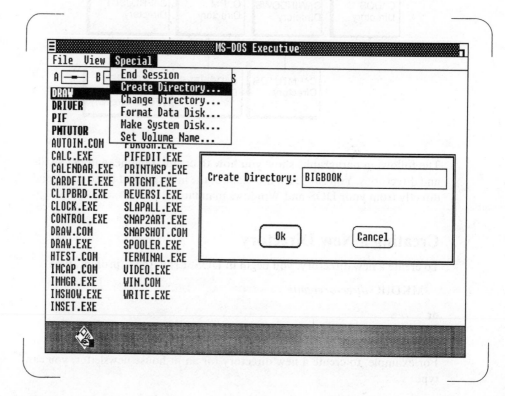

Deleting a Directory

You can delete a directory from the hard disk if you first delete all the files stored in that directory. To delete (remove) a directory from DOS, at the C prompt, type

RMDIR*directoryname*

or

RD*directoryname*

For example, after you have finished a particular book project, copied all the files from the directory named BIGBOOK to floppy disks for backup, and deleted the files from the hard disk, you type

   RD\BIGBOOK

This command tells the program to remove the directory named after the backslash.

If you are using Windows, you can also remove directories by using the File menu's "Delete..." command.

Changing Directories

To change to another directory, in DOS, from the C prompt, type

   CD*directoryname*

In other words, the command says to change to the directory name that is typed after the backslash.

If you are using Windows, you can switch between directories using the Special menu's "Change Directory..." command. You also can double-click any subdirectory name (shown in bold in the MS-DOS Executive window) to move down the hierarchy, or you can click the root directory name to move up the hierarchy (see fig. 2.4). Note that subdirectory names appear in bold. You use this same convention for changing directories in all the PageMaker dialog boxes that list file names (see fig. 2.5). Refer to table 2.1 for a summary of the mouse and window operations.

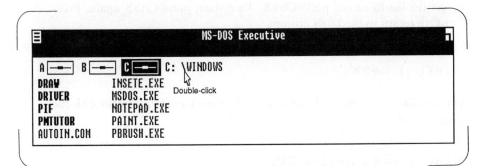

Fig. 2.4. Moving up the hierarchy in the MS-DOS Executive window.

Fig. 2.5. *Moving up the hierarchy in a dialog box listing.*

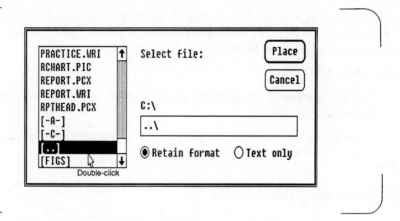

Listing All Directories

You can view the complete list of directories and subdirectories on your disk by typing

     TREE

You must type this command at the C prompt from DOS because Windows has no equivalent command. To view the names of the files in each directory, type

     TREE /F

(Notice that, in this command, you use a normal slash—not a backslash.)

To get the list to pause, press Ctrl-S. To restart, press Ctrl-S again. Press Ctrl-C to return to the DOS prompt.

You can get a printout of the same list, shown in figure 2.6, by typing

     TREE /F >PRN

You will find this command useful for maintaining a record of your disk-file organization.

Naming and Copying Files

File names on any MS-DOS system can be no longer than eight characters, but you can add a three-character extension or suffix. The file name and extension take the form of *nnnnnnnn.nnn*.

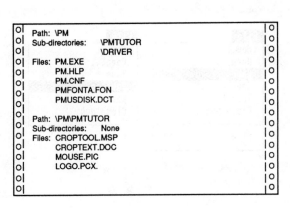

Fig. 2.6. *A directory list printed by the TREE command.*

Just as the first part of the name can be shorter than eight characters, the suffix can be shorter than three characters. A suffix cannot be longer than three characters, however, and is always separated from the rest of the file name with a period. Some file names may have no suffix, but the suffix helps PageMaker know what type the file is. (See Chapters 3 and 5 for lists of suffixes used by different types of files.)

The PageMaker program automatically gives all PageMaker publication files the suffix .PUB unless you specify a different extension when saving the file. Like directory names, a file name can include a hyphen but not spaces or special characters such as

" / \ [ ] : | < > + = ; ,

Normally, the program you are using creates new files when you use the "Save" command, when you open a file and save it with a new name, or when you use the DOS or Windows COPY command. The methods and commands for saving files vary among programs. In PageMaker, the commands for saving are on the File menu (see fig. 2.7).

Copying a File from One Disk or Directory to Another

Sometimes you need to copy a file from one disk or directory to another. First, you change to the disk or directory in which the file is stored. Then you type

COPY *filename disk*:*directory**filename*

Fig. 2.7. Use
*PageMaker's "Save" and
"Save as..." commands to
create new files.*

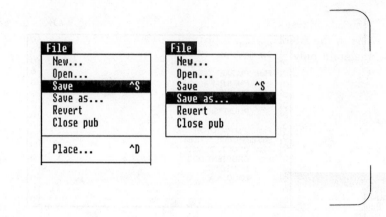

For example, to copy the file named NEWS11-7.PUB from the directory
named NEWSLTTR on the hard disk to the floppy disk in drive A, first type

    CD C:\NEWSLTTR

Pressing Enter changes you to the NEWSLTTR directory if you are not already there. Then type

    COPY NEWS11-7.PUB A:

You can accomplish the same effect from the A drive by first typing

    A:

Press Enter, and then type

    COPY C:\NEWSLTTR\NEWS11-7.PUB

This sequence of commands copies the file NEWS11-7.PUB from the
NEWSLTTR directory on the hard disk to the floppy disk in drive A and
gives the file the same name. A copy of the file remains on the hard disk.

To copy a file from one directory to another (*target directory*) on the hard
disk, first change to the directory where the file is stored; then type

    COPY *filename* C:*targetdirectory*

For example, to copy the file named CHAPTER1.DOC from the directory
named WORD to the directory named BIGBOOK, first type

    CD\WORD

to change to the WORD directory. Then type

    COPY CHAPTER1.DOC C:\BIGBOOK

This action results in two copies of the file: one in the WORD directory and one in the BIGBOOK directory. To keep your hard disk "lean" and help maintain only one active version of your text files, you should delete the CHAPTER1.DOC file from the WORD directory.

You also can use the Windows "Copy..." command under the File menu to copy files (see fig. 2.8).

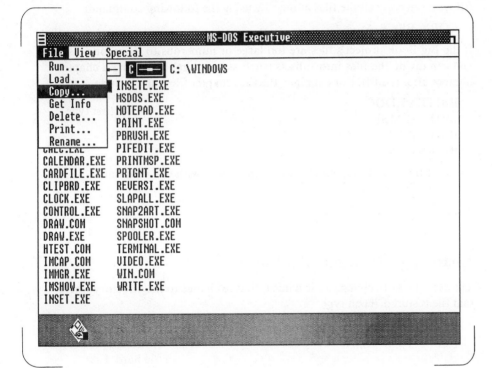

Fig. 2.8. The Windows File menu.

Efficiency Tip

Copying Files

You can copy groups of files by using an asterisk or question mark as a *wild card* when you name the files to be copied. For example, to copy to the floppy disk in drive A all the files from the NEWS11-7 directory on the hard disk, you change to the directory NEWS11-7 and then type

COPY *.* A:

To copy only the PageMaker publications from the directory to the floppy disk in drive A, you type

COPY *.PUB A:

Be sure that you're working in the PageMaker directory.

You can easily copy all the files related to a single publication or project in one step if you make every related file name begin with the same characters. For example, if all the files used in the Big Book project began with the letters BB, you can copy all the files at once by using the following command:

COPY BB*.* A:

If the Big Book project's files are too large or numerous to fit on one disk, you can divide the files into subsets (such as chapters) by adding a chapter number after the BB. For example, the first chapter files may include

BB1TEXT.DOC
BB1FIG1.MSP
BB1FIG2.PIC
BB1FIG3.IMG

All these files can be copied to the disk in drive A with one command:

COPY BB1*.* A:

Changing the Name of a File

The easiest way to change a file name is first to change to the directory where that file is stored. Then type

RENAME *oldfilename* *newfilename*

or

REN *oldfilename* *newfilename*

For example, to change the file named STORY1.DOC to STORY1.TXT, you type

REN STORY1.DOC STORY1.TXT

In other words, change the name of the file STORY1.DOC to STORY1.TXT. (Chapter 3 shows you the differences these two suffixes make when you enter a file in PageMaker.)

You also can use the Windows "Rename..." command under the File menu to rename a file (see fig. 2.8).

Deleting a File

When specific projects are complete, you can free some space on your hard disk by copying the files from the hard disk to a floppy disk for backup. Then you can delete the files from the hard disk. To delete a file, first change to the directory in which that file is saved; then type

ERASE *filename*

or

DEL *filename*

To delete groups of files, you can use the same shortcuts you take when you copy files. For example, to delete all the files with the suffix .BAK, you type

ERASE *.BAK

You also can use the Windows "Delete..." command under the File menu to delete files (see fig. 2.8).

Making Subdirectories for Publication Projects

If you are accustomed to working on floppy disks only, you probably have experienced the problem of running out of space on a disk when it is filled with files. On the other hand, you may not have experienced having so many files on your floppy disk that you cannot see all of them listed at once on your screen.

When working with a hard disk, you are less likely to run out of storage space; but you can easily create so many files that you cannot view the complete list of files at once on the screen. More than one screen full of names to display all the files can be simply an inconvenience. A more serious production problem is that you won't be able to keep track of all the files used in creating each document. For this reason, you should set up a separate directory or subdirectory outside the PM and WINDOWS directories for each major project or long document. A directory map set up for a busy production network is shown in figure 2.9.

Starting Procedures

Up to this point, all the commands have been entered directly from the DOS operating system or from the MS-DOS Executive under Windows. Once PageMaker is installed, you can start the program in several ways. At first, you start PageMaker simply to explore the program. Eventually, when you

Fig. 2.9. *Map of directory system with subdirectories devoted to specific projects.*

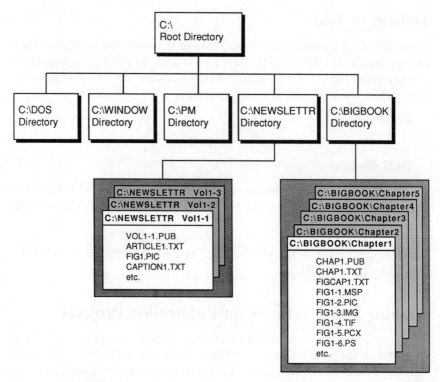

are working on a project, you will want to use some of the commands just described to set up a project directory and move all the text and graphics files you need into that directory before you start PageMaker (see Chapters 3 and 5).

Once you start PageMaker or before you use some of Microsoft Windows' functions, however, you need to be familiar with the basic window and mouse operations used in this book. These are summarized in table 2.1

Starting PageMaker from DOS

If you are using the run-time version of Windows, which came on your PageMaker disks, you can start PageMaker by changing to the directory where you installed the PageMaker program and typing **PM**. For example, if your program is in the directory named PM, you type two commands to start the PageMaker program:

CD\PM
PM

Table 2.1
Basic Mouse and Window Operations

Operation	Action
Mouse Operations:	
Point	Position mouse pointer over object
Click	Point at object and quickly click main mouse button once
Double-click	Point at object and quickly click main mouse button twice
Drag	Point at object, hold down main mouse button as you move mouse; release mouse button when object or pointer is in desired location

Window Operations:

With PageMaker and many other programs, you often see only a small part of the full page in the screen window. You can move the screen image around inside the window.

With scroll bars:

Operation	Action
 Click on arrow	Move image in small increments
 Click in gray area of scroll bar	Jump up or down in window in larger fixed increments
 Drag white portion of scroll bar	Move any distance

With icons:

Operation	Action
 Use "icon" command	Convert window to icon
Double-click on icon	Open window represented by icon

Operation	*Action*
Pull-down menus:	
Select command on menu	Position pointer over menu title and hold down mouse button to view commands on menu. Continue holding down mouse button and drag pointer down menu. Release mouse button when desired command is highlighted.
Dialog box entries:	
In response to some commands, a dialog box may be displayed. Defaults or current settings are already selected. You can make new entries by using a combination of keys and mouse clicks:	
Click on option button (or on text to right of button)	Make selection. Option buttons often indicate mutually exclusive choices.
Click in check box (or on text to right of box)	Select option. Check boxes often list nonexclusive choices.
Tab to, or click in, text box and type value.	Hold down mouse button and drag cursor over text entry to select, delete, or replace
Click on name in list	Select that name. In some cases, double-clicking selection closes dialog box at same time as selecting item.
Click OK	Close box with changes
Click CANCEL	Close box without recording changes

If your PATH line in the AUTOEXEC file shows

PATH C:\PM;\DOS

you can start PageMaker from any directory by typing **PM**.

If you are running the full version of Windows, you can start Windows and PageMaker with one command from the directory where the Windows program is saved. For example, if the Windows program is in the directory named WINDOWS and the PageMaker program is in the directory named PM, the PATH line in the AUTOEXEC file should show

　　PATH=C:\WINDOWS;C:\PM

To start PageMaker from any directory, you type two commands at once:

　　WIN　PM

Starting PageMaker from the MS-DOS Executive under Windows

If you are running the full Windows program, from the Windows opening screen, you can change to the directory where the PageMaker program is stored. Double-click the mouse on the program file named PM.EXE, shown on the Windows opening screen (see fig. 2.10). As an alternative, you can click once on the file name, PM.EXE; then select the "Run..." command under the Windows File menu. This obvious sequence, however, involves extra steps, which you can bypass by double-clicking to accomplish the same thing. (Many menu commands have similar shortcuts, which are described throughout this book.)

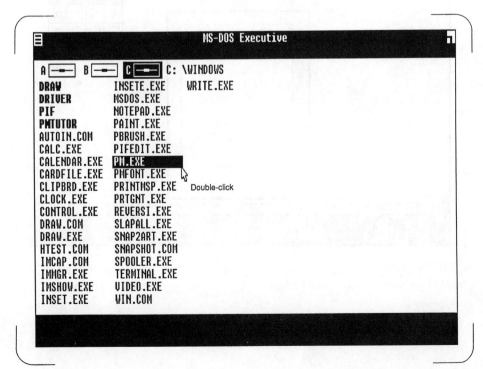

Fig. 2.10. Starting PageMaker from the Windows opening screen.

Also with the full Windows program, you can start other programs under Windows without closing PageMaker. For example, you can open the MS-DOS Executive under Windows without closing PageMaker. You double-click the MS-DOS disk icon at the bottom left corner of the screen and open the Windows Write program as a second window (see fig. 2.11). From the Windows main screen, you can use any of the Windows commands to copy, rename, or erase files. You can also start another program by double-clicking the program name, such as WRITE.EXE. You can go back and forth between PageMaker and most other programs on the screen; however, programs that require a great deal of memory cannot be run at the same time. While you are using PageMaker, you should try to keep the icon area clear to let the program use as much memory as possible.

Fig. 2.11. Running PageMaker and Windows Write at the same time.

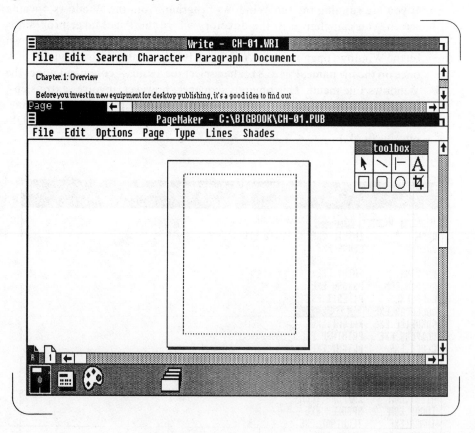

Opening a Document

If you have already created a PageMaker document and saved it on the disk, you can start PageMaker and open that document in one step from DOS by typing

PM *filename*

If the file is not in the current directory, you can include the directory path in the command:

PM C:*subdirectoryname**filename*

If you have installed the full Windows program, you can open a publication directly by typing

WIN PM *filename*

or

WIN PM C:*subdirectoryname**filename*

If you are already running the full Windows program, you can open a PageMaker document from the MS-DOS Executive by double-clicking on the program name: PM.EXE, in the \\PM directory.

At a Glance

How To Start PageMaker

If you do not have the full Windows program (if, for instance, you are using the run-time version supplied by Aldus), type

PM

or

PM *filename*

If you do have the full Windows program, from DOS you type

WIN PM

or

WIN PM *filename*

From the MS-DOS Executive under Windows, double-click the program name, PM.EXE.

When you start PageMaker, the opening screen displays the Aldus logo and information about your version of PageMaker. A row of menu titles is displayed along the top of the screen. You can use the "New..." command or the "Open..." command under the File menu (see fig. 2.12) to start a new publication or open one that has already been started and saved.

Fig. 2.12. Using the "New..." or "Open..." command under the File menu.

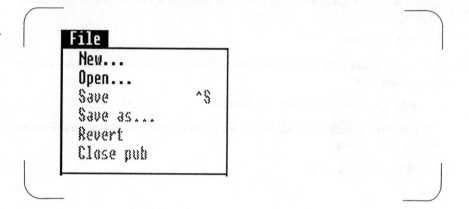

A New Document

You use the "New..." command to start a publication from scratch. The first display that you see is the "Page setup" dialog box. You can use this box to specify overall characteristics of the document. The "Page setup" dialog box appears when you start a new document or use the "Page setup" command (see fig. 2.13). These options are explained in Chapter 6.

Fig. 2.13. The "Page setup" dialog box.

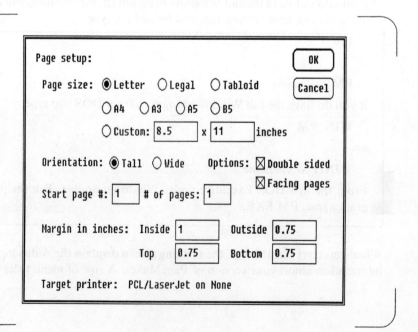

Dialog Box Operations

Click on an option button to make a selection.   Orientation: ⦿ Tall ◯ Wide

Tab to or click in an entry box and type a value.   Inside [1]   Outside [0.75]

Click on a name in a list to select the name.   [OK]

Click "OK" to close the box with changes.   [Cancel]

Click "Cancel" to close the box without recording any changes.

You can make changes to the page setup before the document is open or keep PageMaker's defaults and simply click "OK". Once you close the "Page setup" dialog box, PageMaker displays the blank page 1 of the new document (see fig. 2.14). Later, you can use the "Page setup..." command to redisplay the dialog box and make changes to some selections.

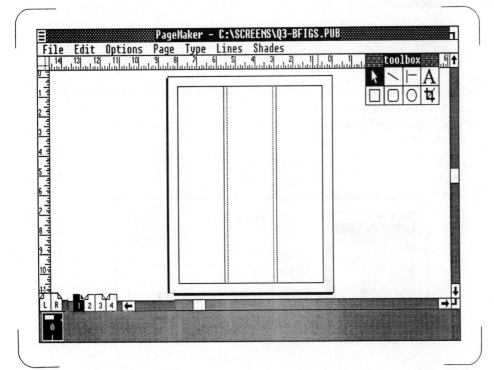

Fig. 2.14. Display of blank page 1 of a new document.

A Previously Created Document

When you use the "Open..." command, PageMaker displays a dialog box that shows the list of PageMaker files on your disk. To choose the name of the file you want to open, first find the file name in the window (see fig. 2.15).

1. If the file name is not visible, drag the scroll bars to move down the list.

2. Click [-A-] or [-B-] or [-C-] to view the list of files on other drives.

3. Click [..] to view the list at the next higher directory level (see fig. 2.16).

4. Click a directory name (shown in brackets) to view the list at the next lower directory level (see fig. 2.17).

5. Double-click a directory name (in brackets) to view files within a subdirectory.

6. Click "Open copy" to make a duplicate of the file as you are opening it.

7. Click "Cancel" to stop the "Open..." command.

When you find the name of the publication you want to open, click on the file name to highlight it and then click "Open". You also can simply double-click the file name. PageMaker displays the page that was displayed when the file was last saved.

Fig. 2.15. *Selecting a file name in the "Open..." command dialog box.*

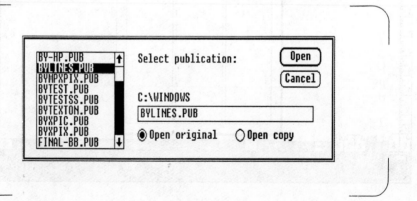

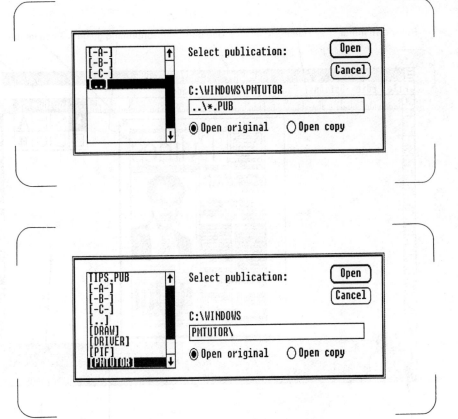

Fig. 2.16. Viewing files at the next higher directory level.

Fig. 2.17. Viewing files at next lower directory level.

The Publication Window

Once a new or existing publication is open, PageMaker displays pages in the publication window (see fig. 2.18). A quick look at the different elements of the publication window can give you an idea of the versatility of PageMaker.

The title bar shows the name of the publication and includes the System menu box. Pull-down menu titles on the menu bar list PageMaker's command categories. In the figure, the toolbox is pulled down to display graphics tools and a text tool. The page image shows the outline of the edges of the paper; the nonprinting guides on the page indicate margins, columns, or grid lines. The surrounding area serves as a *pasteboard* for storage of text and graphics that have not yet been positioned on the page. The pointer shows the current position of the mouse and is used for selecting commands and objects on the page or pasteboard.

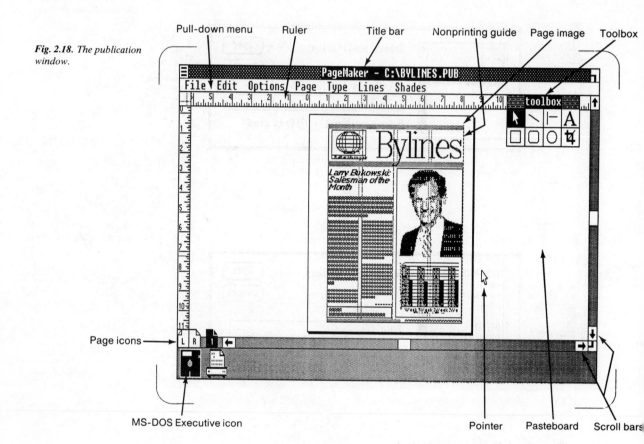

Fig. 2.18. *The publication window.*

Pull-down menu   Ruler   Title bar   Nonprinting guide   Page image   Toolbox

Page icons

MS-DOS Executive icon

Pointer   Pasteboard   Scroll bars

The scroll bars and rulers can be turned on or off. The page icons at the bottom of the screen show where you are in the document by highlighting the page number. Click on a page icon to turn to that page. The L and R pages are master pages. If you are working under the full Windows program, the icon for the MS-DOS Executive window is displayed at the bottom left corner of the screen.

You can view and work on a display of one page at a time or two *facing* pages at a time. Facing pages are the two pages you see when you open a document that is printed and bound (see fig. 2.19). In the "Page setup" dialog box, select "Double sided" to work on a single page or "Facing pages" to work on facing pages.

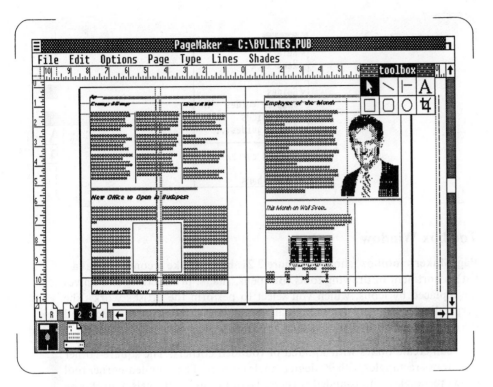

Fig. 2.19. Facing pages.

This chapter covers the essential elements of the publication window. Look for more information about working in this feature throughout the book.

Pull-Down Menus

Menu titles appear along the menu bar at the top of the screen. When you position the pointer over a menu title and hold down the mouse button, the menu *drops down* on the screen to show all the commands under that menu. You select a command by *dragging* the pointer down until the desired command is highlighted. Then you release the mouse button.

Some commands also have keyboard shortcuts, which are given on the menu (see fig. 2.20). A caret (^) before a letter represents the Ctrl key. To execute the command, hold down the Ctrl key while you type the letter shown. A check mark in front of a command indicates a toggle switch (an on/off option). The feature is on if it is checked; you can turn off the feature by selecting the command. The feature is off if it is not checked; you turn on the feature by selecting the command. Ellipses (...) following a command indicate that a dialog box asking you for more information is displayed when you select the command. The dialog box also offers you a chance to cancel the command.

Fig. 2.20. *A pull-down menu.*

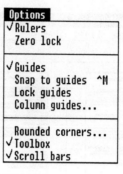

```
Options
√ Rulers
  Zero lock

√ Guides
  Snap to guides   ^M
  Lock guides
  Column guides...

  Rounded corners...
√ Toolbox
√ Scroll bars
```

Toolbox Window

PageMaker's toolbox, shown in figure 2.21, is much like a conventional artist's assortment of drawing tools. But pens, rulers, protractors, and knives are replaced by icons, which you select to perform the artist's work. The perpendicular-line tool draws lines at any angle divisible by 45 degrees, and the diagonal-line tool draws lines at any angle.

You can create boxes with squared or rounded corners: The square-corner tool draws rectangles with 90-degree-angle corners. The rounded-corner tool draws rectangles with rounded corners. To draw circles or ovals, you choose the oval tool.

In addition, you can use the pointer tool to select objects or the text tool to edit or type text. Finally, you use the cropping tool to trim edges from graphics that you bring in from other programs.

To select any tool in the toolbox, click on the tool, or use the keyboard shortcuts shown in table 2.2.

Table 2.2
Keyboard Shortcuts for the Toolbox

Keys	Tool
Shift-F1	Pointer tool
Shift-F2	Diagonal-line tool
Shift-F3	Perpendicular-line tool
Shift-F4	Text tool
Shift-F5	Square-corner tool
Shift-F6	Rounded-corner tool
Shift-F7	Oval tool
Shift-F8	Cropping tool

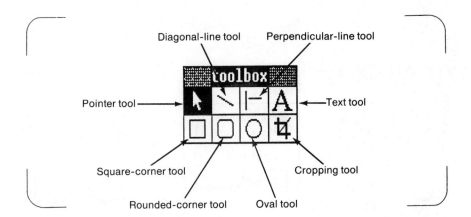

Fig. 2.21. The toolbox.

The graphics created with tools from the toolbox can be modified through the options under the Lines menu. Two-dimensional objects like boxes and circles can take any fill pattern listed under the Shades menu.

The toolbox is a separate window on the screen. You can drag the window by its title bar to any position on the screen. You can also close the window by selecting the "Toolbox" command on the Options menu. To redisplay the toolbox after you close the window, select the "Toolbox" command under the Options menu again.

Microsoft Windows Commands (the System Menu)

The top left corner of the screen shows a small square with three black bars. This is the System menu icon. The System menu lists the commands that are accessible from any program running under either the full or the run-time version of Windows (see fig. 2.22). These commands control the windows and supply useful information.

Controlling the Windows

If two or more windows are open on the screen, you can adjust the size of each one with the "Size" command on the System menu. First, select the "Size" command on the System menu in the window whose size you want to change (see fig. 2.23); then click on the edge of the window and drag the mouse up or down. You will see a line moving on the screen, showing how the edge will be moved when you next click the mouse.

Fig. 2.22. The System menu.

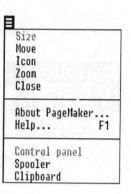

Fig. 2.23. Changing the size of a window with more than one window on the screen.

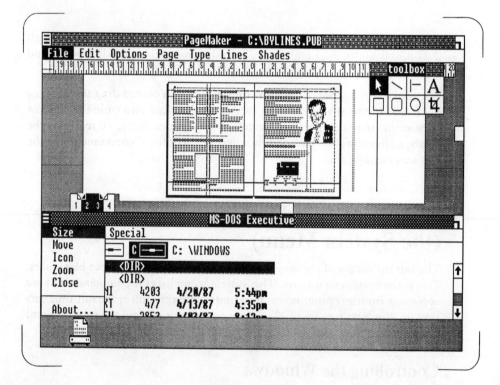

If two or more windows are open on the screen, you can enlarge one window to full-screen size by using the "Zoom" command on the System menu. To reduce the window to a portion of the screen, use the "Zoom" command again.

When two or more windows are displayed, you can rearrange them with the "Move" command. First, select the "Move" command under the System menu of the first window you want to move; then click on the second window. The two windows swap places.

You use the "Close" command under the System menu to close a window and leave the program that is running in that window. When you use this command, most programs (including PageMaker) prompt you to save the file if you haven't already done so.

You can close a window entirely without leaving the program by using the "Icon" command under the System menu. When you select the "Icon" command, the selected window closes and is replaced by an icon at the bottom of the screen (see fig. 2.24). (The window you most recently clicked on is the one selected; its title bar is a solid color rather than a pattern.) To change any icon back to an open window, simply double-click the icon.

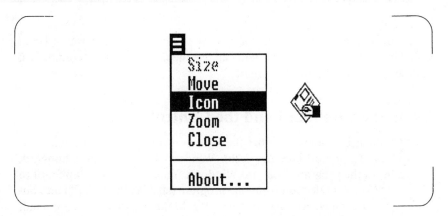

Fig. 2.24. The "Icon" command and resulting icon.

Using the System Menu To Help Control Printing

Microsoft Windows has a built-in spooler for printers. You can send more than one file to print and go on working while the current file is being printed. In other words, when you issue the File menu "Print..." command from any program, that program sends the printing information to the spooler rather than directly to the printer. As soon as the spooler has all the printing information, you can resume working on your file or go on to another task within the Windows environment.

While you are working, the spooler keeps track of which jobs are printing on which printers. When one job is printed, the spooler sends the next job in the queue to print. The System menu "Spooler" command lets you see what printers are being used and what jobs are currently printing or in the queue (see fig. 2.25).

Fig. 2.25. List of print jobs in the spooler queue.

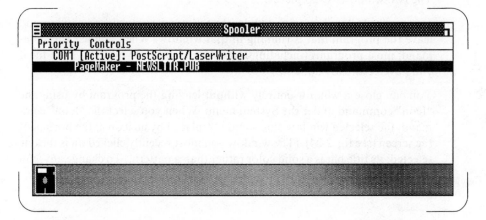

You can use the commands on the Priorities menu to change the order in which jobs will be printed, and you can use the Controls menu commands: "Pause," "Resume," and "Terminate."

Using the Clipboard and the Control Panel

The "Clipboard" command under the System menu shows the current contents of the Clipboard (see fig. 2.26). Windows has only one Clipboard, shared by all the programs that use Windows. You can use the Clipboard to "Cut" or "Copy" a selection from one program (such as PC Paint™) into another program (such as PageMaker). PageMaker's "Place..." command, however, serves this function more conveniently in most cases.

You can open two PageMaker documents in two different windows, and use the Clipboard to move objects from one document to another.

The "Control panel" command under the System menu lets you adjust basic options, such as the background color of the screen, the mouse speed, and the printer connections (see fig. 2.27). If this command is not shown on your menu, or if the command is shown in gray, you can activate the Control Panel by executing the CONTROL.EXE program from the MS-DOS Executive under Windows.

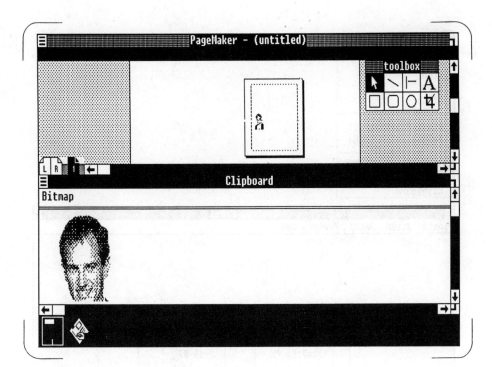

Fig. 2.26. The Clipboard
window with a
PageMaker window.

Control of the Display

As already mentioned, you often can see only a part of a page or a document in one window at a time. In PageMaker, you have three different ways to move the page image around the screen. You can use the scroll bars to scroll vertically and horizontally. You can use the Page menu commands to jump to enlarged views of a particular area or reduce the page image to a smaller size. You can use the *grabber hand* to move the image in any direction. These techniques are described in the following paragraphs.

Using the Scroll Bars

PageMaker's scroll bars operate the same way other scroll bars work under Windows (described in table 2.1). To move the image on the screen in small increments, you click on an arrow. You click in a gray area of a scroll bar to jump up or down in the window in larger fixed increments. You drag the white portion of the scroll bar to move any distance. The position of the white box on the scroll bar indicates the position of screen image relative to the whole page and the pasteboard (see fig. 2.28).

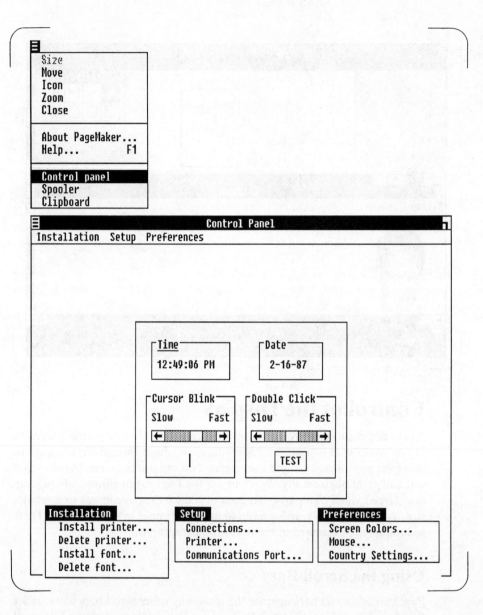

*Fig. 2.27. The Control
Panel and menus.*

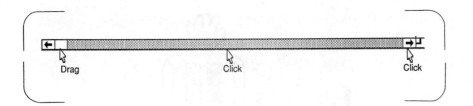

Fig. 2.28. PageMaker's scroll bars.

The distance the image moves when you click on the gray part of the scroll bar or on an arrow varies depending on the view you are using. The increments are smaller in enlarged views (such as 200%) than in reduced views (such as "Fit in window").

You can turn off the scroll bars so that they are not displayed, by selecting the "Scroll bars" command under the Options menu. This way, you can see more of the page at once, and you can use any of the techniques described next to move around on the screen. When the scroll bars are turned off, the page icons are also hidden; but you can use the "Go to page..." command under the Page menu to change pages.

To turn on the scroll bars and display them again, select the "Scroll bars" command again. This toggle switch shows a check mark next to the command when the scroll bars are on.

Using the Grabber Hand To Move the Screen Image

In any view, you can use the grabber hand to drag the image in any direction. Hold down the Alt key while you press the main mouse button. When the pointer changes to a hand (see fig. 2.29), you can drag the pointer in any direction to move the page image on the screen. If you hold down both the Alt key and the Shift key, the grabber hand moves either horizontally or vertically, not diagonally.

Efficiency Tip

Moving Around on the Page

The quickest way to move around on the screen is to use the grabber hand for diagonal or small movements.

Fig. 2.29. *The Alt key and the grabber hand.*

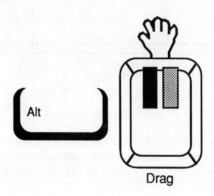

Using the Page Menu To Change the Screen View

The Page menu offers five commands for changing your view of the page. Each of these commands also has a Ctrl-key equivalent:

"Actual size"	Ctrl-1
"75% size"	Ctrl-7
"50% size"	Ctrl-5
"Fit in window"	Ctrl-W
"200% size"	Ctrl-2
"Fit in pasteboard"	Ctrl-Alt-W

If your mouse has two or more buttons, you can use the secondary button to change views quickly. Pressing the secondary mouse button changes the view from any other view to "Actual size" of the page. The "Actual size" image is centered at the position of the pointer on the screen. If you are already in the "Actual size" view, pressing the secondary mouse button changes to a "Fit in Window" view.

Holding down the Shift key and pressing the secondary mouse button changes from any other view to a "200% size" view. The "200% size" image is centered at the position of the pointer on the screen. If you are already in 200% size, pressing the secondary mouse button changes you to an "Actual size" view.

(See the Microsoft Windows installation guide for information about selecting the primary and secondary mouse buttons.)

Efficiency Tip

Changing Views of the Page

Use the secondary mouse button to toggle between "Actual size" and "Fit in window".

Use the Shift key with the secondary mouse button to toggle between "Actual size" and "200% size".

Use the secondary mouse button to jump from "Fit in window" view to close-up views of particular areas of the page by placing the pointer at the spot you want to see before you click. For example, toggling from "Actual size" to "Fit in window" and back to "Actual size" (of another part of the page) can be faster than using the scroll bars or the grabber hand when moving diagonally for long distances.

Changing the Appearance of the Mouse Pointer

The appearance of the mouse pointer changes depending on what you are doing (see fig. 2.30). Any pointer can be used to select menu commands, toolbox options, or page icons, or to use the scroll bars. In addition, the appearance of the pointer indicates what other functions can be performed.

You use the arrow pointer, which appears whenever the pointer tool is selected in the toolbox, to select objects on the page. The I-beam appears whenever the text tool is selected in the toolbox. You use the I-beam to select portions of a block of text and to position the text insertion point. A crossbar appears whenever one of the graphics tools is selected in the toolbox. You use the crossbar to draw lines, boxes, and circles. When the cropping tool is selected in the toolbox, the pointer changes to the cropping icon. You use this icon to trim the edges of a graphic from another program.

The mouse pointer also takes on different appearances when you use the "Place..." command to get text or graphics from other programs. The text icon places text from another file. The pencil icon means that you are bringing a graphic from a draw-type program. You use the paintbrush icon to place a graphic from a paint-type program. When you are placing a scanned image, the pointer becomes a box containing an X. The hourglass icon is displayed while the program is processing. You must wait until the hourglass changes back to one of the other icons before you can continue working.

Fig. 2.30. Changes in appearance of the pointer.

Icon	Name	Description
	Pointer:	Selects objects on the page
	I-beam:	Selects portions of a block of text, positions the text insertion point
	Crossbar:	Draws lines, boxes, circles and ovals
	Cropping Tool:	Trims the edges from a graphic that is placed from another program
	Text Icon:	Places text from another file
	Pencil Icon:	Places a graphic from a draw-type program
	Paintbrush Icon:	Places a graphic from a paint-type program
	X Icon:	Places a scanned image
	PS Icon:	Places an Encapsulated Postscript file
	Hourglass:	Displayed when the program is processing -- you must wait until the hourglass changes back to one of

Selecting with the Pointer and Text Tools

Many commands used in PageMaker operate only on objects that have been selected on the page. You select the objects as soon as they are drawn or placed on a page, or you select objects with the pointer tool and the text tool.

The three methods of selecting objects with the pointer tool are shown in figures 2.31, 2.32, and 2.33.

- Position the pointer over text or a graphic and click once to select the text or graphic. If the handles are not displayed as expected, the object may be buried under other objects, and you must use the "Send to back" and "Bring to front" commands to dig out the object, as described in Chapter 6 (see fig. 2.31).

- Hold down the Shift key, and click the pointer on several objects to select them all (fig. 2.32).

- Position the pointer at one corner of the area that includes the objects to be selected and drag the pointer diagonally to the opposite corner. Objects that are not completely encompassed are not selected (fig. 2.33).

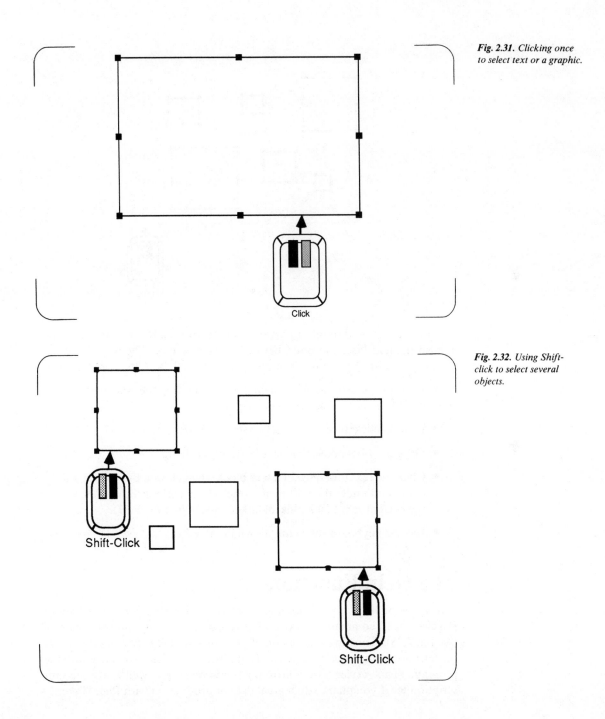

Fig. 2.31. Clicking once to select text or a graphic.

Fig. 2.32. Using Shift-click to select several objects.

Fig. 2.33. Dragging the pointer to select an area.

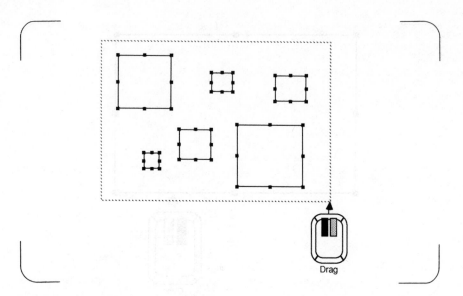

Drag

The text tool is used to select portions of text within a block of text or to establish the text insertion point before typing new text. The methods of selecting text with the text tool are shown in figures 2.34, 2.35, 2.36, and 2.37.

- Position the I-beam beside a character, and drag the I-beam to the end of the desired selection (see fig. 2.34).

- Double-click a word to select it (see fig. 2.35).

- Drag the I-beam over the text to select it (see fig. 2.36).

- Click the text tool once in a text block, then choose the "Select all" command under the Edit menu to select the entire article, such as the current text block plus all linked blocks (see fig. 2.37).

- Use the keyboard shortcuts shown in table 2.3.

The Help Function

Two types of help are offered under the System menu. First, the "About PageMaker..." command tells you what version of the program you are using (see fig. 2.38). Knowing the version of your program is important if you use the telephone hotline offered by Aldus to resolve problems you have with the program. (This service, available to registered owners, is well worth the subscription fee if you plan to do a great deal of production with PageMaker.)

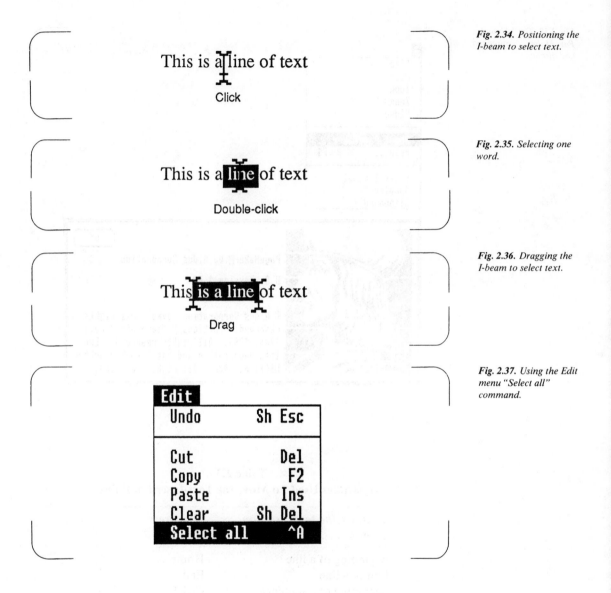

This is a|line of text

Click

Fig. 2.34. *Positioning the I-beam to select text.*

This is a line of text

Double-click

Fig. 2.35. *Selecting one word.*

This is a line of text

Drag

Fig. 2.36. *Dragging the I-beam to select text.*

Edit	
Undo	Sh Esc
Cut	Del
Copy	F2
Paste	Ins
Clear	Sh Del
Select all	^A

Fig. 2.37. *Using the Edit menu "Select all" command.*

Fig. 2.38. *The "About*
Page Maker..." command
and display.

PageMaker® by Aldus Corporation

U.S. Version 1.00

© Aldus Corporation, 1986. All rights
reserved. Portions © Microsoft Corp.,
1984, 1985. All rights reserved. Eng-
lish Hyphenation and Database © Houghton
Mifflin, 1986. All rights reserved.

Table 2.3
Keystrokes Used To Move the Text-Insertion Point

To move the text insertion point to . . .	*You press . . .*
Beginning of a line	Home
End of a line	End
Beginning of a sentence	Ctrl-Home
End of a sentence	Ctrl-End
Left one character	Left arrow
Right one character	Right arrow
Left one word	Ctrl-left arrow
Right one word	Ctrl-right arrow
Up one line	Up arrow

Down one line	Down arrow
Up one paragraph	Ctrl-up arrow
Down one paragraph	Ctrl-down arrow
Up one screen	PgUp
Down one screen	PgDn
Top of story	Ctrl-PgUp
Bottom of story	Ctrl-PgDn

The second source of help is the "Help..." command, also under the System menu. This command produces what most of us think of when we hear that a program offers on-screen help.

The "Help..." command under the System menu gets you into a tiered help system. The first dialog box displays a list of the main topics covered by the "Help..." command (see fig. 2.39). When you double-click one of these topics, you see a second list of the topics covered under the main topic you selected (see fig. 2.40). When you double-click a topic on this second list, you see detailed information on the topic (see fig. 2.41). Click "Cancel" to return to the publication window.

Basic Steps in Creating a Document

The steps of creating a document fall into three divisions: planning and designing your document, constructing the text and graphics with programs other than PageMaker, and producing the final version in PageMaker. Planning a document includes designing and formatting. You may decide things like page size, typeface, location of figures, and general appearance on the page. Some of these decisions can be applied in the word-processing and graphics programs that you use to create the document. The remaining specifications are made in PageMaker. After you know the basic steps in creating a document, you can understand how the detailed steps explained in the rest of this book fit into the overall process.

IMPORTANT NOTE: Save your files often.

While you are working on a document, it is stored in the memory of the computer. Each time you save the document, the version that is in memory is copied to the disk. If the power fails or something else forces you to restart the computer, anything in the computer's memory is erased; but whatever you have saved on the disk is preserved. For this reason, save your document often while you are working.

Fig. 2.39. List of "Help..." command topics.

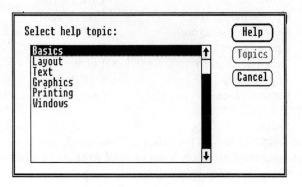

Fig. 2.40. A secondary list of "Help..." command topics.

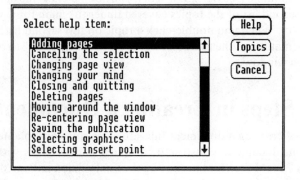

Fig. 2.41. Help information.

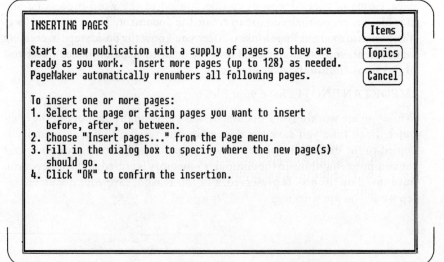

PageMaker also saves on disk interim versions of the document every time you insert, remove, turn a page, or touch the icon of the page you are on. These interim versions do not replace the last version you saved on the disk, but they are available when you reopen a document after a system failure.

PageMaker has a more sophisticated recovery program than any other desktop publishing program. PageMaker's recovery program is similar to the recovery program of a large database. When you use PageMaker's "Revert" command to cancel your current edits and revert to the last saved version, you go back to the latest version you saved with the "Save" or "Save as..." command. Interim versions saved automatically by PageMaker are ignored by the "Revert" command.

Efficiency Tip

When To Save a Document

- When you finish a page—before turning to another page

- When you finish placing a long text file

- When you finish placing, sizing, and cropping a graphic

- As you are working, every 15 minutes or so

- Before you print

- Before you globally change type specs or format

- After you make any changes to the master pages

The following overview of the steps involved in producing a document includes references to other chapters, which discuss each step in more detail.

1. Develop design specifications.

   Traditionally, design specifications have been hand-written or typed and illustrated in rough pencil sketches. However, you can use PageMaker as a design tool for developing specifications (see Chapter 9). This step includes deciding what type of printer you will use for the final production because the choice of printer affects your type specifications (see Chapters 7 and 8).

2. Prepare text and graphics by using other programs.

Although you can build documents from scratch using PageMaker alone, most PageMaker documents are composed of text and graphics that have been created in other programs (see Chapters 3 and 5.)

3. Start a new document.

After the text and graphics have been prepared in other programs, you start PageMaker and begin building the document. In this step, you may begin with a new file, or you may begin with a *template* file, which is already set up with the design specifications (see Chapters 6 and 9).

4. Create the master pages.

The master pages include the running heads and running feet and any other elements that appear on every page. These pages also may contain the underlying *grid*—a network of lines that appear on the screen but are not printed. This grid is used to align objects consistently on all pages of the document (see Chapters 6 and 9).

5. Change the grid as necessary on individual pages.

The elements set up on the master pages can be changed on individual pages of the document as you are working (see Chapters 6 and 9).

6. Place the text and graphics in the document.

On each page of the document, you use the "Place..." command to get text and graphics that have been created in other programs (see Chapters 3, 5, and 6).

7. Print the document.

You should expect to print a document many times before you print the final version. Even if you have edited thoroughly the text and graphics before placing them on a page, you still need to print drafts of the PageMaker publication to review for format and alignment. PageMaker is a WYSIWYG program: "what you see (on the screen) is what you get (on the printed page)." However, you always find some differences between the screen and the printed page because of the differences in resolution. These discrepancies cannot be seen until you print the publication. (You will find detailed information about printing in Chapter 7.)

8. Close the publication.

You can close one PageMaker file without leaving the PageMaker program altogether by using the "Close pub..." command under the File menu. You also can close the current publication by using the "New..." or "Open..." commands under the File menu. If you have already saved your document, PageMaker closes the publication and opens another publication when you use these commands. If you have not already saved your document, PageMaker displays a dialog box asking whether you want to save the document before you close it and open another.

9. Close PageMaker.

When working in a full Windows environment, you can run other programs without closing PageMaker. When you do want to leave PageMaker, however, you use the "Close" command under the System menu. PageMaker automatically checks to see that you have saved your current document. If you have not, PageMaker displays a dialog box asking whether you want to save the publication as well as close PageMaker (see fig. 2.42).

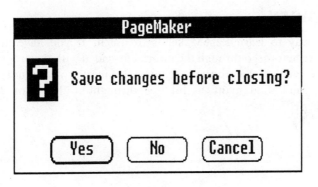

Fig. 2.42. Confirmation for saving a document.

When you leave PageMaker under the full Windows program, you return to the Windows opening screen or to a full screen view of the other windows that are already open. When you leave PageMaker under the run-time version of Windows, you return to DOS.

10. Close Microsoft Windows.

    To leave the full Windows program, choose the "Close" command
    from the System menu of the Windows MS-DOS Executive
    screen. The Windows program always asks you to confirm that
    you want to end the session (see fig. 2.43).

*Fig. 2.43. Confirmation
for ending a session.*

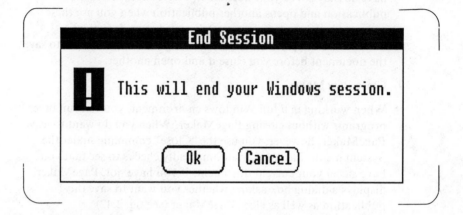

End Session

! This will end your Windows session.

(Ok)   (Cancel)

Summary

The best way to learn PageMaker is to use it. If you have never used
PageMaker before, go through the tutorial provided with the program to get
a quick overview of the program's features. No matter what your level of experience, you'll find many useful tips throughout this book for using
PageMaker efficiently.

Sources of Text

3

One of PageMaker's distinguishing features is its capability to import text from word-processing programs. In many cases, PageMaker can preserve the formatting done in the word processor, for example, type specifications, tabs, and paragraph alignment. This chapter shows you both how to import text from word-processing programs and how to type text into PageMaker.

Although you learn how to type text on a page, the goal of this chapter is to help you use your own word processor to prepare text for PageMaker. In most projects, you begin publications with word processing. In this chapter, you see how PageMaker handles text formatted in a word-processing program. After seeing what you can do with PageMaker and by knowing your word processor's capabilities, you can decide whether you should put more time in formatting during the word-processing step or later on in PageMaker.

The steps that precede placing text into PageMaker—such as setting up column guides—are presented in Chapter 6. In Chapter 4, you learn how to change the appearance of the text with paragraph formats and type specifications after it is placed on the page in PageMaker. If you have never used PageMaker, you should read both this chapter and the next. Then, before you launch your first major publication project, try placing a few files of your own.

Typing and Bringing Text into PageMaker

The three ways of bringing text into PageMaker are

- Typing text directly using PageMaker's text tool

- Importing text typed with a word-processing program (or other programs that save data as text) with the "Place..." command

- Pulling in text from the Windows Clipboard with the "Paste" command

You will see the pros and cons of each of these methods in the following sections.

Typing Text

Because typing and editing text in PageMaker are relatively slow processes, most PageMaker publications are composed of text typed in a word-processing program and then placed in PageMaker. Generally, you use PageMaker's text tool for editing text rather than for typing text from the keyboard. On occasion, however, you can use the text tool to type short segments of text. In this chapter, you see how the text tool operates as an input device. The text tool's more common uses as an editing tool are described in Chapter 4. (See Chapter 1 for a discussion of the differences between PageMaker and word-processing programs.)

To type text on a page in PageMaker, you first select the text tool—the letter A in the top right corner of the toolbox. When you click the pointer on the text tool, the mouse pointer changes to an I-beam. You click the I-beam anywhere on the page to set an insertion point and start typing (see fig. 3.1).

Fig. 3.1. Starting to type on a PageMaker page.

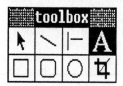

Click

Typed text begins at the text insertion point.

The position of the typed text varies depending on where you click the I-beam to set the text-insertion point. For instance, if you click the I-beam on an empty part of the page between two column guides, the text will begin at the left column guide and automatically wrap at the right column guide (see fig. 3.2). The typed text will be in the default format, which is usually flush left 12-point Times roman type (see table 3.1).

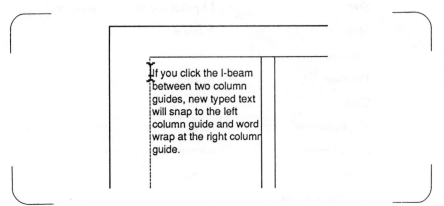

Fig. 3.2. Typed text.

If you click the I-beam between two column guides, new typed text will snap to the left column guide and word wrap at the right column guide.

If you click the I-beam within an existing block of text, the typed text is inserted within that text block. This text has the same format as the text immediately to the left of the insertion point.

If you click the text insertion point on the pasteboard or a page with no column guides, the typed text begins wherever you click the insertion point. If you are working on a pasteboard, the text assumes the margin-to-margin width defined in the "Page setup" dialog box. If you click the I-beam on a page with no column guides, the new typed text wraps at the right margin.

You have already seen that text typed directly into PageMaker with the text tool takes the default characteristics unless you specify otherwise. Table 3.1 lists the default settings for all text in PageMaker. Figures 3.3, 3.4, and 3.5 show the dialog boxes illustrating the default settings.

Suppose that you want to change the typeface for only the next text typed. First, you click the I-beam to position the text insertion point; then, you use the commands under the Type menu and type the text. In this case, you are setting new specifications for the current insertion point only.

To change the default settings so that the new specification carries over to all new insertions, select the pointer tool in the toolbox. Then use the Type menu's commands to change any of the settings shown in figures 3.3, 3.4, and 3.5. (Chapter 9 includes more tips about when to change PageMaker's default settings.)

Table 3.1
PageMaker's Text Defaults

Specification	Default
Font name	Times (or similar, if available on the target printer)
Size	12 point (or next size smaller)
Style	Normal
Leading	Auto
Position	Normal
Case	Normal
Hyphenation	Auto
Pair kerning	Above 12 points
Indents	None
Spacing between paragraphs	Zero
Paragraph alignment	Left
Tab stops	Every half inch

Fig. 3.3. "Type specifications" dialog box with PageMaker's default settings.

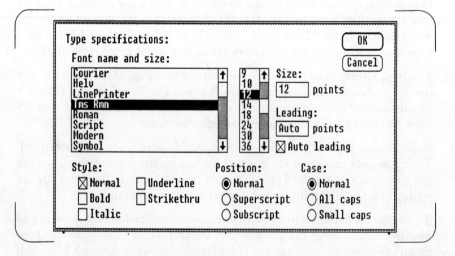

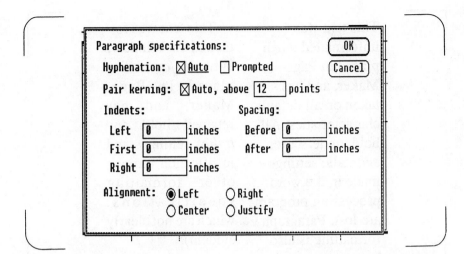

Fig. 3.4. "Paragraph specifications" dialog box with PageMaker's default settings.

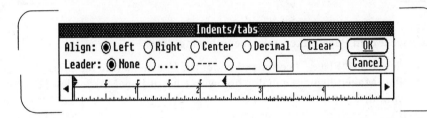

Fig. 3.5. "Indents/tabs" dialog box with PageMaker's default tab settings.

Importing Text with the "Place..." Command

You use the "Place..." command to import text typed in a word processor or any data saved as text-only (ASCII) from a spreadsheet or database program. If the text has been formatted in a word-processing program supported by the PageMaker program, PageMaker preserves some of that formatting (see "Sources of Formatted Text," in this chapter).

If the text to be placed is not already formatted in a word-processing program or if Pagemaker does not support the word processor and cannot preserve its formatting, the text takes on PageMaker default formats and type specifications when it is brought into PageMaker. Figure 3.6 shows examples of formatted and unformatted text placed on a page in PageMaker (see also "Using the Drag-Place Feature" in Chapter 6).

Fig. 3.6. Unformatted (left) and formatted (right) text placed in PageMaker.

This text was unformatted when placed in Page-Maker, and has taken on all default characteristics. All bold, underscore, and italic settings made in the word processing program are lost. Paragraph formatting is also lost.

This text was for-matted in Windows Write *before* being placed in Page-Maker, and has retained **bold** and *italic* settings and justification (among other formatting specifications, which are not clearly evident).

To place text in PageMaker, take the following steps:

1. Select the "Place..." command under the File menu (see fig. 3.7). PageMaker displays a dialog box with a list of PageMaker files on your disk.

2. In the dialog box, find the name of the text file you wish to place (see fig. 3.8).

   - If the file name is not visible drag the scroll bars to move down the list.

   - Click [–A–], [–B–], or [–C–] to view the list of files on other drives.

   - Click [..] to view the list at the next higher directory level.

   - Click a directory name (shown in brackets) to view the list at the next lower directory level.

   - Double-click a directory name (in brackets) to view the files within a subdirectory.

3. Choose the "Text only" option if you want to convert formatted text to unformatted text as it is placed. Choose "Retain format" to keep all formatting.

4. Select the file name by double-clicking on it. Double-clicking is a shortcut for clicking on the file name to select it and then clicking on "Place...".

The pointer changes to the text icon, which represents the top left corner of a column of text.

5. Position the text icon at the top of the column where you want the text to appear and click.

The text takes on the width of the column in which the text is placed and stops flowing at the bottom of the column or when the text runs into another object on the page (see fig. 3.9).

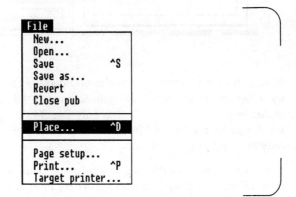

Fig. 3.7. The File menu with "Place..." selected.

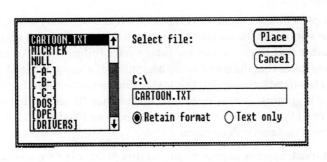

Fig. 3.8. The "Place..." command dialog box.

Fig. 3.9. The page before (left) and after (right) placing text.

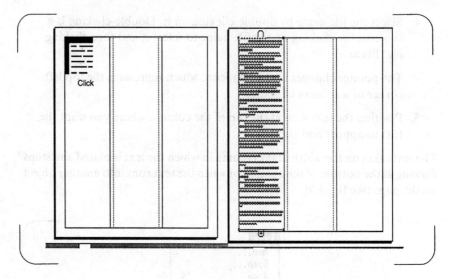

Notice that you change directories and disks with the "Place..." dialog box by using the same techniques you learned in Chapter 2 for the "Open..." dialog box. The difference is that only PageMaker publications are listed in the dialog box with the "Open..." command. The "Place..." command lists only text and graphics files.

When first placed on the page, your text appears as a block framed in horizontal lines at the top and bottom. These lines are called *windowshades*. In the middle of each windowshade is a *handle*, which looks like a square with a plus sign or a pound sign inside. A black sizing square is located at each end of a windowshade (see fig. 3.10). These windowshades appear whenever you select a text block with the pointer tool.

One complete document can be composed of text from many different source files. The symbols in the handles indicate whether the displayed text is linked to any other text in this document (again refer to fig. 3.10). An empty top handle indicates that the block is the beginning of a story or file. A plus sign (+) in the top handle means that this text is continued from another block and is not the beginning. A plus sign in the bottom handle means that more text follows this block. A pound sign (#) in the bottom handle indicates the end of text from this particular source.

The text block handles appear when you first place text on a page and when you select the text block with the pointer tool. The handles disappear when the text block is no longer selected.

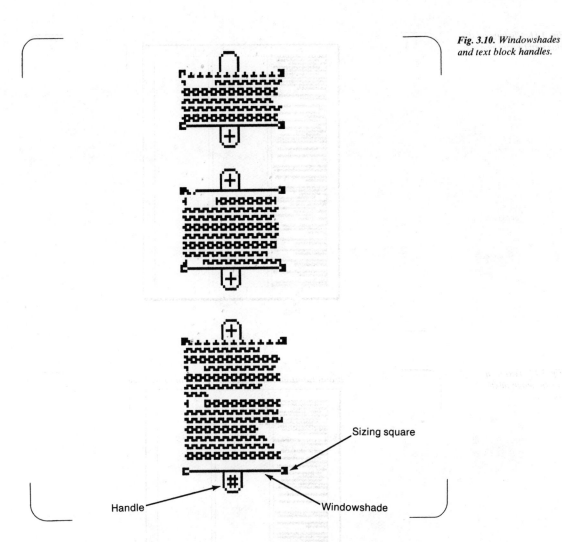

Fig. 3.10. *Windowshades and text block handles.*

Sizing square

Handle

Windowshade

Continuing Text from One Column to Another

To continue text from one column to the next, click on the plus sign in the bottom handle of the column or block (see fig. 3.11). When the text icon appears, position it at the top of the next column and click again (see fig. 3.12).

You can continue placing text across all the columns of the page until a pound sign (#) appears in the bottom handle indicating that you have no more text to place or until you fill the page (see fig. 3.13).

Fig. 3.11. Clicking on the plus sign to continue text.

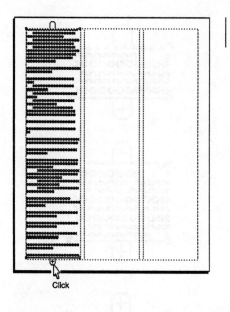

Click

Fig. 3.12. Text icon positioned in next column.

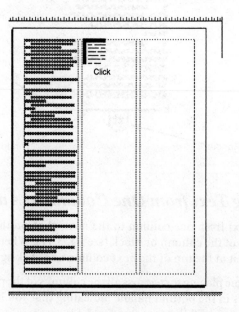

Click

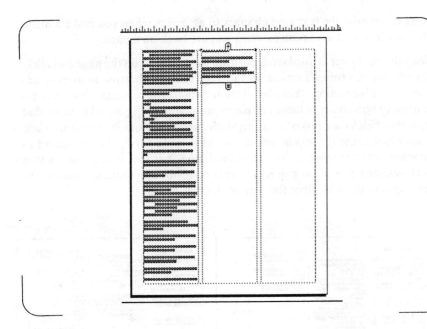

Fig. 3.13. Pound sign indicating the end of the text.

Efficiency Tip

Using Different Views

Work in the "Fit in window" view when placing text from another program, but work in "Actual size" when typing or editing text. The text is *greeked* in the "Fit in window" view so that you are unable to read the letters as you are typing. (To change how greeking is done, consult the disk file README.TXT.)

(Text may be greeked in the "75% size" and "50% size" views as well, depending on the resolution of your screen and the point size of the text.)

Continuing Text from One Page to Another

When the page is filled but the last block on the page still shows a plus sign in the bottom handle, you can continue the text to the next page just as you continue text from one column to another. To continue text to another page, first click the plus sign in the bottom handle of the last column on the page to get the text icon. You then have the following options:

- Click on the icon of the page number to which you want to go

- Select the "Go to page..." command from the Page menu

- Select "Insert pages..." from the Page menu to create a new page

Don't worry that the text icon changes to an arrow when you make a menu selection. The text icon returns when you are back on a page.

When the next page is displayed, position the text icon on the page and click. The text file continues flowing on the page until the bottom margin or another object is reached. Text placed from a single file remains connected, regardless of how many columns or pages are spanned. Figure 3.14 shows that when text blocks are linked in a single file, any insertions or deletions made in one block cause the text in linking blocks to move forward or backward to accommodate the change. Notice in the figure that text moves only within blocks already placed on pages. The text does not automatically flow on to new pages unless you place the text on the new pages.

Fig. 3.14. Adding material within linked blocks of text causes other text to shift.

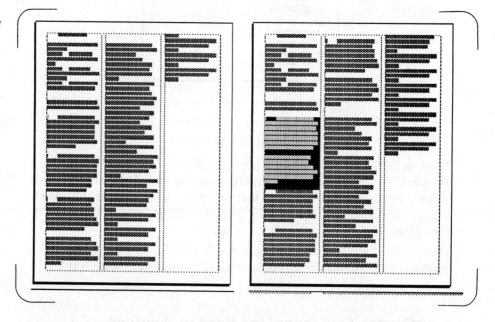

The length of the last text block changes if all the text has been placed. Otherwise, the length of the last block does not change until you adjust the length manually and continue placing the text.

Breaking a Column of Text into Several Blocks

A column of text can include more than one text block. You can have several text blocks when a column is composed of text placed from different files, when the text is typed as separate blocks, or when the text is deliberately broken up to accommodate graphics (see fig. 3.15).

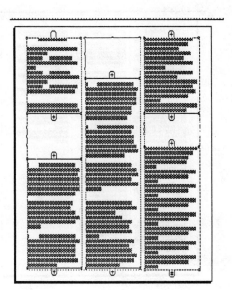

Fig. 3.15. Columns composed of several blocks of text.

Suppose that you want to break into two blocks the text shown in the middle column of figure 3.16. Follow these steps:

1. Select the block to be broken up so that you display its handles.

2. Drag the bottom handle up to shorten the block (see fig. 3.17).

3. Click on the plus sign in the bottom handle to get the text placement icon.

4. Click the text placement icon anywhere in the column below the first block (see fig. 3.18).

The text continues flowing as a second block of text, and a space is left between the two blocks (see fig. 3.19).

Fig. 3.16. *Text block before breaking.*

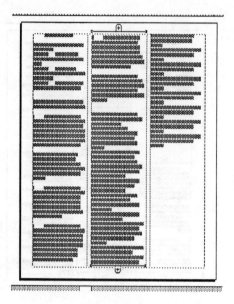

Fig. 3.17. *Text block after shortening.*

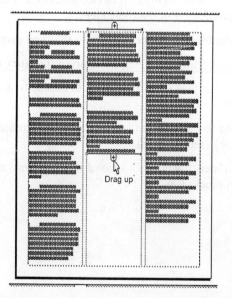

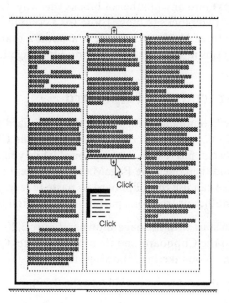

Fig. 3.18. *Text icon ready to continue text.*

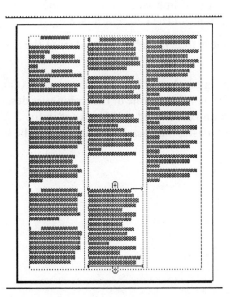

Fig. 3.19. *Divided text block.*

You can break text into any number of blocks this way. Generally, you need to break text into two blocks to make room for a column-wide graphic (as in fig. 3.19) or into three blocks to wrap text around a graphic. You will find more production tips in Chapter 6, "Creating Full-Page Layouts."

Pasting Text from the Clipboard

Using the "Paste" command brings from the Clipboard text you have put there with the "Cut" or "Copy" command. Because the Clipboard is a Windows feature, you can put text in the Clipboard while you are working in another program and then open the PageMaker document to paste the text on the page. You also can use the Clipboard to paste text from one PageMaker publication to another or from one part of a publication to another.

Suppose that you start with the page shown in figure 3.20. You want to copy a block of text to the Clipboard and then paste that text onto another page of your document. You take the following steps:

1. First select the text to be copied (see fig. 3.20).

2. Choose the "Copy" command from the Edit menu (see fig. 3.21). PageMaker automatically copies the selected text to the Clipboard.

3. You can use the "Clipboard" command under the System menu to view the contents of the Clipboard (see fig. 3.22).

4. Finally, choose the "Paste" command from the Edit menu (see fig. 3.23).

If you select the pointer when you paste, the pasted text appears in the center of the screen. You can then use one of the techniques described in the following section to position the pasted text block (as in fig. 3.23). If you select the text tool when you paste, the pasted text appears at the text insertion point.

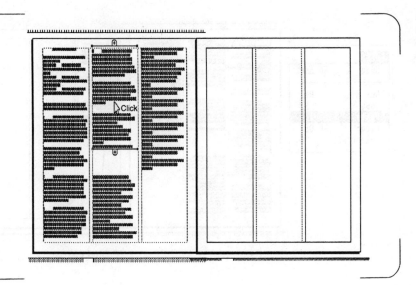

Fig. 3.20. *Text block in column 2 selected to cut and paste.*

Fig. 3.21. *Selecting the "Copy" command.*

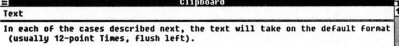

Fig. 3.22. *Viewing the contents of the Clipboard.*

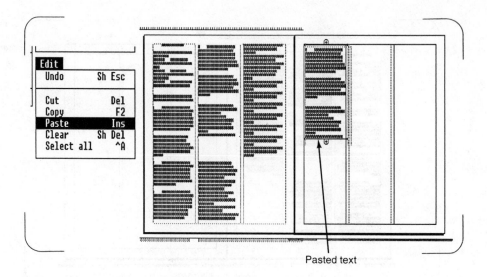

Fig. 3.23. *The "Paste"*
command and the final
result.

Pasted text

Controlling the Position
and Size of Text Blocks

Whether text is typed, placed, or pasted, it becomes part of a text block on
the page. A page can contain any number of text blocks, as illustrated in figure 3.24. A full page of single-column text with no graphics might consist of
one text block, but a two-column page of text must have at least two text
blocks—one in each column. A page with four columns of text and two figures might contain six or more blocks of text. You can move a block of text
or change its size by the following techniques.

Moving a Text Block

You use the pointer tool from the toolbox to move a block of text. Click anywhere on the block and hold down the mouse key as you drag the block in
any direction (see figs. 3.25 and 3.26).

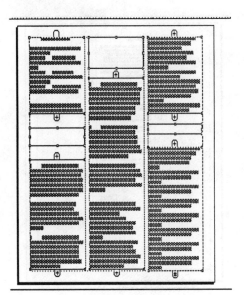

Fig. 3.24. *A page composed of several blocks of text.*

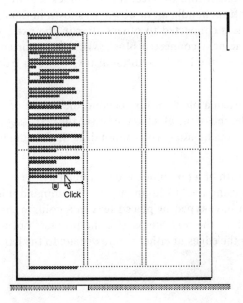

Fig. 3.25. *Block of text ready to be moved.*

*Fig. 3.26. Block of text
after being moved.*

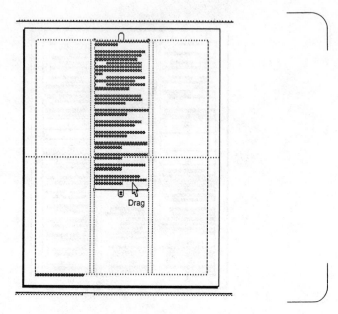

Changing Text Block Length and Width

Once your text is on the page, you can easily change the length of the text block. Use the pointer tool to select the text block and display the handles; then drag the bottom handle up or down, as shown in figures 3.27 and 3.28. If this text block is connected to others after it, the extra text flows automatically into the next connected block when you shorten the first block. When you lengthen the block, additional text flows in from the next connected block.

You cannot lengthen a block of text beyond the extent of the text itself. In other words, if the end of the block is the end of the text—signified by a pound sign (#) in the bottom handle—you cannot drag the bottom handle down any farther.

Normally, the width of a text block is determined by the column guides that you have set up using the "Column guides..." command under the Options menu. Once you have typed or placed text in a column, however, you can change the width of the text block. Use the pointer tool to select the text block; then drag the edges of either windowshade to the left or right.

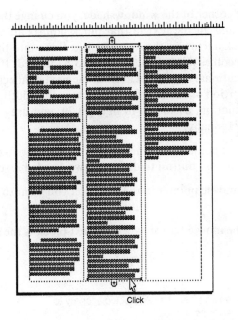

Fig. 3.27. Block of text before shortening.

Click

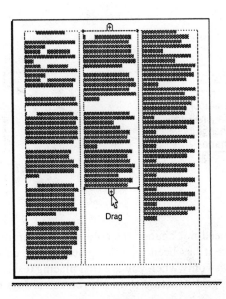

Fig. 3.28. Block of text after shortening.

Drag

By dragging the corner of the windowshade, you change the width of the entire text block; and all the text in that block adjusts automatically. If you make a text block narrower, the overflow text flows into the next connected text block or becomes part of the text yet to be flowed. If you make a text block wider, additional text flows in from the next connected block or from the unflowed portion of the text file. To change the width and the length of a block in one motion, as shown in figure 3.29, you drag the corner of the windowshade diagonally:

1. Position the pointer over the corner of a windowshade and hold down the mouse button to display a two-headed arrow.

2. Drag the mouse pointer in the direction you want to shape the text block.

3. Release the mouse button when the text block is the shape you want.

Fig. 3.29. Dragging the text handle diagonally to change text width and length.

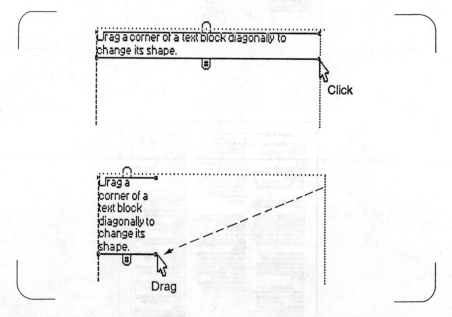

Notice that you need not change the column guides in order to change the width of text once it has been typed or placed in the column. The column guides are necessary only when you are first placing text, and they are a part of the document's grid structure to which you can always return.

Working with Text on the Pasteboard

Normally, you will be placing text from outside files directly into columns in PageMaker. Under some conditions, however, you may want to place text directly on the pasteboard. For instance, you may want all the text to fit on one page; but when you fill the last column, you can see that more text remains in the source file. In figure 3.30, text was flowed onto the pasteboard to see how much overflow needed to be accommodated or edited out. Text that you place on the pasteboard takes on the default width, which is determined by the page margins rather than the column guides.

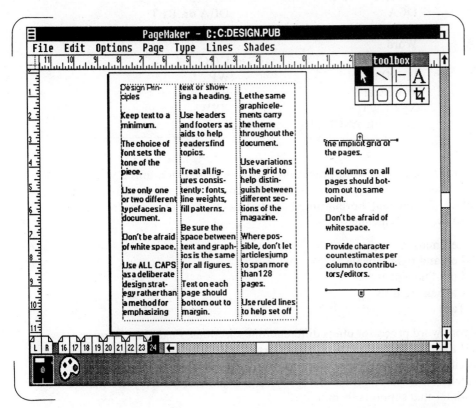

Fig. 3.30. Text flowed to the pasteboard.

Importing Formatted Text

As long as you select the "Retain format" option in the "Place..." command dialog box, PageMaker preserves the formatting of text from such word-processing programs as Windows Write, Microsoft Word, WordPerfect®,

WordStar®, MultiMate™, Lotus Manuscript™, and XyWrite™. In addition, PageMaker reads IBM Document-Content Architecture (DCA) files like those created by IBM DisplayWrite™ 3, SAMNA Word™, Volkswriter® 3, and WordStar 2000. These file names must have the appropriate suffixes so that the files can be converted properly when placed in PageMaker with the "Place..." command. Table 3.2 lists the suffixes.

Table 3.2.
Suffixes for Different Word-Processing Programs

Word Processor	Suffix
DCA	.DCA or .RFT
Windows Write	.WRI
Word	.DOC
Multimate	.DOC
WordPerfect	.WP
WordStar 3.3	.WS
XyWrite III	.XYW
Text-only ASCII files	.TXT

Be sure to save your word-processing files with these extensions if you want PageMaker to translate text-formatting commands when you use the "Place..." command. Formatting characteristics that are preserved from most word processors include

Left margin
Left and right indents
First-line indent
Carriage returns
Tabs

If your word processor offers different font selections, PageMaker may convert the type specifications. If the target printer does not support the type specifications set with that word processor, PageMaker substitutes a close match but remembers the initial specifications and uses them if you switch to a printer that supports them.

The right margin of your text is changed to match PageMaker's column width, with right margin indents preserved from some word processors. But PageMaker ignores specialized formatting commands such as running heads and running feet, footnotes, and the side-by-side command of Microsoft Word.

The examples in figures 3.31 and 3.32 demonstrate how PageMaker preserves formats from compatible word-processing programs. You can use Page-Maker tools to implement any type specifications and formatting options that are not supported by the word-processing program or not preserved in PageMaker (see Chapter 4).

Windows Write

This text was typed in Windows Write, in 10-point Times.

This paragraph has no indent. The ruler line was set with a normal (flush-left) tab at .5 inches and a decimal tab at 2 inches.

    Flush left   Decimal
    text   100.00
                    Centered Bold Text

                            Flush-right Italic Text
                            Bold Italic Text

This paragraph has a normal indent at .25 inches in the word processor.

This paragraph has a reverse or "hanging" indent of .25 inches in the word processor.

This line was set up with a left indent at 1 inch.

This line was set up with a right indent at 1 inch.

This line was set up with left and right indents of 1 inch.

This paragraph is justified in the word processor. The default font and the menu list of fonts changes depending on what printer is selected. The menu in this case offered:

```
Courier 12
Helvetica 14
LinePrinter 8
Times Roman 8 and 10
```

You can specify any size of text.

Fig. 3.31. Formatted Windows Write text placed in PageMaker.

If your word processor is not represented in these examples or if you want to test formatting commands that are not shown here, you should make your own test file and place it in PageMaker.

Importing Unformatted Text

Although you should try to do as much formatting as possible in your word-processing program, sometimes your only sources of text are unformatted text files. You can place unformatted text in PageMaker and format with PageMaker's tools. The three common sources of unformatted text are ASCII files from any word processor, data saved in ASCII format from a

Fig. 3.32. *Formatted Microsoft Word text placed in PageMaker.*

Microsoft Word

This text was typed in Microsoft Word, in 10-point Times.

This paragraph has no indent. The ruler line was set with a normal (flush-left) tab at .5 inches and a decimal tab at 2 inches.
Flush left   Decimal
text   100.00
                                   Centered Bold Text

                                                                    Flush-right Italic Text
                                                                    Bold Italic Text

This paragraph has a normal indent at .25 inches in the word processor.

This paragraph has a reverse or "hanging" indent of .25 inches in the word processor.

This line was set up with a left indent at 1 inch.

This line was set up with a right indent at 1 inch.

This line was set up with left and right indents of 1 inch.

This paragraph is justified in the word processor. The default font and the menu list of fonts changes depending on what printer is selected. The menu in this case offered:

`Courier 12`

Helvetica 14

Times Roman 8 and 10

You can specify any size of text.

spreadsheet or database program, and text that has been telecommunicated through a central mailbox facility. You also can convert formatted text to unformatted text by choosing the "Text only" option on the "Place..." command dialog box.

Initially, unformatted text takes on the default type specifications and format (see table 3.1). The default specifications also are applied to formatted text files if you place them by selecting the "Text only" option in the "Place..." command dialog box.

Efficiency Tip

When To Use the "Text only" Option

If your word processor is not capable of specifying the fonts you want in your publication, adjust the default settings in PageMaker to match the specifications for your publication's text body. Then place files by selecting the "Text only" option to change the format of text.

By changing the default settings first, you can see immediately how the text fills each page. This method is better than placing all the text in the wrong font first and then using the "Select all" command to change the type specifications.

Even if your word processor is not supported directly by PageMaker, you can still place your text files in PageMaker if those files have been saved with the "Text only" option that most word processors offer. If your word processor does not offer this option, you may not be able to place your files in PageMaker.

Most spreadsheet programs and database packages offer the option of saving data as text-only ASCII files. If your program uses the tab character as the delimiter, you can use your word-processing program or PageMaker to set tabs on the ruler line. The data should then fall into columns.

If the other program uses commas or some other delimiter, you must convert these delimiters to tabs before the data can be arranged in columns. Sometimes the text-only files include quotation marks around fields that happened to use the delimiter as part of the data. In either case, you should probably prepare the data with a word-processing program, especially if the text is long.

Text can be telecommunicated from one computer to another, either directly or through a mailbox facility. If you are telecommunicating directly from one computer to another, you can preserve the formatting that is set up in many word-processing programs. If you are sending your text through a mailbox facility, however, the text should probably be stored in ASCII format (text-only) so that you will receive text in this unformatted state.

Just like data saved from spreadsheets, you can either format the telecommunicated text using your word-processing program or place the text in PageMaker to be formatted directly within the program.

PageMaker's text-importing capability is file-extension sensitive. If the extension (.DOC, .TXT, .DCA, and so on) does not appear in the dialog box, you will get another dialog box prompting you for the extension.

Summary

As you can see, the process of placing text in PageMaker is relatively simple. Use the "Place..." command to bring in long text files from other programs. Use the "Paste" command to bring in text that was cut or copied from another part of the publication. Use the text tool from the toolbox to type text.

Build a test file using your own word processor to see how PageMaker handles the text when you place it on a page. Try placing the same test file under each of the two options, "Retain format" and "Text only", to see how they differ.

Once you are familiar with how PageMaker handles your files, do as much preparation as you can in the word-processing program before placing the text in PageMaker. Once the text is in PageMaker, you can use the commands and techniques explained in the next chapter to edit the text and to change the formatting of the text.

Formatting and Editing Text 4

In Chapter 3, you learn that PageMaker retains some of the text formatting set up in the word-processing program used to prepare the text. In most documents, you will probably do still more formatting and editing after placing text on the page in PageMaker. This chapter explains how to use Page-Maker's text tool and Type menu to select text and change its format and content.

In practice, the procedures and steps described in this chapter are part of the page-layout process presented in Chapter 6. They are described here in order to give you an idea of the range of formatting options available through PageMaker and to help you decide how much formatting and editing to do in advance, using your word processor, and how much to do directly in PageMaker. As stressed in Chapters 1 and 3, you should usually do as much formatting and editing as possible during the word-processing stage because PageMaker's graphic WYSIWYG screen processing makes the program slower in text editing than programs that specialize in word-processing functions.

An anecdote can serve to illustrate this point. A company sent its editors to a one-day PageMaker class, hoping that they would be able to produce a 200-page product catalog within two weeks. The next day, the editors began their project. They used an optical character reader to scan in the catalog from the preceding year and placed the scanned-in text files in PageMaker. They decided to make format conversions at the same time that they edited the text with updated information, performing all tasks in PageMaker.

Two hundred hours later, the end was not in sight. (This length of time was due, in part, to the editors' lack of proficiency with PageMaker, as well as to PageMaker's slow editing.) Finally, the editors decided to go back to the originally scanned-in text files and edit them in their word-processing program.

The editors used global searches for needed conversions and then went through and edited the text with updated information. They accomplished all these tasks with the word processor in only 10 hours; placing the edited text files in PageMaker took another 10 hours. In only 20 hours, the editors finished the entire job; but they had already lost four weeks by using the wrong approach initially.

So why do any formatting in PageMaker? There are at least two good reasons. For example, your word processor may not be capable of producing the type of formatting called for in your design specifications. Therefore, before you decide what format to use, you may want to wait until you can see the whole page on the screen in PageMaker. Or perhaps the division of responsibilities and the skills on your team are such that the person typing the text in the word processor does not know the final format, and the person using PageMaker does all formatting.

In any case, you can learn a lesson from the troubles of the catalog production team. Before you embark on any large project with PageMaker, place a few pages of text in PageMaker and try performing some of the formatting and editing steps that are described in this chapter. Format some text according to the design specifications for your document. Then, make lists of the specifications that cannot be done at the word-processing stage and of those that are not retained when the text is placed in PageMaker. After these steps, you can decide how much formatting to save for the layout steps with PageMaker.

Selecting Text with the Text Tool

In Chapter 3, you learned that to display handles and move or reshape a whole block of text, you use the pointer tool to select the block. To format or edit text, you select it with the text tool.

You select the text tool either by clicking on the large A in the toolbox or using the keyboard shortcut, Shift-F4. When you select the text tool, the pointer changes to an I-beam icon, as shown in figure 4.1. You use this I-beam to position the text-insertion point for entry of new text, as described in Chapter 3, or to select text that is already on the page, as described next.

Fig. 4.1. The text tool
I-beam icon.

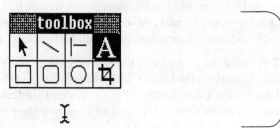

Selecting Text within a Block

The most generally applicable method of selecting any amount of text within a block is to drag the I-beam over the text you want. In other words, you put the I-beam next to the first part of the text you want to select. Then, you hold down the mouse button as you drag the I-beam to the end of the text to be selected. If necessary, the screen scrolls as you drag the I-beam down a column. When you release the mouse button, the selected text appears in reverse video (see fig. 4.2).

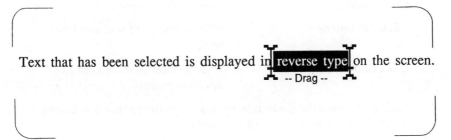

Text that has been selected is displayed in reverse type on the screen.

-- Drag --

Fig. 4.2. Selecting text by dragging the I-beam.

To place the text-insertion point within a text block, you click once with the I-beam between two characters. To select a whole word (including the space that follows), you double-click (click the mouse twice) with the I-beam on that word. To select a whole paragraph, triple-click (click the mouse three times) with the I-beam in the paragraph. To select an entire text file (all the linked text blocks that were brought from the same text file, such as one story or article), you click the I-beam anywhere in a text block; then you choose "Select all" from the Edit menu.

You can use many shortcut methods to select text groups, including segments that cross multiple blocks of linked text. These methods, described in table 4.1, involve clicking the mouse once, twice, or three times, either alone or with special keys. For example, to select the end of a text file, you click the I-beam once to put the text-insertion point in front of the first word or character you want to select; then you press Shift-Ctrl-PgDn.

Selecting a Whole Text File

To select all the text in a series of linked text blocks, you use the "Select all" command, as shown in figure 4.3. To issue this command, select the text tool and click once anywhere in any single block that is part of the continuous file. Then, you either specify "Select all" on the Edit menu or use the keyboard shortcut, Ctrl-A.

Table 4.1
Shortcuts for Moving the Text-Insertion Point and Selecting Text

Key/Click Sequence	Result
Click once	Selects next point of insertion for new text from keyboard
Click-drag	Selects a range of text character-by-character or line-by-line
Click twice	Selects whole word
Click-twice-drag	Selects a range of text word-by-word
Click-Shift-click	Selects all the text between two insertion points

Each of the preceding selection methods sets the anchor point from which the following keyboard commands operate:

Shift-left arrow Shift-right arrow	Extends or decreases the selection one character at a time to the left or right of the anchor point
Shift-Ctrl-left arrow Shift-Ctrl-right arrow	Extends or decreases the selection one word at a time to the left or the right
Shift-Home or Shift-up arrow Shift-End or Shift-down arrow	Extends or decreases the selection one line at a time
Shift-Ctrl-Home Shift-Ctrl-End	Extends or decreases the selection one sentence at a time
Shift-Ctrl-up arrow Shift-Ctrl-down arrow	Extends or decreases the selection one paragraph at a time
Shift-PgUp Shift-PgDn	Extends or decreases the selection a fixed distance determined by the view and the resolution of your screen
Shift-Ctrl-PgUp Shift-Ctrl-PgDn	Extends or decreases the selection to the beginning or the end of the article

(If your keyed selections require a jump to another page, PageMaker displays the new page.)

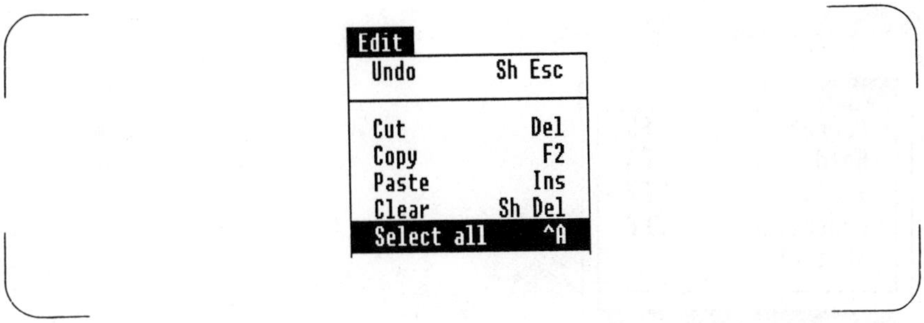

Fig. 4.3. The "Select all" command.

```
Edit
 Undo       Sh Esc

 Cut           Del
 Copy           F2
 Paste         Ins
 Clear      Sh Del
 Select all      ^A
```

After selecting text by any of the techniques explained in the preceding paragraphs and in table 4.1, you may perform the tasks described throughout this chapter.

Changing Type Specifications

Type specifications determine the appearance of the characters of text—the font of the text. All the options for defining the type specifications of selected text can be entered in the "Type specifications" dialog box, shown in figure 4.4. Some of these options are repeated as commands on the Type menu and also have shortcuts for entering them through the keyboard.

As explained in Chapter 3, you can change the default type specifications by using the Type menu commands when the pointer tool is selected. You can change the defaults when the text tool is selected, as long as no text is selected and the text insertion point is not positioned on the page. The default specifications apply to new text typed in PageMaker and to unformatted text files that are brought into PageMaker.

You also can use the Type menu commands to change the specifications for text that is currently selected with the text tool. When you first display the Type menu or any of its associated dialog boxes, the screen shows the options that apply to the current selection. If the current selection includes more than one format, the appropriate selection box or entry in the dialog box is blank.

Changing Type Specifications through the Dialog Box

When you give the "Type specs..." command, the screen displays the "Type specifications" dialog box. Here, you define the font name and size, leading, style, position, and case of the selected characters (again see fig. 4.4). These specifications define what a character will look like.

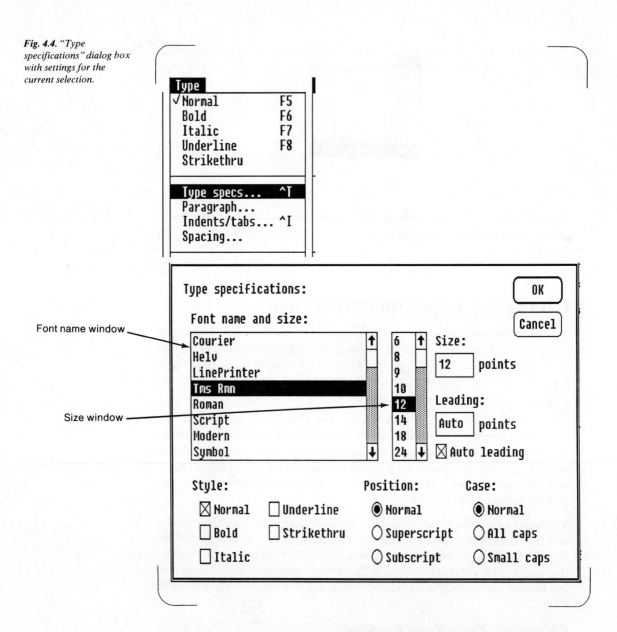

Fig. 4.4. *"Type specifications" dialog box with settings for the current selection.*

The "Font name and size" heading in the "Type specifications" dialog box is a slight misnomer. To be more correct, the heading should read "Typeface and size". Technically speaking, a *font* is a specific combination of typeface, size, and style. A *typeface* is the more general family name. For example, 10-point Times italic is a different font from 12-point Times italic, but both are the same typeface (Times).

Typefaces and sizes are displayed in scrolling windows in the "Type specifications" dialog box. To select a typeface, you use the scroll bars, if necessary, to display the name you want and then click on that name to highlight it.

The typefaces that appear in the dialog box are determined by the printer you have and the typefaces you have installed. If you have installed more than one kind of printer, or if you have installed more typefaces than the current printer or cartridge can handle, you should select only faces for which your printer is set up.

To select a size, you scroll to any number in the size window and click on that number. In the "Size" box itself, you also can specify any size from 4 to 127 points—not just the sizes listed on the scrolling menu. Not all printers, however, handle all sizes of every typeface. (For a detailed discussion of printer fonts, see Chapter 8.)

Leading is a measure of the distance from the base of one line of text to the base of the next line, as illustrated in figure 4.5. If you specify "Auto" in the "Leading" box, PageMaker sets the leading and automatically adjusts it if you change the point size of the text. If you enter a specific value for the leading, when you change the point size, you may need to change the leading, too.

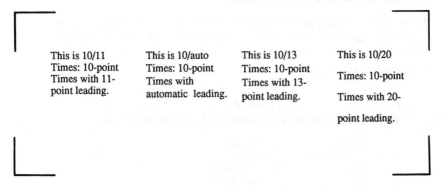

Fig. 4.5. Examples of leading.

This is 10/11
Times: 10-point
Times with 11-
point leading.

This is 10/auto
Times: 10-point
Times with
automatic leading.

This is 10/13
Times: 10-point
Times with 13-
point leading.

This is 10/20

Times: 10-point

Times with 20-

point leading.

With automatic leading selected, PageMaker sets leading at 120 percent of the point size—to the nearest half point. For example, 10-point type gets 12-point leading.

To achieve a particular look, you may want to specify the leading precisely as part of the design specifications (see Chapters 8 and 9). Changing the leading is also a way of fitting copy into a defined space. For example, you can adjust the leading in order to squeeze text on a tight page, to expand text to fill an area, or to force two columns to the same length. Leading may be adjusted in half-point increments.

The five styles listed in the "Type specifications" dialog box also appear as commands on the Type menu. The most common styles have keyboard equivalents: the F5 key sets normal text, F6 sets text in boldface, F7 sets italic, and F8 sets underscores.

The options for the "Position" of text include "Normal", "Superscript", and "Subscript". Superscripts and subscripts may affect the leading where they occur. Some printers cannot print superscripts and subscripts in all sizes.

You can automatically convert any text to "All caps" (all capital letters) or to "Small caps". Small caps are 70 percent the height of full caps (see fig. 4.6).

Fig. 4.6. All caps and small caps.

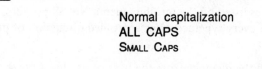

Normal capitalization
ALL CAPS
SMALL CAPS

Using Keyboard Shortcuts

Table 4.2 provides a list of keyboard shortcuts for changing type specifications. You turn off selected style settings for selected text by using the same function key that turns on the setting. (Remember that these switches are called toggle switches.)

Table 4.2
Keyboard Shortcuts for Changing Type Specifications

Key(s)	Action
F5	Normal style
F6	Boldface
F7	Italicize
F8	Underscore
Shift-F9	Decrease point size
Shift-F10	Increase point size
Ctrl-L	Align on left
Ctrl-C	Align in center
Ctrl-R	Align on right
Ctrl-J	Justify

Defining Paragraph Formats

Type specifications define the appearance of each character; but paragraph specifications determine the alignment of the text (left, right, centered, or justified); the spacing between characters; and hyphenation. A paragraph in PageMaker includes all the text between two hard carriage returns. A hard carriage return occurs wherever you press the Enter key while you are entering text. The computer distinguishes between these returns and the soft (or changeable) returns that occur with automatic wordwrap. For example, if you change the width of the text, the soft returns shift to new positions; but the hard carriage returns still mark the ends of lines and, by definition, the ends of paragraphs.

Paragraph specifications apply to whole paragraphs, regardless of how much text is selected. In other words, when you select one of the commands that affect whole paragraphs ("Paragraph...", "Indents/tabs...", or "Spacing..."), the options you choose apply to all the text for any paragraph in which the text-insertion or selection point is positioned (see fig. 4.7).

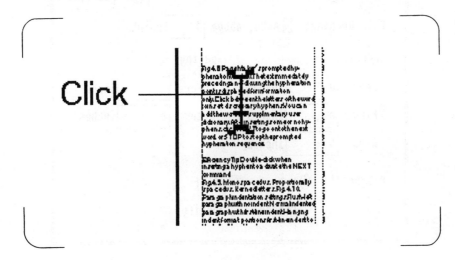

Fig. 4.7. Paragraph specifications applied to whole paragraphs.

Choosing Paragraph Specifications

When you choose the "Paragraph..." command from the Type menu, the "Paragraph specifications" dialog box appears (see fig. 4.8). Here, you select the options that affect hyphenation, kerning conditions (the space between letters) for the entire paragraph, paragraph indentation, spacing between words, and paragraph alignment (left, right, centered, justified).

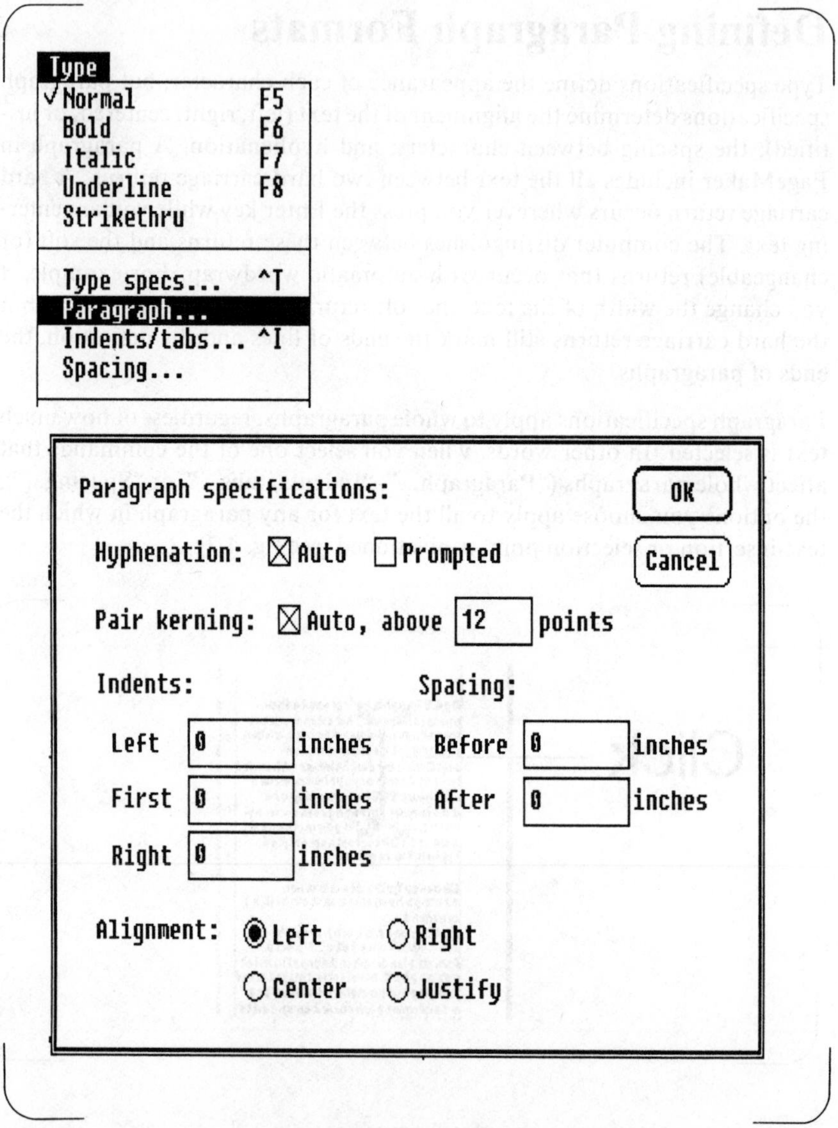

Fig. 4.8. The Type menu
and "Paragraph
specifications" dialog
box.

```
┌─────────────────────────────┐
│ Type                        │
│ √ Normal          F5        │
│   Bold            F6        │
│   Italic          F7        │
│   Underline       F8        │
│   Strikethru                │
│                             │
│   Type specs...   ^T        │
│ ▓ Paragraph...              │
│   Indents/tabs... ^I        │
│   Spacing...                │
└─────────────────────────────┘
```

```
┌────────────────────────────────────────────────┐
│  Paragraph specifications:            ┌──────┐  │
│                                       │  OK  │  │
│  Hyphenation:  ⊠ Auto  ☐ Prompted     └──────┘  │
│                                      ┌────────┐ │
│  Pair kerning: ⊠ Auto, above │ 12 │  │ Cancel │ │
│                              points  └────────┘ │
│                                                 │
│  Indents:                Spacing:               │
│                                                 │
│  Left   │ 0 │ inches     Before │ 0 │ inches    │
│                                                 │
│  First  │ 0 │ inches     After  │ 0 │ inches    │
│                                                 │
│  Right  │ 0 │ inches                            │
│                                                 │
│                                                 │
│  Alignment:  ◉ Left     ○ Right                 │
│              ○ Center   ○ Justify               │
│                                                 │
└────────────────────────────────────────────────┘
```

Changes made in the "Paragraph specifications" dialog box are not reflected in the text on-screen until the dialog box is closed.

Controlling Hyphenation

Usually, PageMaker automatically hyphenates text as you are typing it or placing it on the page. The program does so by looking up each word in a

Houghton-Mifflin dictionary of more than 90,000 terms. The process seems instantaneous as you are working. With the options in the "Paragraph specifications" dialog box, you can turn off hyphenation, add terms to the dictionary, and control hyphenation on a case-by-case basis. Following are descriptions of these options.

Using the "Auto" and "Prompted" Options

"Auto" on, "Prompted" off is the default setting for hyphenation. This selection invokes the automatic hyphenation.

When both automatic hyphenation and prompted hyphenation are on, PageMaker hyphenates words according to hyphenation information provided in the dictionary. If the program cannot find a word in the dictionary, PageMaker prompts you to hyphenate the word manually by clicking points within the words as they appear in the prompted hyphenation window (see fig. 4.9). Prompted hyphenation applies to justified text only; you will not be prompted to hyphenate unjustified text.

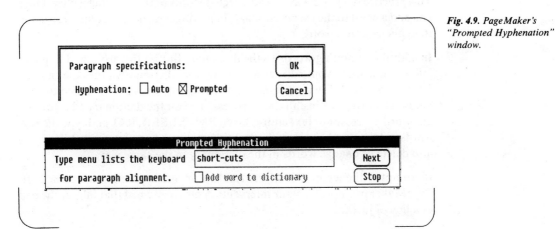

Fig. 4.9. PageMaker's "Prompted Hyphenation" window.

When prompted hyphenation is turned on, you proceed as follows:

1. Wait for PageMaker to identify and display a word that the program cannot hyphenate automatically. The text immediately preceding and following the hyphenation point is displayed for information only.

2. To insert discretionary hyphens, you click between the letters of the word at the correct locations for hyphenation.

3. You may add the word to a supplementary user dictionary by selecting that option.

4. After inserting some—or no—hyphens, you click either "Next" to
   go on to the next word or "Stop" to stop the prompted
   hyphenation sequence.

Faster Prompted Hyphenation

To activate the "Next" command, double-click when inserting a hyphen. The
few seconds you save per word can add up to hours saved for long documents
with many foreign or technical terms.

When you are placing justified text, you can work with prompted hyphenation on. However, to place all the text quickly, work with this feature off and
then turn it on for selected text only. In other words, you can apply prompted
hyphenation to specific text selections after placing all the text. Wait until you
see that certain terms are causing bad line breaks; then activate prompted hyphenation for only that portion of the text.

This practice is a good way to add selected words to the user dictionary. Once
you add a word to the user dictionary, PageMaker does not prompt you again
to hyphenate that word.

In addition to adding words to the dictionary during the prompted hyphenation sequences, you can also update the dictionary—the file named
PMUSUSER.TXT, which comes on the program disks and is copied to your
hard disk during the installation process. To edit the dictionary file, you use
any word processor or text editor. Open PMUSUSER.TXT and type the new
words, adding hyphens in each place where a word can be divided. You can
also delete or change words in the dictionary in the same way.

If prompted hyphenation is selected and automatic hyphenation is turned off,
PageMaker prompts for your intervention on every word that falls at the end
of a line of justified text.

If both hyphenation options are turned off, PageMaker does no hyphenating
on its own. If the text was hyphenated in the word-processing program, however, the discretionary hyphens set there still result in line breaks in
PageMaker.

Using Discretionary Hyphenation

To insert discretionary hyphens manually within words, you press Ctrl and
the hyphen key simultaneously. You can insert these discretionary hyphens
by using the word processor before the text is placed in PageMaker, or after
the text is placed in PageMaker. Discretionary hyphens "behave" in the same

way as automatic hyphens: They appear on-screen and in print only when they fall at the end of a line.

You delete discretionary hyphens as you do any other character—by selecting them and pressing the backspace key.

Using Kerning

Kerning refers to the fine adjustments that are made to the space between certain combinations of letters in order to achieve a balanced look. When kerning is not active, each character is assigned a specific width determined by the font selection and the character itself. For example, all 10-point Times italic *A*'s have the same width.

When kerning is turned on, the spacing between two letters is adjusted slightly in accordance with the values stored in PageMaker's table of "kerning pairs." For example, in figure 4.10, the space between the characters **AV** is smaller than the space between the characters **VE** because of the shapes of the letters. If the spacing between the different pairs is not adjusted or kerned, the **A** and **V** will seem to be farther apart than the **V** and **E** are. For this reason, kerned text generally looks better than text that is not kerned.

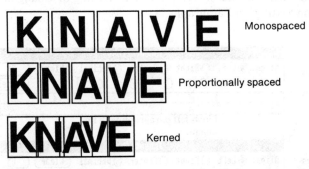

Monospaced

Proportionally spaced

Kerned

Fig. 4.10. Monospaced, proportionally spaced, and kerned letters.

The "Pair kerning" option in the "Paragraph specifications" dialog box activates automatic kerning for all text above 12 points in size. You may change the point size below which kerning is turned off, or you may turn off kerning entirely for a whole document or selected paragraphs.

Efficiency Tip

Use Automatic Kerning for Large Fonts Only

Your pages will be printed more quickly if kerning is turned off for small point sizes. If you do not want to turn off kerning, you can set it to a number higher than any point size you are using.

Not all printers support kerning, but PageMaker offers kerning capability for the printers that can support it. For more information on the pros and cons of kerning and ways to kern the spaces between letters manually, see Chapter 8.

Indenting Paragraphs

The "Paragraph specifications" dialog box enables you to set paragraph indents. You also can set or change indents by using the "Indents/tabs..." command. The only difference between these two alternatives is that you can specify decimal increments for indents with the "Paragraph..." command, but you are limited to fixed increments on the ruler line if you use the "Indents/tabs..." command. Any changes made to the "Indents/tabs" ruler line are reflected in the "Page specifications" dialog box, and vice versa.

You may use three different indentation settings for any paragraph: left indent, first-line indent, and right indent. Figure 4.11 shows how different indentation settings affect the text and what those settings look like in the dialog box and on the ruler line. Notice that you can use these settings to create a hanging indentation. In the third example, the "Left" indent is set at 0.25 inches, and the "First" line indent is set at −0.25 inches. (For a description of how to change the ruler line, see the section called "Setting or Changing Tabs and Indentation Settings in Paragraphs.")

Fig. 4.11. Paragraph indentation settings.

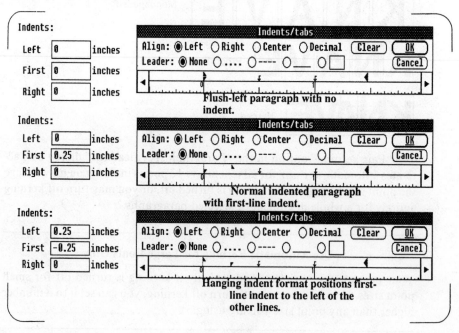

The unit of measure shown in the dialog box reflects the current setting of the "Preferences" command on the Edit menu. You can use this command to work in inches, picas and points, centimeters, or ciceros (see Chapter 9).

Setting the Spacing between Paragraphs

You specify the spacing between paragraphs in the "Paragraph specifications" dialog box, as shown in figure 4.12. Wherever a new paragraph occurs, PageMaker adds to the usual spacing between lines the amounts entered in the "Before" and "After" boxes. Stated more precisely, the values you enter for spacing between paragraphs is added wherever a hard carriage return appears in the text.

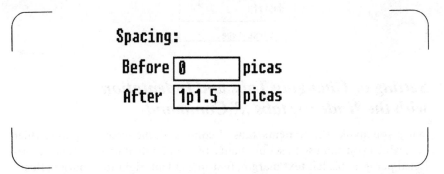

Fig. 4.12. Specifying spacing between paragraphs.

This method of defining breaks between paragraphs yields more flexible results than using extra carriage returns (empty lines) or changing leading in order to add space between paragraphs. When you have two or more hard carriage returns in a row, the spacing value is added twice or more. If you are accustomed to double-spacing between paragraphs, you may want to experiment with the spacing setting on short documents before you decide to strip out all double carriage returns in your text.

Aligning Paragraphs

PageMaker offers four alignment options for paragraphs: flush left, flush right, centered, or justified. To specify alignment, you use the "Paragraph specifications" dialog box, select the alignment directly on the Type menu, or use the keyboard shortcuts for paragraph alignment (see fig. 4.13). Any changes made through the menu or keyboard also are reflected in the dialog box.

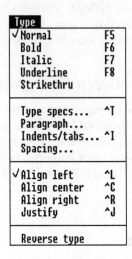

Fig. 4.13. The Type menu with keyboard shortcuts for paragraph alignment.

Setting or Changing Tabs and Indentation with the "Indents/tabs..." Command

When you invoke the "Indents/tabs..." command, the screen displays a ruler line, which you can use to set or change tabs and indentation settings for selected paragraphs: left text margin, first-line indent, right text margin, flush-left tab, flush-right tab, center tab, and decimal tab (see fig. 4.14). Changes made to the indentation settings on the ruler line are also reflected in the "Paragraph specifications" dialog box. You can define indentation by entering numeric values in the "Paragraph specifications" dialog box, but you can achieve the same results by clicking and dragging icons on the ruler line.

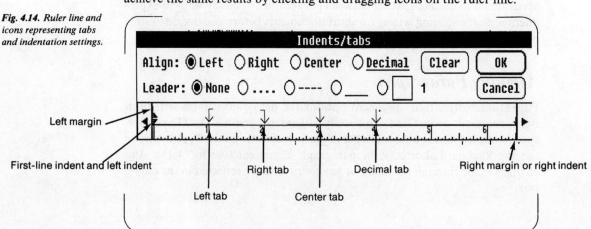

Fig. 4.14. Ruler line and icons representing tabs and indentation settings.

PageMaker sets default tabs every half inch on the ruler line. If you set tabs in the word-processing program, then, when you place the text, PageMaker's ruler lines change to reflect those settings.

To change the ruler line, you select the text and then choose the "Indents/tabs..." command on the Type menu. When the ruler line window appears, you can move the window and use the scroll bars to put it over the text you want to format (see fig. 4.15). (This procedure is not necessary if you want to base all your settings on measured values rather than on the screen image.)

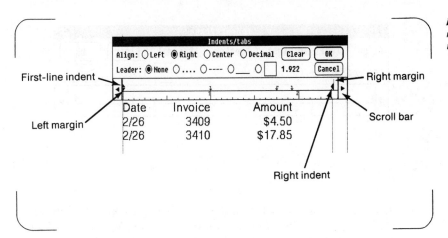

Fig. 4.15. Placing the ruler line window over the text to be formatted.

The "Indents/tabs" ruler is always displayed in the scale that matches the screen view; the ruler shows a wider measure in the "Fit in window" view than in "Actual size", for example. When you are working in close views, you may not be able to see both the left and right margins at once in the "Indents/tabs" dialog box. Use the scroll arrows at the ends of the ruler to see extensions of the measure.

Efficiency Tip

Position the "Indents/tabs" Ruler over the Column

The "Indents/tabs" dialog box is a window that can be moved on the screen by dragging the title bar with the pointer. You can also use the scrolling arrows at each end of the ruler to move it inside the window.

For convenience in setting tabs and indents, position the zero point of the "Indents/tabs" ruler over the left column guide of the text (see fig. 4.15).

Adding and Deleting Tabs

To add a tab, you first define the type of tab: click left, right, center, or decimal (see fig. 4.16). Then you select the leader option. A tab *leader* is a character that fills in the space between two tab stops. You can select a line of periods, hyphens, or underscores; or you can define your own leader characters by clicking the fourth option and typing one or two (alternating) characters in the box, as shown in the figure.

Fig. 4.16. Setting tabs on the ruler line.

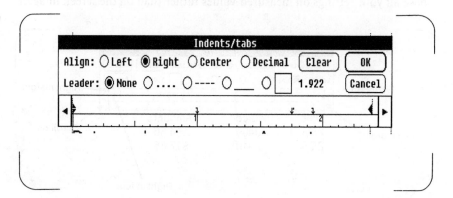

After defining the tab, you set it on the ruler line by clicking just above the ruler line in the location where you want to set the tab. When you set a tab, the numeric value of the new tab position appears in the ruler line window.

Once you set a tab stop, you can move it or delete it; but you cannot change the tab's alignment (left, right, center, or decimal) or leader settings. If you want to change these settings, you must delete the tab and create another one with new settings.

Settings are limited to the increments on the ruler line. The number of increments per unit of measure depends on the size in which you are working on the screen. For example, when working in "200% size", you can use finer increments than when you work in a reduced view of the page.

To delete individual tabs, you click on the tab marker and hold down the mouse button as you drag the tab down to the bottom of the ruler line. You can clear all the tabs at once by clicking "Clear" in the ruler window.

Moving a Tab or Indentation Marker

To move a tab, you click on the tab marker and hold down the mouse button as you drag the tab horizontally along the ruler line. As you move a tab, the ruler line window displays the current ruler measure.

You can copy a ruler line from one paragraph to subsequent paragraphs. Select the text you want to affect, beginning with the paragraph with the ruler you want to copy and including the subsequent paragraphs that you want to match the first one. When the ruler line appears, it shows only the settings that apply to the first paragraph selected (see fig. 4.17). Make any change to the ruler, such as adding a tab; and then close the ruler line window. The new ruler line will apply to all the selected text. (You must make at least one change to the ruler line in order for any changes to be registered in the text.)

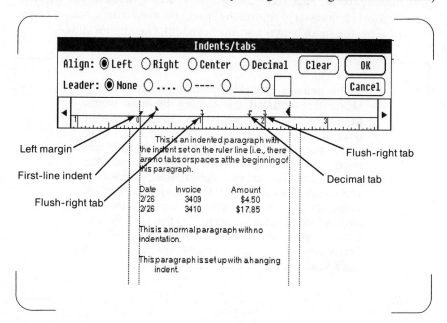

Fig. 4.17. *Ruler line showing settings for first selected paragraph.*

You cannot set more than 20 tab stops on the ruler line. If you try to add a tab and find that PageMaker does not accept it, the ruler line may already have 20 tabs set.

Changes made on the ruler line are not reflected on the screen until you close the ruler line window. Changes made to the ruler line affect only the selected text. Changes made with the pointer tool selected or with the text tool selected but no text selected become the new default values.

Once tab stops are set on the ruler line, text that already has tab characters falls into place below each tab stop. You add tab characters to align text by positioning the I-beam for text insertion and pressing the tab key.

Controlling Spacing

In unjustified text, the amount of space between words and letters is determined by the font and kerning tables. In justified text, on the other hand, infinitesimal amounts of space are added or deleted between letters and words in order to make the text fit between the left and right margins (see fig. 4.18). The "Spacing..." command on the Type menu enables you to control the amount of space added or deleted between words and characters. During the justification process, PageMaker adjusts the spaces between words, hyphenates words when necessary, adjusts the spaces between letters, and, if necessary, expands the space between words beyond the maximum allowed.

Fig. 4.18. *Process of justification.*

In the process of justifying this paragraph, Page-Maker first adjusted the spacing between words (within the limits specified on the "Spacing..." dialog box). After this process, words that extended past the end of each line were broken at the hyphens (if any were inserted by PageMaker's automatic hyphenation process when the text was placed). Next, to make the line exactly flush at the right margin, spacing was adjusted between letters within the words (within the limits specified in the "Spacing..." dialog box). Finally, if the line was still not flush at the right margin, Page-Maker extended the space between words *beyond* the limits specified in the "Spacing..." dialog box.

Efficiency Tip

Getting Fewer Hyphens

Turn on hyphenation for justified text. If you want fewer hyphens, turn off justification (use flush-left text) or expand the allowance for word and letter spacing in the "Spacing..." command dialog box.

To adjust the ranges allowed for spacing, you select the "Spacing..." command on the Type menu and then, in the "Spacing attributes" dialog box that appears, specify the spacing values as percentages. For example, 100 percent is equal to one normal space, as defined for that font (see fig. 4.19). You may specify

- The "Minimum", "Desired", and "Maximum" spaces allowed between words. PageMaker starts with the desired space between each word on the line, and expands or condenses from that point within the limits specified as minimum and maximum for justified text. For text that is not justified, the spacing specified in the "Desired" box is used throughout.

- The minimum and maximum allowed for spacing between letters when text is justified. These settings do not apply to text that is not justified (0% is assumed).

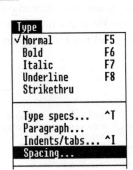

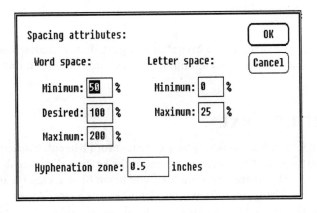

Fig. 4.19. Type menu and "Spacing attributes" dialog box.

The "Hyphenation zone" is the acceptable area along the right margin within which the program will hyphenate a word. The figure you enter for the "Hyphenation zone" is an absolute value rather than a percentage and applies to unjustified text only. When hyphenating unjustified text, PageMaker takes one of two actions:

- If the word begins within the hyphenation zone and does not fit on a line, the program carries the word to the next line (that is, does not hyphenate the word).

- If the word begins to the left of the hyphenation zone, PageMaker hyphenates the word.

In other words, the "Hyphenation zone" setting enables you to control the minimum line length of unjustified text. A narrow hyphenation zone results in a great deal of hyphenation. The wider the hyphenation zone, the more ragged the right margin is (see fig. 4.20). When hyphenation is turned off, the hyphenation zone is limited only by the length of the longest word in the text. Lines may be shorter than the hyphenation zone, and the text may be very ragged.

Fig. 4.20. Effects of hyphenation zone on unjustified text.

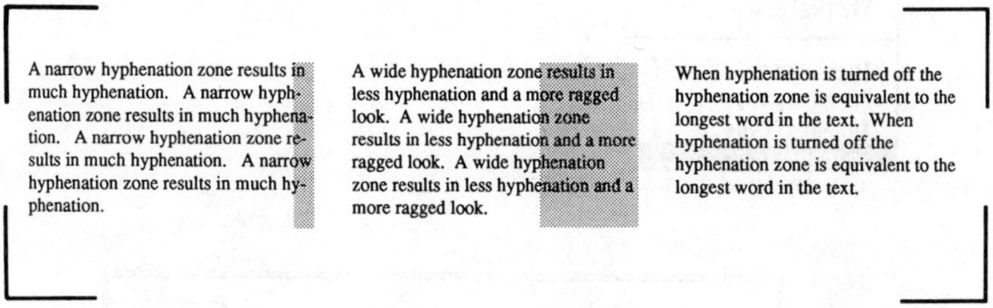

A narrow hyphenation zone results in much hyphenation. A narrow hyphenation zone results in much hyphenation. A narrow hyphenation zone results in much hyphenation. A narrow hyphenation zone results in much hyphenation.

A wide hyphenation zone results in less hyphenation and a more ragged look. A wide hyphenation zone results in less hyphenation and a more ragged look. A wide hyphenation zone results in less hyphenation and a more ragged look.

When hyphenation is turned off the hyphenation zone is equivalent to the longest word in the text. When hyphenation is turned off the hyphenation zone is equivalent to the longest word in the text.

Note that the variables set in the "Spacing attributes" dialog box apply to the entire article or text file containing the text-insertion point or text selection.

Editing Text

To edit text in PageMaker, you use the text tool I-beam. You can replace text or insert new text by entering the text at the keyboard, as you do with a word processor. If you are replacing text, you begin by marking the text you want to replace. Then, you type new text from the keyboard. As soon as you begin typing, the marked block of text is deleted; you do not have to delete the block before you begin typing.

If you want to keep all existing text and insert new text, you position the I-beam where you want the new text to begin. As you type, existing text shifts to make room for the inserted text. Although in some instances you may need to replace or insert text in these ways, remember to use the Edit menu's commands (or their keyboard equivalents) to cut, copy, and paste text through the Windows Clipboard.

Chapter 2 describes methods of moving around on the screen or through documents. For your convenience, table 4.3 lists the shortcuts mentioned in that chapter.

Table 4.3
Shortcuts for Moving Around on the Screen or in a Document

Key/Click Sequence	Result
Click once	Selects next point of insertion for new text from keyboard
Left arrow Right arrow	Moves the insertion point one character at a time to the left or right of the current point
Ctrl-left arrow Ctrl-right arrow	Moves the insertion point one word at a time to the left or right
Home or up arrow End or down arrow	Moves the insertion point one line at a time
Ctrl-Home Ctrl-End	Moves the insertion point one sentence at a time
Ctrl-up arrow Ctrl-down arrow	Moves the insertion point one paragraph at a time
PgUp, PgDn	Moves the insertion point a fixed distance determined by the view and the resolution of your screen
Ctrl-PgUp, Ctrl-PgDn	Moves the insertion point to the beginning or end of the article

(If your keyed selections require a jump to another page, PageMaker displays the new page.)

Summary

Now that you have seen (in this chapter and Chapter 3) the wide range of formatting options that PageMaker provides, you can compare PageMaker's features with the capabilities of your word-processing program and decide how to approach any large publication project. Remember that the goal is to do as much formatting in the word processor as possible, as long as PageMaker retains that formatting when you place the text on the page.

Few word processors, however, have the full range of options available through PageMaker for selecting typefaces and sizes and for controlling the amount of space between words, letters, and lines of text. Chapter 6 provides more tips about efficient methods of applying these specifications in the page layout stage. Chapters 8 and 9 offer suggestions on when to modify the defaults for these settings, and Chapters 10 through 14 contain examples of the settings used in specific documents. Before you move into the multifaceted design and layout steps, read the next chapter to learn about the sources of graphics for a PageMaker publication.

Graphics 5

One of the characteristics of PageMaker and the other new page-composition programs is their capability to incorporate graphics and text on a page. PageMaker contains some graphics tools and also enables you to import graphics created in other programs, such as Windows Draw, In*a*Vision™, AutoCAD®, 1-2-3, Symphony®, Windows Graphics Device Interface (GDI) metafiles, Windows metafile (WMF), Encapsulated PostScript (EPS) formats, Windows Paint®, PC Paintbrush, and Publisher's Paintbrush™. You also can import scanned images that are saved as PC Paintbrush files or in TIFF format.

This chapter familiarizes you with the alternatives available for adding graphics to a page and helps you decide how to prepare graphics in other programs. You learn how to create graphics by using PageMaker's tools and how to import graphics created in other programs. The differences among graphics from various sources are explained, and the function of the cropping tool is discussed. You also learn how to use the pointer tool to select, move, and scale (resize) graphics. Chapter 6 presents the specific applications for the procedures introduced here.

Creating and Importing Graphics

In PageMaker, you have three ways of generating graphics. You can use PageMaker's built-in graphics tools. You can use the "Paste" command to bring in graphics from Window's Clipboard; and you can use the "Place..." command, which brings in graphics created in other programs.

Creating Graphics with the Toolbox Drawing Tools

All PageMaker's built-in graphics tools appear as icons in the toolbox. The toolbox itself, shown in figure 5.1, is actually a window. You can move the toolbox to any position or hide it entirely (by issuing the "Toolbox" command from the Options menu).

Fig. 5.1. The Options
menu and the toolbox.

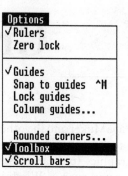

The toolbox provides eight tools. You have already seen how to use the text tool and how to use the pointer tool to select, move, and size blocks of text. In this section, you find out how to draw straight lines and create boxes, circles, and ovals with the toolbox's five drawing tools:

- The diagonal-line tool

- The perpendicular-line tool

- The square-corner tool

- The rounded-corner tool

- The oval tool

When you select one of the five drawing tools, the pointer changes to a crossbar. All five drawing tools work the same way: You place the crossbar at one corner of the graphic area on either the page or pasteboard, and you hold down the mouse button as you drag the crossbar to the opposite end of the desired area (see fig. 5.2). As long as you hold down the mouse button, you can keep adjusting the size of the object. Once you release the mouse button, the graphic is set. To change the size or position of a completed graphic, you must switch to the pointer tool, as described in this chapter.

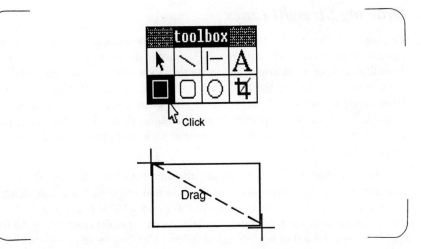

Fig. 5.2. Drawing a graphic.

By selecting line patterns from the Lines menu, you can further define any object you create with PageMaker's built-in tools. You can fill two-dimensional objects with patterns from the Shades menu (see fig. 5.3). These menus affect only graphics created in PageMaker; they cannot be applied to graphics imported from other programs. Drawn objects have the default settings for line style and shade: hairline width and no fill pattern, respectively. You can change these settings either before or after you draw the object (the following sections explain how to make these changes).

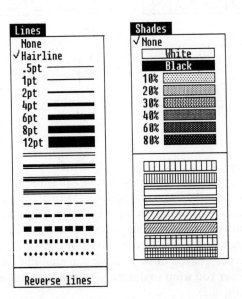

Fig. 5.3. The Lines and Shades menus.

Drawing Straight Lines

You use both the diagonal-line tool and the perpendicular-line tool to draw straight lines. What is the difference? Using the diagonal-line tool, you can draw lines that cross at any angle; using the perpendicular-line tool, you can draw only lines that, as the tool name indicates, are perpendicular to each other or are drawn at a 45-degree angle. To draw a square or rectangle, for example, you choose the perpendicular-line tool. If, on the other hand, you are drawing a figure with lines that angle at various degrees, you choose the diagonal-line tool.

The diagonal-line tool and perpendicular-line tool are activated from the tool-box (see fig. 5.4). When you use the diagonal-line tool, the diagonal lines begin and end exactly at the crossbar points (see the left side of fig. 5.4). With the perpendicular-line tool, however, the line that results from dragging the tool is always vertical or horizontal or follows a 45-degree angle (see the right side of fig. 5.4). That is, a perpendicular line begins at the crossbar point and ends at the 45-degree increment nearest the ending crossbar location.

Fig. 5.4. Using the perpendicular-line and diagonal-line tools.

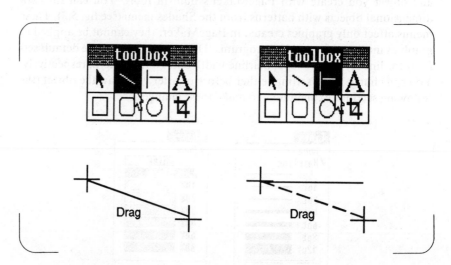

Because the perpendicular-line tool creates lines that are perpendicular to each other or angled at 45 degrees, you use this tool when figures contain only these types of lines. However, if you need to draw a figure that contains lines that are perpendicular to each other, lines that are angled at 45 degrees, and lines that are angled at other degrees, you can use the diagonal-line tool to draw all three types. As you draw with the diagonal-line tool, hold down the Shift key whenever you want to draw a perpendicular line or a line angled at 45 degrees (see fig. 5.5).

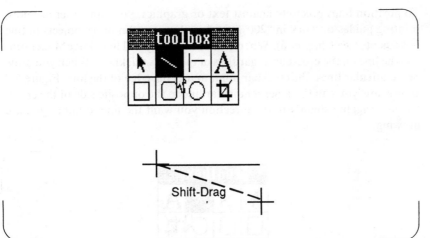

Fig. 5.5. Forcing perpendicular lines with the diagonal-line tool.

Lines drawn with the diagonal- or perpendicular-line tool have small black squares as handles at each end when the lines are first drawn or when they are selected with the pointer tool (see "Selecting, Moving, and Scaling Graphics with the Pointer Tool"). To change a line's length or angle, you drag one of these corner handles. To move a line to another position, you drag anywhere on the line except a corner handle. To change the line style of one line or several selected lines, you make a different selection on the Lines menu.

When changing the length or angle of any line with the pointer tool, you can use the Shift-key option (see fig. 5.6). If you hold down the Shift key as you drag one of these handles, you force the line to follow a 45-degree path. You can stretch a line or even change a diagonal line to a vertical or horizontal line (top and middle of figure 5.6). If you do not hold down the Shift key while dragging, you can stretch the line in any direction, including changing the angle of a line drawn with the perpendicular-line tool (bottom of figure 5.6).

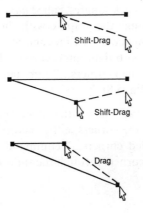

Fig. 5.6. Stretching lines with the pointer tool.

To position lines precisely against text or graphics, you can either use non-printing guides or work in "200% size" so that you can move objects in fine increments (see Chapter 6). When you draw a diagonal line, PageMaker centers the line on the crossbar, regardless of the line's thickness. When you draw perpendicular lines, the crossbar point marks the edge of the line. Figure 5.7 shows how you can flip a perpendicular line to the opposite side of the cross-bar by dragging slightly in the direction you want the line to fall as you are drawing.

Fig. 5.7. *Flipping a perpendicular line to one side of the crossbar.*

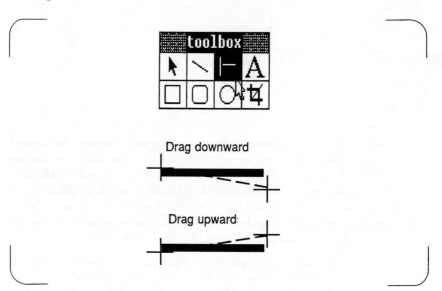

Creating Boxes

You use both the square-corner and rounded-corner tools to draw boxes. As soon as a box is created, and any time it is selected with the pointer tool, the box is framed in eight small black squares, called *handles*. These handles must be displayed when you change the graphic with the "Rounded corners..." command or with any option under the Lines and Shades menus. The square-corner tool produces boxes with right-angle corners, but you can make them rounded by using the "Rounded corners..." command on the Options menu after the box is drawn (see fig. 5.8).

The rounded-corner tool draws boxes with rounded corners. You can change the degree of roundness of the corners, either before or after you draw the box, by using the "Rounded corners..." command. You can also change rounded corners to square corners through the same command.

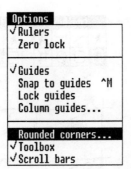

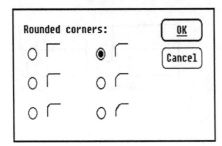

Using these tools, you can draw rectangles in any proportion, as shown in the top example in figure 5.9. If, however, you hold down the Shift key while you are drawing, you draw squares (see the middle example in fig. 5.9). After drawing a rectangle, you can change it to a square by selecting the rectangle with the pointer tool and then holding down the Shift key as you click or drag any handle, as shown in the bottom example of figure 5.9.

You also can change the shape and size of a box by using the pointer tool to select the object and then dragging one of the handles. The corner handles can be dragged in any direction to change both dimensions of the box, and the handles in the middle of each side of the box can be dragged horizontally or vertically to change one dimension only.

You can change the style of the border around the boxes by using the Lines menu, and you can fill a box with any pattern from the Shades menu.

All the boxes you draw in PageMaker have horizontal and vertical edges. You cannot create trapezoids or parallelograms in PageMaker. If you use the lines tools to create a polygon, you cannot fill it with a pattern. You can, however, use other graphics programs to create polygons and then import them to PageMaker, as described in this chapter.

Fig. 5.9. *Drawing*
squares.

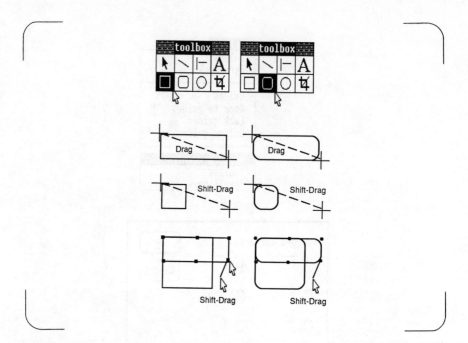

Creating Circles and Ovals

The oval tool enables you to draw circles as well as ovals (ellipses). When using this tool, you drag the crossbar diagonally to define the rectangular area into which the circle or oval will fall (see fig. 5.10). If you hold down the Shift key while you are dragging the crossbar, you create a circle.

When a circle or oval is first created, and any time it is selected with the pointer tool, the graphic is framed in eight handles. These handles are used to scale the object, by dragging them with the pointer tool (see "Creating Boxes").

Circles and ovals take on the default line style and fill shade, but you can change these settings for selected objects by using the Lines and Shades menus.

You can change an oval into a circle by selecting the oval with the pointer, then holding down the Shift key as you click on any handle. All ovals drawn in PageMaker have horizontal and vertical axes. If you want an oval to have a diagonal axis, you must create the oval in another program and import it into PageMaker. Also, you cannot draw arcs (segments of circles, as used in pie charts) in PageMaker, but you can import arcs drawn in other programs.

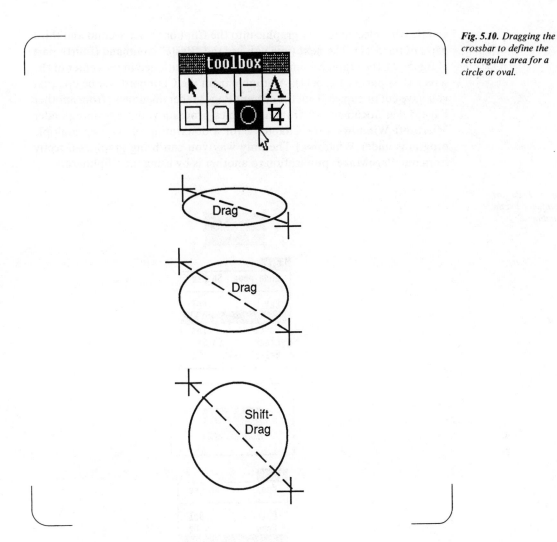

Fig. 5.10. *Dragging the crossbar to define the rectangular area for a circle or oval.*

Pasting Graphics from the Clipboard

Besides using PageMaker's graphics tools to create an object, you can cut, copy, and paste objects through the Windows Clipboard. The Clipboard is a temporary storage area, which contains the objects that were most recently cut or copied in the Windows environment. The contents of the Clipboard are replaced each time the "Cut" or "Copy" command is used, and the Clipboard is erased when you close Windows.

To use the Clipboard, you first select one or more objects on the screen (see top of fig. 5.11). With the "Cut" and "Copy" commands under the Edit menu, you put the selected text or graphic into the Clipboard (see second and third parts of fig. 5.11). The next time you use the "Paste" command (fourth part of fig. 5.11), the graphic from the Clipboard is positioned in the center of the screen (last part of fig. 5.11). A graphic from the Clipboard can be one that you have cut or copied from the current PageMaker document, from another PageMaker document, or from a graphics program you are running under Microsoft Windows. (See Chapter 2 for a description of running multiple programs under Windows.) The only way you can bring graphics directly from one PageMaker publication to another is by using the Clipboard.

Fig. 5.11. Pasting graphics from the Clipboard.

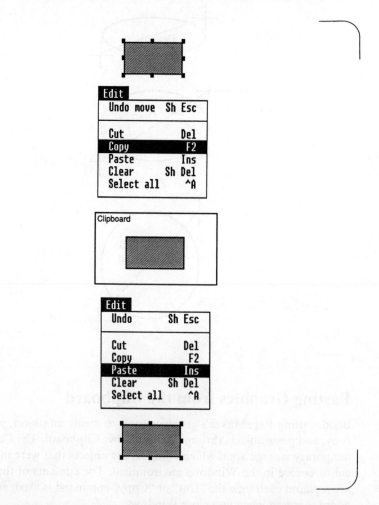

You also can use the Clipboard to make exact duplicates of a graphic. Figures 5.12 through 5.15 show how this technique is used in creating drop shadows. First, you draw the top layer of the graphic, using one of PageMaker's tools.

Then you use the Shades menu to create a fill pattern (see fig. 5.12). With the "Copy" command, you create a duplicate graphic in the Clipboard; and with the "Paste" command, you bring the duplicate back onto the same Page-Maker page (see fig. 5.13). To select the shadow pattern, you use the Shades menu. Then, move the shadow to the desired position (see fig. 5.14). Finally, select the "Send to back" command on the Edit menu (see fig. 5.15).

Importing Graphics Created in Other Programs

Besides creating graphics with PageMaker and pasting them through the Clipboard, you can use the "Place..." command to import graphics created in other programs. For many documents, PageMaker's graphics tools alone are sufficient—especially when all the graphics are part of the design and you have no illustrations. Otherwise, for heavily illustrated material, programs other than PageMaker are the primary sources of graphics. These graphics can be scaled and cropped in PageMaker, but you cannot change their lines or patterns using PageMaker's menus. You must edit the graphics using their originating program.

Importing Different Types of Graphics

To meet different needs, PageMaker imports four kinds of graphics from other programs. These four types are object-oriented (or vector) graphics, bit-mapped graphics, scanned images, and PostScript graphics. With these four formats, you can create reports containing AutoCAD designs, newsletters with illustrations created through Windows Paint, magazines containing pictures scanned from photographs, and many other kinds of illustrated materials. With all PageMaker's options for importing graphics, you have the capability of producing high-quality graphics for many types of documents.

Object-Oriented Graphics

Object-oriented graphics are composed of separate objects—such as boxes, lines, and ovals—that can be moved independently. PageMaker's built-in graphics are object-oriented graphics, and you can import object-oriented graphics from other programs. Object-oriented graphics are sometimes called *vector graphics* because the lines and patterns that you see are actually stored as mathematical formulas for the vectors that compose the image. A *vector*, shown in figure 5.16, is a line defined by a starting point, a directional angle, and a length.

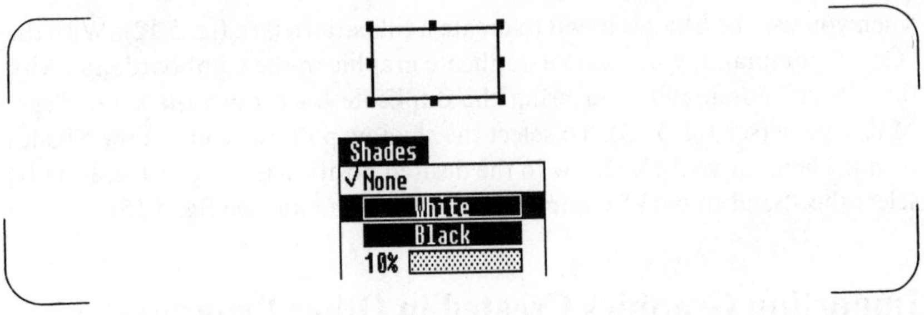

Fig. 5.12. *Drawing the top layer of a drop-shadow graphic.*

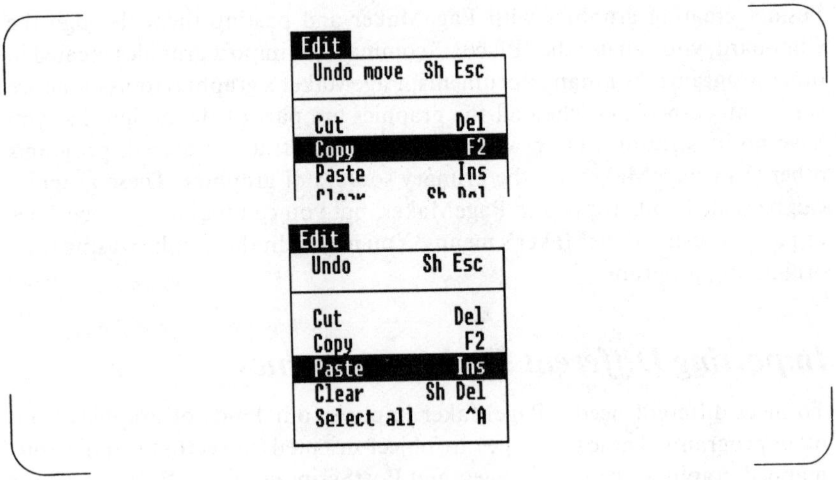

Shades
✓ None
White
Black
10%

Fig. 5.13. *Copying the graphic to the Clipboard and back to PageMaker.*

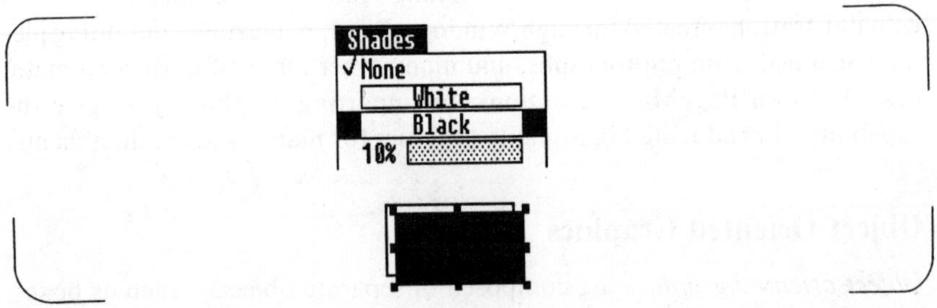

Edit
Undo move   Sh Esc

Cut   Del
Copy   F2
Paste   Ins
Clear   Sh Del

Edit
Undo   Sh Esc

Cut   Del
Copy   F2
Paste   Ins
Clear   Sh Del
Select all   ^A

Fig. 5.14. *Moving the drop-shadow to the desired position.*

Shades
✓ None
White
Black
10%

Fig. 5.15. *Using the "Send to back" command for the final graphic.*

Send to back   ^B

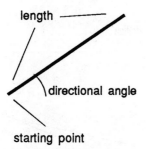

length ———————

directional angle

starting point

Fig. 5.16. A vector.

Object-oriented graphics are created with drafting programs, draw-type programs, and spreadsheet graphics. Programs that produce vector graphics which can be placed in PageMaker include Windows Draw (see fig. 5.17), In*a*Vision, AutoCAD, 1-2-3 (see fig. 5.18), Symphony, Windows Graphics Device Interface (GDI) metafiles, and Encapsulated PostScript (EPS) formats (see fig. 5.19).

Fig. 5.17. Two graphics created in Windows Draw.

Fig. 5.18. A graph created with 1-2-3.

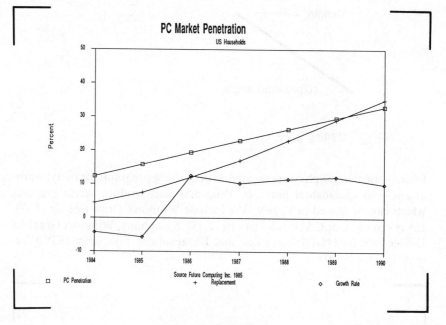

Fig. 5.19. Graphics drawn with Adobe's Illustrator program to create Encapsulated PostScript (EPS) code.

Because these vector graphics are defined mathematically, they are smoothed during the printing process to create crisp line art and precise fill patterns. Therefore, vector graphics are considered better-quality images than bit-mapped graphics.

Bit-Mapped Graphics

Bit-mapped graphics are composed of a pattern of dots, or *pixels*, rather than being stored as mathematical formulas. This type of graphic comes from a paint-type program, such as Windows Paint, PC Paintbrush, or Publisher's Paintbrush. Figure 5.20 shows a bit-mapped graphic drawn with Windows Paint.

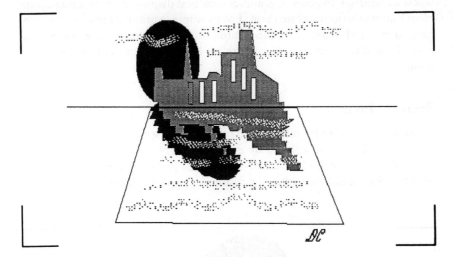

Fig. 5.20. A bit-mapped image drawn with Windows Paint.

Because bit-mapped images are composed of dots, rather than whole objects, bit-mapped images cannot be broken easily into separate elements (boxes, circles, lines). Objects are not *layered* one above the other as they are in PageMaker. Instead, when a circle is drawn on top of a square, for example, where the two objects overlap, the dots that compose the circle actually replace the dots that composed the square.

Bit-mapped images are not smoothed like vector graphics are when printed. Therefore, bit-mapped graphics are generally considered inferior to vector graphics for most line art. Bit-mapped images, however, are superior for scanned images and for "fine art" images that call for air-brush effects.

Efficiency Tip

Use Object-Oriented Graphics if Possible

Use object-oriented graphics rather than bit-mapped graphics whenever possible. Bit-mapped graphics have a jagged appearance and take much longer to print.

When bit-mapped graphics are required, do not include text in the file in the paint program. Place the graphic portion in PageMaker and use PageMaker's text tools to add captions and labels.

NOTE: On-Screen vs. Printed Bit-Mapped Images: Some bit-mapped graphics may seem distorted on the screen, but they print well if the original graphic was not distorted. In general, graphics look best displayed on the same equipment that was used to create them. For example, a graphic created on equipment using a Hercules Graphics Card may look distorted when placed, using PageMaker, on equipment with an EGA graphics card or a different monitor.

Scanned Images

Scanned images are also bit-mapped images, but they can be stored at higher resolutions than those allowed by most paint-type programs. Good-quality scanned images can look like half-tones when printed, even though the images may look coarse on your low-resolution screen (see fig. 5.21).

Fig. 5.21. A scanned image.

PageMaker v.1.0a has the capability to place and print gray-scale and tag image file format (TIFF) files. Scanned images can be saved in the .IMG format
created by the scanning program, in one of the paint-type formats supported
by PageMaker, or in Microsoft's tag image file format with the suffix .TIF in
the file name. Scanners that create images which can be saved in one of these
formats include those made by Canon, Datacopy Corporation, DEST Corporation, Microtek Lab, Inc., and Ricoh Systems, Inc.

Scanned images are often stored at 300-dots-per-inch resolution, so scanned
image files can be quite large, sometimes larger than 256K. Rather than incorporating such large images into the publication, the PageMaker publication stores the image at the low resolution shown on your screen. The scan
file, however, is linked to the publication; and when you print the publication,
PageMaker looks for the original scan file on the disk in order to print at high
resolution.

For this reason, storing the scanned-image file in the same directory as your
publication is a good idea. If you copy the publication to another disk, copy
the scanned image, too. Without the scan file, the image is printed at low resolution, even on high-resolution printers. If PageMaker cannot find the scan
file when you print the publication, the program prompts you to specify another disk or directory (see fig. 5.22).

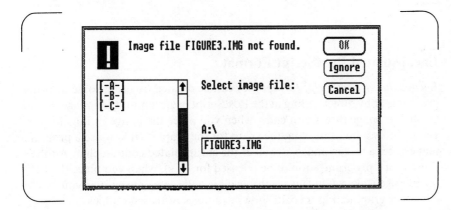

*Fig. 5.22. PageMaker
looks for the scan file
when printing the
PageMaker publication.*

Efficiency Tip

Scanning Resolution

If your scanner offers a choice of resolutions, choose the one that matches
your printer's resolution. The image may seem rough on low-resolution
screens but should look better when printed (see fig. 5.23).

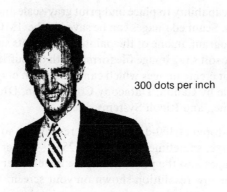

Fig. 5.23. Scanned images at 72 and 300 dots per inch.

300 dots per inch

72 dots per inch

Encapsulated PostScript Format

Encapsulated PostScript format files can be created by using some drawing programs or by direct coding in the PostScript programming language. If you create the image directly in code, when you place the image in PageMaker, you see only a box reserving the space for the graphic. If you use a program that creates a screen image as well as the encapsulated code (such as Adobe's Illustrator™ program, soon to be released for PCs), when you place the EPS file in PageMaker, you can see the graphic and scale or crop it as you would any other graphic. Figure 5.19 shows examples of these graphics.

Efficiency Tip

Primary Source of EPS Files

You can use Adobe's Illustrator program on a Macintosh to create graphics and save them in Encapsulated PostScript format (IBM Windows version). Then you can telecommunicate that EPS file as text from the Macintosh to a PC and place the graphics in PageMaker.

Importing Graphics with the "Place..." Command

You use the "Place..." command to bring in graphics created in other programs. The entire graphics file is placed in PageMaker as a single graphics object, regardless of how large the graphic is or how many different objects are in the original source file. If the graphic includes text, PageMaker retains the font settings specified in the graphics program.

Figure 5.24 lists the types of graphics programs that PageMaker supports and shows the icons for each type. You can determine the type of graphic in two ways. Files created by object-oriented graphics programs usually end with the suffix .PIC, .PLT, .WMF, or .EPS in the name shown in the "Place..." command dialog box; and the placement icon looks like a pencil or like a box containing the letters PS (for an Encapsulated PostScript file). File names that represent bit-mapped graphics usually end with the suffix .MSP, .PCX, .TIF, or .IMG; and the placement icon looks like a paintbrush or a box containing a crosshair.

Graphics Program	Suffix	Icon
EPS-format (Encapsulated PostScript)	.EPS	
Scanned Image	.IMG .TIF	
MacPaint	.PNT	
PC Paintbrush	.PCX	
Publisher's Paintbrush	.PCX	
Windows Paint	.MSP	
AutoCad	.PLT	
GDI metafiles	.WMF	
In-a-Vision	.PIC	
Lotus 1-2-3	.PIC	
PC Paint	.PIC	
Symphony	.PIC	
Windows Draw!	.PIC	
Windows Graph	.	
HP Graphic Galery	.TIF	
Dr. Halo DPE	.TIF	
Hotshot	.PCX or .EPS	
HPGL plotter files	.PLT	

Fig. 5.24. File-name extensions and placement icons for different types of graphics.

Figures 5.25 and 5.26 illustrate the steps involved in placing graphics from other programs onto a page in PageMaker.

1. Select the "Place..." command on the File menu.

2. Find in the dialog box the name of the graphics file you want. Use the scroll bars to scroll through the list of names. If you do not see

the name of the file you want, click on the drive ID, type the path name, and press Enter. Then click on the file name and place it. The "Retain format" and "Text only" options have no effect on graphics files (see fig. 5.25).

3. Once you find the name of the file you want to place, select the name by double-clicking on it. The pointer changes to one of the graphics placement icons shown in figure 5.24.

4. Put the icon where you want the top left corner of the graphic to appear; then click. Let the snap-to column guides help you position the graphic placement icon. PageMaker displays the placed graphic framed in eight handles (see fig. 5.26).

Placed graphics initially have the same length and width that they had in the original program, but you can change the image's size or trim off edges, as described in the following sections.

Fig. 5.25. Finding the name of a graphics file.

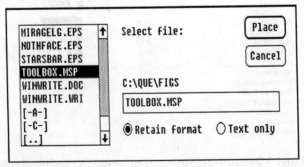

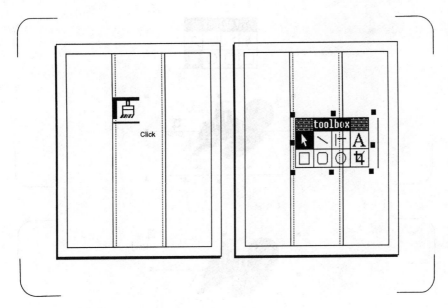

Fig. 5.26. Positioning a
graphic image on the
page.

Trimming Graphics with the Cropping Tool

The cropping tool trims edges from a graphic without changing the size of the
rest of the graphic. You can crop, or trim the edges from, graphic objects that
are brought in from other programs; but you cannot crop graphics that are
drawn with PageMaker's built-in graphics tools.

To crop a graphic, you select the cropping tool in the toolbox, and then select
the graphic. You next click the cropping tool on the graphic to display the
handles (see fig. 5.27). Then, you put the cropping tool over any handle and
drag. You can trim horizontally or vertically by dragging one of the middle
handles; you can trim diagonally by dragging one of the corner handles (see
fig. 5.28).

If you hold down the Shift key while dragging one of the corner handles, the
cropped image retains the proportions of the original image. If you crop too
much off a graphic, you can drag the handles to enlarge it again.

The full image is stored with the PageMaker publication, and you always
have the option of returning to the original full-size image by using the cropping tool to expand the graphic by dragging one of the handles. You can also
move the image around inside the crop frame by placing the cropping tool
anywhere on the graphic, except on a handle, and dragging (see fig. 5.29). In
the figure, the image is moved to the left but retains the same proportions.

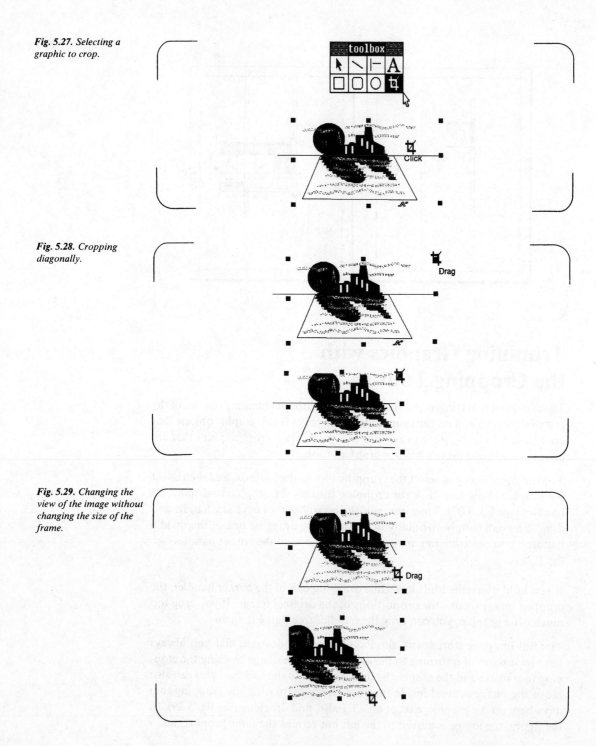

Fig. 5.27. Selecting a graphic to crop.

Fig. 5.28. Cropping diagonally.

Fig. 5.29. Changing the view of the image without changing the size of the frame.

Selecting, Moving, and Scaling Graphics with the Pointer Tool

You can use the pointer tool to select, move, or scale graphics after you draw or place them on the screen. You cannot select, move, or scale a graphic while any of the other graphics tools are selected. With the other tools, you can only draw new graphics or make menu selections.

To select a single graphic object, you click the pointer tool on any part of the object. The graphic displays the handles (see fig. 5.30). To select one or more objects at a time, you hold down the Shift key and click each object (see fig. 5.31). To select all the objects within a rectangular area, you hold down the mouse button as you drag the pointer tool diagonally from one corner of the area to the opposite corner (see fig. 5.32).

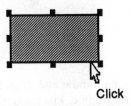

Click

Fig. 5.30. Selecting a single graphic object.

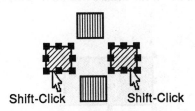

Shift-Click   Shift-Click

Fig. 5.31. Selecting more than one graphic object at a time.

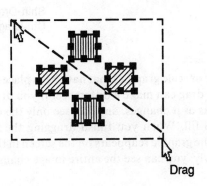

Drag

Fig. 5.32. Selecting all the graphic objects within a rectangular area.

After selecting a graphic object, you can move or scale it by using the pointer tool. To move one or more selected objects, you click the pointer tool on any part of the selection except the handles and drag the object or group to the new location. When you hold down the mouse button to move a graphic object, the pointer becomes a four-directional arrow.

To move a graphic object that has no fill pattern (that is, Shade = None), you must place the pointer somewhere on the border. To move a selection along horizontal or vertical lines, you hold down the Shift key as you drag (see fig. 5.33).

Fig. 5.33. Moving a graphic.

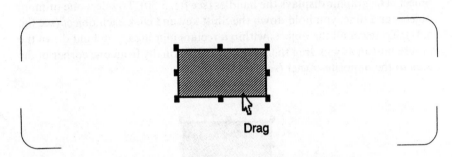

Drag

If you place the pointer on a handle and drag, as shown in figure 5.34, you scale (stretch or shrink) the graphic. The pointer changes to a two-directional arrow when you hold down the mouse button to scale a graphic.

Fig. 5.34. Scaling a graphic.

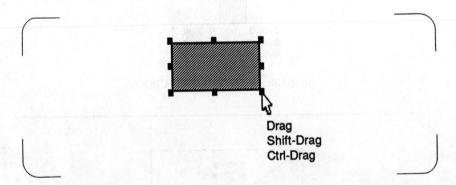

Drag
Shift-Drag
Ctrl-Drag

When you move or scale graphics that have been placed from other programs, the speed of the drag can make a difference. If you drag quickly, the graphic image disappears as it changes, and you see only the outline of the area that the graphic will fill. When you finish dragging the object and release the mouse button, the graphic reappears on the screen in the new size or location. If you drag slowly, you can see the entire image changing as you work.

Efficiency Tip

Watch Your Pointer

When drawing, moving, or scaling a graphic, always be sure that the pointer's appearance reflects your intentions before making a change: A crossbar indicates that you are about to draw a new object. A four-headed arrow indicates that you are about to move the selected object(s). A two-headed arrow indicates that you are about to scale an object.

Two-dimensional objects have eight handles: one at each corner and one in the middle of each side. When you drag one of the handles that falls in the middle of a side, you stretch the graphic along one axis only. In other words, you stretch the graphic out of proportion. When you drag one of the corner handles, you can stretch the graphic in two directions at once.

If you hold down the Shift key while dragging a corner handle, you can bring about several effects:

1. If you used PageMaker's tools to draw the graphic (see fig. 5.35),

    • Lines become or remain horizontal or vertical

    • Boxes become or remain squares

    • Ovals become circles; circles remain circles

2. If you have imported the graphic from another program, you size the graphic exactly proportionally (see fig. 5.36).

When changing the size of some bit-mapped images in PageMaker, you may notice that parts of the image show a moiré pattern: a grid of perpendicular and diagonal lines. You can avoid this effect by using PageMaker's "magic stretch" feature, which jumps to fixed reduction and enlargement settings. The higher the resolution of your printer, the finer the adjustments you can get in "magic stretch." First, you select the graphic with the pointer tool. To retain original proportions, you hold down the Shift key as you are stretching. To activate "magic stretch" and jump to the best scales for printing, you hold down the Ctrl key as you are stretching (see fig. 5.37 for results of both).

Fig. 5.35. Effects of the Shift key on graphic objects created in PageMaker.

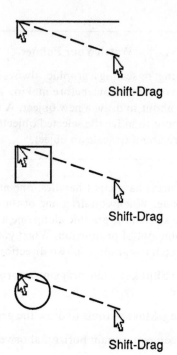

Shift-Drag

Shift-Drag

Shift-Drag

Fig. 5.36. Effects of the Shift key on graphic objects created in another program.

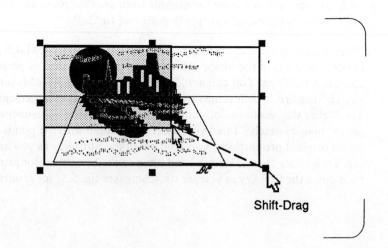

Shift-Drag

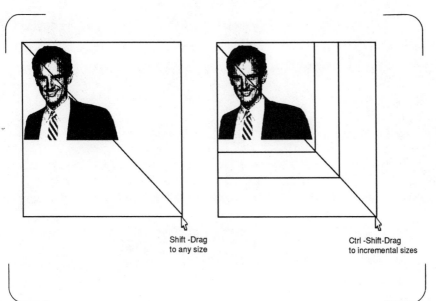

Shift -Drag
to any size

Ctrl -Shift-Drag
to incremental sizes

Fig. 5.37. Proportionate *scaling and "magic stretch."*

Summary

Now that you know what alternatives are available for adding graphics to a page, you can make decisions about whether to use PageMaker or another program to create graphics. Chapter 9 offers more specific advice about making design specifications for graphics from diverse sources. Chapter 6 takes you through all the steps involved in laying out a publication, incorporating the information you learned in Chapters 3 through 5 and providing tips about using PageMaker's tools during the layout process.

Creating Full-Page Layouts 6

After using other programs to prepare text and graphics, you are ready to begin using PageMaker in the page-layout process. This chapter takes you through all the steps involved in building full-page layouts. The discussion begins with the "New..." command, which is used to create a PageMaker publication, and then moves through setting up a grid for the page layout and placing text and graphics on the pages.

You have already glimpsed parts of the page-layout process described in this chapter. Chapters 3, 4, and 5 explain how to use other programs to prepare text and graphics and how to bring the text and graphics into PageMaker. You have learned that before starting to build the PageMaker publication, you should do as much editing and formatting as possible in the word processor and that you should use other programs to create complex graphics. Those chapters also describe the process of using PageMaker's tools to create text and graphics.

This chapter begins by explaining how to open a new PageMaker publication and then takes you through the following steps:

1. Entering page-layout specifications in the "Page setup" dialog box

2. Specifying standard layout elements on the master pages

3. Using the Page menu commands to change views of the publication

4. Arranging text and graphics on a page

5. Editing text and graphics in PageMaker

These steps are described from the production perspective. The beginning assumption is that the design specifications for the publication are already known and that the task is simply to build the publication according to those specifications. In Chapter 9, some of these same steps are reviewed from the designer's perspective, and basic design principles are discussed. Part III of this book (Chapters 10–14) provides examples of how these basic design principles have been applied in PageMaker publications.

Entering Page-Layout Specifications

When you begin creating a document by using the "New..." command on the File menu, PageMaker displays the "Page setup" dialog box (see fig. 6.1). You use this box to specify the size of the sheets of paper you will be using, the orientation of the printed image, the text margins, the number of pages, and the starting page number. You also indicate whether you will print the document and bind it as a two-sided publication.

Fig. 6.1. The "Page setup" dialog box with default settings.

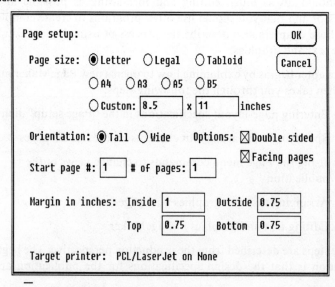

Before making your selections in the "Page setup" dialog box, you should plan the design of your document. Why? Because the page's size, orientation, and margins may affect your design specifications for the text and graphics (see Chapter 9). Figure 6.2 shows how the settings in the "Page setup" dialog box affect a page. Double-sided facing pages are displayed. The "Page size" is defined in solid lines; the "Orientation" is "Tall". The inside margin measure is applied to the right margin of left-hand pages and the left margin of right-hand pages. The dashed lines on the inside and outside margins indicate that a column guide is on the margin. The top and bottom margins are shown as dotted lines.

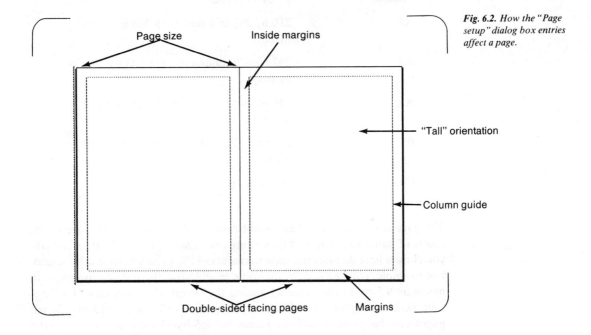

Page size   Inside margins

"Tall" orientation

Column guide

Double-sided facing pages   Margins

Fig. 6.2. How the "Page setup" dialog box entries affect a page.

At any time during the production process, you can change the "Page setup" options, such as double-sided printing, number of pages, and starting page number. To do so, you use the "Page setup..." command on the File menu. The following sections explain what happens when you change these settings after you have started building the document.

Specifying Page Size

PageMaker offers seven predefined page sizes that match the standard paper sizes, but you can specify any size up to 17 by 22 inches. The measurements that correspond to PageMaker's list include three standard American paper sizes and four European standards (see table 6.1).

Table 6.1
Standard Paper Sizes in PageMaker

Option	Size
Letter	8.5 by 11 inches
Legal	8.5 by 14 inches
Tabloid	11 by 17 inches
A4	210 by 297 millimeters (8.268 by 11.693 inches)
A3	297 by 420 millimeters (11.693 by 16.535 inches)
A5	148 by 210 millimeters (5.827 by 8.268 inches)
B5	250 by 176 millimeters (6.929 by 9.842 inches)
Custom	Any size up to 17 by 22 inches

The page size you specify here is not necessarily the same as the size of the sheets of paper that you will be feeding into a laser printer. Rather, the size you choose here dictates the measurements of the page border on the screen. For example, you can specify tabloid size and print the publication pages in pieces on 8.5-by-11-inch sheets by using the "Print..." command's "Tile" option, which is explained in Chapter 7. Figure 6.3 shows how 12-by-22-inch pages can be printed in four pieces on 8.5-by-11-inch paper, using the "Print..." command's "Tile" option.

If you choose a page size smaller than the sheets of paper on which you print, PageMaker prints the image in the center of the paper. You can use the "Crop marks" option in the "Print..." command's dialog box to print crop marks to indicate the final trim size on the larger paper (see fig. 6.4).

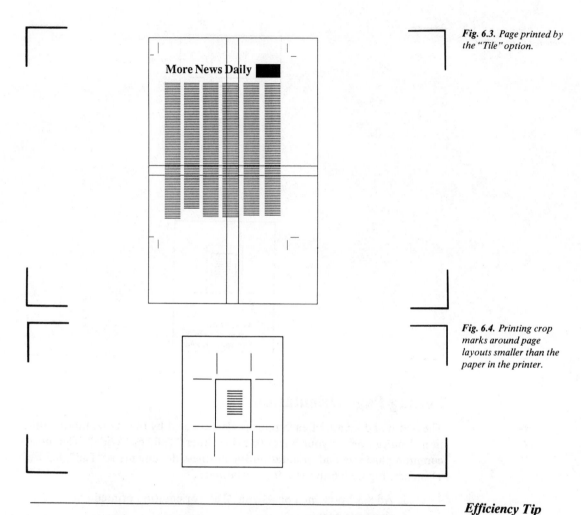

Fig. 6.3. Page printed by the "Tile" option.

Fig. 6.4. Printing crop marks around page layouts smaller than the paper in the printer.

Efficiency Tip

Specifying a Page Size Larger than the Final Trim Size

Although the page size is usually the same size as the publication once it is mass-produced, bound, and trimmed, you can specify larger page sizes for special layouts. Figure 6.5 provides an example. In the "Page setup" dialog box, 8.5-by-11-inch page size is specified for a document that will eventually be trimmed to 4 by 5 inches. Nonprinting guides, margins, and columns are used to define the 4-by-5-inch layout area, and the area beyond that is used to print project control information, crop marks, registration marks, and instructions to the printer. The printed pages show crop marks that are created with the perpendicular-line tool on the master pages—because the automatic crop marks feature would not show the true trim size in this case.

Fig. 6.5. *Page size compared to paper size.*

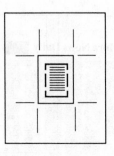

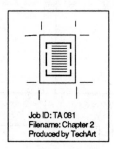

Job ID: TA 081
Filename: Chapter 2
Produced by TechArt

Setting Page Orientation

The width and length of each page is also affected by the "Orientation" option. You can orient your pages to print either "Tall" or "Wide". The most common page size and orientation for business documents is "Tall", 8.5 by 11 inches. Figure 6.6 shows a few variations:

a. An 8.5-by-11-inch page with "Tall" orientation printed one sheet per page

b. An 8.5-by-11-inch page with "Wide" orientation printed one sheet per page

c. An 11-by-17-inch (tabloid) page with "Tall" orientation printed four sheets per page

d. An 11-by-17-inch page with "Wide" orientation printed four sheets per page

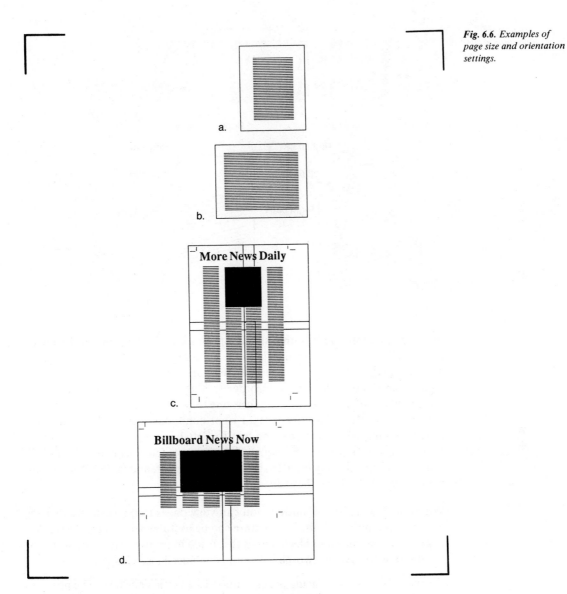

Fig. 6.6. *Examples of page size and orientation settings.*

Working with Double-Sided Publications

The "Double sided" option does not cause pages to be printed on both sides of the paper as it comes out of the printer. Rather, you use this option if you want to reproduce the final pages as a two-sided document, using either xerographic or offset printing equipment. See figure 6.7 for examples.

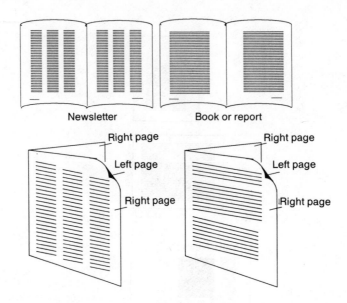

When you choose the "Double sided" option, PageMaker applies the measure specified for the inside margin to the left margin of odd-numbered pages and to the right margin of even-numbered pages. The inside margin is often wider than the outside margin in order to allow for binding. Double-sided documents also have two master pages: one for even-numbered, or left-hand, pages, and one for odd-numbered, or right-hand, pages. You can set up different running heads and running feet for left-hand and right-hand pages. Figure 6.8 shows the screen display for a single-sided document; figure 6.9 shows the screen display for a double-sided document; and table 6.2 describes the differences between these documents.

With the "Facing pages" option, you can view pages that face each other in double-sided publications. This feature can be useful when you are designing pages with graphics that bleed across the inside margin or when you want to be sure that the overall two-page layout is balanced (see Chapter 9).

You can also use the "Facing pages" option as an efficiency tool. The process of laying out and changing pages is much quicker when you can see two pages at once.

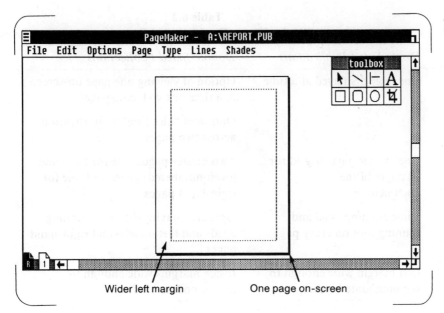

Fig. 6.8. A single-sided document.

Wider left margin   One page on-screen

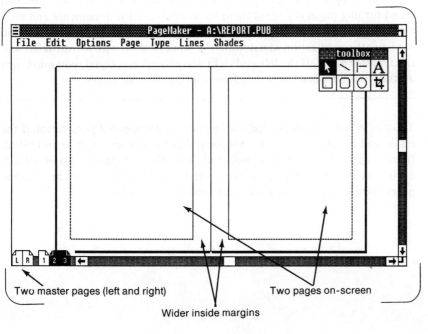

Fig. 6.9. A double-sided document.

Two master pages (left and right)   Two pages on-screen

Wider inside margins

Table 6.2
Single- Versus Double-Sided Documents

Single-Sided Publications	Double-Sided Publications
One page displayed at a time	Option of viewing one page on-screen at a time or two facing pages
	Option of "bleeding" an illustration across two pages
One master page or grid for all pages of the document	Two master pages: one for left-hand (even-numbered) pages and one for right-hand pages
Same running head and running foot on every page	Option of having different running heads and feet on left- and right-hand pages
Left margin wide enough to accommodate binding	Inside margins wide enough to accommodate binding

Efficiency Tip

Double-Sided Option for Single-Sided Publications

When building long single-sided documents, you can reduce the time you spend turning pages if you set them up as double-sided documents and view facing pages as you are working. If the right and left margins are equal, you can print the publication as a double-sided publication with identical left and right master pages. If the left and right margins are not equal, you must turn off the "Double sided" option before printing the final pages.

You can set up a double-sided document as a single-sided publication if the inside and outside margins are the same and the master pages are identical. In most cases, however, you should use the "Double sided" option for any document that you plan to make double-sided and turn off the "Facing pages" option if you want to work on one page at a time.

Efficiency Tip

Turn Off the "Facing Pages" Option for Heavy Pasteboard Use

If your page layouts will not be affected by what is on the facing pages of a double-sided publication, and if you expect to use the pasteboard heavily as a work area during production, turn off the "Facing pages" option and work on one page at a time.

In any case, work with the "Facing pages" option on while you are setting up the master pages. This practice will help you align running heads and feet and horizontal guides on the two pages.

Designating the Number of Pages

PageMaker's default is set to create a one-page document. However, you can designate the number of pages before you start building the document. If you do not know how many pages the publication will have, you can add or delete pages as you work by using the "Insert pages..." or "Remove pages..." commands on the Page menu. (Once you open a new document, you cannot change the number of pages through the "Page setup" dialog box; you must use the "Insert pages..." command.)

Efficiency Tip

Always Enter a Page Estimate or Limit

If you do not know exactly how many pages you need, enter a rough estimate in the "Page setup" dialog box. This way, you can go through the publication quickly by clicking on the page icons at the bottom of the screen. If you need more pages, add them with the "Insert pages" command on the Page menu. If you do not use all the pages, use the "Remove pages..." command on the Page menu (described in this chapter) before printing. (PageMaker prints all pages of a document, including blank ones.)

A PageMaker document can be up to 128 pages long, but you will find working with smaller files more efficient. In long files, when you turn pages or make text edits that carry over to subsequent pages, response time is slow. Dividing a long document into sections or chapters is good practice because you can work faster on smaller files. Another advantage is that you can set up a different running head and running foot for each chapter. (Running heads and feet are usually entered on the master pages, so they cannot be changed in the middle of a file.)

Another important consideration when you are deciding how many pages a single file will have is the size of the final publication in bytes. You want to be able to back up your publications on floppy disks for storage and transport purposes. Therefore, you need to keep the size of your files less than 330K for single-sided low-density disks or less than 730K for double-sided high-density disks.

Efficiency Tip

Check the File Size as You Work

When creating large publications, save your file frequently while you work; and open the MS-DOS Executive window periodically to see how large your publication is (see fig. 6.10). Do not build a publication file that is too large for a floppy disk to hold; break large documents into sections or chapters.

In PageMaker V1.0a, you can use the "Save as..." command to reclaim space in a publication that you created by editing, cutting, pasting, and deleting pages. You can reclaim as much as 30 percent of the publication's size.

Fig. 6.10. Viewing the list of files and their size in the MS-DOS Executive window while you are working in PageMaker.

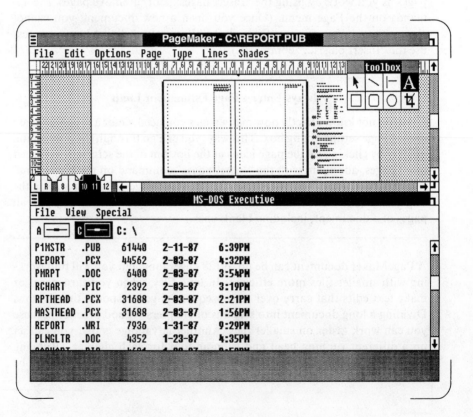

You can start a document with any page number, up to 9999. For example, if you fill one file with 128 pages, the maximum allowed, you can continue building a second file that starts with page 129. You also can specify the starting page number for publications that are divided into sections, with the first section starting on page 1 and the second section starting on page 20, for example. You can change the starting page number of the document at any time. PageMaker then shifts all the page numbers in the document to match the new sequence. This process may cause left-hand pages to become right-hand pages in double-sided documents, however.

Efficiency Tip

Controlling Left-hand and Right-hand Page Positions

When preparing a document for double-sided printing, be sure to account for and print every page, including blank left-hand pages that are needed to force new sections or chapters to start on right-hand pages. Having a numbered sheet for every page of the document also helps whoever is printing or copying the document before binding.

Specifying Page Margins

The page margins entered in the "Page setup" dialog box affect all pages of a document, and this setting cannot be altered for individual pages. To change the margins on individual pages, you must move the column guides.

Margins are measured from the edges of the page. That is, margins are measured from the page size, which is not necessarily the paper size, as explained earlier in this chapter. The margins should reflect the limits to be used for text and column settings on numbered pages rather than the limits allowed for graphics and master-page elements (see fig. 6.11). Margins also should be within the image area of your target printer.

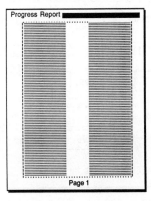

Fig. 6.11. Margins defining the limits of the text area and excluding running head and foot.

The margins are displayed in the measure specified by the "Preferences..." command on the Edit menu (see fig. 6.12). To specify margins, you use decimals, unless the unit of measure is specified as inches, picas and points, or ciceros (a European measure). For example, you enter a measurement of 4 picas and 6 points as *4p6*, as shown in table 6.3.

Fig. 6.12. Using the "Preferences..." command to determine the unit of measure for the margins in the "Page setup" dialog box.

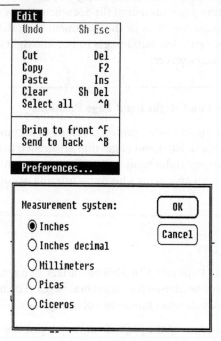

Table 6.3
Equivalent Measures:
Inches, Millimeters, Picas and Points, and Ciceros

Page Size	Inches	Millimeters	Picas	Ciceros
	.04	1		
	.167		1p0	
	.177			1c0
	.25	6.36	1p6	1c4.9
	.5	12.7	3p0	2c9.9
	.75	19.06	4p6	4c2.8
	1	25.4	6p0	5c7.8
A5	5.827	148	34p11.6	
B5	6.929	250	41p6.9	39c1.4
A4, A5	8.268	210	49p7.3	
Letter, Legal	8.5	215.9	51p0	
B5	9.842	176	59p.07	55c6.7
Letter, Tabloid	11	279.4	66p0	
A4	11.693	297	70p1.9	
Legal	14	355.6	84p0	
A3	16.535	420	99p2.6	
Tabloid	17	431.8	102p0	

You can override the current unit of measure in the "Page setup" dialog box (or any dialog box) by entering a one-character abbreviation for the unit of measure you want to specify (see fig. 6.13). To specify inches, enter an i after the number (for example, *0.75i*). To specify millimeters, you enter an m after the number (as in *19.06m*). To specify picas and points, enter a p between the number of picas and the number of points (for instance, *4p6*). To specify ciceros, enter a c between the number of ciceros and the number of points (as in *4c2.8*). (Note: Early versions of PageMaker use a d rather than a c in the measurement specifications for ciceros.) The unit of measure shown on the publication ruler line always reflects the current unit of measure, as set with the "Preferences..." command on the Edit menu, regardless of the unit of measure you enter in a dialog box (see also "Choosing the Unit of Measure" in this chapter).

Specifying the Target Printer

The "Page setup" dialog box shows what printer is currently the target printer (see fig. 6.14). If the specified printer is not the one you will be using for your final document, you should change the target printer before you start build-

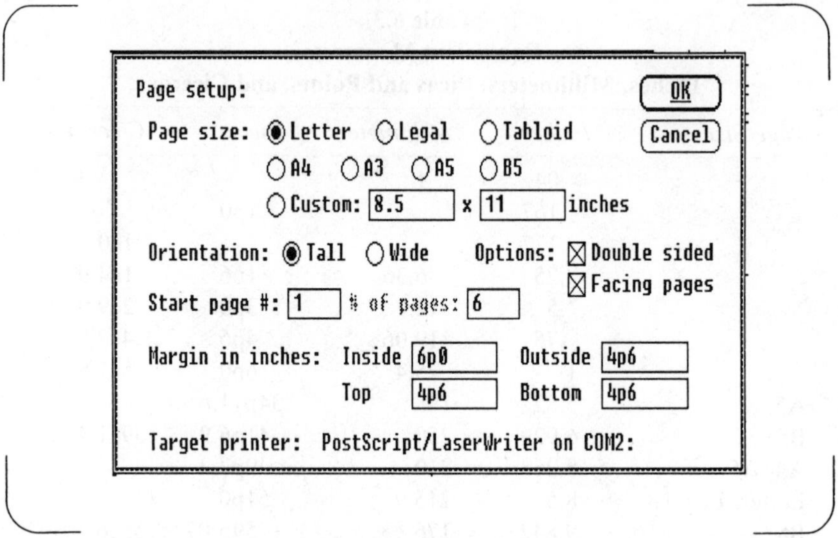

Fig. 6.13. *Overriding the current unit of measure in the "Page setup" dialog box.*

Fig. 6.13. *Overriding the current unit of measure in the "Page setup" dialog box.*

ing your document. You change the target printer by selecting the "Target printer..." command on the File menu. Or before you print, you select the target printer in the "Print" dialog box (see Chapter 7).

Before making this choice, answer these questions: Does your installation have more than one type of printer? Are you using a font cartridge system, and do you have more than one cartridge? In both these cases, you should define the target printer that you will be using for the final printouts *before* you start a new document, and you should stick with that setting throughout the production cycle. Otherwise, the publication may look different when it is printed.

For a discussion of the differences among printers, the methods available for installing and selecting them, and the ways printers can affect your document design and production, see Chapter 7.

After you enter the initial specifications in the "Page setup" dialog box, PageMaker displays a blank page with the default setting for column guides (see fig. 6.15). This page is page 1 of your document. You can begin building a document immediately by using the "Place..." command to bring in text and graphics that you have prepared in other programs or by using PageMaker's built-in graphics and text tools.

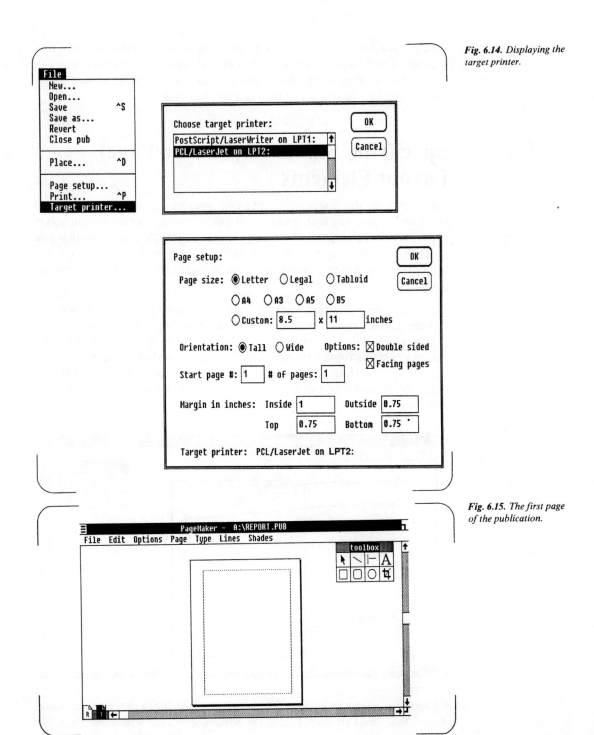

Fig. 6.14. Displaying the target printer.

Fig. 6.15. The first page of the publication.

Usually, however, you will want to begin by defining the master pages so that you can fit each page layout to an overall grid system. At any time, you can go back to the "Page setup" dialog box by choosing the "Page setup..." command from the File menu and then change the options.

Specifying Standard (Master-Page) Layout Elements

PageMaker divides publications into two types of pages: master pages and numbered pages. Any text, graphics, or guides that you set on a master page appear on every page in the document. Any text, graphics, or guides that you set on a numbered page are printed on that page only. If your document is longer than two pages, you can save time by making basic settings on master pages.

Figure 6.16 shows elements that are usually on master pages. These elements include column guides, running heads and running feet, and nonprinting guides, which define the basic grid system underlying the document's design. Settings made on the master pages can be changed on individual pages when necessary. You can move column guides, suppress running heads and running feet, hide all guides, or call the original master page settings back to the current page display.

Fig. 6.16. Master page elements.

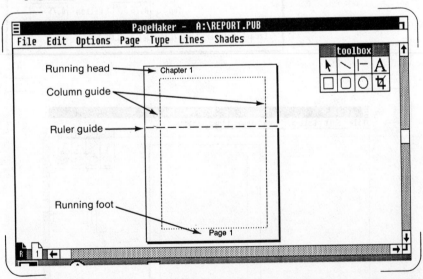

To turn to a master page, you click on the page icon for the left or right master page. These icons are displayed at the bottom left of the screen (see fig. 6.17).

You also can use the "Go to page..." command on the Page menu. Once on the master page, you can use the techniques described in this chapter to set the column guides and other grid lines shown in figure 6.16.

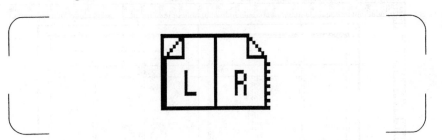

Fig. 6.17. Page icons for the master pages.

Figure 6.18 shows how left and right master pages affect numbered pages. Elements set up on the right-hand master page appear on every page of a single-sided document but only on odd-numbered pages of double-sided documents. Elements set up on the left-hand master page appear on all even-numbered pages of double-sided documents. If you select the "Double sided" and "Facing pages" options in the "Page setup..." dialog box, you can work on both master pages at once (see fig. 6.19). Because elements defined for one master page do not affect the other, you must build two master pages for double-sided documents.

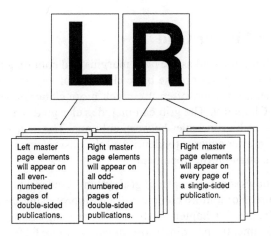

Fig. 6.18. Effects on numbered pages of left-hand and right-hand master-page settings.

Fig. 6.19. *Left and right master pages on-screen.*

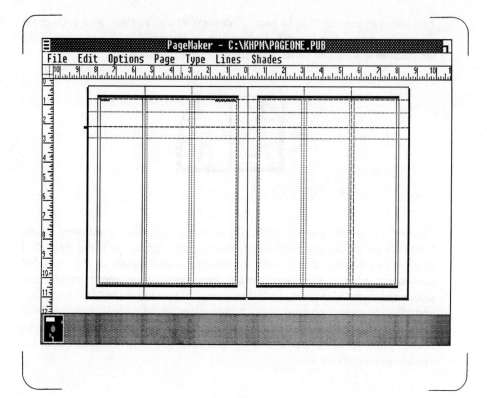

Creating a Master Grid

We usually think of a grid as the page margins and column guides for a publication. Of course, these are the basic elements of any grid system. Professional designers, however, often use much more elaborate grid systems, as described in Chapter 9. The grid can include ruler guides as well as graphic elements such as hairline rules between columns. The principle in designing a grid for the master pages is to identify all the basic elements that appear on every page throughout the document.

Figure 6.20 shows some examples of grid systems used in a book, a newsletter, and a brochure. For a more complete discussion of using the grid system in design, see Chapter 9. Chapters 10 through 14 provide examples of grids used in various documents, including those shown in figure 6.20.

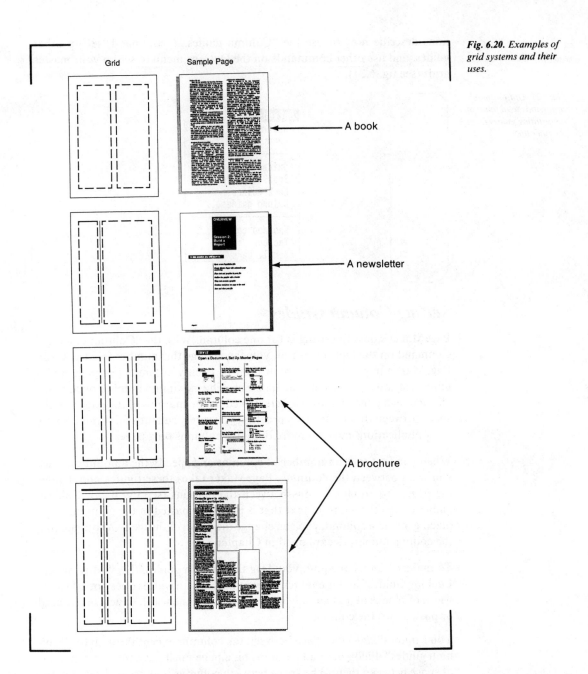

Grid

Sample Page

A book

A newsletter

A brochure

Fig. 6.20. Examples of grid systems and their uses.

The grid for left-hand pages may differ from that for right-hand pages. More likely, however, the grid itself will be the same on all pages; only the text of the running heads and running feet differs between pages. The following sections describe how to use the "Column guides..." command, set up other guides, and use other commands on the Options menu to set up your master grids (see fig. 6.21).

*Fig. 6.21. Options menu
commands used to set up
nonprinting guides from
the ruler line.*

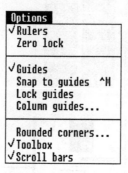

Setting Column Guides

PageMaker's default setting is for one column. With the "Column guides..." command on the Options menu, you can change this number (see fig. 6.22). PageMaker imposes a maximum limit of twenty columns per page and a minimum column width of one-half inch. The maximum number of columns allowed on a page therefore is determined by the margins of the page and the space between the columns. In practice, you rarely run into this limit because most publications have no more than five columns on a page.

When you first select a number of columns and specify the amount of space you want between the columns, PageMaker takes these figures and divides the page into equal columns between the margins (see fig. 6.23). Column guides define the width of text that is placed or pasted in the column. After placing text in a column, you can change the width of the text without moving the column guides, as explained in Chapter 3.

To make columns unequal, you drag the column guides. (See "Moving and Locking Guides" in this chapter.) Changing column widths does not affect the width of blocks of text already on the page, only the width of new text placed or pasted into the column.

You cannot change the space between the columns except through the "Column guides" dialog box; all columns on a page must have the same amount of space between them. The space between columns is given or entered in the unit of measure currently selected through the "Preferences..." command on the Edit menu. Note that the space between columns is ignored in one-column layouts.

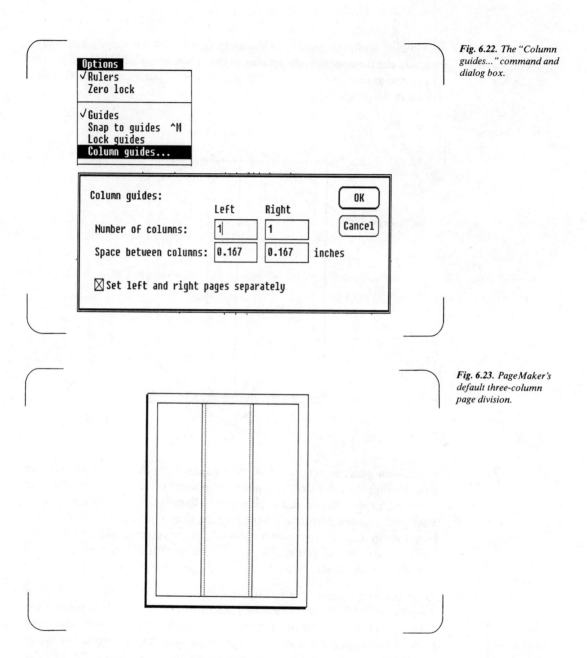

Fig. 6.22. The "Column guides..." command and dialog box.

Fig. 6.23. PageMaker's default three-column page division.

Creating Nonprinting Guides

Nonprinting guides include all the various dotted and dashed lines that are displayed in PageMaker but are not printed. These include page margins, column guides, and ruler guides, as shown in figure 6.24. To specify page margins, you use the appropriate options in the "Page setup" dialog box. To set up column guides, you use the "Column guides..." command, which is described in the preceding section.

Fig. 6.24. Nonprinting guides.

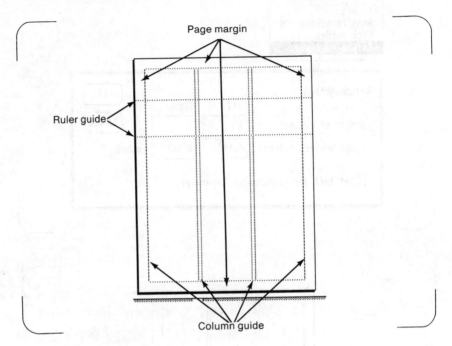

In addition, you can drag up to 40 ruler guides from the ruler lines. To drag a guide from the ruler line, you place the pointer on the ruler line and hold down the mouse button until the pointer changes to a two-headed arrow. Then you drag the pointer onto the page, as shown in figure 6.25. You drag from the top ruler line to create horizontal guides; you drag from the left ruler line to create vertical guides. The dotted-line marker on the ruler line helps you position the guide.

Ruler guides are useful for positioning objects on a page but do not affect directly the width of text (as column guides do) or the length of text (as the bottom page margin does). You can reposition column guides and ruler guides by dragging them on the page. Page margins, however, cannot be moved except with the "Page setup..." command (described in "Specifying Page Margins" in this chapter).

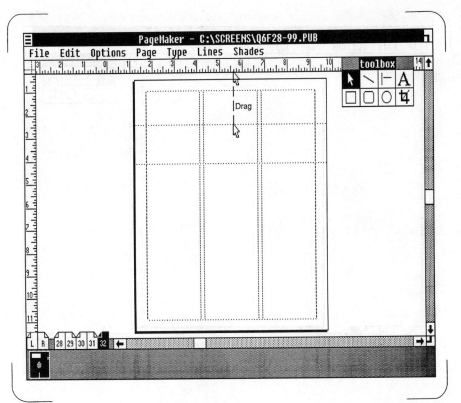

Fig. 6.25. Dragging nonprinting guides from the ruler lines.

At a Glance

Three Types of Grid Lines

Page margins, column guides, and other nonprinting guides help align objects on a page. All three types of guides have a snap-to effect. Only column guides and ruler guides can be moved by dragging them on the page. Only column guides cause text to wrap. Only the bottom page margin affects the length of the columns.

Moving and Locking Guides

To move a column guide or ruler guide, you put the pointer over the guide and hold down the mouse button. When the pointer changes to a two-headed arrow, you can drag the guide to a new location (see fig. 6.26). Displaying the ruler lines before moving column guides is good practice: You can use the rulers to help position the column guides precisely.

Fig. 6.26. Moving column guides.

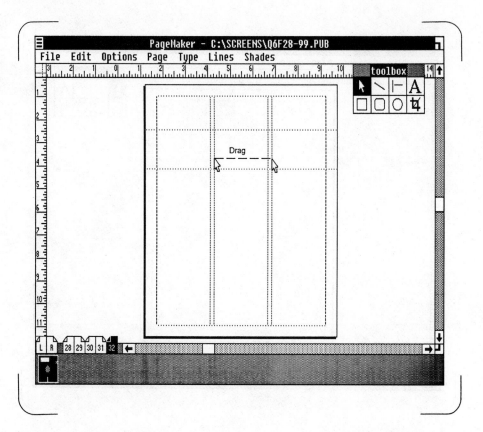

Figure 6.27 shows an example of a publication in which the column guides were moved to create "custom" layouts. The example is taken from Part III of this book. On the left side of the figure, the middle column guides of a two-column layout have been moved to the left to create a narrow left column and a wide right column. In the center example, columns have been arranged to create a wide right column and two narrow columns. In the example on the right, the column guides have been moved to create two columns: a wide left column and a narrow right column.

To be sure that you do not move any guide inadvertently, you can use the "Lock guides" command on the Options menu. This command works like a toggle switch. When the toggle is on, the command is checked on the menu; and when the command is off, it is not checked. The "Lock guides" setting holds for every page of the publication.

You can remove a ruler guide by dragging it off the page. To remove a column guide, however, you must use the "Column guides..." command and dialog box.

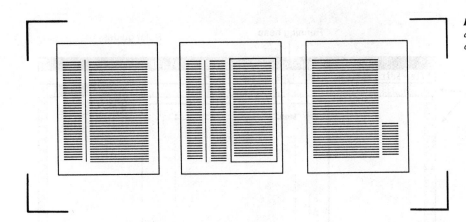

Fig. 6.27. Examples of documents with custom column settings.

Typing Running Heads and Running Feet

Text entered on the master pages appears on every page of the document unless the text is suppressed (see "Hiding Master Page Items" in this chapter). This text can include running heads and running feet as well as automatically produced page numbers.

You can type or place text on a master page the same way you type or place text on any other page (see Chapter 3). Usually, you type the text directly on the master pages because it is short and does not have to be part of a continuous flow between the master page and other pages. Following is a typical sequence for building a master page, an example of which appears in figure 6.28:

1. Set the column guides.

2. Display the rulers and position guides that are part of the grid, including horizontal guides for positioning the running heads and feet on the master pages.

3. Type the running head between the column guides and then drag it to the top of the page.

4. Add graphic elements.

5. Type the running foot between the column guides and then drag it to the bottom of the page.

Fig. 6.28. Building a
master page.

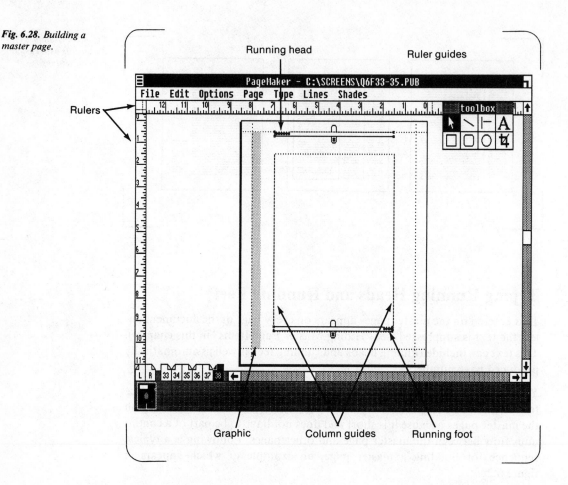

Rulers

Running head

Ruler guides

Graphic   Column guides   Running foot

Efficiency Tip

Use Margins To Control Placed Text

Place the running heads and feet outside the page margins, as shown in figure 6.29. Use the top and bottom margins to define the length of the columns when you place text on other pages.

If you have already placed ruler guides and customized column settings on several pages before you define the master page elements, those pages retain their original settings and do not pick up the master settings, unless you use the "Copy master guides" command, described in the section "Copying Master Guides."

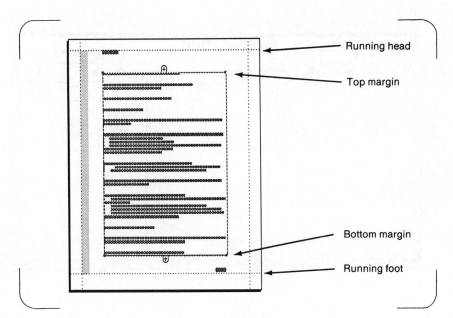

Fig. 6.29. Running heads
and running feet outside
the page margins.

Running head

Top margin

Bottom margin

Running foot

Numbering Pages Automatically

You create a page number by pressing Ctrl-Shift-3 (Ctrl-#) on a page you
have selected with the text tool. When you press this keystroke combination,
a zero appears at the text-insertion point on the master page, as shown in figure 6.30. You can format the page number as you would any other text—by
selecting the page number with the text tool and setting type specifications.

Page numbers usually appear in a running head or foot on the master pages,
but you can make PageMaker print page numbers anywhere on any page. If
you enter the page numbers by pressing Ctrl-Shift-3 on the master pages, on
subsequent pages the page numbers appear in the location set on the master
pages. You also can set up page numbers by pressing Ctrl-Shift-3 on individual pages within a publication.

The most easily referenced parts of any book are the outer edges of the pages:
the top or bottom left of even-numbered pages, top or bottom right of odd-
numbered pages. Figure 6.31 shows how using these four positions makes
page numbers and section names easy to find.

Fig. 6.30. Setting up automatic page numbering by pressing Ctrl-Shift-3.

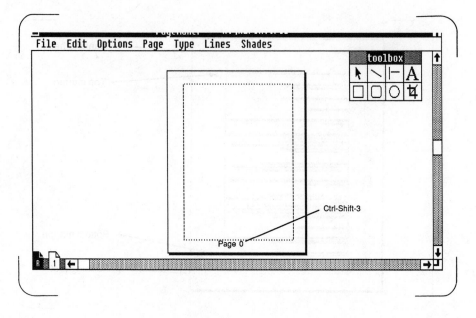

Fig. 6.31. Four common page-number locations.

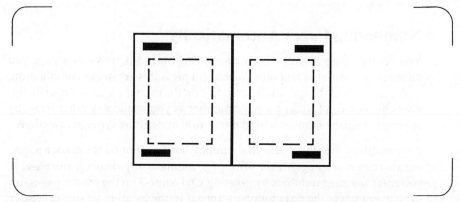

Adding Graphic Elements to Master Pages

In addition to containing text and guides, master pages can include graphics created in PageMaker or imported from other programs. For instance, the grid system may include hairline rules between columns. Figures 6.32 and 6.33 show some examples from Part III of this book; these examples incorporate graphics on the master pages. Figure 6.32 shows pages that use PageMaker graphics to set off the grid. Figure 6.33 shows pages that incorporate a logo created in a graphics program.

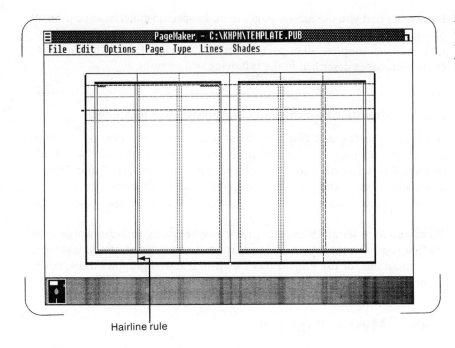

Fig. 6.32. Examples of master pages including hairline rules and other graphics drawn in PageMaker.

Hairline rule

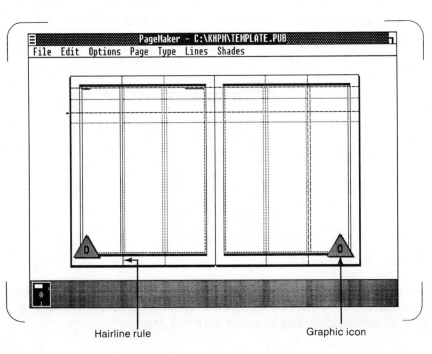

Fig. 6.33. Master pages including graphics from other programs.

Hairline rule   Graphic icon

Remember that you use master pages to make specific material appear on all or most pages of a document. Once you are on a numbered page of the document, you can suppress all or parts of the master-page elements by using one of the techniques described in the following two sections.

Repeating Elements from One Master Page to Another

After setting up text and graphics on one master page, you can copy them to another master page. The procedure is the following: Use the "Select all" command to select the entire group, and then use the "Copy" and "Paste" commands to copy and paste the group onto the second master page.

When you have set up the master pages, you are ready to begin working on the first page. Use the "Place..." command to bring in graphics and text from other programs, or use PageMaker's built-in text and graphics tools, as described in Chapters 3 through 5.

Hiding Master-Page Items

After building your master pages, you can eliminate all the master guides, text, and graphics from an individual numbered page by turning off the "Display master items" command on the Page menu (see fig. 6.34).

Fig. 6.34. The "Display master items" command controls the display of all master elements.

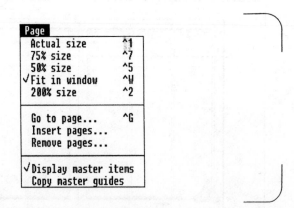

You can use the "Display master items" command to eliminate all the master elements. Then, you can use PageMaker's text and graphics tools to add back only the elements you want to use on a selected page.

Efficiency Tip

Suppressing Parts of the Master-Page Elements

If you want to suppress only some of the master-page elements, you can hide them by covering them with white boxes: rectangles created with Page-Maker's square-corner tool and given a Shade of White and a Line style of None. Figure 6.35 provides an example in which a white box at the top of the page hides the running head.

This trick does not work with all printers; some printers cannot print reverse type or white boxes.

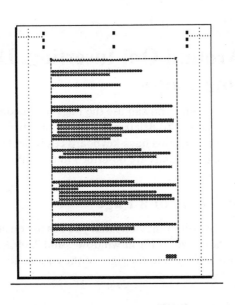

Fig. 6.35. Using a white box to hide the running head.

Copying Master Guides

Suppose that you have suppressed all the master elements by turning off the "Display master items" command. Or suppose that, on a numbered page, you have moved any of the column guides or ruler guides initially set up on the master pages. With the "Copy master guides" command, you can restore these guides. This command is useful in several situations:

- When you want to restore the master guides after changing them

- When you want to display the master guides on a page that you built before setting up the master page.

If you have already placed ruler guides and customized column settings on several pages before you define the master page elements, those pages retain their original settings and do not pick up the master settings unless you use the "Copy master guides" command.

- When you are using more than one grid system or column layout in a document.

For example, if you want some pages to contain three equal columns and other pages to have a particular custom column setting, you set up the custom columns on the master pages and use the "Column guides..." command to switch to three columns (see Chapter 9).

Moving Around On, Inserting, Deleting, and Turning Pages

While building a document, you can use the Page menu commands to move around on a page, to add or to delete pages, or to turn from one page to another. Most of these commands have keyboard equivalents or mouse shortcuts. The Page menu commands are described in the following sections.

Changing the Views of a Page

The Page menu lists five different views that you can use on any page: "Actual size", "75% size", "50% size", "Fit in window", and "200% size". The menu shows the keyboard shortcuts to the right of the commands (see fig. 6.36).

Fig. 6.36. Keyboard shortcuts shown on the Page menu.

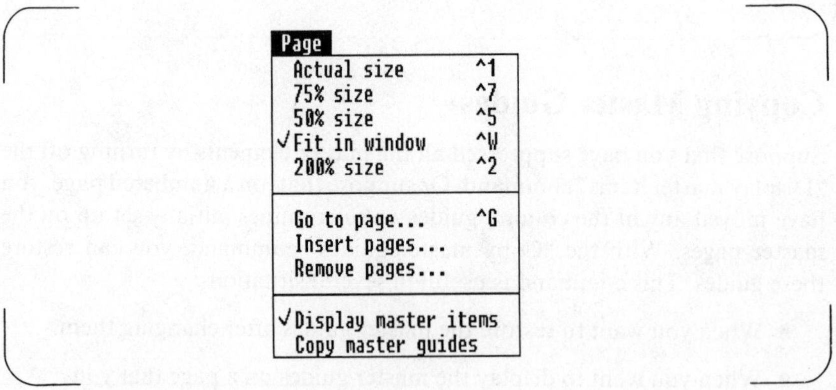

Page	
Actual size	^1
75% size	^7
50% size	^5
√Fit in window	^W
200% size	^2
Go to page...	^G
Insert pages...	
Remove pages...	
√Display master items	
Copy master guides	

In addition to using those shortcuts, you can click the secondary mouse button to switch to an "Actual size" view of the pointer's position on the page or to toggle between "Actual size" and "Fit in window". Hold down the Shift key and click the secondary mouse button to switch to a "200% size" view of the pointer's position.

To move around on the screen in any view, you do one of the following:

- Use the scroll bars.

- To move the page on the screen, hold down the Alt key as you drag the grabber hand.

- To jump the text tool (the I-beam) from one place to another within a text block (and thereby jump to a new view of the page), use the keyboard shortcuts described in Chapter 4.

Efficiency Tip

Start a Page in the "Fit in window" View

Start building each page by working in the "Fit in window" view, letting the snap-to effect of the guides help you place text and graphics from other programs. To type or edit text or to draw graphics with PageMaker's tools, change to "Actual size", "75% size", or "50% size". Change to "200% size" to work with small type (eight points or less) and to align graphics and text precisely without guides.

Efficiency Tip

Save Pages in Different Views

Some layout artists save the finished pages in their documents in "Fit in window" view and the unfinished pages in a close-up view of where they left off with that page. This way, the layout artist can page through a document quickly, making finishing touches after the first complete run through. (Each page is saved with exactly the same view it last had.)

Inserting and Removing Pages

While you are working, you can insert and delete pages by using the "Insert pages..." and "Remove pages..." commands on the Page menu. With either command, you enter the number of pages to be inserted or deleted (see fig. 6.37).

Fig. 6.37. Inserting new pages.

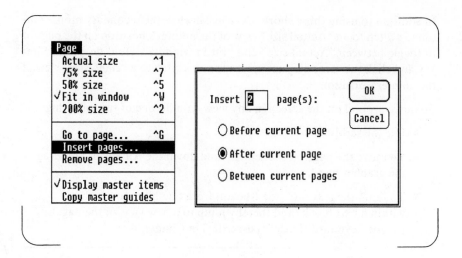

Page insertions and deletions in the document are reflected in the page count displayed in the "Page setup" dialog box. Chapter 3 describes how to continue text from one page to another when you are using the "Insert pages..." command.

When you delete pages, PageMaker warns you that you cannot restore their contents. If you delete a block of text from the middle of a multipage flow of text from the same source, PageMaker "preserves the link" between adjacent blocks. For example, in figure 6.38, the text, before the deletion, flowed through three columns. After the middle block of text is deleted, the text flows from the first column to the third column. To delete pages without losing their contents, you move the page contents to the pasteboard area and then delete the pages.

Efficiency Tip

Enlarge Your View of the Pasteboard

When working with big graphics or large blocks of text on the pasteboard, you can obtain a wider view of the pasteboard by holding down the Shift key as you select the "Fit in window" option (see fig. 6.39). This technique works if you select the option from the menu or if you press Shift-Ctrl-W but not when you use the secondary mouse button to change the "Fit in window" view.

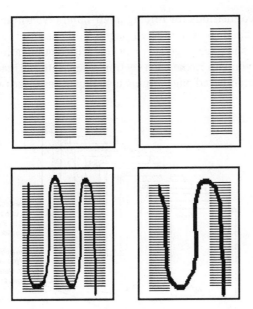

Fig. 6.38. *Preserving the link between adjacent blocks after deletion.*

Fig. 6.39. *Pressing Shift-Ctrl-W to get a wider view of the pasteboard area.*

PageMaker has two methods for forcing a left-hand (even-numbered) page to become a right-hand (odd-numbered page). You can insert a blank page in front of the left-hand page. If you are working with a publication consisting of many sections, you can make each section a separate file, each of which starts with an odd-numbered page. Figure 6.40 illustrates these two methods.

Fig. 6.40. Two ways of forcing new sections to start on right-hand pages.

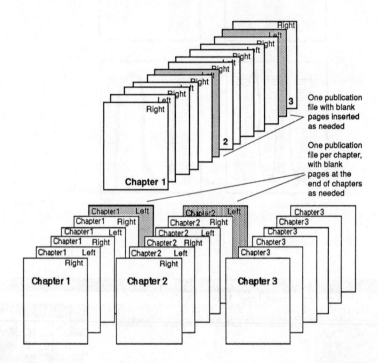

If you insert pages between two facing pages, any items that extend across the boundaries between the two pages remain on the left-hand page. If you delete a left-hand page from a facing-page set and some elements overlap both pages, PageMaker deletes those elements. If you delete pages so that two new facing pages have more than 40 ruler guides (the maximum allowed for a pair of facing pages), PageMaker deletes some of the ruler guides on the right-hand page.

If you insert an odd number of pages into a double-sided, facing-page layout, elements that were formerly set up to bleed from the left-hand to the right-hand page of a pair bleed onto the pasteboard. In figure 6.41, for example, elements bleed across pages 54 and 55. When a new page is inserted, the elements bleed from page 55 (the old page 54) onto the pasteboard, and the connection with page 56 (the old page 55) is lost (see fig. 6.42).

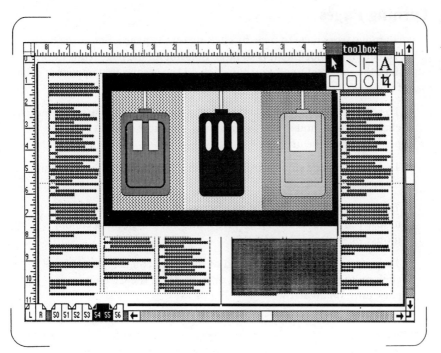

Fig. 6.41. Before one page is inserted between facing pages, the figure "Three Mice" bleeds across pages 54 and 55.

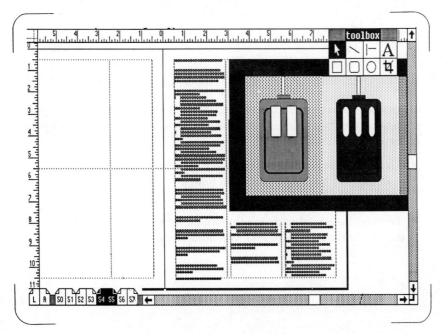

Fig. 6.42. After one page is inserted, the figure bleeds onto the pasteboard.

Turning Pages

You can move from page to page by clicking on the page icons at the bottom of the screen. If the document is so large that not all the page icons fit on the bottom of the screen at once, you can click on the arrows that appear at each end of the page icons (see fig. 6.43). Use one of the following methods:

- To scroll one page icon at a time in the direction of the arrow, you click the main mouse button once with the mouse pointer positioned on the arrow.

- To keep the page icons scrolling, you hold down the mouse button on an arrow.

- To jump half the number of page icons shown, you place the mouse pointer over the scroll arrow and click with the secondary mouse button.

- To jump to the beginning or end of the page icon list, you either click on the third mouse button or hold down the Ctrl key and click once on an arrow.

Fig. 6.43. Scrolling
through the page icons in
large documents.

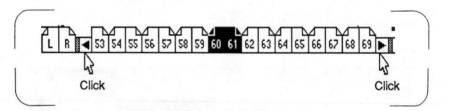

You can also jump to other parts of the document by using the "Go to page..." command on the Page menu, or you can use keyboard shortcuts to jump one page forward or back at a time:

- To jump forward one page (or two pages in a double-sided document with facing pages), you hold down the Ctrl key and press the tab key.

- To jump backward one page (or two pages in a double-sided document with facing pages), you hold down the Ctrl and Shift keys while you press the tab key.

Changing Pages

You can change pages by using the keyboard shortcuts for jumping through an article with the text tool. In other words, you can jump to the end of an article in order to jump to the page on which the article ends. With the text tool selected and the I-beam placed within a block of text, you press Ctrl-PgUp to jump to the beginning of that text file. To jump to the end of a text file, you press Ctrl-PgDn.

Developing Efficient Procedures

Up until this point, you have learned that you should build master pages before creating individual pages, and that you can easily add or remove pages or hide master items on selected pages. Chapters 3 through 5 explain how to place text and graphics on the pages by using the "Place..." command or PageMaker's text and graphics tools. When actually building a document, however, you will find it helpful to study various methods or sequences of operations before deciding on the one that suits you best.

Starting with a Blank Page

Once you build the master pages as described in the previous sections, you begin the task of placing text and graphics on each page. Following is a typical sequence of steps for each page:

1. Verify that the master-page elements are appropriate for the current numbered page. If column guides or ruler guides need to be changed for this page, make adjustments as needed before placing text and graphics on the page. Commands that are used in this step include "Column guides...", "Rulers", and "Display master items".

2. If your design specifications limit you to only one or two variations in text and graphic formats, change the default settings to match the most common specifications. Remember that you change the default settings for text and graphics by making menu selections while the pointer tool is selected.

3. Place text and graphics on the page. Following are general guidelines:

- Work in "Fit in Window" view at first to lay out the entire page. Then change to "Actual size" view to make fine adjustments.

- Use the "Snap to guides" feature to help you position text and graphics against the guides on the page.

- Use the "drag-place" feature to scale a graphic as you are placing it or to override the column width when placing text (see "Using the Drag-Place Feature").

4. Save your work often. Press Ctrl-S to execute the "Save" command, or click the current page icon to cause a "minisave." For more information on these two alternatives, see "Reversing All Changes Made Since the Last Save" in this chapter.

The most efficient approach to building a publication varies according to the type of publication you are producing and your own personal preferences. In some cases, you assemble all the elements on one page at a time, refining every detail of that page layout before you go on to the next page. In other cases, you quickly position all or part of the elements on each page, working through the entire publication once before you go back and make fine adjustments. The question of whether to place text or graphics first also depends on the design of the publication as well as personal choice. More tips on positioning text and graphics are provided in the sections that follow.

In most cases, you should place all the text in the document before you go back and do any text editing that was not done with the word processor. If you are placing unformatted text, be sure that the default paragraph format and type specifications match those specified for the bulk of the text so that you can fit the copy roughly on the pages as you go along. As explained in Chapter 3, you can change the defaults for text by making selections on the Type menu with the pointer tool selected from toolbox.

You should finish placing one whole text file before you start placing another. Doing so is not a requirement; you can work with as many "loose ends" of unplaced text as you like. In practice, however, you may find that working with more than two text files at a time is confusing.

Using the Snap-To Effect

All guides—page margins, column guides, and ruler guides—have a snap-to effect. They pull the pointer, icons, and the edges of a graphic or block of text into position against the guide when you bring the object close to the guide (see fig. 6.44). This capability is extremely useful when you want to align objects quickly and precisely, especially when you are working in reduced views such as "Fit in window".

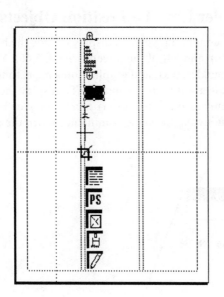

Fig. 6.44. The snap-to effect on icons, blocks of text, and graphics.

Sometimes, you may prefer to work with the snap-to effect turned off—for example, when you are forcing something into a position outside the basic grid structure. Suppose that you are drawing a hairline rule between two columns. You do not want the crossbar or the rule to snap to either column guide. To turn off the snap-to effect, you use the "Snap to guides" command on the Options menu (see fig. 6.45). Turning "Snap to guides" on and off has no effect on text and graphics already on the page.

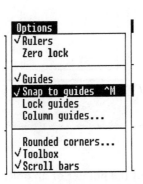

Fig. 6.45. Turning off the snap-to effect.

Using the Ruler Line To Position Objects

With the "Rulers" command, you can display or hide the horizontal and vertical rulers at the top and left of the screen (see fig. 6.46). You use these ruler lines to help place guides, text, and graphics on a page; to measure distances; and to draw or scale graphics to fit an area. To display the rulers, you select the "Rulers" command on the Options menu. This command is a toggle switch; that is, you invoke the same command to turn the rulers on or off.

Fig. 6.46. *Using the "Rulers" command to display or hide the ruler line.*

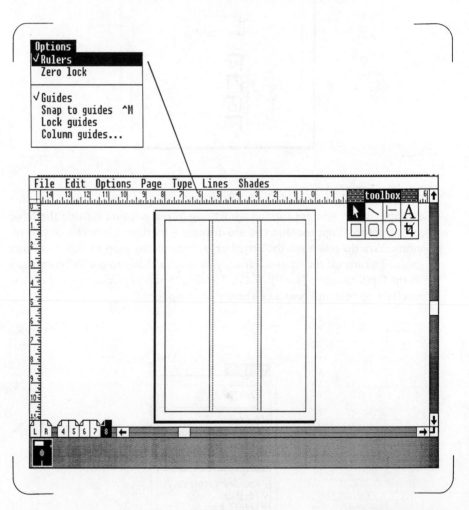

The position on-screen of the pointer or an object being moved is indicated by dotted markers on the rulers, as illustrated in figure 6.47. These markers can be especially helpful in aligning objects or drawing a graphic to exact size.

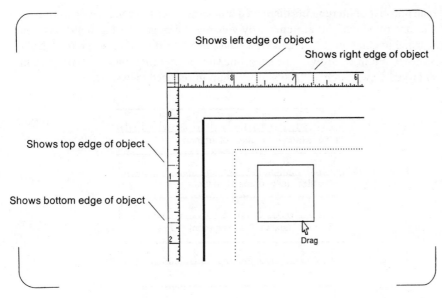

Shows left edge of object

Shows right edge of object

Shows top edge of object

Shows bottom edge of object

Drag

Fig. 6.47. Markers on the ruler line show positions of pointer or objects being moved, cropped, or scaled.

The screen must display the ruler lines before you can move the zero point and create nonprinting guides on the page, as described in the section "Creating Nonprinting Guides."

Choosing the Unit of Measure

The "Preferences..." command on the Edit menu enables you to set the unit of measure displayed on the ruler (see fig. 6.48). You can change the preferred unit of measure at any time without affecting the document itself; only the ruler line and other displays that show measurements change. You may choose to work with one unit of measure throughout the production, or you may want to switch among the different measures (for example, use picas for margins and columns, and inches for scaling figures).

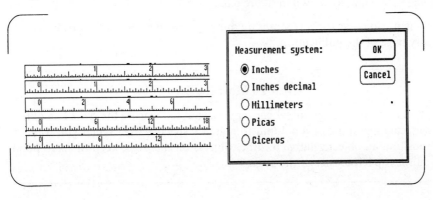

Measurement system:

- ● Inches
- ○ Inches decimal
- ○ Millimeters
- ○ Picas
- ○ Ciceros

OK

Cancel

Fig. 6.48. The "Preferences..." command dialog box and equivalent measures on the ruler line.

The number of increments displayed along the ruler line varies, depending on the size in which you are currently viewing the page (see fig. 6.49). As you learned in Chapter 2, you can view pages in five different scales, from "200% size" to "Fit in window". The ruler line shows finer increments of measure in enlarged views, such as "200% size", than in reduced views.

Fig. 6.49. Increments on the ruler line in different views of the page.

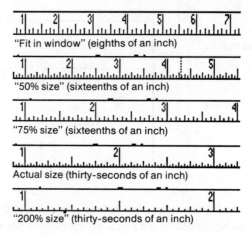

Changing the Zero Point

The *zero point* is where the top and left rulers intersect and begin measurement. Usually, the zero point falls at the top left corner of the page. In double-sided publications viewed with the "Facing pages" option, the zero point falls at the top right corner of left-hand pages.

Before you can change the zero point, the ruler line must be on the screen. To move the zero point, you put the pointer on the intersection point of the rulers and hold down the mouse button as you drag the marker to the new zero point location (see figs. 6.50 and 6.51). The measures on the ruler line then shift to the new point, as shown in figure 6.52.

When you move the zero point on one page, the new position appears on every page of the publication.

Efficiency Tip

When To Move the Zero Point

You move the zero point whenever you want to measure the size of an object or scale a graphic or a column to match a specific size. When you want to position an object relative to other objects on the page, keep the zero point at the top left corner of the page.

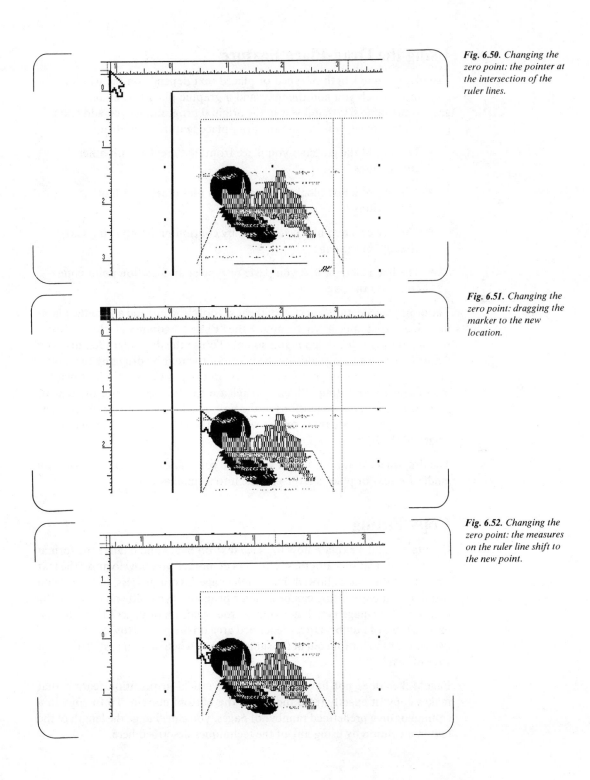

Fig. 6.50. Changing the zero point: the pointer at the intersection of the ruler lines.

Fig. 6.51. Changing the zero point: dragging the marker to the new location.

Fig. 6.52. Changing the zero point: the measures on the ruler line shift to the new point.

Using the Drag-Place Feature

Usually, the line length of typed or placed text depends on the width of the column in which you add the text, and a graphic placed from another program is the same size that it was in the original program. As you add text and graphics to a page, you can use the drag-place feature to control

- The size of the graphics you place from files created with other applications

- The size of a text block you place from files created with other applications

- The size of a text block you place by continuing or adjusting text already on the page

- The line length of text you paste or type at an insertion point you create on the page

The drag-place feature works with the text tool (I-beam) and any of the placement icons that appear when you use the "Place..." command (the text icon, pencil icon, paintbrush icon, and so on). To use the drag-place feature, you define the size of the graphic or the width of the text by dragging the mouse diagonally. An outline of a box appears on the page as you hold down the mouse button and drag. When you release the mouse button, the text or graphic takes on the dimensions of the box. If you drag the I-beam, the new text you type or paste takes on the width of the box but is not limited to the length of the box.

The drag-place feature is useful whenever you want to override the column guides for text or place a large graphic into a small area.

Copy Fitting

Chapters 3 and 4 explain how to place text on pages and change the format or type specifications. But these chapters do not tell you how to make the text actually fit the space allowed. During the page-layout process, however, you will find that copy fitting can be a major problem. What do you do when the text for a four-page newsletter runs to four and a half pages? How do you make a table of numbers fit a predefined area on the page? How can you force two columns to bottom out at the same measure when they consist of different sizes of text?

PageMaker does not have an automatic vertical-justification feature that makes copy fit exactly from the top to the bottom margin. To fit copy in a column or on a predefined number of pages, you can change the length of the text in a column by using any of the techniques described here.

The most direct method of forcing text to fit a designated number of pages or of making two columns the same length is to adjust the length of the text in each column by dragging the bottom windowshade handles up or down. For example, if the text of a four-page price list is two or three lines too long to fit, you might decide to add one line of text to each column by dragging the windowshades to extend below the bottom page margin. If an article falls a few lines short of filling a two-column page, you might drag the bottom handle of the longer column up to make the two columns end at the same measure on the page.

This technique of dragging the bottom windowshade can also be used to eliminate "widows" and "orphans." These are the terms used to describe single lines of text that are separated from the rest of their paragraph by a column break, a page break, or an illustration. An *orphan* is the first line of a paragraph that continues to the next column or page. A *widow* occurs when the last line (or part of a line) of a paragraph falls at the top of a column or a page.

Letting single lines remain isolated from the rest of a paragraph is usually considered bad form. Some editors consider two lines to be widows or orphans when they are separated from the rest of the paragraph, and these editors insist on keeping at least three lines of a paragraph together before or after a column break. To force an orphan into the next column or page, you drag the bottom windowshade up. To pull a widow into the bottom of a column or page, you drag the windowshade down.

If you have strict standards about making text meet the bottom margins, or if your extra text is too long to make fit by extending the bottom margin on each page, you may need to use one of approaches described next. Remember, however, that you always need to search for widows and orphans after making any changes that affect the position of the text.

One way to change the amount of space that the text occupies is to change the width of the text. Another way is to change the point size. Chapters 3 and 4 describe the steps involved in both these operations. They are fine for copy fitting if you are designing the document as you go along or designing the text deliberately to fit the space allowed. However, for very long documents or documents that must match the design specifications, changing the width or size of the text is the least preferable method of fitting copy.

A better approach is to change the leading (the space between the lines) through the "Type specifications" dialog box (see fig. 6.53). If you use small increments, this method is the least disruptive to the basic design. (Page-Maker allows increments as small as one-half point.) Besides, if the text is divided into many columns or text blocks throughout the document, making copy fit by changing the leading is much faster than changing the width of every text block. (You cannot globally change the width of all text in a publication once the text has been placed. You must adjust each text block individually.)

Fig. 6.53. Changing leading to fit copy.

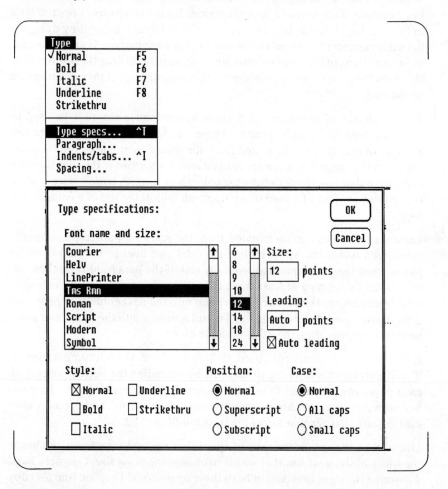

Change Leading To Fit Copy

To change all the leading in copy, you use the "Select all" command to select the copy with the text tool inside the text area. Then, you go through the document and reset the leading on individual headings where necessary.

If you are trying to fit a table of tabbed entries into a space of a specific width, you can change the tabs and, if necessary, the type size. To fit a tabbed table into a space of a set length, you can adjust the leading as described previously. Another method is illustrated in figure 6.54. You can adjust the "Spacing" settings in the "Paragraph specifications" dialog box, which appears when you select the "Paragraph..." command on the Type menu. This setting controls the amount of space between paragraphs. Each line of the table is treated as a "paragraph" with space before or after.

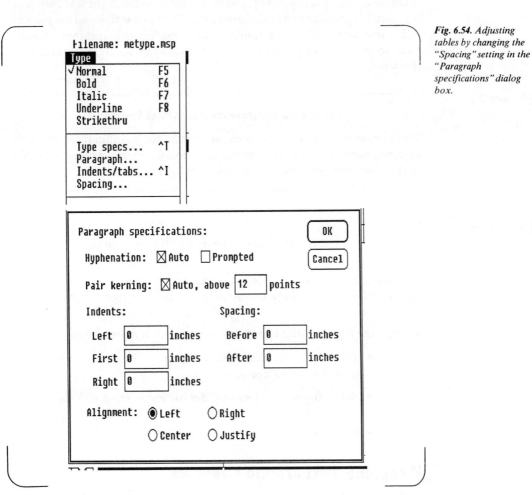

Fig. 6.54. Adjusting tables by changing the "Spacing" setting in the "Paragraph specifications" dialog box.

For suggestions on how to fit copy before the page layout stage, see Chapter 8.

Positioning Graphics

Usually, you should place graphics first as you go along; and before going on to a new page, you should fit the text around those graphics. Ideally, each page should be complete before you go on to the next. In practice, however, this guideline does not always apply. For example, to be sure that the text will fit the number of pages allowed, you may want to place all the text first, leaving space for graphics to be positioned later. Or suppose that you are working with a brochure which uses graphics as the primary communicators. You may want to position all the graphics first and wrap the text around them afterward.

Efficiency Tip

Placing Large Graphics from Other Programs

If you know that a graphic is much larger than the position reserved on the page, you can place the graphic on the pasteboard and size or crop the graphic there before moving it onto the page layout.

Efficiency Tip

Using PageMaker's Tools To Draw Graphics

When you use one of the tools from the toolbox to draw graphics, you can save time in the long run by positioning the crossbar carefully when you start and not releasing the mouse button until you are sure that the graphic is the correct size.

If you make a graphic the wrong size, you can fix it in two ways:

- Press Shift-Del immediately to remove the graphic; then draw the object again.

- Select the pointer tool in order to change the graphic's size or position.

Wrapping Text around Graphics

You wrap text around graphics by dividing the text into blocks of different widths. Remember that the best approach is to build each page completely before going on to the next. You will find, however, that many approaches to laying out a page are available. Figures 6.55 and 6.56 show two different methods of wrapping text around a graphic.

The first method (see fig. 6.55) involves placing the text first. The steps are

1. Place the text in the column.

2. Roll up the windowshade to make room for the graphic.

3. Position and size the graphic.

4. Continue the text in a narrow column next to the graphic.

5. Roll up the windowshade to the area just below the graphic.

6. Continue the text in the column below the graphic.

7. Move the blocks as necessary to align them.

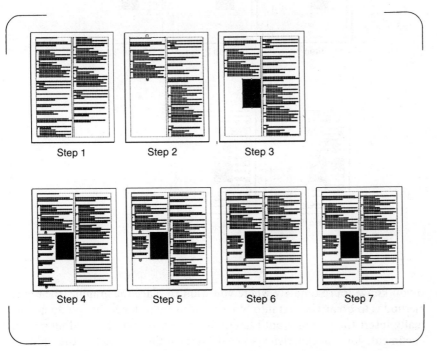

Fig. 6.55. Wrapping text by placing text first.

Step 1   Step 2   Step 3

Step 4   Step 5   Step 6   Step 7

The second method (see fig. 6.56) involves placing the graphic first. These steps are

1. Place and size the graphic in the column.

2. Place the text in the column above the graphic. The text stops flowing when it reaches the graphic.

3. Continue the text beside the graphic. The text block automatically matches the width available in the column.

4. Adjust the length of the text block next to the graphic.

5. Continue placing the text below the graphic.

6. Move the blocks as necessary to align them.

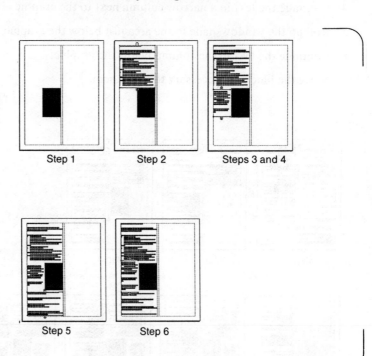

Fig. 6.56. Wrapping text after placing a graphic first.

If you know approximately where you want to place the graphic, the better method is to break the text into blocks as you enter it, even if you do not actually insert the graphics until later. Otherwise, if you are building a large document, you will experience some delay each time you adjust the width or length of blocks that affect the position of text on subsequent pages.

Handling Figure Captions

In most cases, you want text blocks to be linked continuously throughout a document, an article, or a story. Figure captions are an exception to this rule (see fig. 6.57). After placing a caption next to a graphic, you do not want

PageMaker to move that caption if you edit the text preceding the caption. Editing has two effects on captions:

- Edits made in linked blocks can push or pull captions away from graphics (see top of fig. 6.57).

- Edits made in unlinked blocks can flow text around both caption and graphic (see bottom of fig. 6.57).

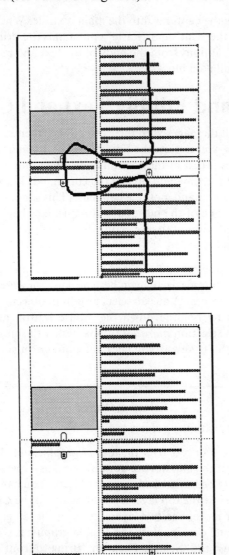

Fig. 6.57. Effects of editing on captions in linked and unlinked text blocks.

Three methods of separating captions from text are available:

- You can type each caption individually in PageMaker.

- You can use a word processor and type all the captions in a separate caption file. Then, you place that file as a separate stream from the rest of the text. This procedure is useful if you do not know exactly where you will put each figure in the final document.

- You can type the captions into the main text file. When you place the text, use the "Cut" and "Paste" commands (described next) to separate the captions from the body of the text and make them individual unlinked blocks.

Selecting and Editing Text and Graphics

After laying out all the pages with their essential elements, or while you are still building pages, you can use the Edit menu's commands to edit text or to work with graphics. Most of these commands affect only the object (or objects) you select at the time you invoke the command. If you select nothing when you give the command, nothing happens. (This statement may seem obvious, but, in fact, one of the most common mistakes beginners make is to execute a command without first selecting the object on which they intended to use the command.)

You are told how to select and edit text and graphics in Chapters 3 through 5, but the steps are summarized again here because they are an integral part of the page-layout process. You can select groups of objects that include both text and graphics by holding down the mouse button and dragging the pointer to create a selection *marquee* (a box with a flashing dotted outline) or by holding the Shift key as you click the pointer on several objects (see fig. 6.58).

At a Glance

Selecting Objects

Selecting objects with the pointer tool:

1. Put the pointer tool over the text or graphic and click once to select it. (If the handles are not displayed as expected, the object may be buried under other objects. You can select objects below the top layer by holding down the Ctrl key as you click. For more than two layers, continue holding down the Ctrl key and clicking until the desired graphic is selected. You can also use the "Send to back" or "Bring to front" commands to dig out the object, as described in the sections under "Layering Objects.")

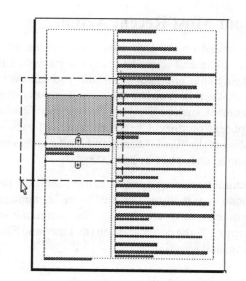

Fig. 6.58. Selecting a group of objects with the pointer tool.

2. To select adjacent objects in an area, place the pointer at one corner of that area and drag the pointer diagonally to the opposite corner. (Objects that are not completely encompassed are not selected.)

3. Hold down the Shift key as you click on several different objects, one at a time. You may select more than one object at a time this way, and they do not have to be adjacent.

4. You may use a combination of the two preceding methods: hold down the Shift key and either click to select one object at a time or drag to select groups of objects.

5. To deselect an object from a selected group of objects, you hold down the Shift key and click on that object.

6. To select all the objects on the current page or facing pages, including the pasteboard, you use the "Select all" command.

Selecting text with the text tool:

1. Place the I-beam beside a character and drag it to the end of the desired selection.

2. To select a word, double-click it.

3. To select a paragraph, triple-click it.

Chapter 4 lists more keyboard shortcuts for selecting text with the text tool.

Undoing Your Most Recent Action

The "Undo" command on the Edit menu reverses the action taken immediately before the command is invoked. That is, immediately after making a mistake or changing your mind about an edit, you can use the "Undo" command to reverse that action. You should work cautiously when making major changes to a document, such as changing the type specifications or formatting a whole block of text or story. Check the results of each action as you go along. The wording of the "Undo" command itself changes to describe the last action—for instance, Undo move or Undo stretch.

If PageMaker cannot reverse your last action, the Edit menu displays the words cannot undo in gray instead of the "Undo" command in black. Some of the actions you cannot reverse include the commands on the File menu (except "Page setup..."), the commands on the Lines and Shades menus, view changes, scrolling, and selecting.

Reversing All Changes Made Since the Last Save

With the "Revert" command, which is on the File menu, you can reverse *all* the edits or changes you made since the last time you saved the document. In other words, you can use this command to restore a publication to the state it was in the last time you used the "Save" or "Save as..." command. If you have not used either command since the last time you used the "Open..." command, you restore the publication to the condition it was in before you opened it. PageMaker automatically saves a temporary copy of your file—called a "minisave"—on disk whenever you click a page icon, add or delete a page, or change the page setup. You can revert to the last minisave by holding down the Shift key as you select the "Revert" command on the File menu.

Efficiency Tip

Use the "Save" and "Revert" Commands

Save your documents often while you are working. Doing so enables you to use the "Revert" command to reverse your most recent changes.

Using "Cut", "Copy", "Clear", and the Backspace Key

The "Cut", "Copy", and "Clear" commands and the backspace key affect all the blocks of text and graphics selected with the pointer tool or the phrases of text selected with the text tool.

Both the "Cut" (Del key) and "Copy" (F2 key) commands put the selected object (or objects) in the Windows Clipboard. The "Cut" command removes the selected objects from the page, whereas the "Copy" command leaves the objects on the page and puts a copy of them in the Clipboard. The Clipboard is a temporary storage area that is active while you are working, but its contents are lost the next time you use the "Cut" or "Copy" command or when you leave Windows.

The Clipboard remains active throughout each Windows session. For example, suppose that you use Windows Draw to draw something. Then you copy the graphic to the Clipboard and open a PageMaker publication without leaving Windows. With the "Paste" command, you can pull the graphic from the Clipboard onto the page in PageMaker.

Similarly, you can use the Clipboard to paste selected objects from one PageMaker document into another. Figure 6.59 shows three windows open at once: they show two different PageMaker documents and the contents of the Clipboard.

Efficiency Tip

Working with Two PageMaker Publications at Once

To open two PageMaker documents at once under the full retail version of Windows, you start the PageMaker program and open one publication. Then, you open the MS-DOS Executive Window by double-clicking the disk icon at the bottom of the screen. Go to the directory where the PageMaker program is stored, and double-click PM.EXE to start the PageMaker program a second time.

This procedure can be handy if you need to paste elements from one publication to another. But the procedure doubles the demand on the memory and slows the whole system because two complete PageMaker programs are running at once. When you finish pasting from one publication to the other, close one of the PageMaker windows.

When you use the "Clear" command and the backspace key, PageMaker removes the selected object from the page but, as is not the case with the "Cut"

Fig. 6.59. *Using the*
Clipboard to move
objects from one
PageMaker document to
another.

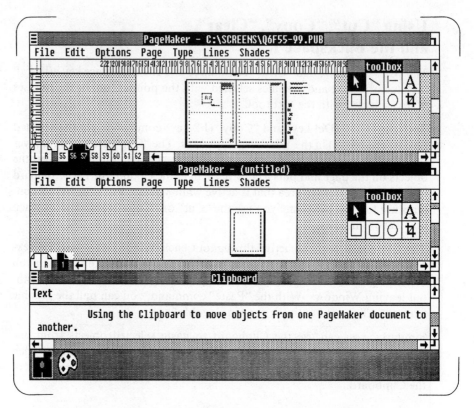

command, does not put the objects into the Clipboard. The only way to re-trieve objects after using the "Clear" command or the backspace key is to in-voke the "Undo" command immediately.

Efficiency Tip

Preserving the Clipboard Contents

When you specifically do not want to replace the contents of the Clipboard, use the "Clear" command or the backspace key to delete text or graphics. Otherwise, use the "Cut" command and let the Clipboard serve as a tempo-rary backup for later retrieval of the objects.

To remove objects from a page for indefinite storage and retrieval, move them onto the pasteboard instead of the Clipboard.

Retrieving Objects with the "Paste" Command

By using the "Paste" command (Ins key), you can retrieve whatever was last put in the Clipboard with the "Cut" or "Copy" command and place that material on the page, usually in the center of the screen.

When objects are first pasted on the page, they are already selected. That is, you can see the handles of the pasted graphics and text. If you are pasting a group of objects, you can move them as a group by dragging the entire selection immediately after pasting it on the page (see fig. 6.60). Otherwise, if you click the pointer off the selection, the object is no longer selected.

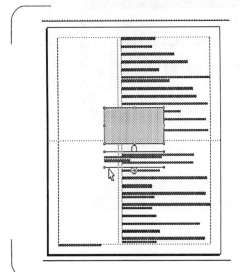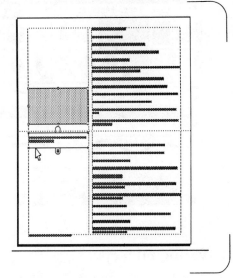

Fig. 6.60. Dragging a group of items immediately after they are pasted from the Clipboard.

The "Paste" command is most often used to paste objects from one part of a PageMaker document to another or from one PageMaker document to another. To move graphics or text from another program into PageMaker, you will find using the "Place..." command more convenient.

This rule has one exception. Suppose that you want to select only a small part of a word-processing document or a drawing from another program. Rather than place the entire file and crop, or cut off, the excess parts, a more convenient technique is to go into the word-processing or graphics file under the Windows umbrella, select the desired parts, and copy them to the Clipboard. Then open the PageMaker document and paste. Figure 6.61 shows an example of PageMaker and a paint program being used together. At the top of the figure, the PageMaker document is open. The paint program in the mid-

dle of the figure is open as a second window on the screen. The third part of
the figure shows the contents of the Clipboard with an object from the paint
file about to be pasted into PageMaker.

Fig. 6.61. Working in two different programs at once and pasting through the Clipboard.

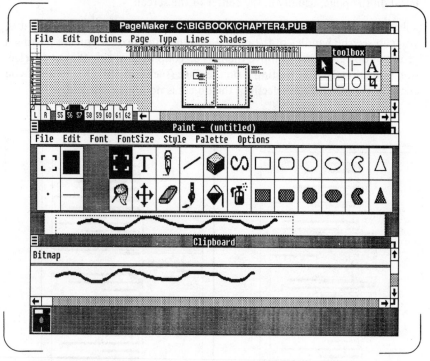

Layering Objects

PageMaker is a three-dimensional system in the sense that in addition to placing objects next to each other, you can layer objects, one on top of the other,
as shown in figure 6.62. Usually, the first object placed, drawn, or typed in a
series becomes the bottom layer; and the last object is the top layer. Often,
you will want to change the order of the layers, and you can do so by using
the "Send to back" and "Bring to front" commands on the Edit menu. You
also can work down through the stack by pressing Shift-click to select objects
below another object.

Placing Objects in the Background

The "Send to back" command sends a specific object to the bottom layer in
a series. For example, you can use this command to make shaded boxes the

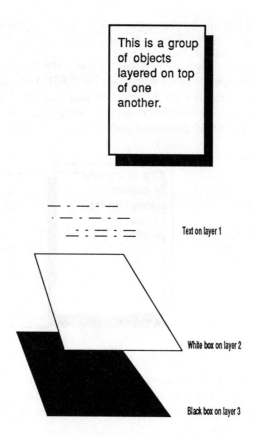

Fig. 6.62. *Examples of layered objects.*

background for a particular area. You can also use the "Send to back" command to access objects several layers below the top layer. (This procedure is an alternative to holding down the Ctrl key as you click to select objects on different layers, as explained in "Selecting and Editing Text and Graphics" in this chapter.)

Bringing Objects to the Foreground

The "Bring to front" command makes a selected object come to the top layer, in front of any other unselected objects. When you are arranging a series of objects on the screen, you may find this command a useful alternative to the "Send to back" command.

The "Bring to front" command is especially useful when you are dealing with more than two layers of objects. When only two objects are layered, you can select the top one by clicking it with the pointer. Then, you use the "Send to back" command to uncover the object below.

When many objects are layered, however, the pointer tool cannot get to an object through the other layers (see fig. 6.63). You may be able to select the target object easily with the selection marquee (by dragging the pointer tool to get the flashing selection marquee). After editing or moving the object, use the "Send to back" command if necessary.

Fig. 6.63. Using the marquee to select buried objects.

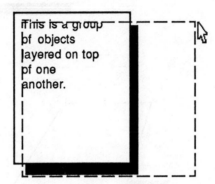

When you edit text or move a graphic, it automatically becomes the top layer on that page. You may need to use the "Send to back" command to return the text or graphic to the proper order, even though you did not use the "Bring to front" command.

Summary

This chapter takes you through the sequence of steps that you follow when building any publication with PageMaker:

1. Open a new publication.

2. Set up the master page elements and nonprinting grid lines.

3. Use the guides to arrange text and graphics on each page.

The next chapter explains the process of printing the publication. Together, Chapters 3 through 7 present all the commands and steps required for a complete production cycle *except* the design process. Part II offers basic guidelines to help you design your own publications, and Part III provides examples of publications that have been designed for efficient production, as well as for usefulness and pleasing appearance.

Printing 7

Your ultimate goal in the production process is to print your publication on a high-resolution printer. Sometimes this output becomes the distribution copy or copies. More often, the output becomes the *camera-ready pages* from which the document is reproduced with photocopying or offset-printing equipment. In this chapter, you learn the differences among various printers' capabilities. You learn how to install the printer (during the process of installing Windows or PageMaker), how to select the printer for a publication (if you are using more than one printer), and how to print a publication. You also learn how to add new fonts to your printer and to the list of fonts in the "Type specifications" dialog box.

Your choices of printers are increased by PageMaker's capacity to use three different types of fonts: bit-mapped fonts, vector fonts, and outline fonts. Bit-mapped fonts are either screen fonts or printer fonts that are displayed and printed as solid fonts. Being solid images, bit-mapped fonts take up more memory than the other two types and print more slowly. The printed results, however, are typically crisper and more true to the font design than other types of fonts. Vector fonts are like stick-figure replicas of fonts. The vector fonts are useful for speed or screen display of type larger that 24 points. Programs that output to plotters—CAD, for example—use vector fonts frequently. Outline fonts are just that—font outlines that the printer interprets and prints like solid bit-mapped fonts. Outline fonts print faster and can be scaled, so they are more flexible. These fonts are especially useful with PostScript printers, although the HP LaserJet also uses many outline fonts because of their printing speed.

Knowing Your Printers

The printing devices available for personal computers fall into six broad categories: character printers, plotters, dot-matrix printers, ink-jet printers, laser printers, and phototypesetters. Of these, only the last two types are normally used for final printing of a PageMaker publication. One reason is that only laser printers and phototypesetters can handle outline fonts and so produce typeset-quality publications. Another reason is that laser printers and phototypesetters can print at much higher resolutions than dot-matrix printers and ink-jet printers.

The term *laser* is not the distinguishing feature between laser printers and phototypesetters; typesetters also use laser technology to create the image on the drum. The primary difference between laser printers and phototypesetters is the method used to lay the image on the paper. Laser printers work the way most photocopiers work. The laser printer places electrostatic charges on a drum; the charges are transferred to the paper, and the paper picks up black (or color) toner in the pattern of the charges. Phototypesetters also lay a pattern of charges on the paper, but the image is set on photosensitive paper and then developed by a chemical process.

Publications created with PageMaker can be printed on dot-matrix and laser printers and typesetters that are supported by Microsoft Windows, including the following:

- Apple LaserWriter and LaserWriter Plus®
- Hewlett-Packard LaserJet and LaserJet Plus
- Allied Linotronic 100 and 300 typesetters

Before designing publications for PageMaker, you should become familiar with the capabilities of your printer. Not all printers can take advantage of all PageMaker's features (reverse type and white lines, for example). Some printers produce graphics and text at higher resolution than other printers. The list of fonts available varies among printers also. Generally, you will want to design your publications with your final-copy printer in mind.

High or Low Resolution

One difference among printers is the resolution in which they print. *Resolution* is a measure of the density in which text and graphics are printed and is usually specified in dots per inch. Laser printers, such as the LaserWriter and LaserJet, print at 300 dots per inch. This resolution is considered high compared to dot-matrix printers, which print at 120 dots per inch, but is considered low compared to typesetting equipment, which prints at 1,200 or 2,400 dots per inch.

The higher the resolution, the smoother the appearance of the edges of text and graphics. The lower the resolution, the greater the jaggedness of the edges. Some printers have a range of settings for resolution, as shown in table

7.1. Most printers can print pages of text at the higher resolutions. Pages containing graphics, however, may overload some printers' processing capabilities unless the printers are set to lower resolution for graphics. (Lowering the graphics resolution does not impair the resolution of text unless the fonts are bit-mapped.)

Table 7.1
Resolutions of Some Printers Compatible with PageMaker

Printer	Resolution Settings
LaserWriter	300
LaserJet	300, 150, or 75
Linotronic 100	1200, 900, 600, or 300
Linotronic 300	2400, 1200

Built-in Fonts

Another major difference among printers is their number of built-in fonts (see table 7.2). A font that is built into the printer is always available for any publication. Sometimes the fonts are available in replaceable cartridges that can be inserted into the printer. For example, the Hewlett-Packard LaserJet has one built-in font (12-point Courier), and you can add more fonts on cartridges. The choice of fonts depends on which cartridge is loaded in the printer and selected in the "Target printer..." command dialog box. The Apple LaserWriter, on the other hand, has four built-in typefaces (Courier, Times, Helvetica, and Symbol), each available in any size and style (normal, bold, italic, and bold italic).

PageMaker includes both the width tables and screen fonts for all the fonts listed in table 7.2, as well as some additional downloadable fonts. A width table assigns the space allowed for each alphabetic character, number, and symbol in a given font. A screen font is a bit-mapped version of the outline font used in printing the text. The screen fonts are used to display the text on the screen.

Downloadable Fonts

Fonts that are neither built into the printer nor built into the printer's cartridges can be downloaded to the memory of some printers. You must purchase downloadable fonts from the printer manufacturer or a software developer who makes downloadable fonts. Adobe Systems is one of the pri-

Table 7.2
Built-In Fonts of Some Printers Compatible with PageMaker

Printer	Fonts
LaserWriter	Times, Helvetica, Courier, Symbol (all sizes, all styles)
LaserWriter Plus	Times, Helvetica, Courier, Symbol, Avant Garde, Bookman, New Century Schoolbook, Helvetica Narrow, Palatino, Zapf Chancery, Zapf Dingbats (all sizes, all styles)
LaserJet and LaserJet Plus Cartridge A	Helvetica 14 point Times 10-point normal Times 10-point bold Times 10-point italic Times 10-point bold italic Times 8-point normal Courier 12-point normal Line printer 8-point light
Cartridge B	Helvetica 14 point Times 10-point normal Times 10-point bold Times 10-point italic Times 10-point bold italic Times 8-point normal Courier 12-point normal Line printer 8-point medium
Linotronic 100	Times, Helvetica (all sizes, all styles)
Linotronic 300	Times, Helvetica (all sizes, all styles)

mary sources for downloadable PostScript fonts. Bitstream is a popular source of downloadable fonts for the Hewlett-Packard LaserJet Plus, Series II, and 500 Plus printers. (You cannot download fonts to a LaserJet.)

The steps involved in downloading fonts to a printer are described in this chapter after the discussion on installing the printer. See the section "Downloading Soft Fonts to the Printer."

Installing the Printer

The first step in installing any printer is to use a cable to hook up the printer to your computer. These steps are described in the manufacturer's instructions for your printer. After you connect your printer (or printers) to the computer by cable, you must perform other steps to install your printer's driver through the Windows installation program or the Control Panel before you can print a publication. If you already have Windows installed and want to install PageMaker only, PageMaker does not install the printer drivers.

The installation program displays a list of printers supported by the program and prompts you to select the printers you are using. (These installation steps are described in detail in Chapter 2.) Select all the types of printers that you may use for your publications, whether the printers are hooked up to your computer or to another computer that you will use for final printing. Then, as you are building your publication, you have the advantage of being able to access any printer's list of typefaces in the "Type specifications" dialog box, not just the list that applies to your draft printer, for example.

The second opportunity you have to define your printer setup is through the Windows Control Panel, where you can add printers to the list of available printers and change printer connections. After you have installed several printers, you can use PageMaker's "Target printer..." command to set up the specific printer for a particular publication before you start; you also can change the target printer in the "Print..." command's dialog box. Because PageMaker composes the publication for the target printer, you must specify the target printer before you start the publication.

The following sections describe these last two methods of adding or selecting a printer through PageMaker's commands.

Adding Printers and Printer Connections with the Control Panel

After installing PageMaker, you can use the "Control panel" command on the System menu to install a new printer driver or change the connections. The "Control panel" command on the System menu appears at the top left corner of all application windows running under Windows. If the "Control panel" command is not available on your System menu—that is, if the command appears in gray on the System menu—you can activate the Control Panel by running the CONTROL.EXE program from the MS-DOS Executive window (see fig. 7.1).

Fig. 7.1. Using the
"Control panel"
command on the System
menu.

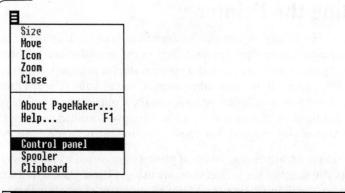

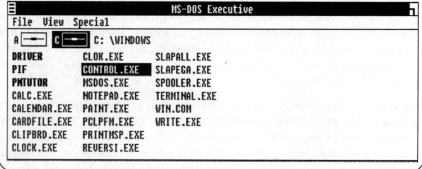

When you call for the Control Panel, the screen displays a window with three
menu titles along the menu bar: Installation, Setup, and Preferences, as
shown in figure 7.2. You use the Installation menu to install or remove printers or fonts. Through the Setup menu, you can specify or change the connections assigned for each printer. The Preferences menu affects the screen colors
and mouse operations but does not affect printing.

Adding a Printer Driver

In order for the "Target printer..." command to list a printer, you need to install the printer driver for that printer. A *driver* is software that "translates"
information sent from your computer into a form the printer can recognize.
Microsoft Windows comes with many printer drivers. Aldus supplies with
PageMaker several printer drivers that replace those that come with Microsoft Windows. The printer manufacturer also supplies a driver that may update or supplement the drivers that come with Windows and PageMaker.

When you connect a new printer to your system, you may need to use the
Control Panel to add the driver for that printer (if you didn't install the driver

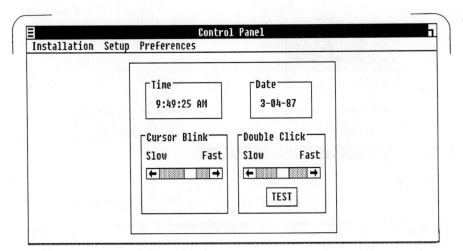

Fig. 7.2. The Control Panel menus.

during the Windows or PageMaker installation procedures). You also use the Control Panel to install a new driver that updates an older driver you have already installed. In this case, you first delete the old driver and then add the new driver. For instance, early versions of PageMaker included a driver to replace the Windows driver for LaserWriters. The first release of the package suggested that you delete the drivers named HPLASER.DRV and HPLASERP.DRV, which came with Windows, and replace these drivers with the driver named HPPCL.DRV supplied by Aldus.

To replace a driver, you first use the "Delete Printer..." command on the Control Panel's Installation menu (see fig. 7.3). This command removes the driver name from the list of printers and from all menus. Then, you use the "Add New Printer..." command from the same menu to select the new drivers (see fig. 7.4). To add a printer driver, use just the "Add New Printer..." command. These menu commands simply copy or remove the files, called printer drivers, on the hard disk.

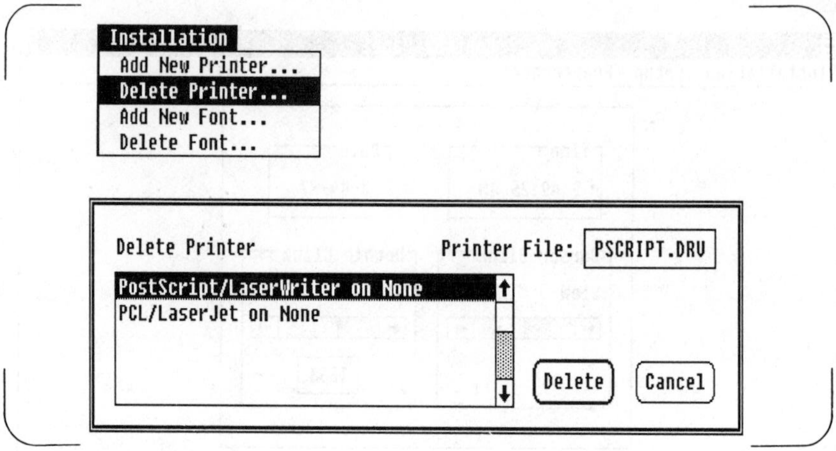

Fig. 7.3. Using the "Delete Printer..." command.

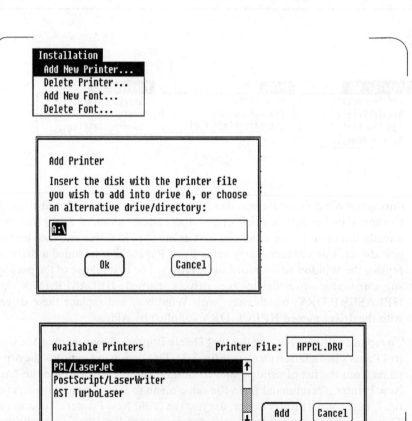

Fig. 7.4. Using the "Add New Printer..." command.

You can install the printer driver from the PageMaker disk or from the printer manufacturer's disk that contains a Windows driver. After you select "Add New Printer...", you are prompted to insert the disk that contains the printer-driver file or to type the name of another drive or directory where that file is stored. You insert the disk and click "OK". Scroll through the list of printers shown, select the one you want, and click "Add".

Changing Printer Connections

If you change the cable connections between your computer and printer, you must use the "Connections..." command on the Setup menu to tell Windows and PageMaker where to send the printed pages (see fig. 7.5).

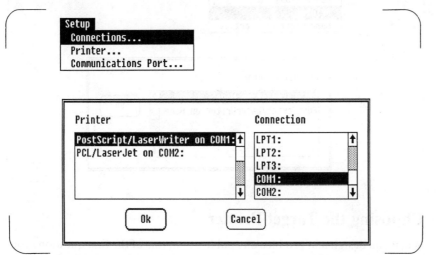

Fig. 7.5. *Using the* "Connections..." *command.*

You must connect your printer to a port. Typically, LPT1, LPT2, or LPT3 are parallel ports; and COM1 and COM2 are serial ports. You can install the same printer driver twice and connect it to different output ports. This practice saves the time needed to reconnect the printers. Suppose, for example, that you are using a LaserJet with the F cartridge and a Series II printer with two cartridges. Both printers use the same driver; but because they are set up differently, installing the driver twice makes sense. You also may want to install a driver twice if you regularly save or print a file to disk for telecommunicating.

If your system has only one communications port but you use two different printers, you may need to change the cable connections each time you change printers. You not only change the physical cable connection, you also must use the Control Panel's "Connections..." command to declare the change.

Changing the Default Printer

You use the "Printer..." command on the Setup menu to specify the default printer used by PageMaker and all Windows applications (see fig. 7.6). This printer is the default printer unless you change PageMaker's default with the "Target printer..." command. You also use the "Target printer..." command to specify the printer for a particular publication without changing the default printer for all new publications.

Fig. 7.6. Using the "Printer..." command on the Setup menu.

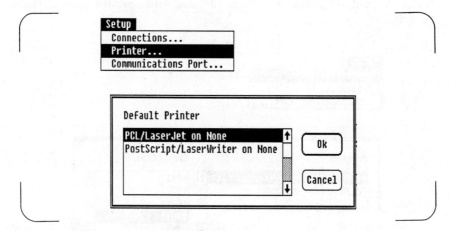

Choosing the Target Printer

When you design and produce any publication, one of the first questions you need to ask yourself is this: What printer will be used for the final camera-ready pages?

In many cases, you will use the same printer through the entire production sequence, from early proofs to final masters. In fact, most installations probably have only one printer, or only one type of printer even if they have more than one printer available.

If your system has only one printer with one set of fonts, you can set the target printer once during the program installation process and never change it. If your system has more than one printer but the printers are all the same type—for example, all Hewlett-Packard LaserJets with the same cartridge—you can use the "Target printer..." command on the File menu to change from one printer to another at any time, either before starting a publication or at any time during production.

You also use the "Target printer..." command on the File menu if you have more than one type of printer or a cartridge printer with more than one font cartridge available. In this instance, you specify the printer and cartridge you are using before you build your publication (see fig. 7.7).

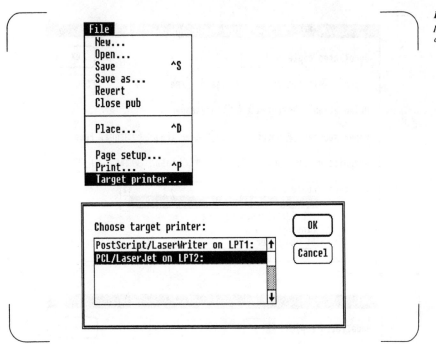

Fig. 7.7. The "Target printer..." command and dialog box.

The "Choose target printer" dialog box lists the names of only the printers you specify during the initial Windows and PageMaker installation steps. If you add another printer to your system, you must use the Control Panel to add the new printer to the list in the "Choose target printer" dialog box (see the section called "Adding Printers and Printer Connections with the Control Panel").

Depending on the type of printer you select as the target printer, PageMaker displays a dialog box that lists the available options and fonts for the printer selected. You can set the default values for number of copies, orientation, paper size, and paper tray here, and change these settings for individual publications in the "Page setup" dialog box. Figures 7.8 and 7.9, for example, show the dialog boxes for the Apple LaserWriter Plus and Hewlett-Packard LaserJet Plus, respectively.

Notice that the "Orientation" for both is "Portrait" rather than "Landscape". Some PageMaker dialog boxes list these options as "Tall" and Wide". "Portrait", or "Tall", orientation is the way you normally print on a piece of letter-size paper. The longer measurement (11 inches on an 8.5-by-11-inch page) is the vertical measurement. "Landscape" is the same as a "Wide" orientation; the longer measurement is the horizontal measurement. You can choose either "Portrait" or "Landscape" for any size paper.

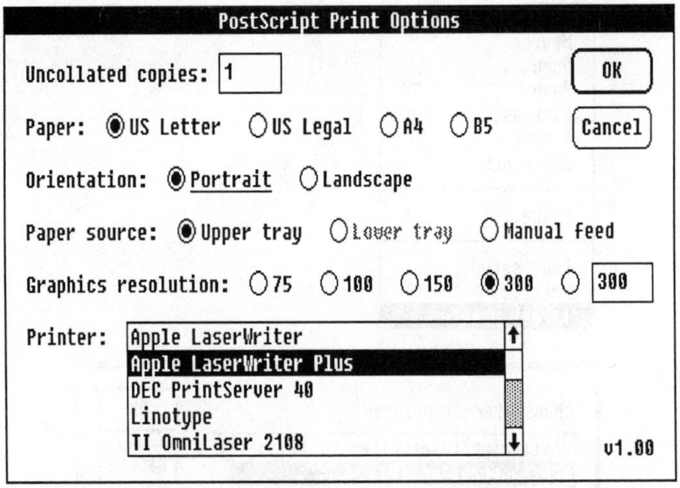

Fig. 7.8. The dialog box for the Apple Laser Writer Plus printer.

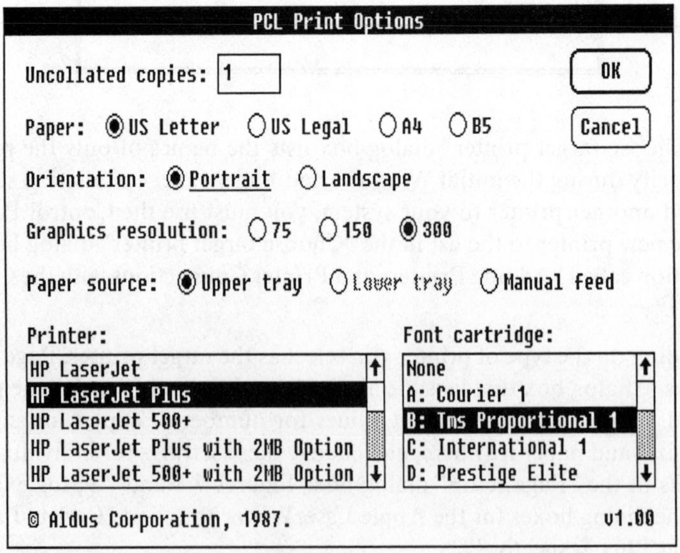

```
┌─────────────────────────────────────────────────┐
│              PostScript Print Options             │
│                                                   │
│  Uncollated copies: [1    ]          ┌────────┐   │
│                                      │   OK   │   │
│  Paper: ●US Letter ○US Legal ○A4 ○B5 └────────┘   │
│                                      ┌────────┐   │
│  Orientation: ●Portrait ○Landscape   │ Cancel │   │
│                                      └────────┘   │
│  Paper source: ●Upper tray ○Lower tray ○Manual feed│
│                                                   │
│  Graphics resolution: ○75 ○100 ○150 ●300 ○ [300]  │
│                                                   │
│  Printer: ┌─────────────────────────────┐▲        │
│           │Apple LaserWriter            │         │
│           │Apple LaserWriter Plus        │         │
│           │DEC PrintServer 40           │         │
│           │Linotype                      │         │
│           │TI OmniLaser 2108            │▼        │
│                                          v1.00    │
└─────────────────────────────────────────────────┘
```

Fig. 7.9. The dialog box for the Hewlett-Packard LaserJet Plus printer.

```
┌─────────────────────────────────────────────────┐
│                 PCL Print Options                 │
│                                                   │
│  Uncollated copies: [1    ]          ┌────────┐   │
│                                      │   OK   │   │
│  Paper: ●US Letter ○US Legal ○A4 ○B5 └────────┘   │
│                                      ┌────────┐   │
│  Orientation: ●Portrait ○Landscape   │ Cancel │   │
│                                      └────────┘   │
│  Graphics resolution: ○75 ○150 ●300               │
│                                                   │
│  Paper source: ●Upper tray ○Lower tray ○Manual feed│
│                                                   │
│  Printer:                    Font cartridge:      │
│  ┌──────────────────────┐▲   ┌──────────────────┐▲│
│  │HP LaserJet           │    │None              │ │
│  │HP LaserJet Plus       │    │A: Courier 1      │ │
│  │HP LaserJet 500+      │    │B: Tms Proportional 1││
│  │HP LaserJet Plus with 2MB Option│C: International 1│ │
│  │HP LaserJet 500+ with 2MB Option│▼ D: Prestige Elite│▼│
│                                                   │
│  © Aldus Corporation, 1987.              v1.00    │
└─────────────────────────────────────────────────┘
```

Your Printer May Restrict Orientation

Some printers do not print well in "Landscape" orientation. For some reason, they have to work harder, take longer, and sometimes drop information. In printers like the LaserJet, some downloadable fonts cannot be combined on a single page in either "Portrait" or "Landscape".

Printer and font-cartridge names are shown in scrolling windows. In the dialog box in figure 7.9, you can choose from 21 cartridges (see Chapter 8 for examples of the different fonts on each cartridge) and from graphics resolutions of 75, 150, or 300 dots per inch. Letters have more jagged edges at the lower resolutions, but the quality of text is not lowered, and the pages are printed faster. Lower resolutions are good for printing drafts during the production process. Also, some pages with complex graphics or large bit-mapped images cannot be printed at 300 dots per inch without overloading the printer's memory.

Efficiency Tip

Printing at Lower Resolutions

Use lower-resolution printing during the early stages of a project for faster printing of draft copies.

If you run into memory-overload problems printing a publication at 300 dots per inch, try printing it at 150 or 75 dots per inch.

If you change a publication's target printer from one type of printer to another after the publication is assembled, the new printer may substitute fonts automatically (replace fonts it does not have with those it does have); and the printed results may differ from what you see on the screen.

Caution

Switching Printers Can Cause Problems

Switching a publication from a PostScript printer to a non-PostScript printer, or vice versa, may cause unexpected changes in the page layouts.

Using the "Print..." Command

The "Print..." command is used throughout the production process to print both preliminary versions and final copies of publications. Because this command is so frequently used, it has a keyboard alternative: Ctrl-P. Invoking the command causes PageMaker to display a dialog box in which you specify the number of copies and range of pages to be printed, as well as other special options described in the following sections and shown in figure 7.10. These options include printing miniature "Thumbnails" of each page, printing crop marks on pages that will be trimmed for final production, printing large-format pages on smaller pieces of paper, reducing or enlarging pages, and changing the target printer.

Fig. 7.10. The "Print..." command and dialog box.

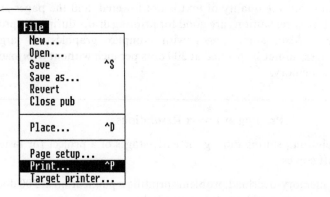

Efficiency Tip

Save Your Publication Often

Immediately before issuing the "Print..." command, you should save your publication. During the time needed to print a large bit-mapped image, for example, some complex pages can cause a printer to malfunction and force you to reboot your computer. When you reboot, you lose some data. Even if you lose only one page of edits, you can save a significant amount of time by saving before you begin to print.

Specifying the Number of Copies

You can specify the number of copies that you want to print of each page and indicate whether you want to collate them or print them in reverse order. If you print one copy in reverse order— that is, print the last page first—when you pick up the publication from the printer's tray, the pages will be in the correct order (see fig. 7.11).

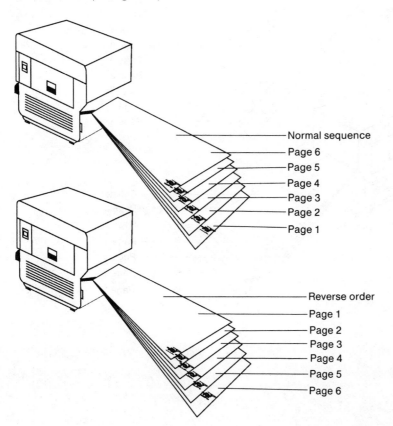

Fig. 7.11. By printing in reverse order, you get copies sorted in the correct order for reading.

If you are printing more than one copy and choose the "Collate" option, PageMaker prints one complete copy of the entire publication before printing the next copy. This option is handy when you want to review the first copy while the other copies are printing or if you are printing final copies for distribution.

Collating saves you the time you would spend sorting the copies manually, but the process often involves significantly longer printing time. When copies are not collated, the printer processes each page only once and prints multiple copies immediately from the same drum image. During collation, the printer must process each page for each copy—that is, reprocess the drum image for each sheet of paper printed (see fig. 7.12).

Fig. 7.12. Collated and uncollated copies.

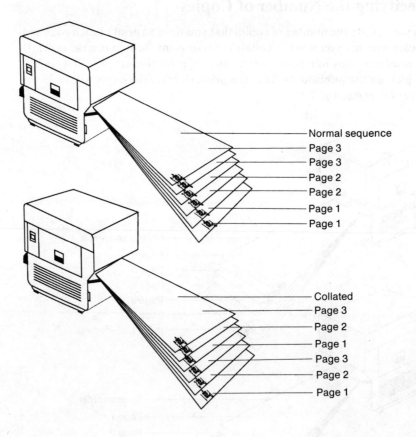

Normal sequence
Page 3
Page 3
Page 2
Page 2
Page 1
Page 1

Collated
Page 3
Page 2
Page 1
Page 3
Page 2
Page 1

Printing a Range of Pages

Suppose that you need to make changes that affect just a few pages or that you want to print the finished parts of a publication that is still in process. In these cases, you can print a specific range of pages. You enter the beginning and ending page numbers in the "Print" dialog box.

Printing Miniature Pictures of Each Page

The "Thumbnails" option enables you to print miniature pictures of each page, with facing pages paired, as shown in figure 7.13. Not all printers support this option. For example, LaserJet printers and clones and dot-matrix printers do not print thumbnails, but PostScript and DDL printers do. If your current target printer does not have thumbnails capability, this option looks gray in the dialog box. Thumbnails can be handy reminders of the contents of a publication, and they can be used as planning tools during the design and production process, as described in Chapter 9.

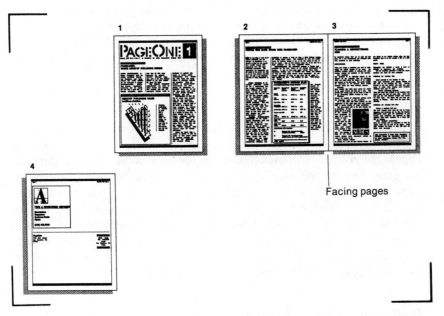

Fig. 7.13. Example of publication printed with the "Thumbnails" option.

Facing pages

Using Crop Marks

You can use the "Crop marks" feature to generate automatically the marks traditionally used to indicate where the pages will be cut when trimmed to their final size (see fig. 7.14). This option is useful when you are printing on a paper size larger than the page size specified for the publication. You also can use "Crop marks" when you are printing a reduced page size, using the "Scaling" factor described later in this chapter.

Fig. 7.14. Printing crop marks when page size is smaller than paper size.

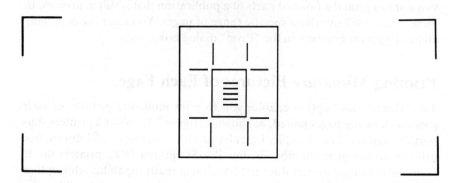

Fig. 7.14. Printing crop marks when page size is smaller than paper size.

Printing Parts of Pages

With the "Tile" option, you can print pieces of large pages on smaller paper. A common application of the "Tile" option is to print tabloid-size (11-by-17-inch) pages on 8.5-by-11-inch paper, as shown in figure 7.15. You can assemble the "tiled" papers into one piece for reproduction, or you can use them as proof sheets only. (You can print the final version of a tabloid page on a Linotronic typesetter's 12-inch wide roll of photosensitive paper, without using the "Tile" option.)

When "tiling" pages, you can select the "Auto" option and specify by how much you want the images on each tile to overlap (up to one inch in PageMaker V1.0a). You need to account for the fact that most printers cannot print closer to the edge of the paper than approximately 1/3 inch, and some printers cannot print closer than 1/2 inch. You also can let parts of the printed images overlap when you assemble them into one large page. You can select the "Manual" option and define the limits of each tile piece by moving the zero point on the ruler line. For example, you print one "tile" with the zero point at the top left corner of the page; then, you move the zero point to mark the top left corner of the next tile and print again.

Reducing and Enlarging Pages

Some printers print in percentage reductions or enlargements between 25 and 1,000 percent. Figures 7.16 and 7.17 provide two examples of reductions. The top left corner of each page, as shown on the screen, remains the top left corner of the printed pages, and all enlarging or reducing is done to the right and down the page.

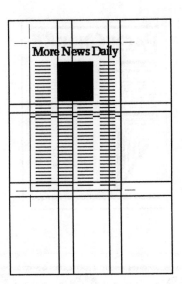

Fig. 7.15. A tabloid-size page printed on 8.5-by-11-inch paper with the "Tile" feature and a full page printed with crop marks on a Linotronic typesetter.

Fig. 7.16. *Page printed at 40 percent.*

Fig. 7.17. *Page printed at 60 percent.*

The results of printing enlargements are predictable: If you scale a page to be larger than the printer paper, you lose part of the right and bottom edges of the page.

The results of printing reductions may not be what you expect. Only the elements that actually touch the page on the screen appear on the printout. Elements that overlap both the page and pasteboard are printed, but elements that fall totally onto the pasteboard are not printed in a reduction. In figure 7.18, the black box and the text block that hang over into the pasteboard will be printed because they both touch the page, but the hairline rule at the right will not be printed.

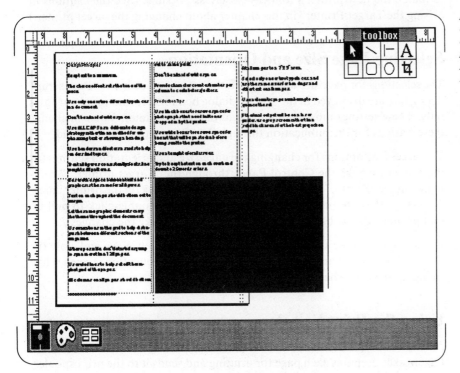

Fig. 7.18. Elements overlapping both page and pasteboard are printed; elements in pasteboard only are not printed.

Efficiency Tip

Working in Large Scales

Suppose that you are using very small point sizes throughout a document or that you have more columns than will fit on an 8.5-inch-wide page. In these cases, you can work in larger point sizes on a tabloid-size page on the screen and then print the publication at 50 percent to fit on an 8.5-by-11-inch page.

Changing the Target Printer

The "Printer" window of the "Print" dialog box displays the currently se-lected (highlighted) target printer, along with a list of other printers that have been installed on your system (see fig. 7.10). You can change the selection there by clicking on another printer name (if other names are displayed). If you change the type of printer for a publication, the text will be recomposed to match the new printer's fonts as closely as possible. (See the cautions in "Using the Target Printer" in this chapter about changing the target printer.)

Selecting Page Size and Orientation

The selections for page size and orientation that you made in the "Page setup" dialog box are displayed in the "Print" dialog box for informational purposes only. These settings must match those of the target printer. You can change these settings for the publication through the "Page setup..." command.

You access the options for changing the page-size and orientation settings for the printer through the Control Panel, through the "Target printer..." com-mand, in the "Print..." dialog box, or with a double-click on the printer name. To change these settings, you select the printer and double-click to pull up that printer's dialog box of options. Then you can make the changes.

Do not change these settings while a publication is open. Save and close the publication first. Changing these settings while the publication is open is like changing steering wheels while you are driving.

Using the Print Spooler

After you complete your entries in the "Print" dialog box and click "OK", PageMaker prepares each page for printing and sends it to the print spooler, which is part of the Microsoft Windows operating environment. The print spooler enables any program running under Windows to perform all its print processing quickly and store the results on the computer's hard disk. This way, you can resume working with the program while printing is in progress.

Efficiency Tip

Saving Time Spooling and Printing

You can allocate more RAM to the spooler so that it works faster. Before you begin printing, choose the "Spooler" command from the System menu and select "Priorities". Then choose "High" instead of the default "Low".

Small print jobs take almost as long to spool as to print. Spooling is most beneficial for long jobs (10- to 100-page files). You can turn off your spooler in the WIN.INI file so that print jobs go directly to the printer. For some networks with their own spoolers, this adjustment is necessary.

While PageMaker is preparing each page for printing, the program displays a dialog box with a changing message about the current status of the printing process (see fig. 7.19). When PageMaker finishes its part of the printing process, you can resume working on the publication or running any other program under Windows.

Caution

Terminating Printing

If you close the Windows environment, you terminate the printing process.

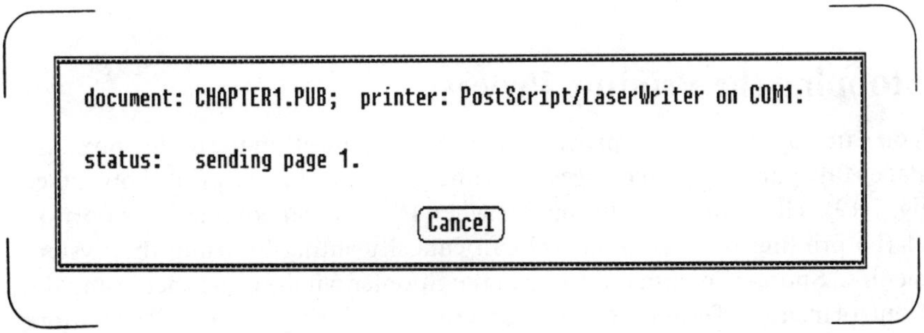

```
document: CHAPTER1.PUB;  printer: PostScript/LaserWriter on COM1:

status:   sending page 1.

                   ( Cancel )
```

Fig. 7.19. Dialog box showing the status of the printing process.

While you go on working, the spooler manages all the jobs that wait to be printed. You can use the "Spooler" command on the System menu to display the list of jobs that are printing or waiting to be printed, to cancel the printing of selected jobs, or to change the order in which publications will be printed. The dialog box in figure 7.20 shows that the publication named CHAPTER1.PUB is being printed on the PostScript printer attached to the COM1 port. Nothing else is printing or waiting to be printed on COM1 or COM2 (a PCL printer).

Fig. 7.20. *The "Spooler"*
command and dialog
box.

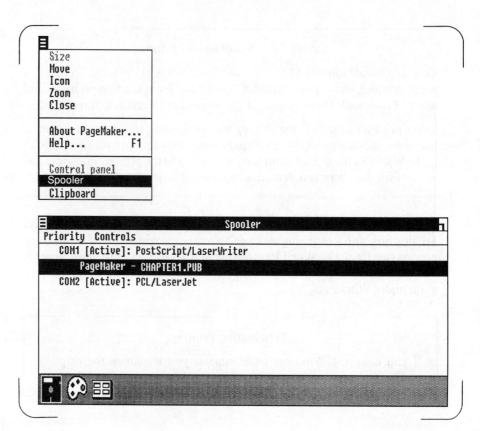

Stopping the Printing Process

You can stop the printing process by clicking "Cancel" in the dialog box that
PageMaker displays while pages are being formatted for the print spooler (see
fig. 7.19). The dialog box disappears when PageMaker completes its portion
of the printing process. You still can cancel printing by using the System
menu's "Spooler" command to open the Spooler window and then using the
Control menu's "Terminate" command to stop printing (see fig. 7.21). If more
than one publication is in the queue for printing, you can use this command
to terminate selected publications before they start printing.

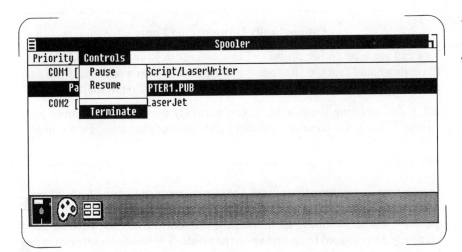

Fig. 7.21. *Using the Spooler's "Terminate" command to stop printing.*

Downloading Soft Fonts to the Printer

Besides the fonts that come with your printer, you can buy more fonts on disks from various sources. These fonts are sometimes called *soft fonts* because they are not "hard-coded" into chips in the printer or in the printer font cartridge. They are also called *downloadable fonts* because to use these fonts, you need to send, or download, them to the printer before you print the page or publication. The following sections describe the difference between permanent and temporary downloading and explain how downloading is achieved.

Downloading Permanently or Temporarily

The first step involved in using a soft font is to follow the manufacturer's instructions, which usually involve running a utility program for downloading the fonts to your printer or your hard disk. This utility program comes with the font. In this step, the downloaded fonts are assigned numbers by which the printer identifies the fonts. In this step, you also specify whether the fonts are to be permanently or temporarily downloaded. Permanently downloaded fonts are used most often for body text in smaller sizes (10, 12, or 14 points). Temporarily downloaded fonts usually are specialty fonts, like headlines or decorative fonts, which are used less frequently.

To say that a font is *permanently* downloaded is slightly misleading. More accurately, the only truly permanent fonts are hard-coded into the chips; and these fonts, by definition, are not downloadable. They are resident in the printer's ROM or in a cartridge.

Efficiency Tip

Automatically Downloading Fonts

You can use a batch file or lines of instructions in your AUTOEXEC.BAT file to download fonts to your printer at the start of your workday. If you use the batch-file method, you need to turn on your printer first so that it is ready.

Batch downloading is advisable if you normally use the same number and style of fonts, as for company letters or publications that always use a specified type style.

In reference to downloadable fonts, the term *permanent* refers to a work session. At the beginning of a session, you download a font into the printer's memory, where the font remains until the printer is turned off. Because permanently downloaded fonts remain in the printer's memory, it can print publications more quickly. The amount of memory remaining for processing each page, however, is limited by the number of fonts downloaded. In particular, you may experience problems printing pages with graphics when several fonts are downloaded.

Temporarily downloaded fonts are sent to the printer's memory while a publication is being printed. When the printer finishes printing the publication, the temporarily downloaded font is flushed out of the printer's memory. Printing tends to be slower with temporarily downloaded fonts because the fonts are downloaded each time the publication is printed. Temporarily downloaded fonts have the advantage of releasing memory space when the font is not being used.

Efficiency Tip

Erase Permanent Fonts

If you permanently downloaded any fonts at the beginning of the day, and you run into memory problems when printing pages with graphics that do not use those fonts, you can flush the fonts out of the printer's memory by turning off the printer. When you turn the printer back on, print the pages with graphics first, before you permanently download the fonts again.

Most printers can handle no more than 16 soft fonts per page and 32 soft fonts per publication. (Even this maximum depends on the size of the font because larger fonts take up more memory.) These limits are considerably smaller for printers with limited memory available. For example, a 512K printer may be able to hold only 10 different text-size fonts, which are 9 or 10 points in size. The advantage of temporarily downloading fonts is that the printer's memory is completely cleared between print jobs. With permanently downloaded fonts, you must turn the printer off, then on again, in order to clear the memory.

Some printers—PostScript printers, for instance—can print any size of a specific typeface and style once the font is downloaded; but other printers require that each combination of size, typeface, and style be downloaded as a separate font. As stated in Chapter 4, a font is a particular combination of typeface and style (and sometimes point size). To use the entire family in the Palatino typeface on a PostScript printer, for example, you need to download four different styles: normal, boldface, italic, and boldface italic. For design suggestions, along with other production considerations in choosing fonts for publications, see Chapter 8.

Creating a PFM File for Windows

The second step in using a soft font is to let the Windows environment "know" that the new font is available. To do this, you must have a *printer font metrics*, or PFM, version of the font. Some manufacturers provide these versions on their disks. If you do not have a PFM file, you can use the PCLPFM program that comes on PageMaker's Drivers disk to create the file for Hewlett-Packard printer fonts.

Follow the manufacturer's instructions for copying the fonts from the manufacturer's disk to your hard disk. Copy the fonts into the Windows directory or into a new font subdirectory you create. Make a note of the identification numbers the installation program assigns during this process.

Next, copy the files named PCLPFM.EXE and PCLPFM.PIF from the PageMaker Drivers disk into the same directory. Use the PCLPFM program to create a PFM file for each font to be downloaded. Start the PCLPFM program from DOS or from the MS-DOS Executive window. When prompted, type the name of the downloadable file, as provided by the vendor. The PCLPFM program creates a file with a name based on the manufacturer's name for the font file. If another file of the same name already exists, you are given the chance to change the name of the new file or replace the existing file name.

After you create a PFM file for every downloadable font you want to use, add the list of names to the WIN.INI file in the \WINDOWS directory. To do this, you open the WIN.INI file as text-only in any word processor that lets you save unformatted files. Find the line that lists the printer you want to use with the downloadable fonts—for example,

   [HPPCL,LPT1]

Following that line, you can copy the text from the APPNDWIN.INI file created by the PCLPFM program (versions 1.03 and later); or you can type the list of downloadable fonts, one per line, beginning each line with the word *SOFTFONT*, as shown in figure 7.22. After typing the word **SOFTFONT**, you enter the font number assigned when the font was downloaded to the printer and to the hard disk, according to the manufacturer's directions. Then you type an equal sign and the full path name to the PFM file. For example, to list a PFM file for the font named HV10B#RP in the subdirectory NEWFONTS, you type

SOFTFONT3=C:\NEWFONTS\HV10B#RP.PFM

Entries like this one create permanently downloaded fonts, which are downloaded to the printer when you start Windows. To create temporarily downloaded fonts, you add a comma followed by the full path name to the manufacturer's font file—for example,

SOFTFONT3=C:\NEWFONTS\HV10B#RP.PFM,C:\NEWFONTS\HV10B#R8.SFP

What if the soft font was not downloaded to the printer and assigned a number during any of the manufacturer's downloading processes? In this case, you can use, after the word *SOFTFONT*, any two-digit number that is not already used by another soft font. These fonts will always be temporarily downloadable, but they cannot be permanently downloaded unless their font numbers are also assigned through the printer's downloading program (that is, in addition to the WIN.INI listing).

Using Downloadable Fonts

The third step in using a soft font is to select it in the "Type specifications" dialog box and try using the font in a publication. If you have trouble printing the publication, any of several problems may be the reason:

- The names you entered in the WIN.INI file do not match the PFM file names.

- The page has graphics that cannot be processed when the fonts are permanently downloaded.

- You have used too many fonts on one page or in one publication.

Remember that different typefaces, styles, and sizes take up different amounts of memory and that different types of graphics also make different demands on memory. Before you design a long publication with downloadable fonts, try printing one or two sample pages with representative graphics

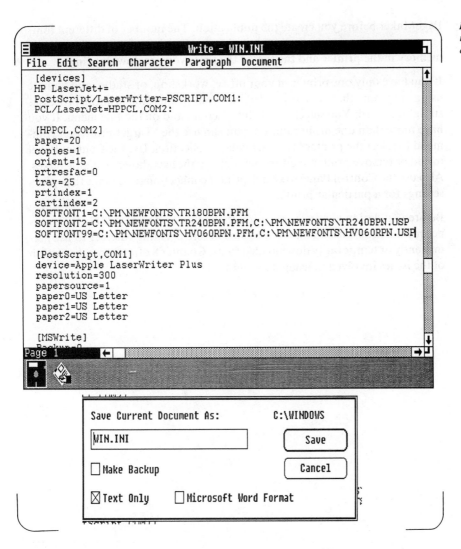

Fig. 7.22. Lines entered in the WIN.INI file to set up downloadable fonts.

as well as text that uses all the fonts called for in the design. If you have trouble printing these sample pages, change your design by reducing the number of fonts you use or by simplifying the specifications for illustrations.

Summary

As you can see, the printing process can be simple if you are using only the fonts that are built into your printer. If you want to add downloadable fonts for your publications, the process involves several steps outside of

PageMaker before you create the publication. The number of different fonts you can use on one page or in one publication is limited by the amount of memory in the printer and the size of the fonts you are downloading.

If you have only one printer in your office, workshop, or studio, and you are using only fonts that are hard-coded into your printer, the printing process is straightforward: You select the "Print..." command on the File menu. If you have more than one printer option, you can use the "Target printer..." command to select the printer for a particular publication. Use the Control Panel to add or remove printer and font names from the lists shown in dialog boxes. Also use the Control Panel to switch printer connections or change the option settings for a particular printer.

Before you design a large publication that calls for downloadable fonts, experiment a little with them. Do the same before deciding whether to use permanently or temporarily downloaded fonts. Chapter 8 offers more discussion of the issues involved in using different fonts.

II

Designing and Producing Different Types of Publications

Part II focuses on how you can apply to your PageMaker documents the typography and design concepts used by professional typesetters and text designers. You'll learn what fonts, sizes, and styles of type are available for your printer, how fonts are installed, and how new fonts are created. Part II discusses selecting fonts for a document along with defining and illustrating leading and kerning. Finally, in Part II you'll learn how to design a PageMaker document, how to use master pages and template systems, and how to prepare pages for an offset printer.

Part II at a Glance

Typography ▮8

Designers and typographers have a unique way of describing the text in a document in terms of fonts, leading, and kerning. In this chapter, you learn how to view a PageMaker publication in these terms and how to set up your design specifications by using PageMaker's menus. You learn how to estimate the amount of text that will fit on each page and how to make fine adjustments in spacing to fit copy into a defined space.

This chapter also explains what fonts are available for each printer and how new fonts can be added to the menus. You see the importance of knowing what fonts, sizes, and styles are available for your printer before you start the design process.

Whether you, as a designer or typographer, are writing the design specifications for a document or actually using PageMaker to set up the master template, you need to know how PageMaker works before you make your design specifications for a publication. In this chapter, not only do you learn something about how professional typesetters and designers determine what fonts to use in a document; you also learn how to specify them for a production team that will be using PageMaker.

Fonts and Type

The word *font* comes from the French word *fondre*, which means to melt or cast. The term once referred literally to the trays of cast metal letters that printers used to compose a document. Each tray or font included all letters of the alphabet for a specific typeface-style-size combination (see fig. 8.1). For example, one tray held only 10-point Times italic letters, another tray held only 10-point Times bold, and so on. A font, then, was a particular combination of typeface, style, and size.

Fig. 8.1. *A font, or tray of cast metal letters, from 1747.*

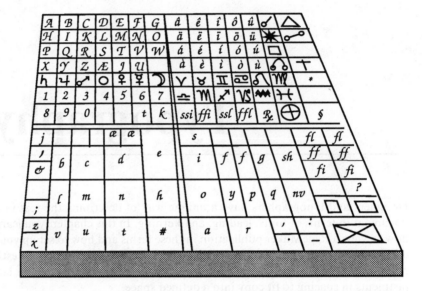

More recently, however, the word *font* has come to be defined more loosely to mean the name of a typeface, such as Times or Helvetica. This is the meaning of the word in PageMaker's "Type specifications" dialog box. This definition is rational for the new computer fonts that are based on formulas, such as PostScript fonts. Each letter of the alphabet is *cast*, or designed, only once in order to define the shape of the letter. This information is then stored as a complex curve-fitting equation. A printer that uses a programming language, such as PostScript or DDL, to create text can produce any size of a typeface for which the printer "knows" the shape of each letter.

When you hear that a certain printer is limited to a certain number of fonts per page or per document, you must know which meaning of the word *font* applies. For some printers, a limit of four fonts means four typefaces: for example, Times, Helvetica, Courier, and Palatino. Other printers are limited to four fonts in the more traditional sense: 10-point Times roman, 10-point Times italic, 10-point Times boldface, and 10-point Times boldface italic.

When creating the design specifications for the type in a PageMaker publication, the designer needs to be specific about the type of printer as well as the fonts (typefaces, sizes, and styles). The next section provides some tips about selecting fonts for documents.

Typeface

In the traditional sense, a *typeface* is a family of type that has the same basic shape for each letter. The typeface Times, for example, includes all sizes and styles of type that are variations of the same basic family of designs for each letter of the alphabet. Typefaces are broadly grouped into two kinds: serif and sans serif, examples of which are shown in figure 8.2. The word *serif* refers to one of the fine cross strokes that project across the ends of the main strokes of a letter (across the top and bottom of the *h* or the *p*, for example); *sans serif* means "without serif."

Times is a serifed typeface.
Helvetica is a sans serif typeface.

Fig. 8.2. Serifed and sans serif typefaces.

Typefaces are often distinguished on another scale as either body-copy typefaces or display typefaces. *Body-copy typefaces* are commonly used for most text, especially the main body of a document, and are legible in small point sizes. *Display typefaces*, on the other hand, are used primarily in display ads and logos, headings in documents, and headlines in newsletters. Display typefaces can be ornate and are usually set larger than 12 points (see fig. 8.3).

Body type can be as small as 9 points.
Body type can be as large as 12 points.

Display typefaces

are usually designed for larger sizes.

Fig. 8.3. Display type and body-copy type.

When used on computers and laser printers, typefaces are often divided into groups on a third scale: bit-mapped fonts and curve-fitting (outline) fonts (see fig. 8.4). *Bit-mapped fonts*, which are printed as patterns of dots, may appear jagged at the edges when printed (the way the screen fonts appear on your screen). Some bit-mapped fonts are designed to be printed at higher resolutions, and these fonts can look as good as curve-fitting fonts when produced on most laser printers. Bit-mapped fonts are harder to scale to different sizes, so the font designer must develop a different set of designs for each size. Stored as a pattern of dots, these fonts usually take up a great deal of space in the printer's memory while a page is being printed.

Fig. 8.4. Bit-mapped font and curve-fitting (outline) font.

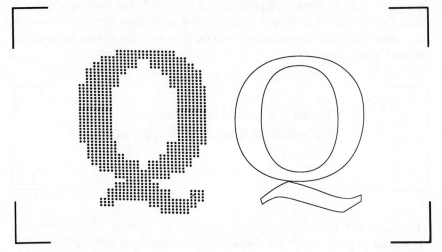

Curve-fitting fonts (also called *outline* fonts) are defined by curve-fitting mathematical formulas. These typefaces can be scaled to any size or made boldface or italic by changing a few variables in the formulas that define the shapes of the letters. PostScript, for example, is a curve-fitting language, and choosing PostScript fonts when printing with a PostScript printer or typesetter ensures a smooth finished product. Fonts that are stored as formulas take up less space in the printer's memory than do bit-mapped fonts, so you can download more of these fonts at one time.

The list of typefaces or fonts in PageMaker's "Type specifications" dialog box varies depending on which printer drivers you have installed and which fonts you have added (or deleted). PageMaker supports a wide range of typefaces, sizes, and styles that not all printers can handle. By using the Control Panel's "Add font..." command on the Installation menu, you can add a new screen font to the menus. You cannot, however, print the publication in that font unless you also install it on the printer. (See "Adding and Deleting Screen Fonts on the Menu" and "Using Screen Fonts and Printer Fonts" in this chapter.)

Know Your Printer

If you do not know whether a particular typeface is installed on your printer, select the typeface in the "Type specifications" dialog box. If no sizes are listed for that typeface, it is not installed on the target printer.

In your documents, you can use fonts that your printer does not support. For example, you may specify a PostScript printer as your target printer but take the finished publication to a service bureau for printing on a Linotronic 100 and use your own dot-matrix printer for drafts. When you print these documents, however, the printer either converts the fonts to fonts it supports or prints them as bit-mapped fonts. This substitution may be acceptable for printing draft copies, but the appearance of the document may change significantly when you switch from one printer to another. Through the entire production cycle, use a printer supporting the fonts you are using.

Size

Typesetters measure the size of type in points. The point system derives from the French word *poindre*, "to prick." A *point* was the smallest possible mark that a printer could make on a page—about 1/72nd of an inch. Therefore, an inch contains approximately 72 points.

Originating during the same time period in which the words *font* and *serif* were introduced, the term *leading* once referred to thin strips of metal (lead) that were inserted between lines of type to add vertical space in a column or tray of set type. For example, a type specification of 10/12 Times roman ("ten on twelve Times roman") calls for 10-point Times roman letters with two points of leading between lines.

This system of measure is the same as the picas and points listed in the "Preferences" dialog box and used on the ruler lines (see Chapter 6). The larger 12-point unit, the pica, is used to measure distances on the page but is not usually used in defining type size. A 1.5-inch measure on the page is measured as 9 picas, for example, but a 1.5-inch high character is measured as 108 points.

Originally, the size of type was measured as the full height of the cast letter or type block. This measurement included some space above and below the letter so that two lines of type would not touch each other. Because the width and exact position of the type on the block was determined by the original designer of the typeface, the apparent sizes of the letters may vary greatly among different typefaces. Figure 8.5 shows 36-point letters from an assortment of typefaces. Note the differences.

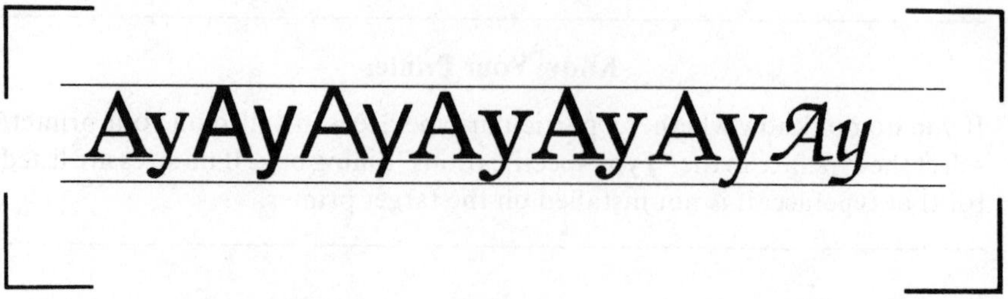

Fig. 8.5. Letters with the same nominal size that look different in different typefaces.

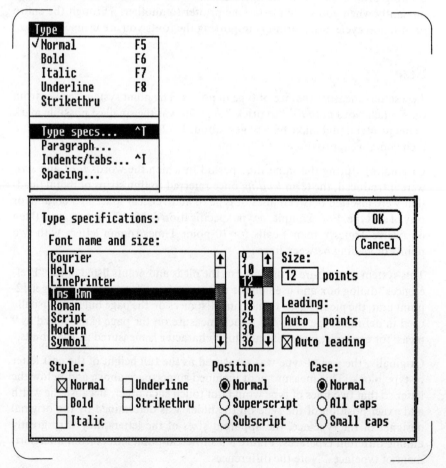

Fig. 8.5. Letters with the same nominal size that look different in different typefaces.

The "Type specifications" dialog box, shown in figure 8.6, displays the sizes available for each typeface. With PageMaker, you can specify any size between 4 and 127 points, in half-point increments. Usually, however, you will want to use the sizes supported by your printer. PostScript printers can handle any size, including sizes larger than 127 points. You can also import Encapsulated PostScript files that use larger fonts.

Fig. 8.6. The "Type specifications" dialog box.

Generally, body copy is set between 9 and 12 points in size. Headlines are usually larger. Business cards and classified ads can be smaller, using 7 or 8 point sizes. Text smaller than 6 points is difficult to read in most typefaces and is rarely used.

Style

The third basic element of the traditional font is style. Different styles listed on the Type menu and in the "Type specifications" dialog box include normal, boldface, italic, reverse, and small caps. Figure 8.7 provides some examples. (Variables such as the underscore, superscript, and subscript are not considered styles per se, and their use does not usually depend on the design specifications.)

Black type:
Normal
Bold
Italic
Bold Italic
Small Caps

Reverse type:
Normal
Bold
Italic
Bold Italic
Small Caps

Fig. 8.7. Examples of type styles available on a PostScript printer.

As is the case with size, not all printers support all the styles shown on the PageMaker menus. Generally, you will want to use the styles that your printer supports. You need to become thoroughly familiar with the capabilities and limitations of your own printer. Avoid being shocked by last-minute discoveries of what your printer *cannot* do.

Some downloadable typefaces are available in *families*, each style of which must be installed separately. For instance, you install the boldface style of a typeface separately from the italic set. The style then appears in the list of typefaces, as shown in figure 8.8. A display of I Helvetica Oblique (I indicates italic) means that the font Helvetica Oblique has been designed and customized as italic rather than derived from normal Helvetica by automatic formulas. Therefore, you get better-looking type by choosing Helvetica Oblique than by choosing Helvetica and making it italic through the Type menu. If you choose a customized typeface style such as Helvetica Oblique and also choose the Italic style setting on the Type menu, you produce a double-italic effect, which may be hard to read.

Fig. 8.8. *Style as part of the typeface name on the menu.*

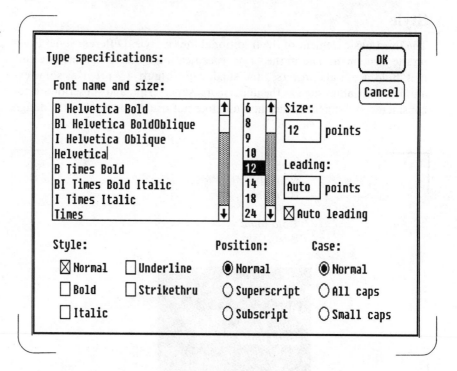

PageMaker's Font List

Chapter 4 explains using PageMaker's "Type specs..." command to change type specifications. This chapter examines the "Type specifications" dialog box in terms of the typefaces and fonts listed there. You learn how to change the default font and add or delete typefaces and fonts to or from the list in the dialog box.

Changing the Default Font

The default font is usually 12-point Times roman or the closest equivalent available for the target printer. If 12-point type is not available, PageMaker uses the next smaller available size. The default font determines the appearance of new text typed directly into PageMaker and of unformatted text (with the file name extension .TXT) placed in PageMaker from another program.

Figure 8.9 illustrates the process of changing the default font during a work session. You select the pointer tool in the toolbox before you make a new selection under the "Type specs..." command.

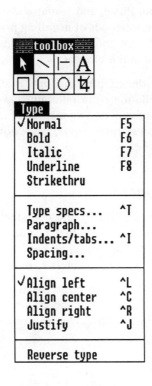

Fig. 8.9. Changing the default font during the work session.

To change the default font for this and all future PageMaker sessions, you choose the "Type specs..." command on the empty PageMaker screen that is displayed when all publications are closed. This change is saved in the file PM.CFN (or PM.CNF).

Using Screen Fonts and Printer Fonts

When you add a typeface or font to the list in PageMaker's "Type specifications" dialog box, you are adding a screen font to the system. PageMaker then knows what width table and kerning table to use for that font and how to display it. The screen font, however, is a low-resolution, bit-mapped font, which is not the same as the curve-fitting font formula or the high-resolution, bit-mapped font used by the printer.

For a printer to print any font correctly, the printer must also know about the font. You learned in Chapter 7 that a printer font is built into the printer, stored on a font cartridge, or downloaded into the printer's memory. Usually, then, installing a new font is a two-step process: You install it on PageMaker's menus by using the Control Panel, and you also install the new font on the printer. Chapter 7 describes methods of installing printer fonts, but some of the factors that may affect your choice of target printer or fonts for a publication design are described in this chapter.

As mentioned throughout this chapter, the fonts available vary from printer to printer and from installation to installation. Essentially, three types of printer fonts exist, each font with its own method of installation. These three types are built-in fonts, cartridge fonts, and downloadable fonts (see Chapter 7).

Built-in Printer Fonts

Built-in printer fonts are installed by the manufacturer. They are always available for any document, are always high resolution, and are never jagged when printed. Ideally, every font would be built into the printer. Unfortunately, fonts take up space, so most printers have few or no built-in fonts.

Apple's LaserWriter is a PostScript printer that comes with four built-in typefaces: Times, Helvetica, Courier, and Symbol (primarily Greek and mathematical symbols). Each of these can be printed in any size or style on the menu (see fig. 8.10).

Fig. 8.10. LaserWriter's four built-in typefaces.

Times
Helvetica
Courier
Symbol: Σψμβολ

Apple's LaserWriter Plus adds seven more typefaces to the LaserWriter's four: Avant Garde, Bookman, New Century Schoolbook, Helvetica Narrow, Palatino, Zapf Chancery, and Zapf Dingbats (all symbols). Each of these, except Zapf Chancery, can be printed in any size or style on the menu (see fig. 8.11).

Times
Helvetica
Helvetica Narrow
Courier
Symbol: Συμβολ
Avant Garde
Bookman
New Century Schoolbook
Palatino
Zapf Chancery
Zapf Dingbats: ✹✧✩✦

Fig. 8.11. *LaserWriter Plus's 11 built-in typefaces.*

Allied's Linotronic Model 100 and 300 typesetters come with Times and Helvetica built in. All other typefaces are downloaded as the pages are being printed. The number of typefaces that you can download at one time is limited by the amount of memory in the typesetter (as described in "Downloadable Fonts" in this chapter), unless you are using fonts that are permanently downloaded to a hard disk attached to the typesetter.

Cartridge Fonts

Cartridge fonts are similar to built-in fonts in that cartridge fonts are built into removable cartridges rather than hard-wired into the printer itself. The number of fonts available for a specific document depends on the cartridge that is installed at the time of printing.

The Hewlett-Packard LaserJet is a cartridge printer. If you do not have a cartridge, the default font is 12-point Courier. The LaserJet's memory is too limited to accommodate any downloaded fonts. The Hewlett-Packard LaserJet Plus is also a cartridge printer, but its expanded memory enables you to download fonts to the printer.

Downloadable Fonts

Downloadable fonts differ from built-in and cartridge fonts in this way: Because downloadable fonts are not hard-coded into hardware, they take up memory space (RAM) when downloaded to the printer. (Chapter 7 explains how to install downloadable fonts.)

PageMaker supports most of the downloadable fonts sold by various manufacturers. For example, at this writing, Adobe Systems, Inc., is planning to offer a wide range of downloadable fonts for PostScript printers. Bitstream also makes downloadable fonts for Hewlett-Packard printers and others.

Additional fonts can be downloaded to the LaserWriters and Linotronic typesetters, but these printers' memories limit the number of downloadable fonts to no more than four at once (depending on the typeface). This limit applies to individual text blocks in the PageMaker document. In other words, you can have as many downloadable fonts on a page or in one document as you like, as long as each text block has no more than four downloadable fonts.

Adding and Deleting Screen Fonts on the Menu

You can add new screen fonts to the menu by using the "Add New Font..." command on the Control Panel's Installation menu. (Remember that the Control Panel is a Microsoft Windows utility that can be started either by selecting "Control Panel..." from the System menu or by double-clicking CONTROL.EXE in the C:\WINDOWS directory from the MS-DOS Executive Window. See Chapter 7 for more information about using the Control Panel.) To delete fonts from the menu, you use the "Delete Font..." command on the Control Panel's Installation menu.

When you add screen fonts to the PageMaker menu, you must be sure to add those same fonts to your printer. The difference between adding fonts to the menu and adding them to the printer is described next.

Design Considerations

The first decision you must make in the design process is to determine the type of printer you will use for the final production of the document. In addition, you must know the type of font cartridge or the list of downloadable fonts. With this information, you can list all the different fonts available for use in your design specifications.

The second step is to list the fonts that you will use in a particular publication. One reason for limiting the number of fonts used involves design considerations. The best designs use only a few fonts on each page. Another reason for limiting the number of fonts is a practical one. Some printers cannot handle more than a few fonts per page or per cartridge.

A third factor in determining the number of fonts is the number of text elements used in the document. Elements that require differentiation can include the following:

- Chapter openings, section openings, or feature article headlines

- Different levels of headings or headlines

- Body copy

- Figure captions

- Labels within figures

- Footnotes

- Special sections, such as sidebars, summaries, and tables

The type specification process, then, involves merging the two lists: a list of the fonts that are available or that you want to use, and a list of the different type elements within the document (see fig. 8.12).

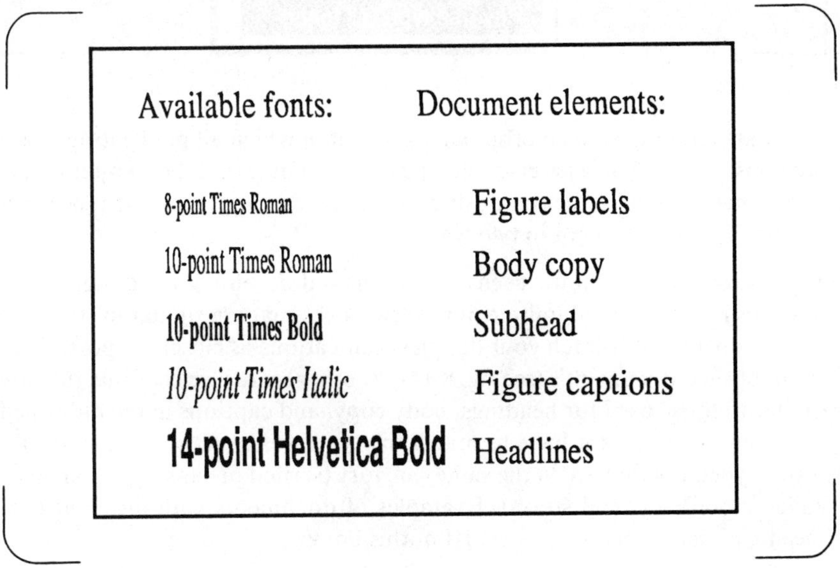

Available fonts:	Document elements:
8-point Times Roman	Figure labels
10-point Times Roman	Body copy
10-point Times Bold	Subhead
10-point Times Italic	Figure captions
14-point Helvetica Bold	Headlines

Fig. 8.12. Beginning the type-specification process.

Efficiency Tip

Print a Type Sample Sheet

If you are not familiar with the different typefaces in the "Type specifications" dialog box, or if you do not know which ones your printer supports, make and print dummy copy, using each of the options on the menu. Figure 8.13 shows type samples.

Fig. 8.13. *A type sample sheet.*

If you are coming from an office environment in which all publications were previously printed on a letter-quality printer, you may find the comparatively wide range of fonts rather confusing. If so, you can approach the type specifications for a document in two ways.

The fastest way to acquire a sense of design and develop good design specifications is to study and imitate published works that are similar in structure to your document. Match your design specifications as closely as possible to the published document's (see fig. 8.14). In other words, select fonts that are similar to those used for headings, body copy, and captions in the published document. You do not have to match the typefaces exactly, but try to substitute typefaces that are in the same category (serifed or sans serif, roman or italic or boldface, and so on). Examples of documents with different type specifications are shown in Part III of this book.

A second approach to creating type specifications is to study the underlying principles that designers and typographers follow. Some of these guidelines are listed here:

1. Do not use more than two typefaces in a document. Usually, one typeface is serifed; the other, sans serif. Use variations in size and style to distinguish among different elements.

2. Use variations in size rather than boldface type to distinguish the different heading levels. One common exception to this rule is the lowest heading level, which may be boldface in the same size and typeface as the body copy.

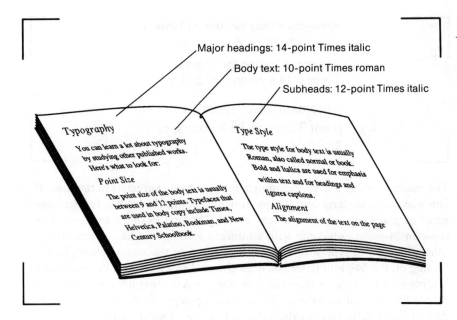

Major headings: 14-point Times italic

Body text: 10-point Times roman

Subheads: 12-point Times italic

Fig. 8.14. Getting ideas for type specifications by studying other published works.

3. Use italic rather than underscores in body copy. (Underscored text is a convention developed for use in documents printed on letter-quality printers that cannot print italic.)

4. Use all caps as a deliberate design strategy rather than as a way to show emphasis or to differentiate heading levels. Use variations in size rather than all-caps text to differentiate headings. One common exception to this rule occurs when the list of available fonts is too limited to accommodate all heading levels. In this case, you can use all caps to distinguish between two heading levels that are the same font.

Few documents can follow all these guidelines without making exceptions to the rules. Some of the most common exceptions have been given with the rules. One mark of a good designer is knowing when and how to break the rules.

Choosing Automatic or Forced Leading

If you are coming from a traditional typesetting environment, you are probably accustomed to specifying the exact leading (the space between lines) as well as the type size. PageMaker, however, has an automatic leading feature. If you do not specify otherwise, the program determines the leading automatically based on the point size of the type. See figure 8.15 for examples.

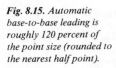

Fig. 8.15. Automatic base-to-base leading is roughly 120 percent of the point size (rounded to the nearest half point).

Automatic leading for 10-point Times is 12 points, or 10/12.

Automatic leading for 12-point Times is 14.4 points, or 12/14.5.

Automatic leading for 14-point Times is 16.8 points, or 14/17.

The leading for any line is determined by the largest characters in that line. If you want to create large initial caps, you must adjust the leading for the large letter or place it as a separate text block. The first example in figure 8.16 shows a 24-point initial cap with automatic leading in a line of text that is otherwise 8-point type with automatic leading. In the second example, the leading on the 24-point letter has been changed to 21 points. (You can use a leading measure smaller than the type size when the text has no letters with descenders or is all uppercase.) To create drop caps like the S in the bottom part of figure 8.16, you cut the letter out or type it on the pasteboard. You make the large letter a separate text block (as shown in the third part of fig. 8.16) and use tabs to indent the first few lines; or you make the first 2 lines a separate text block (for justified text).

Generally speaking, the use of automatic leading is a production convenience rather than a design principle. If you change the point size of all or part of the text, the leading changes automatically to match the new size. When you have a reason, you can override the automatic leading. You can deliberately manipulate the leading to achieve a custom look or to make copy fit a column or a certain number of pages (see "Copy Fitting" in this chapter).

Mixing Typefaces

As stressed in the guidelines, you should stick to one or two different typefaces—usually a serifed and a sans serif typeface—and use variations in size and style to differentiate elements. You will find that using only one typeface whenever possible makes the production process more efficient.

One convenience of using only one typeface (with different sizes and styles) is that you can globally change to any other typeface without affecting the different sizes and styles set up in the text (see fig. 8.17). For example, you can select a whole story or article and change it from Times to Helvetica. You cannot, however, globally change only Times to Helvetica in a block of text that mixes typefaces. Starting with one typeface can be handy if you want to

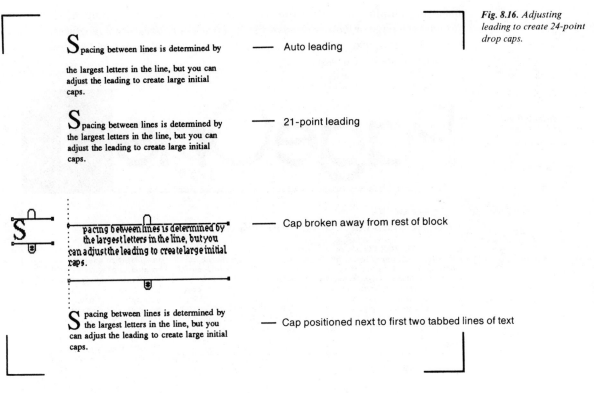

S pacing between lines is determined by —— Auto leading
the largest letters in the line, but you can
adjust the leading to create large initial
caps.

S pacing between lines is determined by —— 21-point leading
the largest letters in the line, but you can
adjust the leading to create large initial
caps.

pacing between lines is determined by —— Cap broken away from rest of block
the largest letters in the line, but you
can adjust the leading to create large initial
caps.

S pacing between lines is determined by —— Cap positioned next to first two tabbed lines of text
the largest letters in the line, but you
can adjust the leading to create large initial
caps.

Fig. 8.16. Adjusting leading to create 24-point drop caps.

generate quickly several variations on a basic design or if you want to use one printer or cartridge for all drafts and then switch to a different printer, cartridge, or downloadable font for the final printing. Another pragmatic reason for using one typeface is that using a single typeface can save formatting time in PageMaker or the word-processing program.

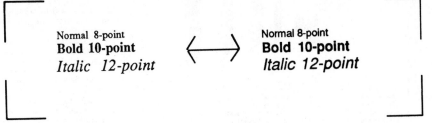

Normal 8-point
Bold 10-point
Italic 12-point   ⟷   Normal 8-point
Bold 10-point
Italic 12-point

Fig. 8.17. Globally changing the typeface for selected text.

At the other extreme, you may have good reasons for using more than two typefaces. For example, you may have to use all the fonts on an eight-font cartridge in order to achieve the required differentiation of text elements. Documents such as magazines and newsletters, which use many changing formats, may employ more than four typefaces throughout the document, although each page or feature or advertisement uses only one or two typefaces. Figure 8.18 shows an example of a document that uses all four typefaces on a Hewlett-Packard cartridge.

Fig. 8.18. Example of a document that uses all four typefaces (eight fonts) on a Hewlett-Packard cartridge.

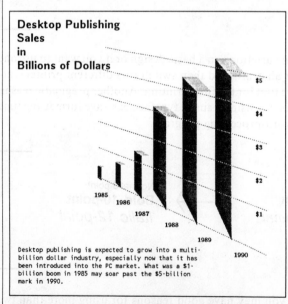

PageOne 1

PAGEMAKER:
WHERE DESKTOP PUBLISHING BEGINS

ALDUS CORPORATION, in Seattle, Washington, leads the desktop publishing industry with PageMaker, page layout software that allows individuals and businesses to produce professional-looking publications in-house. PageMaker's introduction into the market has met with a great deal of industry recognition, particularly from the press. *Infoworld*, the computer industry's influential magazine, gave it the Best Software Product of the Year Runner-Up award for 1985.

THE PHRASE, "DESKTOP PUBLISHING," was coined by Aldus founder and president, Paul Brainerd, who saw that page-layout software would be invaluable to anybody who wanted to produce printed communications, from newsletters, order forms, and annual reports, to proposals, manuals, and magazines. Given the advances in graphics-oriented microcomputers and laser printers, the introduction of PageMaker meant that, for the first time, people could afford to create visually appealing publications with ease.

PAGEMAKER LETS PEOPLE WORK electronically the way professional designers work with conventional pages. With the click of the mouse, or a simple keyboard command, the computer screen becomes a blank page on a pasteboard, accompanied by a toolbox of design aids. A person arranges the page as desired, establishing margins, creating columns of varying widths, adding page numbers, and so on. Then the person fills the page with text and graphics created with other software programs, using on-screen rulers and dotted lines for accurate placement.

INDIVIDUALS AND CORPORATIONS alike have turned to PageMaker as the most reliable way to publish high-quality, low-cost materials, from brochures to 300-page books and technical manuals.

Desktop Publishing Sales in Billions of Dollars

1985
1986
1987
1988
1989
1990

$5
$4
$3
$2
$1

Desktop publishing is expected to grow into a multi-billion dollar industry, especially now that it has been introduced into the PC market. What was a $1-billion boom in 1985 may soar past the $5-billion mark in 1990.

Special considerations also arise when you are using permanently down-loaded fonts. These downloaded fonts are not stored in the printer's perma-nent memory (ROM) or in the printer cartridge, so they take up space in the printer's temporary memory (RAM). Therefore, you usually cannot down-load more than a few fonts at a time; and on some printers, you also may not be able to print high-resolution graphics when the downloaded typeface is required.

Efficiency Tip

Break Pages into Multiple Text Blocks

You can get around a printer's limit for the number of downloadable fonts by breaking text into separate blocks, as shown in figure 8.19. You can print pages that use many different fonts as long as you use temporarily down-loaded fonts (see Chapter 7) and as long as each individual text block on the page uses no more than the maximum number of downloadable fonts for the printer.

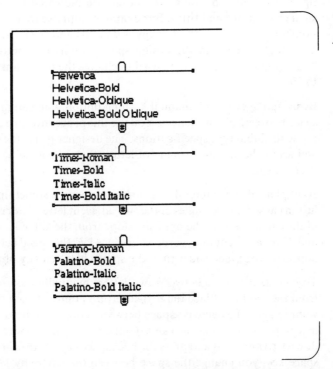

Fig. 8.19. Printing a page with more than three or four downloadable fonts.

Efficiency Tip

Shorten Printing Time

Downloaded fonts can take a long time to print. If time is a concern, stick to the built-in fonts.

Kerning Headlines and Titles

Headlines and titles—such as figure titles, newsletter banners, and advertising copy—should stand out from the body copy of the document. As mentioned previously, you can use size rather than boldface to differentiate and emphasize these elements. Large text is usually kerned.

Kerning refers to the fine adjustments made to the spacing between certain pairs of letters to give the overall text an even appearance. As noted in Chapter 4, the basic kerning formulas are applied automatically to any type above the 12-point size specified in the "Paragraph specifications" dialog box (see fig. 8.20). You can change the point size indicated there in order to kern smaller headings and titles. For example, suppose that you are producing a brochure in which the body copy is 9 points and the headings are 12 points. You might specify in the design specifications for the document that the "Paragraph..." command be used to change the minimum kerning point size to 10.

By using PageMaker's manual kerning option, you can manually adjust the space between any two letters. You use this procedure on a case-by-case basis, not with global type specifications. The designer prints the document and examines the headlines for pairs of letters that appear to have extra space between them.

As explained in Chapter 4, the apparent space is something of an optical illusion caused by the angles of the two adjacent letters. For example, the edges of the capital *A* have the opposite slope from the letter *V*. When the letters *A* and *V* are adjacent in a word, as in *KNAVE*, the space between the *A* and *V* appears to be much wider than the spaces between any of the other letters.

To change the space between two letters manually, you select the text tool from the toolbox. Place the text-insertion point between the two letters you want to kern. To decrease space between letters, you hold down the Ctrl key as you press the backspace key. To increase space between letters, you hold down Ctrl and Shift and press the backspace key. With each press of the backspace key, you change the space between the letters by 1/24th of the usual space assigned to that font (see fig. 8.21).

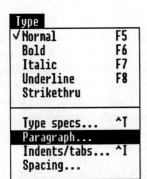

```
Type
√ Normal          F5
  Bold            F6
  Italic          F7
  Underline       F8
  Strikethru

  Type specs...   ^T
  Paragraph...
  Indents/tabs... ^I
  Spacing...
```

```
Paragraph specifications:                    [  OK  ]

Hyphenation:  ⊠ Auto  ☐ Prompted             [ Cancel ]

Pair kerning:  ⊠ Auto, above [ 12   ] points

Indents:                    Spacing:

  Left  [ 0 ] inches         Before [ 0 ] inches

  First [ 0 ] inches         After  [ 0 ] inches

  Right [ 0 ] inches


Alignment:  ⦿ Left    ○ Right
            ○ Center  ○ Justify
```

Fig. 8.21. *Kerning text*
manually.

AV —— Automatic kerning

A̶V —— Ctrl-Backspace to decrease space

A V —— Ctrl-Shift-Backspace to increase space

Handling Captions

In any document, you want to be sure to treat like items consistently, including labels within figures as well as figure titles or captions. Consistency can be difficult to achieve when you are bringing figures into PageMaker from other programs. Will the graphing program be able to match the fonts used in figures from other drawing packages? Will the figure be scaled larger or smaller after it is in PageMaker? The designer needs to specify how captions, figure titles, and figure labels will be handled in each different program that may be a source of illustrations for the document.

To ensure consistency, you may decide to enter all figure titles and captions directly in PageMaker. But you still will have to specify the font you want to use for labels within the figures. Furthermore, you may need to account for changes in the size of type that will result when you shrink or enlarge a figure in PageMaker. As explained in Chapter 5, when you change the size of a graphic imported from another program, you also change the size of the type used in that graphic. If you know that you will be shrinking a figure by 50 percent, for example, the illustrator may need to make the type in the drawing program twice as large as the type in the final document.

Copy Fitting

Copy fitting is the process of making text fit into a predefined area: a column, a page, or a specific number of pages. Chapter 6 explains several methods of fitting copy while you are working in PageMaker. In this section, you learn how a designer estimates how copy will fit before it is placed in PageMaker. Traditionally, professional designers have approached the problems of copy fitting from two angles. First, based on the design specifications, the designers can estimate how many words (or characters) will fill the space allotted. Magazine editors use this method when they ask authors to write articles of a specified word length. Second, the designers can take the text from the author and either estimate how much space the text will fill or make up design specifications that will force the text to fit a specified area.

Before placing a whole document in PageMaker, you should estimate the amount of text that will fit and compare it with the text provided by the authors. Then, if the amount of text provided differs significantly from the amount required, you can force the copy to fit by adjusting the margins in PageMaker before you place the text. As another option, before placing the text in PageMaker, you can edit the copy in the word-processing program to make the copy the desired length.

One traditional method used in both these cases is to refer to the typecasting reference book. This book, available at most bookstores, shows examples of text in various sizes and with different leadings. From these examples, you can choose the look you want for your body copy. Also provided is the average number of characters per pica for each font. The designer gets the character count from the word-processing program or by estimating the number of characters per page or per line of printed copy. The designer also may use a type gauge to measure the type against a specific column width and length to estimate the number of lines of final copy. The designer uses another measuring guide or gauge to determine the number of lines per inch at various leadings. The sequence of calculations goes something like this:

1. Select a font to be used for the text.

2. In the typecasting reference book, look up the average number of characters per pica.

3. Determine the number of characters in the word-processing file.

4. Divide the total number of characters by the average number of characters per pica to estimate the total number of picas required by the text.

5. Divide the total number of picas by the column width in picas to estimate the total number of lines of final copy.

6. Look up the number of lines per inch for the leading you will be using.

7. Divide the total number of lines by the number of lines per inch to estimate the number of inches of final copy.

8. Divide the number of inches of final copy by the number of inches per page to estimate the total number of pages.

Because this method of casting copy or estimating length is tedious and has a wide margin for error, many typesetters use a second method. They lay out one or two sample pages, using stock type samples, and estimate the number of characters that will fit on a page. Often, the character count is converted to an estimated number of words to be assigned to the author. You can use this technique with PageMaker as well. The steps for this method are as follows:

1. Type one paragraph exactly 100 characters (or words) long.

2. Set the type in the specified font.

3. Duplicate the paragraph as many time as necessary to fill the column or page.

4. Count the number of paragraphs required to fill the column or page and multiply that number by 100 to get an estimated character (or word) count per page.

5. Multiply by the number of pages to determine the maximum character (or word) count.

6. Use the word-processing program to count the number of characters in the document.

7. Divide that number by the number of characters per final page to estimate the number of pages.

A third quick method of fitting copy is to take a 100-character paragraph of text and set it in the exact width that will be used throughout the document. Set copies of the same paragraph in different sizes or with different leading, and measure the depth of each variation (see fig. 8.22). You can estimate roughly the total number of column inches for the document by using the following formula:

Total number of column inches for the document =

Inches required per 100 characters ×

$$\frac{(\text{Total number of characters in text files})}{100}$$

Fig. 8.22. Measuring lengths of text in different leading settings.

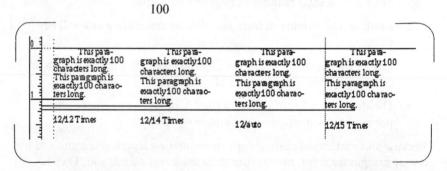

This paragraph is exactly 100 characters long. This paragraph is exactly100 characters long.	This paragraph is exactly100 characters long. This paragraph is exactly100 characters long.	This paragraph is exactly 100 characters long. This paragraph is exactly100 characters long.	This paragraph is exactly100 characters long. This paragraph is exactly100 characters long.
12/12 Times	12/14 Times	12/auto	12/15 Times

None of these copy-casting techniques absolutely guarantees that copy will fit the space allowed. Therefore, you still need to do final copy fitting directly in PageMaker by adjusting one or more of the variables described in the following sections: leading, hyphenation zone, and word and letter spacing (for justified text).

Adjusting the Column Width

If you are accustomed to traditional typesetting techniques, you have probably specified text in terms of the width of each column. PageMaker, however, defines a page in terms of the number of columns and the space between columns. Because you cannot enter the column widths directly, you should define your design specifications in terms of the number of columns and space between them, rather than the width of the text.

Design Tip

Determining the Best Text Width

Following is one rule of thumb for determining the optimum width of text:

> The best line width (column width) is equivalent to 60 characters of the specified font, style, and size.
>
> Columns that are too narrow (much shorter than 60 characters in line length) will have awkward line breaks and hyphenation. Lines that are too long will be hard for the reader to follow.

Adjusting the Leading

Whether you use PageMaker's automatic leading feature or specify the exact leading yourself, you can always make fine adjustments in the leading in order to fit copy into a defined space. Figure 8.23 provides examples. You can specify leading in increments of half a point in the "Type specifications" dialog box. To make copy fit, you can change the leading for the entire document, for selected text elements, or for selected pages.

This paragraph is exactly 100 characters long. This paragraph is exactly 100 characters long.	This paragraph is exactly 100 characters long. This paragraph is exactly 100 characters long.	This paragraph is exactly 100 characters long. This paragraph is exactly 100 characters long.	This paragraph is exactly 100 characters long. This paragraph is exactly 100 characters long.
12/12 Times	12/14 Times	12/auto	12/15 Times

Fig. 8.23. 12-point Times with differing leading specifications.

When adjusting leading, be consistent. Change the leading on all the body copy rather than on individual paragraphs. If you cannot or do not want to change the leading for an entire article or publication, change leading for whole pages and keep it the same across columns on a single page.

Changing the leading is the most common and preferred method of fitting copy after the design specifications are finalized, rather than changing the specifications for typeface, size, or style.

Using Hyphenation and Justification

PageMaker hyphenates text automatically unless you change to prompted hyphenation for selected publications or individual paragraphs by using the "Paragraph..." command and dialog box (see fig. 8.20). Hyphenated text takes up less space than text that is not hyphenated, and justified text tends to take up less space than text that is not justified. This difference occurs because the justification process can reduce the space between words and between characters within words, and unjustified text has standard spacing between words and letters.

Besides using the hyphenation and justification settings to fit copy to a page, you can achieve unusual effects by changing the hyphenation zone on unjustified text. To make this adjustment, use the "Spacing..." command and dialog box. You can use a large hyphenation zone to exaggerate the ragged right margin or to minimize hyphenation without turning it off entirely.

Justified text usually calls for hyphenation, especially when the columns are narrow. Otherwise, justified text that is not hyphenated tends to have more *rivers*: wide areas of white space running down through several lines of type and caused by forced spacing between words (see fig. 8.24).

Fig. 8.24. Justified and unjustified text.

Justified text requires less space than text which is not justified. Justified text requires less space than text which is not justified. Justified text requires less space than text which is not justified.

Justified text requires less space than text which is not justified. Justified text requires less space than text which is not justified. Justified text requires less space than text which is not justified.

Controlling Word and Letter Spacing

You can help fit justified text into a specific space by adjusting the spacing between words and letters. With the "Spacing..." command on the Type menu, you can specify the ranges for adjusting the spaces between words and letters during the justification process. These ranges are given as percentages of "normal" space for the font. Most publishers are likely to accept PageMaker's defaults for these settings rather than change them. You can, however, change these settings to force copy to fit a given space. You may want to change these settings as a deliberate design strategy for special publications, such as advertisements and brochures.

If you think that you can improve your document's appearance by reducing the spacing between words, you should first consider the tradeoffs. With a wide allowance for spacing between words and letters, the "rivers" of white space may seem wide in justified text, but fewer words are hyphenated. Text with a narrow allowance for space between characters and words is likely to be highly hyphenated. Figures 8.25, 8.26, and 8.27 provide examples, with corresponding dialog boxes showing the settings.

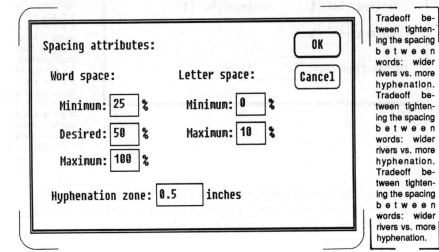

Tradeoff be-tween tighten-ing the spacing b e t w e e n words: wider rivers vs. more hyphenation. Tradeoff be-tween tighten-ing the spacing b e t w e e n words: wider rivers vs. more hyphenation. Tradeoff be-tween tighten-ing the spacing b e t w e e n words: wider rivers vs. more hyphenation.

Fig. 8.25. Normal (default) word spacing.

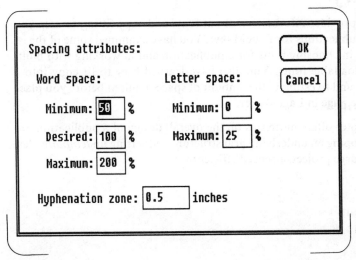

Tradeoff be-tween tighten-ing the spacing b e t w e e n words: wider rivers vs. more hyphenation. Tradeoff be-tween tighten-ing the spacing b e t w e e n words: wider rivers vs. more hyphenation. Tradeoff be-tween tighten-ing the spacing b e t w e e n words: wider rivers vs. more hyphenation.

Fig. 8.26. Tighter word spacing to decrease rivers.

Fig. 8.27. *Wider word*
spacing to decrease
hyphenation.

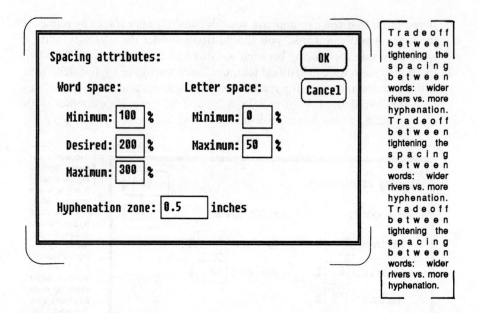

Tradeoff between tightening the spacing between words: wider rivers vs. more hyphenation. Tradeoff between tightening the spacing between words: wider rivers vs. more hyphenation. Tradeoff between tightening the spacing between words: wider rivers vs. more hyphenation.

Unless you have some special effects in mind, you should leave PageMaker's defaults for word and letter spacing alone. Generally speaking, changing word and letter spacing should be the last resort in copy fitting.

Summary

This chapter provides information about fonts and copy fitting to help you design your publications for PageMaker. You have examined some of the issues involved in choosing fonts for a publication and in working with built-in and downloadable fonts. You also have learned how to fit copy into a defined space and to estimate the amount of space required before you place the text on the page in PageMaker.

The next chapter offers more tips on the overall design of a publication, including developing an underlying grid structure and setting up *template* files, which make large projects proceed efficiently.

PageMaker as a
Design Tool

PageMaker, a tremendous design tool in many ways, is outstanding in at least four respects:

- You can use PageMaker to sketch out rough ideas for designs to be reviewed with the rest of your team or your client. (The term *client* can include managing editors, publication department managers, or end-user groups—anyone with whom the designer must share decisions.)

- You can use the structure PageMaker provides for organizing specifications for the production team.

- Using PageMaker, you can create *template* systems to ensure that all parts of a publication follow the same specifications.

- With PageMaker, you have 18 different line styles (each in black or white) and 17 different shade patterns to add designer touches to any document. You can see how these options are used in some of the examples in Part III.

This chapter deals with what you must consider in any document design, with tips about how you can use PageMaker as a design tool. The design considerations are given in the sequence you follow in PageMaker when you build a document from scratch. You first see how you use PageMaker to develop a series of different design ideas for a project. Then, you learn what goes into a template system so that you can create a series of publications with the same design. Finally, you learn how the designer can work ahead of the production team, sketching the layout of each page of the publication before the text and graphics from other programs are placed on the pages. Desktop publishers often play all these roles. If you are the designer, production team, author, and editor, you can learn how to follow the steps of all these professionals.

In practice, some of these steps may be done first on paper rather than at the computer; in fact, the designers on some teams may never touch the mouse. However, whether you—as the designer—are simply writing out the design specifications or actually setting up the master template, you should know how PageMaker works before making your specifications. For example (as mentioned in Chapter 8), you cannot enter the column widths. PageMaker defines a page in terms of the margins, the number of columns, and the space between columns. Your specifications, therefore, should be in terms of the number of columns and the space between, rather than the width of the column itself. (You can move column guides to get an exact width, but you miss the advantages of PageMaker's automatic column guides.)

Traditionally, a designer becomes involved in a production only after the writing is complete or well under way. If the project team is small, however, and the authors are willing, some design specifications can be incorporated in the text during the writing stage. For instance, if you plan the design ahead of time, you can let the authors know whether they should type two carriage returns between paragraphs and indent the first line of each paragraph. Other design details, such as the page size and margins, can be decided later—after the writing but before the text is placed in PageMaker. In other words, you can wait to develop some design specifications until after you learn what text and graphics are required for the publication.

This chapter shows you how to prepare your design specifications in terms of PageMaker's commands and capabilities.

Creating Design Alternatives

You can use PageMaker to create a series of quick "comps" of different designs for a publication before you decide on the final design. A designer's "comp" is a comprehensive layout of a design idea, usually done by hand with pencils, rulers, and colored pens. The advantages of sketching out your ideas with PageMaker rather than using pencil and ruler are threefold:

- Copying and moving elements on a page is easy if you are working on a single design.

- Making copies of the first design and modifying it to create alternative designs is an efficient design practice.

- Showing clients crisp text and graphic elements printed on a high-resolution printer makes an effective presentation.

Identifying the Essential Elements

One of the steps in the design process is to identify the essential elements of the publication to be created. Suppose that you are creating a newsletter, for example. Although the production manager views the elements in terms of articles that must be written by various authors, the designer uses another perspective to view the newsletter. The designer may list the newsletter's design elements as

- Page size and margins

- Underlying grid structure

- Running heads and running feet

- Two different page formats

- Three heading levels

- Four types of graphics

In addition, this particular publication may include one or more of the following special considerations or constraints that affect the design:

- Feature articles requiring special placement

- Sidebars distinct from the rest of the text on a page

For this proposed publication, you use PageMaker as a design tool and let the program's built-in text and graphics features create representations of your basic design elements. For example, use shaded boxes to show where graphics will be placed and crop marks to show the page size. To enhance the design, you use ruled lines; figure 9.1 shows how design ideas for the chapters of a book can be handled in PageMaker's terms. You also may use "greek" text to show the position and size of text on a page. The phrase *greek text*, in this case, refers to any text used to represent the font, but not the content, to be used on a page. Typesetters use standard block paragraphs that are called "greek," but the text looks more like Latin ("Lorem ipsum dolor sit . . ."). This use of the term "greek" differs slightly from that used to describe the appearance or display of text in a "Fit in window" view.

Once you create the basic elements of your publication, you can modify the design or rearrange the elements on the page to develop variations. Rather than create a different PageMaker document to represent each design idea, you use one design document to create and show many pages of different design variations (see fig. 9.2). You can

- Create representations of all the basic design elements once and store them on the pasteboard

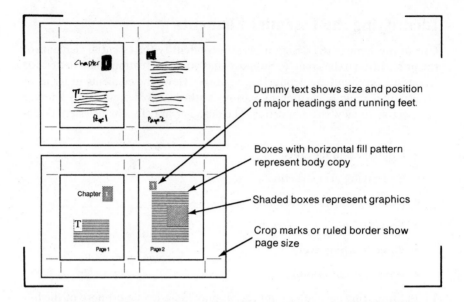

Fig. 9.1. Rough page comps done by hand and made with PageMaker.

Dummy text shows size and position of major headings and running feet.

Boxes with horizontal fill pattern represent body copy

Shaded boxes represent graphics

Crop marks or ruled border show page size

- Use the "Copy" and "Paste" commands to place individual design elements on each page layout

- Change type specifications (specs) of selected text as needed to represent the new design

- Add a new page for each new design idea

Fig. 9.2. Example of a design document with variations.

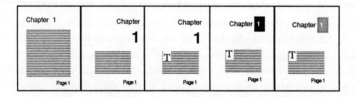

Efficiency Tip

Making Duplicates of the Basic Design Elements

Store all the basic elements on one side of the pasteboard. In starting a new design idea, use the "Copy" and "Paste" commands to move all the basic elements from one side of the pasteboard to the other, and move the duplicated elements on to the new page to create a new design. After completing one design, insert a new page and repeat the copy and paste operation to begin building a second design (see fig. 9.3).

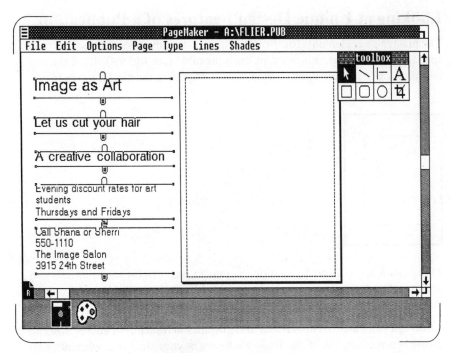

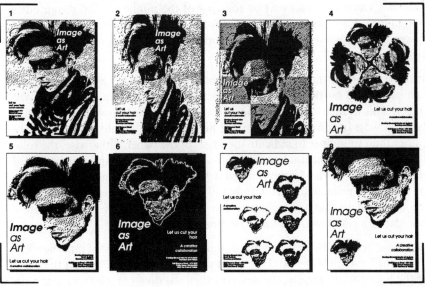

Looking at Unique Design Features of a Publication

The master-page elements for the initial design document should include only specifications that are known and unchangeable (see fig. 9.4). If all the elements of the design are open to change, you may leave the master pages blank.

Fig. 9.4. Master page in a document containing only margins.

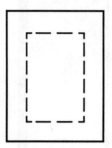

Many elements to be positioned on the master pages of finished publications are considered variable elements during the design phase. You enter these elements directly on the numbered pages of the publication.

Although you place the actual text and graphics in final publications, you can create representations of the basic elements in your design document. You need not know the exact text or contents of the publication to rough out a design idea. You can use dummy text for headlines or headings, unbordered boxes filled with horizontal lines for body copy, and black or gray boxes for figures.

If the trim size of the publication will be smaller than 8.5 by 11 inches, you can use a solid border in the design document to represent the edges of the pages. This border lets you see how the final pages will look when trimmed (see fig. 9.5). In the final publication, however, you should use crop marks rather than solid lines to indicate the edges of the paper. Otherwise, the solid lines may show in the final publication—especially if the pages will be folded into signatures before being trimmed. (A *signature* is a single sheet of paper on which are printed an even number of pages [usually 16 or 32]. The pages are arranged so that the signature can be folded and trimmed to create a booklet or a small section of a larger document.)

After one design idea is chosen, the designer translates that idea into the specifications for PageMaker and the other programs used to construct the parts of the publication. Ideally, the designer then sits down at the computer with PageMaker and builds the basic template system for the final publication.

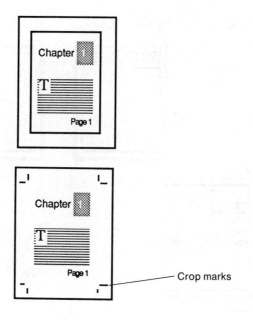

Fig. 9.5. Solid lines showing trim size in design specification, replaced by crop marks in printed copy.

Crop marks

Building a Template

Whenever you start a new publication, you must go through a certain series of steps and commands to set up the pages before you begin placing text and graphics from other programs. In traditional terms, you define the design specifications for the publication. In PageMaker, you make selections in the "Page setup" dialog box and add grid lines and other elements on the master pages.

A template is a PageMaker document that embodies the basic design specifications (see fig. 9.6). The basic grid system for each page appears on the template. The template also includes common elements that will appear within the publication in specific locations or at repeated intervals. A template is set up with all the defaults tailored to match the design specifications for the publication.

After you create a template, you can clone it to create a series of publication files that follow the same design specifications. For instance, a long document may have one template that is cloned to create a series of sections or chapters which follow the same design specifications. A short document produced on a regular basis, such as a newsletter, may have one template from which each issue is cloned. Some documents may be composed of sections that follow different design specifications, requiring a series of templates—one for each different section layout.

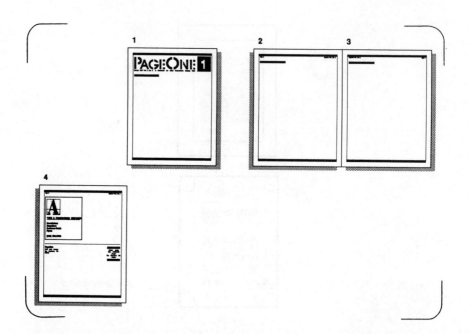

The benefit of using templates is that the activities described in the following
sections are executed only once during the production cycle instead of once
for every new file that composes the full document. As you follow the design
steps for publications, you will soon see how much time you can save by using
a series of templates for large publications.

Defining the Basic Standards for Your Publication

Before you lay out your page grid, you should define the basic defaults and
standards that you will use throughout the publication. These defaults and
standards include defining the page size and orientation, setting the margins,
selecting the target printer, and choosing a unit of measure. After a publication has been opened, these specifications are stored with the publication.

Notice that, in the following sections, these standards are discussed in the sequence in which they appear as you build a template. You must specify page
size, orientation, and margins on the "Page setup" dialog box before you can
set the target printer and unit of measure for a particular publication.

Defining the Page Setup

You define the paper size and orientation through the "Page setup" dialog
box whenever you open a new publication (see fig. 9.7). By setting these stan-

dards in a template, you ensure that all other templates cloned from that template will have the same page-size and orientation settings.

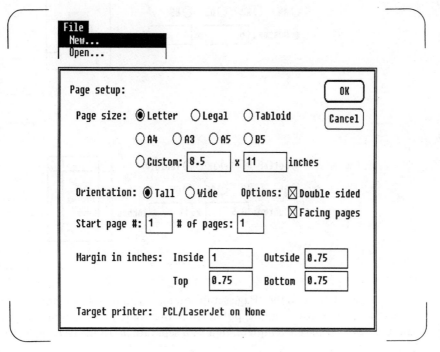

Fig. 9.7. Page size and orientation set for a new publication.

Most publications have the same page size for all sections, but the orientation of the pages may vary from section to section. For instance, you may have a set of appendixes with financial reports that must be printed "Wide" to accommodate many columns of numbers. In this case, you set up two templates: one for all "Tall" pages and one for all "Wide" pages.

Although the page size is usually the same as the final publication after it is mass produced, bound, and trimmed (see fig. 9.8), you can deliberately specify larger page sizes for special layouts. For example, you may specify that you are printing on 8.5-by-11-inch paper and use that setting as the board size for designing a 6-by-9-inch booklet, as in figure 9.9. You can use nonprinting guides, margins, and columns to define the 6-by-9-inch layout area and use the area beyond that to print project-control information, registration marks, and instructions to the printer. The printed pages can also show crop marks that you draw on the master pages because the automatic crop-marks feature won't accurately show the page size in this case.

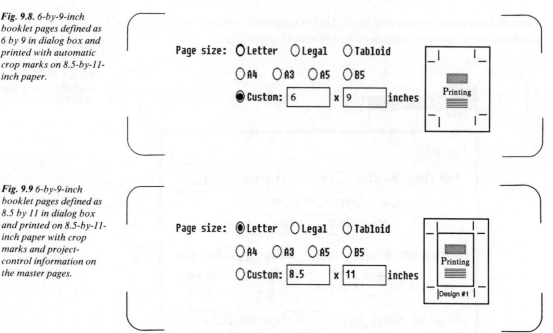

Fig. 9.8. *6-by-9-inch booklet pages defined as 6 by 9 in dialog box and printed with automatic crop marks on 8.5-by-11-inch paper.*

Fig. 9.9 *6-by-9-inch booklet pages defined as 8.5 by 11 in dialog box and printed on 8.5-by-11-inch paper with crop marks and project-control information on the master pages.*

The margins defined in the "Page setup" dialog box apply throughout a publication. Each section of the publication that requires different margins should have a separate template, that is, a separate .PUB file (see fig. 9.10).

Fig. 9.10. *Separate templates for sections of the publication requiring different margins.*

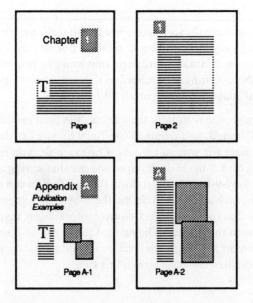

If the margins remain the same throughout but the column guides differ between pages or sections, you can work from one master template and use PageMaker's "Column guides..." command to change column settings. Part III shows you examples of publications with changing column settings.

The margins are not necessarily the same as the limits of the text and graphics that appear on a page. PageMaker lets you position text and graphics beyond the margins. The side margins determine the width of the column guides. The bottom margin determines where text will stop flowing when placed in a column. Other elements that can fall outside your margins are ruled lines around pages, vertical and horizontal rules that are part of the design, and running heads and feet (see fig. 9.11). You must make sure, however, that your printer will print these areas.

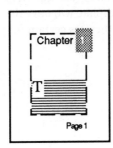 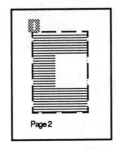

Fig. 9.11. Margins do not limit all text and graphics.

If you are accustomed to defining page layouts by width of text rather than width of margins, you must convert your specifications to the terms used by PageMaker. For example, if you know that you want the text to be 6 inches wide on an 8.5-inch-wide page, the total amount of space available for both the inside and the outside margins is 2.5 inches, or 8.5 minus 6.

In other words, if you know what the margins are and what the page size is, as specified on the "Page setup" dialog box, you can calculate the width of the text with this formula:

Text width = (Page width) – (Inside margin measure + outside margin measure)

On the other hand, if you know the page size and the text width, you can calculate the margin allowance with this formula:

Total space available for inside and outside margins = Page width – text width

You can use variations of these formulas to determine the top and bottom margins or to calculate the measured depth allowed for text on each page.

You can use an expanded version of the following formula to calculate the widths PageMaker will set up for columns when you use the "Column guides..." command:

$$\text{Column width} = \frac{(\text{Page width} - (\text{inside} + \text{outside margin measures}) - (\text{space between columns} \times (\text{number of columns} - 1)))}{\text{number of columns}}$$

Identifying the Target Printer

As you begin to build your template, you should first decide the printer you will use. If you have more than one printer or cartridge available on your system, you make this selection once by defining the target printer in the template with the "Target printer..." command (see fig. 9.12). From that point, all publication files cloned from this template will have the same printer specifications. The target printer selection dictates certain font selections for the rest of the design (see Chapter 8).

Fig. 9.12. The target printer specified in the template.

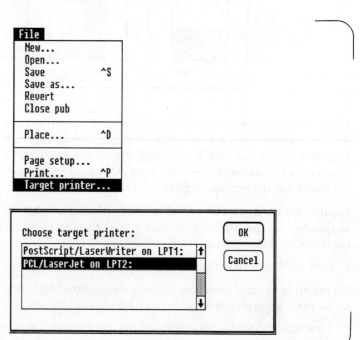

Selecting a Unit of Measure and Displaying Rulers

If you give all your design specifications in the same unit of measure, you can set your preferences in the template so that the same unit of measure applies to all files made from the template. Use the "Preferences..." command under the Edit menu (see fig. 9.13). If you give your specifications in two or more different measures (inches for margins but points for type, for instance), select the unit of measure in which you prefer to view the ruler line.

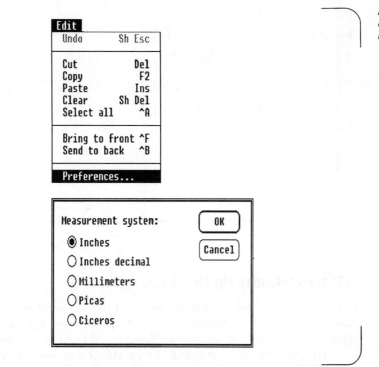

Fig. 9.13. Setting the unit of measure in the template.

During the design phase, you must turn on the rulers to lay out your grid precisely. If you leave the rulers on in the template, they are displayed automatically in all publications made from the template. During the production phase, the automatic ruler lines are convenient for scaling or cropping graphics.

Whenever possible, state your design specifications as a measure from the zero point on the ruler line. Normally, this reference point is the top left corner of the page or the tops of the inside edges of double-sided publications created with the "Facing pages" option (see fig. 9.14). If your design specifications require a different zero point, you should make the position of the zero point on the page a part of the design specifications.

Fig. 9.14. Design specifications in reference to zero point.

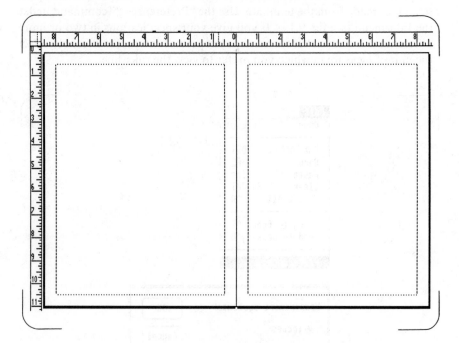

Setting Defaults on the Type Menu

Although most text formatting should occur in your word-processing program, you can set the defaults for the body copy on the Type menu of the template. From then on, all publications cloned from the template retain these settings. Any new text typed in PageMaker and any placed text files (with a .TXT extension) automatically take on the template's default settings.

To change the defaults for an entire publication, make selections on the Type menu after selecting the pointer tool rather than the text tool. These settings are discussed more comprehensively in Chapter 8, "Typography."

Adding Spacing Guides to the Pasteboard

Normally, the spacing within the text is determined by the type specifications set up in the word-processing program. The designer, however, needs to create specifications for the spacing between figures and text, between text and ruled lines, and between text blocks (such as between articles in a news-letter). Rather than express these specifications in numbers only, you can help the production process by setting up spacing guides and storing them on the pasteboard of the template.

You create a spacing guide in one of two ways. The simplest way is to use PageMaker's text tool and "Type specs..." command to create a text block with handles that are separated by the distance called for in the specifications. For example, type the words **Space between articles** and set the text in a point size that makes the text block's handles a measure of the distance. You need to type and format a separate text block for each spacing specification (see fig. 9.15).

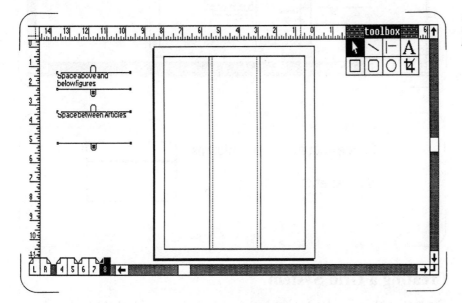

Fig. 9.15. Spacing-requirement boxes on the pasteboard.

When you need to check the spacing between two objects on the page, use the "Copy" and "Paste" commands to copy the spacing guide from the paste-board to the page. Then you can use the spacing guide to position the objects, as shown in figure 9.16. When the two objects are aligned correctly, delete the duplicate guide on the page.

The second method of creating spacing guides is to use Windows Paint or Windows Draw. With this method, you can create one spacing guide that holds all your spacing specifications. Figure 9.17 shows such a box with labels for each section. You can place the guide and its labels in PageMaker as a single object.

Fig. 9.16. Copying the spacing guide to the page to align material.

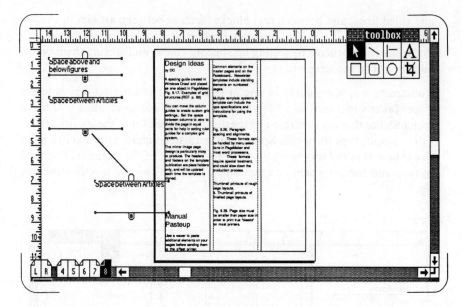

Fig. 9.17. A single spacing guide created in Windows Draw for more than one specification.

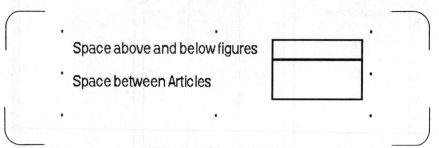

Creating a Grid System

The best publication designs are based on underlying grids that position elements throughout publications. Using PageMaker, you can define the grid and other printing elements, such as ruled lines and folios, on master pages. Nonprinting grid lines in PageMaker include page margins, column guides (up to 20 columns per page), and up to 40 nonprinting ruler guides per page or pair of facing pages.

Simple grid structures that involve one, two, or three columns are relatively easy to work with; but complex grids usually offer more design possibilities (see fig. 9.18). For example, the variety in a one-column grid structure can be achieved only by varying the type specifications and paragraph indentations. A two-column grid structure offers the added possibility of graphics and text expanding to full-page width on selected pages. A three-column grid offers at least three page variations.

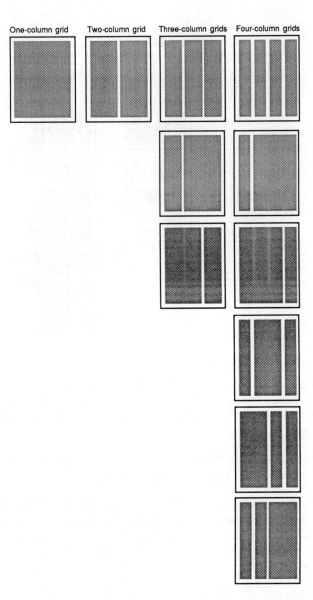

One-column grid   Two-column grid   Three-column grids   Four-column grids

Fig. 9.18. Grid structures showing design possibilities.

For even spacing, you can set up a grid structure automatically with PageMaker's "Column guides..." command. You do not, however, have to leave the column guides fixed to follow the grid. For example, to set up the grids shown in figure 9.19, you first set up three column guides to divide the page in thirds. Then, you move ruler guides to divide the page in thirds. Next, set up two columns and drag the center column guides to the first or second marker, as in the first column of figure 9.19. The second and third columns of figure 9.19 show the same technique applied to a four-column grid.

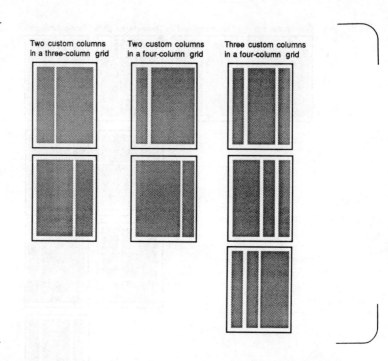

Fig. 9.19. Moving column guides to create custom grid settings.

The spacing between the columns is normally set to a default width of 0.167 inch, or one pica. You can make this space wider if you will be inserting hairline rules between each column, but a good rule is to keep the space between columns less than 2 picas.

Efficiency Tip

Columns as Grid Markers

You can set the space between columns to zero (see fig. 9.20) and use the "Column guides..." command to help divide the page into equal parts. Pull ruler guides into position over the column edges to hold the divisions; then reset the space between columns to create the guides you wish to use to define the text.

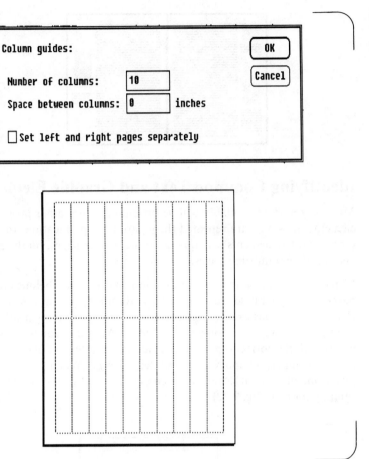

Fig. 9.20. Using columns with no space between as grid markers.

Documents with the same grid on every page are much easier to produce than documents that switch between variations in the grid. A common variation, the mirror-image page layout (see fig. 9.21), is particularly hard to handle. Individual page layout is not difficult, but chaos can ensue if you have to insert or delete a page after the publication is laid out. When you work with mirror-image designs, your best rule of thumb is always to insert or delete an even number of pages to keep intact all the subsequent page layouts.

If you must create mirror-image grid designs, specify all measures starting from the inside edges of the paper. Remember that in double-sided facing-page publications, PageMaker sets the zero point on the ruler lines at the inside margin. On the left master page the zero point is set at the upper right corner, and the right master page shows the zero point set at the upper left corner.

Fig. 9.21. *Mirror-image page design.*

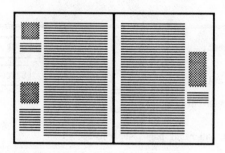

Identifying Common Text and Graphic Elements

Most of your text probably will be brought in from other programs. Some elements, however, are repeated throughout the publication. In a template, these repeated elements can appear on the master pages, on the pasteboard, and on some numbered pages.

Elements that appear in the same position on every page belong on the master pages. Every page holds running heads and running feet, as well as the graphic elements of the basic page design. The master-page running heads and feet of a template, however, are only place holders. Although you position these elements with the correct type specs and alignment, the text of each publication created from the template probably will change. When you clone the template, one of your first steps is to change the text of the running head and running foot (see fig. 9.22).

Fig. 9.22. *The running heads and feet on the template.*

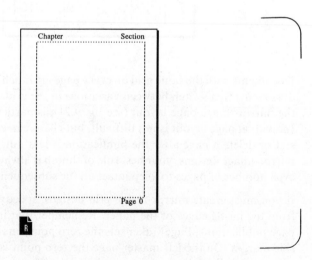

In addition to the elements that belong on the master pages, other elements may be repeated irregularly throughout the publication. You create these items just once and then store them on the pasteboard. Whenever you need the repeated elements, you can duplicate them with the "Copy" and "Paste" commands (see fig. 9.23).

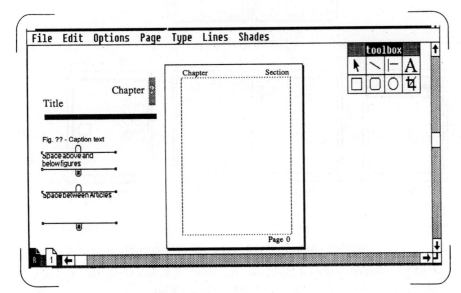

Fig. 9.23. Commonly used elements on master pages and pasteboard.

For example, you can use the pasteboard to store a graphic symbol that appears at the end of every article in a newsletter or magazine. When you reach the end of an article, you simply copy the symbol from the pasteboard. Just as you create textual place holders for the running head and running foot, you create standard dummy text blocks for headlines or captions within the publication and store them on the pasteboard. If your publication will include display ads in predetermined sizes, you can store the right size boxes on the pasteboard. You then duplicate and position the blocks as you lay out the pages.

Adding Standard Elements to Numbered Pages

Besides the elements positioned on the master pages or stored on the pasteboard, your publication may contain elements that appear predictably on certain numbered pages. For example, the template for a newsletter should include the banner from the first page (see fig. 9.24). If all issues of the newsletter are always the same length, you may be able to predict the positions of the subscription information and other permanent features. You also can add place holders for the headline text for feature articles that start on the first page.

Fig. 9.24. Newsletter templates with standing elements on fixed numbered pages.

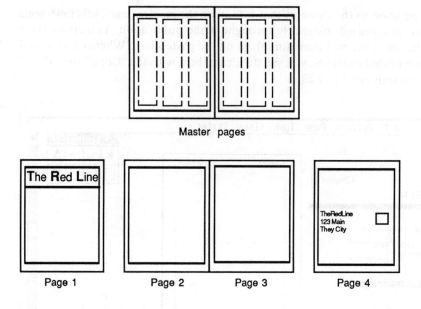

Master pages

Page 1 — The Red Line

Page 2

Page 3

Page 4 — TheRedLine / 123 Main / They City

Efficiency Tip

Storing Dummy Headlines on the Pasteboard

On the pasteboard, store templates for headlines. Use templates that include dummy text and are one-, two-, or three-columns wide.

Determining the Number of Templates Required

You have already seen that a separate template file is required for each unique page size, orientation, and margin setting. In addition, you can use templates to handle any other essential differences among sections of your publication. For example, when the basic format of running heads and feet changes between major sections of a publication, you need more than one template (see fig. 9.25). On the other hand, if the only difference between sections is the number of columns, one template may suffice.

As a rule of thumb, create separate templates if any of the following conditions occurs:

- Page size varies
- Page orientation changes

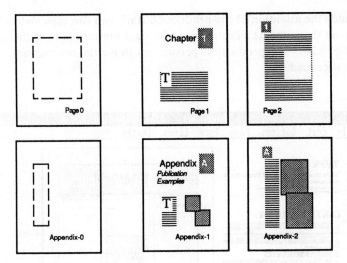

Fig. 9.25. A multiple-template system.

- Master-page elements change (except the text of running heads and feet)

- Basic grid changes

Adding Instructions for Working with the Template

If the person designing the template is not the same person who uses it in production, the designer should list the steps necessary for working with the template. The steps can be simple—serving primarily as reminders of each step. For example, a designer may list the following instructions:

1. Open the template and immediately save it under a new name.

2. Change the running heads and feet on the master pages.

3. Change the volume and date information on the first page, below the newsletter banner.

4. Place the table of contents on the first page before placing the feature article.

5. Delete these instructions.

6. Continue placing text and graphics as specified for the current issue.

To catch the attention of the production staff, you can type instructions directly on the template's pasteboard, the right master page, or the first page (see fig. 9.26). The production person can move the instructions or delete them after reading.

Fig. 9.26. Type specifications and instructions for using the template.

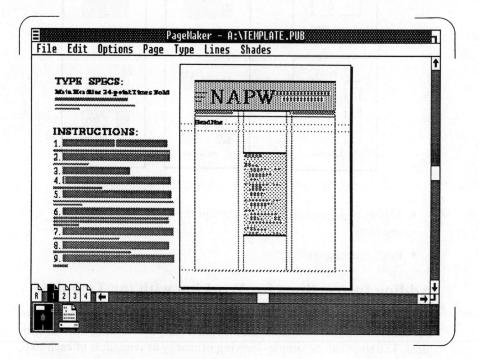

Creating Specifications for Other Programs

Chapter 8, "Typography," presents most of the necessary considerations for selecting fonts for different text elements. You can put some specifications, such as those for the position and format of running heads and feet, directly into your PageMaker template. You can implement other specifications, such as type specifications, with your word-processing program. Line widths and fill patterns can be set up as default values in the PageMaker template. These items also can be stored as predefined elements on the pasteboard or applied in the graphics programs that you use to create the content of the publication.

A designer should have a good idea of the number and sources of graphic elements that go into the publication. Knowing the capabilities and limitations of the available programs, the designer must specify how each illustration is to be treated. What are the size limitations or preferences for the figures, for example? If you are following a grid system, each figure's width must match the increments allowed by the grid. For instance, a two-column grid allows two figure widths (one column wide or full-page width); a three-column grid allows only three different figure widths; a four-column grid allows four widths; and so on.

The designer must answer other questions. What fonts, styles, and sizes will be used in illustrations and their captions? Will the figures be enlarged or reduced during page composition? Will photographs and other special illustrations be pasted up by hand or scanned into the computer? You can simply write out these specifications, or you can use the programs that create illustrations to create figure templates just as you use PageMaker to create publication templates.

Your design specifications for body copy, captions, and figure titles should include directions for paragraph alignment (left, right, justified, or centered) and spacing between paragraphs (see fig. 9.27). The designer must consider convenience and speed of production. Some formats can be handled by menu selections in PageMaker and most word processors. Other formats require special treatment and may slow the production process.

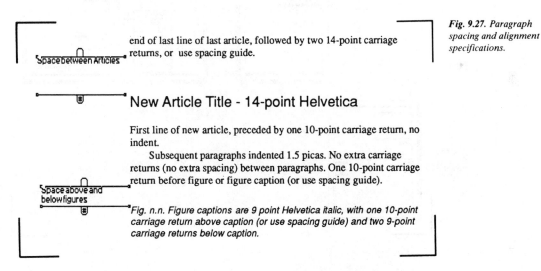

Fig. 9.27. Paragraph spacing and alignment specifications.

Space between Articles

end of last line of last article, followed by two 14-point carriage returns, or use spacing guide.

New Article Title - 14-point Helvetica

First line of new article, preceded by one 10-point carriage return, no indent.

Subsequent paragraphs indented 1.5 picas. No extra carriage returns (no extra spacing) between paragraphs. One 10-point carriage return before figure or figure caption (or use spacing guide).

Space above and below figures

Fig. n.n. Figure captions are 9 point Helvetica italic, with one 10-point carriage return above caption (or use spacing guide) and two 9-point carriage returns below caption.

Designing Page Layouts before Entering Content

Publications with complex grid systems require the designer's attention throughout the production cycle. That attention is especially important for magazines and newsletters that incorporate various sizes of display ads throughout the publication. The designer can work ahead of the production team to specify where ads are to be placed and how articles will jump from one page to another.

Traditionally, a designer would draw pencil roughs of each page, or *thumbnail* sketches. This term originally meant that the sketches could be literally as small as a person's thumbnail because the sketches were intended to be quick to produce. PageMaker's "Thumbnails" option on the "Print" dialog box creates miniature versions of the pages of the publication. (This option is available only on PostScript and DDL printers, not on dot-matrix or the LaserJet printers.) For example, you can make rough page layouts with shaded boxes and article titles for every page of a magazine or newsletter and print the thumbnails as a guide for building the publication (see fig. 9.28). This same rough file can be used as the starting point in placing the finished text and graphics files on each page. Another set of thumbnails may be printed to check the final layouts (see fig. 9.29).

Fig. 9.28. Thumbnail printouts of rough page layouts.

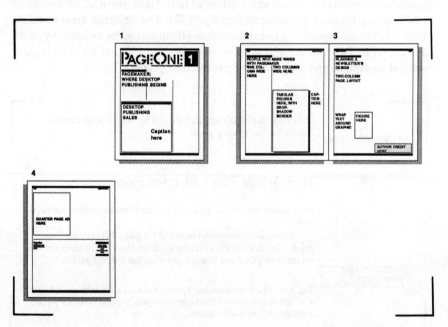

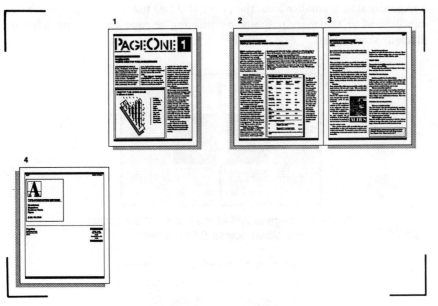

*Fig. 9.29. Thumbnail
printouts of finished page
layouts.*

Efficiency Tip

Build a Page Layout Like a Painting

A publication does not have to be built from front to back, page by page. You can construct a publication in layers, just as painters work on canvas. The painter first pencils the rough outline on the canvas and then gradually adds layers of paint.

In PageMaker, the basic grid system is the painter's penciled sketch. You can use shaded boxes to reserve certain areas for planned graphics and particular articles. The text and graphics that you bring in from other programs to replace the place holders are like the painter's gradually added layers of paint.

During both the design and production phases, you can work on views of facing pages for double-sided publications. Working on both pages can be an advantage when you want to consider the overall impact of the open publication or you want to create graphic images that bleed across from one page to the other.

Be careful when you design page layouts that bleed off the edges of the paper or across facing pages. The top of figure 9.30 shows how part of an image that bleeds across two pages can be lost in the edges of the paper, depending on the type of printer you are using. To solve this problem, you need to specify a page size that is smaller than the paper size (see bottom of fig. 9.30). You can determine the margin limits by printing a page covered by a solid black or shaded box.

Fig. 9.30. Handling bleeds.

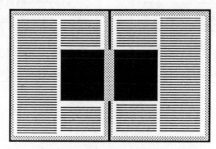

Center of image is lost at the edges of the pages in a bleed across 8.5x11 pages

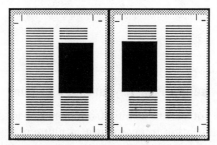

Full image is printed to edges of crop marks when the page size is smaller than 8.5x11

The designer may be called in once more after the PageMaker publication goes to production. (Refer to Chapters 3 through 7 for the production process following the design step.) The final design activities are described in the following paragraphs.

Going beyond PageMaker

For some publications, the final pages for distribution are printed on a laser printer. In most cases, however, you make multiple copies with a photocopier or an offset printer.

After the final pages of the publication are printed on a high-resolution printer, some final preparation may still be required before the pages are ready to be reproduced. This preparation can include manual pasteup of figures that could not be produced on the computer, photograph markup for halftone processing, and tissue overlays to specify multiple-color printing.

Some artwork may be impossible to render using the computer—for example, photographs or original artwork that feature fine charcoal or airbrush techniques. In this case, you leave space for the special artwork on the PageMaker page and paste the artwork by hand on the final version before you make multiple copies of the publication. PageMaker V1.0a can accept gray-scale TIFF scanner images in 16 levels of gray. This sophisticated image storage format is unique to PageMaker.

If you are going to be pasting up many elements, you may want to lay all the pages down on *boards*—heavy white paper that keeps the pages flat and prevents pasted-down elements from peeling up.

If you are using photographs, you can scan them to the computer and then place them on the PageMaker page (see Chapter 5), or the print shop can use a camera to create *halftones*. A halftone is composed of dots, like a scanned image; but most scanned images are saved at low resolutions (between 72 and 300 dots per inch) whereas halftones have many more dots per inch.

You should check with your print shop before you set up pages for halftones. To save time, you can use solid black boxes to reserve space for photographs on the PageMaker pages (as shown in fig. 9.31). Otherwise, you can use a scanned image of the photograph to indicate the exact size and cropping required.

Fig. 9.31. Handling
photographs.

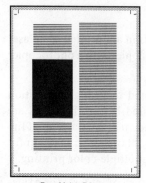

PageMaker Printout

Photograph

Halftone

Negative

Negative Page Image with Photo
stripped in

Final Printed Page

Scanned Images versus Photographs

If the final publication will be printed on a porous paper like newsprint, a 300-dots-per-inch scanned image can look as good as a photographic halftone.

If the final publication will be produced on glossy paper, 300-dots-per-inch scanned images may be too coarse for the final product. You can still scan, place, scale, and crop your PageMaker image to show the camera operator how to handle the original photograph (see fig. 9.32).

Fig. 9.32. Using a scanned image to hold the place of a halftone in the final production.

If the publication will be printed in more than one color, you use one of two different methods to prepare the pages for the print shop. If the areas printed in each color do not overlap, you can overlay tissue paper on the page and mark the colors to be used for each element (see fig. 9.33). If the colors overlap, the process is more complicated. After building the publication in one file, make as many copies of the file as colors to be used. Then, open each copy and delete all the elements that are not to be printed for each color (see fig. 9.34). For instance, if you are using two colors, you make two copies of the publication file. Open one copy and delete all elements except those that will be printed in one color. Then, open the second copy and delete all elements except those that will be printed in the second color. Print each file with registration marks and crop marks, if possible.

Fig. 9.33. *Tissue overlays indicate colors to be used.*

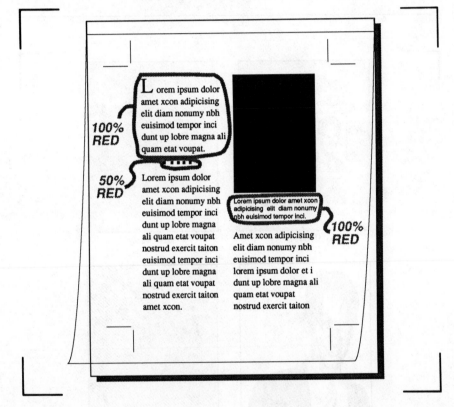

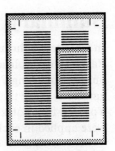

Fig. 9.34. *Color separations supplied on separate sheets of paper.*

Full image printed
for proofing during
production.

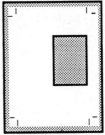

Part of image
prepared for color
#1.

Part of image
prepared for color
#2.

Summary

In Chapters 2 through 9, you have learned all the steps needed to produce a PageMaker publication. In particular, this chapter offers tips for designing a publication using PageMaker's tools. The next part of the book provides examples of more than 30 publications that were produced using PageMaker. You can find notes about how the principles given in Chapters 2 through 9 were applied in each publication.

III

Examples of Publications Created Using PageMaker

The chapters in Part III present examples of publications that were created using PageMaker. These documents illustrate specific applications of the procedures and principles covered throughout the book and demonstrate the wide range of designs possible with PageMaker. You'll be able to develop your own designs with the help of the sample pages, sample templates, and "Page setup" and "Type specifications" dialog boxes provided with many of the examples. Whether you need to create a business report or a brochure, the examples in Part III will help get you started.

Part III at a Glance

Designing and Producing Business Reports, Books, and Manuals

10

In this chapter, you learn some specific design and production ideas that apply to reports, manuals, and books. Whether you are producing a 300-page textbook, a 30-page business proposal, or a 3-page list of illustrated steps for a procedures manual, these publications share many characteristics (see fig. 10.1). For example, these publications are usually longer than the documents in the other categories presented in the following chapters. The full publication normally is composed of several PageMaker files, so these types of documents are good candidates for template systems. Even if your document has fewer than 128 pages, dividing the material into several files still makes good sense in many cases. In this chapter, you will find tips on when and why to divide a document into several files.

Another common characteristic is size. Most business reports and many manuals are published in 8.5-by-11-inch format. Books frequently have smaller dimensions, and this chapter shows you how to prepare a document for smaller finished page sizes.

The publications in this category have similar formats. These documents usually have a one-column format, although some have a second column for headings, captions, and figures. Traditionally, most business reports are single-sided documents, and manuals and books are usually double-sided documents. In this chapter, you learn how and when to use PageMaker's single-sided, double-sided, and facing-pages options.

Fig. 10.1. Examples of the publications in this chapter.

Example 10.1

Example 10.2

Example 10.3

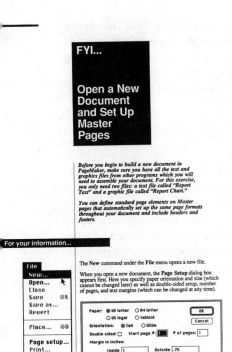

Example 10.4

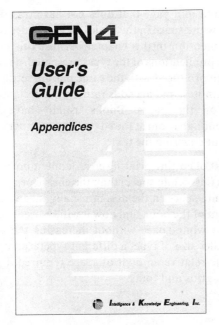

Example 10.5

This chapter focuses on the specific design and production ideas that apply to the types of documents just described. You can apply the same design principles and production tips to any publication in this general category: long publications composed of several sections or chapters. You'll see how the general design principles and production tips have been applied to the examples.

Design Principles

The design principles that have been developed by book designers can be applied to business reports and manuals. For example, because reports and manuals are longer publications, the use of white space and running heads makes the documents more attractive and easier to use. The design principles presented in these examples range from tips for creating the design to page layout to choice of typefaces. By applying these principles, you can produce publications with a professional appearance; they will be uncluttered and unified in design.

Many of these principles apply to all types of publications, not just those in this chapter. Their applications to reports, books, and manuals are described generally in this section, and then the same principles are repeated and applied specifically to the appropriate examples.

Don't be afraid of white space.

White space is any area of a page that does not have text or graphics. The principle of allowing white space in the basic design applies to any document but is worth special mention in this chapter because this principle has not been applied to many publications of the types presented. Traditionally, business reports have been produced with the same margin settings as those used for letters, memos, minutes, and agendas rather than designed specifically to allow white space on the pages. Books usually have minimal white space—leaving only enough room at the edges for the reader's thumbs to hold the book open without covering the text.

Perhaps in the interest of cutting printing costs, contemporary books tend to have smaller margins (less white space) than the classic proportions shown in figure 10.2. More white space in the design usually means more pages. Depending on the content of the book and how it will be used, however, you can increase the apparent white space without increasing the total number of pages by using a smaller size of type, a different typeface, or tighter leading. Figure 10.2 shows the relative amount of space required if you lay out the same text in different grids and fonts.

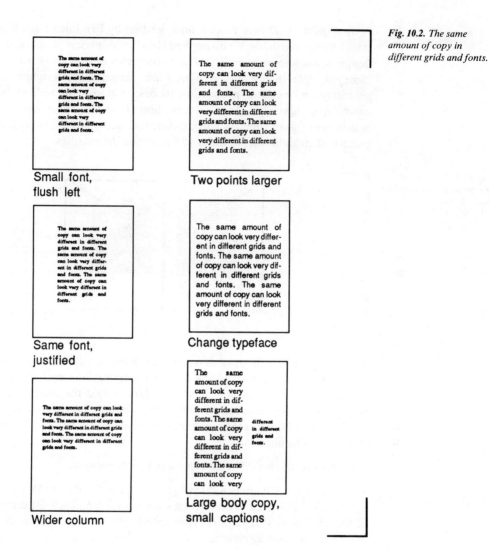

Fig. 10.2. *The same*
amount of copy in
different grids and fonts.

As shown in figure 10.2 and in this chapter's examples, you can often produce the effect of more white space on a page without actually reducing the amount of text or increasing the number of pages. The effect of increased white space is a more attractive and readable publication.

Use a grid system.

The traditions of book design and production are older than any of the other principles discussed in this book. Gutenberg's Bible, for instance, shows traces of the grid system he used to lay out his pages. A few decades later a book named *De Divina Proportione*, written by Fra Luca Pacioli and illustrated by Leonardo da Vinci, applied the rules of classic proportion to book design. Contemporary designers still study this master work and apply the same principles in new book designs. Later, Renaissance designers used basic geometry and rules of proportion to design books (as well as buildings, rooms, and paintings). One classic method of defining the margins of a book is shown in figure 10.3. As you can see, the facing pages are crossed with a pattern of straight lines in order to determine the margins.

Fig. 10.3. Determining the classic proportions for book design.

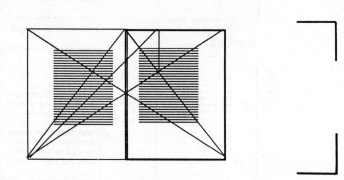

There are many methods of deriving grids based on classic proportions, and you also can develop the grids for your publications by imitating similar documents that you admire. The point here is that the underlying grid for your publication merits some forethought. Chapter 9 and the examples in this chapter show how PageMaker's master-page feature lets you lay out a grid system for a publication.

Use only one or two different typefaces in a document.

As explained in Chapters 8, "Typography," and 9, "PageMaker as a Design Tool," the type-specification process involves listing each different element of the document that requires type specifications. For reports, books, and manuals, the list may include

    Body copy
    Running heads
    Running feet
    Chapter or section titles
    One or more subhead levels
    Figure captions
    Figure labels
    Table headings
    Table data

Each of these elements may be subdivided into several other elements that require more type specifications. In the running feet, for example, you may want the page number in boldface type and the section name in italic. A common tendency is to use a different font for each element—a good idea within limits. The majority of book designers, however, follow the guiding principle of simplicity in design. If you study other published works, you will see that most books use only one or two different typefaces with variations in size and style used sparingly.

Apart from the design principle of simplicity, one reason for having few type changes in a PageMaker publication is that some laser printers are limited to 8 fonts per page or per publication. Some of the examples that follow show how as many as 14 different elements can be distinguished by 8 or fewer fonts.

On the other hand, most current published works use a greater variety of fonts than the traditional business report, which featured, for example, one size of plain Courier and Courier boldface. When you switch your business reports from a letter-quality printer to a laser printer, the wide selection of fonts may seem confusing at first. You will find that the best approach in designing your first reports is to imitate the type specifications used in professionally designed documents that are similar to yours, such as the examples shown in this chapter. Once you become familiar with the underlying design principles, you can easily design your own long documents.

Table 10.1 shows some of the typefaces commonly used in these types of documents. You can see that the more decorative typefaces such as ITC Friz Quadrata and Zapf Chancery are not recommended for the publications in this chapter and that the list of typefaces commonly used in books and manuals is much more limited than the list for business reports.

Use all capitals (uppercase text) as a deliberate design strategy rather than as a method for emphasizing text or showing a heading.

If you are accustomed to using letter-quality printers, you probably have used uppercase type to add emphasis or to distinguish headings. Uppercase letters can still be a part of your deliberate design strategy when other size or style variations are not possible. Do not use uppercase letters, however, just because "that's the way the author typed it." Long headings can be hard to read when the text is all uppercase. Consider changing all-capital headings to upper- and lowercase letters and setting them in boldface or italic.

Only one example in this chapter uses uppercase text as a deliberate design strategy. In Example 10.4 (a manual that uses one template to switch between two grids), the most common head is "FYI..." (to indicate "For Your Information"). All the other heads are short phases ("OVERVIEW," "TRY IT," "NOTES," and "SUMMARY"); they are set in all capitals in order to carry the same "weight" visually as the "FYI..." heads.

Table 10.1.
Typefaces Commonly Used in Reports, Books, and Manuals
(Y = used, N = not used)

Typefaces	Reports	Books	Manuals
ITC American Typewriter	Y	N	N
ITC Avant Garde	Y	N	Y
ITC Benguiat	Y	N	N
ITC Bookman	Y	N	Y
Courier	N	N	N
ITC Friz Quadrata	Y	N	Y
ITC Galliard	Y	Y	Y
ITC Garamond	Y	Y	Y
Glypha	N	N	Y
Goudy Old Style	Y	Y	Y
Helvetica	Y	Y	Y
ITC Korinna	Y	N	Y
ITC Lubalin Graph	Y	Y	Y
ITC Machine	N	N	N
ITC New Baskerville	Y	Y	N
New Century Schoolbook	Y	Y	Y
Optima	Y	Y	Y
Palatino	Y	Y	Y
ITC Souvenir	Y	Y	Y
Times	Y	Y	Y
Trump Mediaeval	Y	Y	Y
ITC Zapf Chancery	N	N	N

Use running heads and running feet to help readers find topics.

This principle is applicable to any long document—including magazines—but the rule is a mandate in reference books and manuals. Besides the page number, you should include the section or chapter name in the running heads or running feet. Place the names near the outer edges of the pages for easy reference. This principle is applied in all but one of the examples in this chapter.

Treat all figures consistently in the fonts, line weights, and fill patterns you use.

In the past, business-report figures came from a single source: one spreadsheet program on a letter-quality printer, or a team of one illustrator and one typesetter. Consistency becomes a more important issue when you start using

PageMaker to assemble graphics from many different sources, such as a spreadsheet program, a drawing program, and PageMaker's built-in graphics tools. Some figures may be used full-sized in the final document, but others may need reducing or enlarging in PageMaker. To keep line weights consistent throughout the publication, you may want to use heavier lines in the drawing program if the figure will be scaled smaller in PageMaker, or use lighter-weight lines if the figure will be scaled larger. If possible, choose fill patterns that are common to all the graphics programs you will be using.

Be sure that your final figures have consistent type specifications. You can standardize captions by making them a part of the word-processing text files instead of the graphics files. For labels within your figures, you may need to establish standards for the fonts to be used in your drawing program. For example, if your report includes many graphs and your spreadsheet program has fewer available fonts than PageMaker, you may want to match the fonts in all your images to the spreadsheet graphics. This principle is included here even though its application is not demonstrated by the examples selected for this chapter. For specific applications, see the examples in Chapter 12.

Be sure that the space between text and graphics is the same for all figures.

Use a spacing guide to position adjacent graphics and text blocks (see fig. 10.4). Because strict standards for positioning graphics may slow the production schedule by requiring meticulous adjustments, you may not want rigid standards. You should, however, know and declare your ideal standards for positioning and your limits of tolerance. Your specification may be as simple as "roughly center the graphic between the adjacent text blocks," but even this simple guideline is worth stating explicitly. Don't assume that graphics will fall naturally into place. The use of spacing guides is described in Chapter 9 and applied in Examples 10.4 and 10.5.

Text on each page should bottom out to margin.

Book designers have traditionally followed the principle that every page should end at exactly the same point. This goal is easy to accomplish for books that are primarily body copy without graphics or subheadings—like the traditional Victorian novel. The principle becomes increasingly difficult to apply the more your document incorporates complicating factors such as

Subheadings within each chapter or section
Figures
Footnotes
Tables that cannot be broken across pages
Limitations for widows and orphans

Fig. 10.4. *Use a spacing*
guide to position graphics
and text.

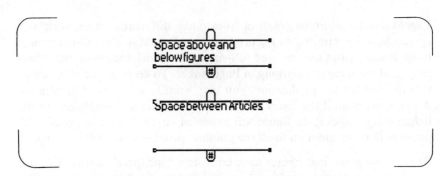

Fig. 10.4. *Use a spacing guide to position graphics and text.*

You can alter the leading (line spacing) around subheadings and the space around figures to make small adjustments in the length of the text on a page. In many documents, however, you will find bottoming out all pages to the same point to be impossible. Alignment can be especially tricky if you follow the common conventions regarding widows and orphans. These terms are used to describe the situation in which one line of a paragraph is separated from the rest of the paragraph by a page break or a column break (see "Copy Fitting" in Chapter 6).

In some documents, you may plan ragged bottom margins as a deliberate design strategy. In general, however, let PageMaker's bottom margin define the maximum length of the text. As shown in the following examples, Page-Maker's bottom margin is not always the same as the limits of text on the page layout: in these examples, the running heads and feet always fall outside the page margins that are defined in the "Page setup" dialog box.

Let the same graphic elements carry the theme throughout the document.

As explained in Chapter 9, PageMaker's master pages can include graphic elements that appear on every page, such as shaded boxes and ruled lines. You can also use graphics to set off headings in the text and to highlight important points. You can see how common graphic elements (black boxes, ruled lines) are applied in Examples 10.2 and 10.4. In many published books, the cover design has no relation to the inside page layouts; but a common graphic theme is often used on the cover as well as inside pages of business reports, catalogs, directories, annual reports, and other documents. This technique is applied in Example 10.1.

Production Tips

The production tips in this chapter can be applied to any long document that is composed of several sections or chapters. The tips help you produce your publications more quickly and efficiently than you might do without following these suggestions. The tips range from creating separate templates for different sections to preparing text in a word processor before you start PageMaker.

Many of these tips apply to other types of publications, such as the magazines and newsletters described in Chapter 11 and the brochures described in Chapter 13. The application to reports, books, and manuals is described generally in this section; then with the examples, the same tips are repeated with explanations of their specific application to that example.

Make each section or chapter a separate PageMaker publication.

Even if your document has fewer than 128 pages (PageMaker's limit for one file), several good reasons exist for breaking a long document into smaller parts and saving each as a separate file.

1. Small files are faster to work with—faster to save and faster to print.

2. You must make separate files of any sections requiring a different page orientation because you cannot mix "Tall" and "Wide" pages in one publication file. For example, an appendix with tables of figures may require a "Wide" format, but the rest of the document appears in "Tall" format.

3. You may want to start with a different master-page grid for different sections of the book (see the following tip).

4. When the document is divided into several PageMaker publication files, you can set different running heads or feet for each section, making an easy reference for readers.

5. If your document is long or includes many graphics, you may need to break the document into sections to keep file sizes small enough to fit a backup on one floppy disk.

6. If different sections of the document will be completed at different times but not necessarily in sequence, you can begin each new section when it is ready. In this way, you can have different sections of the publication in different stages of the production process.

7. You can divide the PageMaker production tasks among several people on the production team.

8. If a file is damaged, you lose only part of the work you have done.

This production practice of dividing a document into parts is especially pertinent to the long publications in this chapter and is more rarely applied in the shorter publications described in Chapters 11 through 14.

Build a master template for all sections.

If the final document will be composed of several files, build a master-template file from which all the other files are cloned. Chapter 9, "PageMaker as a Design Tool," offers suggestions for building template systems. You will see how those ideas are applied in each template used in the examples in this chapter.

If you expect to update sections of the document periodically without reprinting the entire book, include section numbers in the page-numbering system and let each section start with page 1.

This useful production trick may conflict with design ideas and the offset printer's preferences; but using section numbers as part of the page numbering system (1-1, 1-2, 1-3, . . . 2-1, 2-2, and so on) is the best way to handle frequently changed "living" documents, such as procedures manuals. PageMaker's automatic page-numbering feature cannot handle letter suffixes added to inserted pages (23a, 23b, 23c, for instance); but within one section you can number all pages sequentially by using a compound page number that includes a fixed section number and a changing suffix (23.1, 23.2, 23.3).

This tip should be applied only to manuals that are updated frequently. Generally speaking, the best practice is to number all pages consecutively in a document. You can specify the starting page number for each section in the "Page setup" dialog box. None of the examples in this chapter uses compound page numbers.

Prepare all character and paragraph formatting in advance with a word-processing program.

This method of preparation has been set as a goal throughout this book. Ideally, to simplify PageMaker production, you perform all editing and formatting in the word-processing program. Preformatting is especially appropriate for long documents that consist primarily of text. Besides the type specifications, preformatting can include using *hanging indents* to create flush-left heads over indented copy—a format that is often misinterpreted or misdesigned as a two-column format (see fig. 10.5). A hanging indent is a format in which the first line of the paragraph is set flush left and all subsequent lines are indented.

To create the format shown in the top of figure 10.5, set up a hanging indent in the word-processing program with a tab set at the indentation point; then enter a tab at the beginning of each paragraph to indent it. Subsequent lines of the paragraph will be indented automatically as the text wraps.

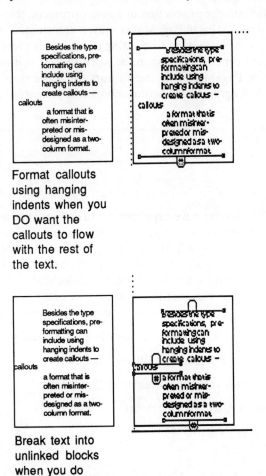

Fig. 10.5. *Preformatting that includes hanging indents.*

Besides the type specifications, pre-formatting can include using hanging indents to create callouts —

callouts

a format that is often misinterpreted or mis-designed as a two-column format.

Format callouts using hanging indents when you DO want the callouts to flow with the rest of the text.

Besides the type specifications, pre-formatting can include using hanging indents to create callouts —

callouts

a format that is often misinter-preted or mis-designed as a two-column format.

Break text into unlinked blocks when you do NOT want the callouts (or figure captions) to flow with the rest of the text.

Test Your Specifications in PageMaker

Before going too far into the production of a long document, test your specifications and plans by placing in PageMaker some text formatted in the word processor so that you can see what formatting elements are preserved. You need not spend extra time formatting in the word processor if most of the formatting is lost in PageMaker. If the authors use more than one word processor, test each program's text before completing your strategy for formatting text.

Examples

The examples in this chapter have been selected to demonstrate a variety of formats and to illustrate various applications of the design principles and production tips that were described in the preceding sections. As noted in those sections, not all the principles and tips that apply to books can be demonstrated in these few examples, but the design principles that are not specifically applied in these examples are illustrated in some of the examples in the chapters that follow. The five examples presented in this chapter are

10.1. A One-Column Format with Graphic Section Openings

10.2. A One-Column Format with Flush-Left Heads

10.3. A Two-Column Tabular Format with Small Type

10.4. One Template Used To Switch between Two Grids

10.5. Section Cover Pages

Example 10.1: A One-Column Format with Graphic Section Openings

The report used in this example is designed to accommodate relatively simple text formatting in a one-column grid that maximizes white space by using wide margins. The text is also more readable because of the narrow column that results from the wide margin settings. This same design can be applied to any business report; the generous running heads (16-point Times with a graphic background) make this design especially applicable to relatively short reports that are composed of many short sections.

This design probably is not good for a reference manual or training guide, however, without considerable expansion of the type specifications table to accommodate a wider variety of subheads and other visual aids. Books and long reports would probably not use running heads as large as the ones in this report, but a similar design could be used on chapter or section opening pages, with a narrower top margin on subsequent pages.

Description of the One-Column Format with Graphics

This limited-distribution report is reproduced in 8.5-by-11-inch format with "Tall" orientation. The grid and graphic elements on the inside pages of this report are designed to carry out a theme that originates with the report cover's design (see fig. 10.6). The final document—one in a series of documents that will be published over time—contains fewer than 128 pages and is stored as one publication file. The text is made up of one source file for each section, a mailing list of names and addresses, and a text file of captions for full-page figures. The figures, not shown here, are reprints of articles from other sources and are pasted in manually.

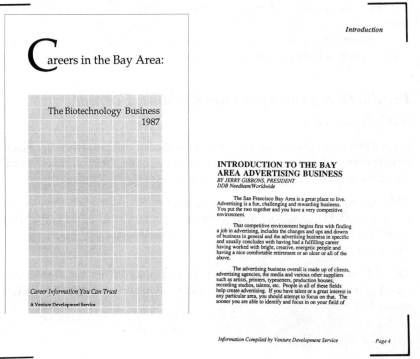

Fig. 10.6. Final printout with a cover-page design that sets the page theme throughout the document.

Caution

Always Obtain Written Permission To Reprint

When you include information or excerpts from other published works, as in Example 10.1, be sure to obtain written permission from the publisher.

Design Principles for One-Column Format with Graphics

All the design principles described at the beginning of this chapter are applied in this report. The two principles that are especially well illustrated by this example are repeated and described here.

Don't be afraid of white space. In this report, the left and right margins are 2.25 inches, and the top margin is 2.5 inches. The running heads and running feet extend beyond these margins to give each page the feel of a full-page grid with a great deal of white space. The relatively short length of each line of text makes the copy easy to read.

Let the same graphic elements carry the theme throughout the document. A gray rectangle crossed with white (reverse) lines is used on the cover, and a smaller gray box with white lines is repeated in the top right corner of every page, as a background for the running heads.

Production Tricks for One-Column Format with Graphics

In final form, this document is double-sided. Because the margins, heads, and feet are identical on every page of the report, it requires only one master page; the publication is set up in PageMaker as a one-sided document.

Although the final number of pages was not known in advance, the plan was not to exceed 32 pages. An initial setup of 32 pages was specified in the "Page setup" dialog box on the template to save repeated use of the "Insert pages..." command.

The wide margins define the limits of the text placed from word-processing files. Figure 10.7 shows how these specifications are set up in the "Page setup" dialog box.

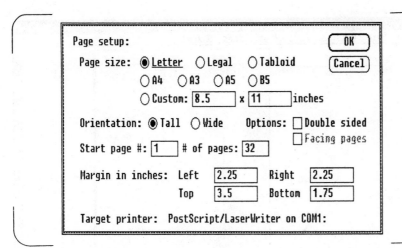

*Fig. 10.7. "Page setup"
dialog box for one-
column format with
graphics.*

The master page of the template includes the graphic that appears in the upper right corner of every page (see fig. 10.8). The normal default for type specifications—flush left 12-point Times—holds for this publication. The first
line of each paragraph is indented by pressing the tab key, with the first tab
set at 0.25 inches. Because the author had originally inserted a blank line between paragraphs, the designer decided to let this convention stand, rather
than use the "Paragraph..." command to set the space between paragraphs.
Figure 10.9 shows that only four different type specifications are used
throughout the publication.

Production Steps for One-Column Format with Graphics

The following steps can be used to produce this publication once the master
template is set up as shown in figures 10.7 and 10.8.

1. Type and format text files in the word-processing program. For
    ease in production, the entire document uses the same ruler-line
    settings. Set all text flush left, and indent each paragraph by
    pressing the tab key, with the first tab set at 0.25 inches. Double
    space between paragraphs. Store the files in the subdirectory for
    this report.

2. Open the PageMaker template document for this series of reports
    and modify the master pages and cover page to reflect the new
    report name. Save the modified template under the new report
    name. (For more information see "Specifying Standard [Master-
    Page] Layout Elements" and other sections in Chapter 6.)

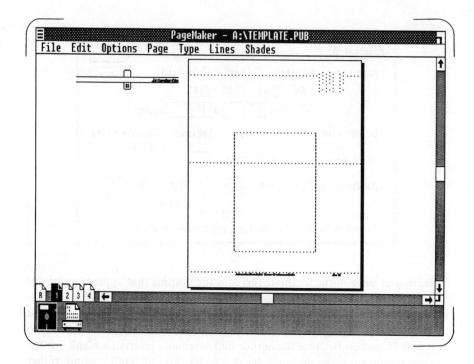

Fig. 10.9. *Type specifications table for one-column format with graphics.*

Chapter Titles   16-point Times Bold Italic, Flush right
                        (all other elements will be flush left)

Level 1 Headings   18-point Times Bold

Bylines   12-point Times Italic

Body copy   12-point Times, first-line indent of .25 inches,
                        extra carriage return between paragraphs

                        Auto leading used throughout

3. Working in "Fit in window" view, place text on consecutive pages in the template until all text is placed. (Consult "Typing and Bringing Text into PageMaker" in Chapter 3.)

4. Return to the beginning of the document, and, working in "50% size", correct the format where necessary and open spaces for figures. Cut the flush-right chapter titles from the text block, and paste them over the graphic in the upper right corner of each

page. Keep a duplicate of the section title on the pasteboard to use on subsequent pages of the same section. During this step, place the captions on the pasteboard, and use the "Cut" and "Paste" commands as needed to copy the captions to the pages (see fig. 10.10). (See Chapters 5 and 6 for full detail.)

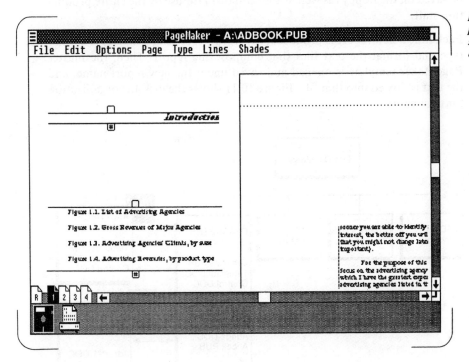

Fig. 10.10. Using the pasteboard to hold section titles and figure captions.

Preparation for Reproduction

All graphics are pasted by hand into page areas reserved for the graphics. All figures are enlarged or reduced photographically to fit the space before pasting. These limited-run reports are reproduced on xerographic equipment at a light setting so that the cut edges of the pasted figures do not show.

Disk-File Organization for One-Column Format with Graphics

The starting point for any new report consists of the two master-template files designed for this series: one PageMaker template (TEMPLATE.PUB) and one template for the word-processing program that is used to type the text (TEMPLATE.DOC). (The times estimated for each step in the production cycle, and the actual times spent on each step, can be entered into a text file named CONTROL.DOC for invoicing or project management.) If you have more than one workstation in your production environment, store the template on a floppy disk designated as the authorized source for any new reports. In this way, enhancements made to the template from any station can be saved on the floppy (as well as the hard disk) for use by the entire production staff.

Each time a new report is produced, the word-processing template is used to type and format the text files that compose the report. Then, the master PageMaker template is opened and saved under the new report name, and the text is flowed into that file. Figure 10.11 shows the disk-file organization for this report.

Fig. 10.11. Disk-file organization for one-column format with graphics.

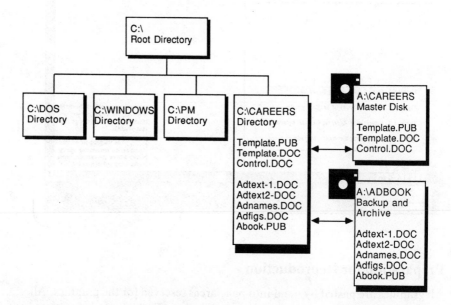

Each report's text files and PageMaker file fit on one floppy disk when the document is complete. This floppy serves as a backup throughout the production cycle, and the same floppy disk becomes the final archived version of the report.

Example 10.2: A One-Column Format with Flush-Left Heads

Designed for easy reference, this manual consists of sections with many subheads. As in Example 10.1, the text is more readable because of the narrow column. In this case, the narrow right column of text is achieved by using a hanging indent. This same design can be applied to manuals, textbooks, and business reports that use many subheads in the text. However, this design probably would not be good for a publication with few subheads.

The production process could be simplified significantly by changing the design slightly to eliminate the use of reverse type. In this particular case, the black boxes with reverse type are printed in a second color of ink, giving the finished pages a lighter feeling than is produced by the black images shown here.

Description of One-Column Format with Flush-Left Heads

This procedures manual identifies subsections with reverse-type heads that appear flush at the left margin. The numbers of the steps in each procedure are printed in boxed reverse type. One text file is created for each procedure. Each new procedure starts on a new right-hand page in this double-sided document. Figure 10.12 shows the final printouts of two pages.

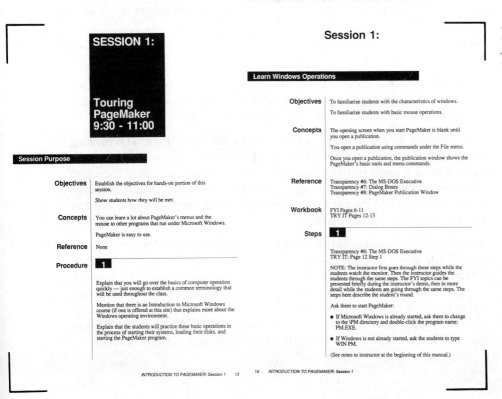

Fig. 10.12. Final printout of pages in one-column format with flush-left heads.

Design Principles for One-Column Format with Flush-Left Heads

All the design principles described at the beginning of this chapter are applied in this report. Four principles that are especially well illustrated by this example are repeated and described here.

Use only one or two different typefaces in a document. This manual uses Helvetica and Times, the two typefaces that are built into the Apple LaserWriter. The full type specifications table is shown in figure 10.13. Only five different fonts are used from these two typefaces. As a result, the final publication looks clean and simple, without distractions from the content.

Fig. 10.13. Type specifications table for one-column format with flush-left heads.

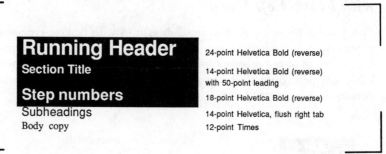

Running Header	24-point Helvetica Bold (reverse)
Section Title	14-point Helvetica Bold (reverse) with 50-point leading
Step numbers	18-point Helvetica Bold (reverse)
Subheadings	14-point Helvetica, flush right tab
Body copy	12-point Times

Don't be afraid of white space. The white space is achieved by reserving the left third of the page for section headings. Extra space is also allowed below headings and between rules and type for each step.

Use running heads and feet to help readers find topics. The running heads give the session number; the running feet show the page number at the outside margin along with the document title and session number. The use of the session number in both running heads and running feet means that each session is a separate PageMaker publication, so the running heads and feet can be entered on the master pages.

Let the same graphic elements carry the theme throughout the document. The graphic theme used is white type on black boxes. These black boxes are printed in a second color when the document is mass produced, giving the final book an attractive and unified appearance. Working with white type can be a production headache, however, because you can "lose" type on the page when it is not on a black box. (See the Efficiency Tip, "Working with Reverse Type," following the production steps for this example.)

Production Tricks for One-Column Format with Flush-Left Heads

The text is first formatted in the word-processing program, and all body copy is formatted with a hanging indent. All the text in this manual uses the same ruler line: the left margin of the section titles is the same as the left margin in PageMaker (see fig. 10.14). From the margin, the first tab is the flush-right tab set at 2.25 inches from the left margin and used by section subheads. The second tab positions the first line of all body copy at 2.5 inches from the left margin—the position of the hanging indent. A third tab is set up for tabs after bullets in short lists.

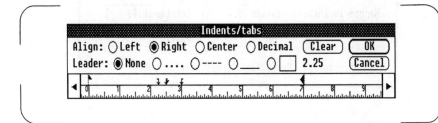

Fig. 10.14. The ruler line used for all text in one-column format with flush-left heads.

The reverse type is set up as normal (black) type in the word-processing program because the word processor does not support reverse type. The specification is changed to reverse type after the document is placed in PageMaker.

Template for One-Column Format with Flush-Left Heads

Figure 10.15 shows the template's margin settings in the "Page setup" dialog box. The master pages of the template for this manual are set up with one column. The master pages show horizontal and vertical ruler guides for positioning the running head and foot and vertical rule. The printed elements on the master page include a vertical rule and the running heads and feet (see fig. 10.16). The running head appears in reverse type on a black backdrop. The pasteboard holds black boxes and the ruled lines used throughout the document.

Fig. 10.15. "*Page setup*"
dialog box for one-
column format with
flush-left heads.

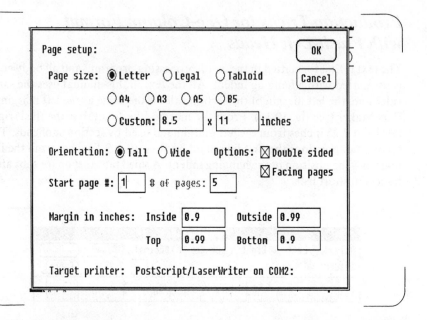

Fig. 10.16. The template,
including repeated
graphic elements on the
pasteboard and on the
master pages.

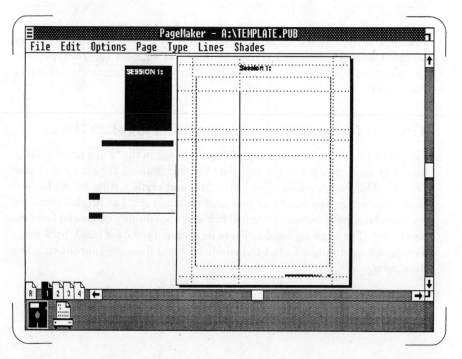

Production Steps for One-Column Format with Flush-Left Heads

The following steps produce this publication:

1. Type and format the text files in the word-processing program, and store them in this manual's subdirectory on the hard disk. Format the text with a hanging indent and the three tab settings shown in figure 10.4.

2. Build one PageMaker template document for this manual, as shown in figures 10.15 and 10.16. Store the template in the manual's subdirectory, and clone the template to continue the manual for each new section or when one section fills more than 128 pages.

3. Working in "Fit in window" view, place text on consecutive pages until all text is placed.

4. Go back to the beginning of the document, and, working with the text tool in "Actual size" view, make the necessary formatting corrections.

5. Return to the beginning of the document and work in "Actual size" view with the pointer tool selected. At the beginning of this sweep, copy the predesigned black box and ruled line (for step numbers) from the pasteboard (as shown in fig. 10.17) of the template into the Windows Clipboard. Avoid using the "Copy" and "Cut" commands for other objects (so as not to replace the Clipboard contents). At each new step number, perform the following:

   - Paste the black box and ruled lines from the Clipboard.

   - Position the black box over the step number.

   - Use the "Send to back" command.

Adjust for widows and orphans on each page (by dragging the bottom windowshade handle of the text) before placing the black boxes on subsequent pages.

*Fig. 10.17. Black boxes
ready to be pasted into
the Clipboard and then
pasted in place on the
pages.*

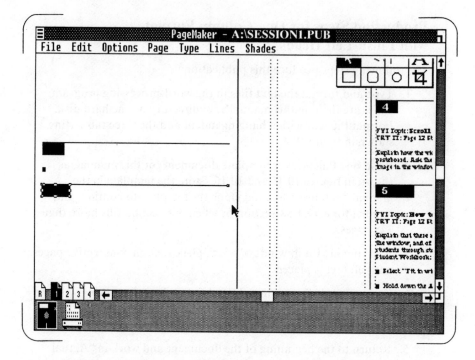

6. Go back to the beginning of the document and sweep through
   with the text tool selected:

   - Select each step number.

   - Choose "Reverse type" from the Type menu.

   - Check the alignment of the black box.

Remember that in order to move the black box, you need to select
the pointer tool. You select the box that is *under* the text block by
holding down the Ctrl key as you click the pointer over the box.
Next, you bring the box to the front, move it, and then send it to
the back again. Repeated switching from the pointer to the text
tool can be time-consuming, and this factor is one of the
inconveniences of working with layered designs.

Efficiency Tip

Working with Reverse Type

When working with reverse type, put a nonreverse character at the end of the
text (see fig. 10.18). This way, if the reverse text falls on a white background
you can still see where the reverse text is in relation to other text and graphics.

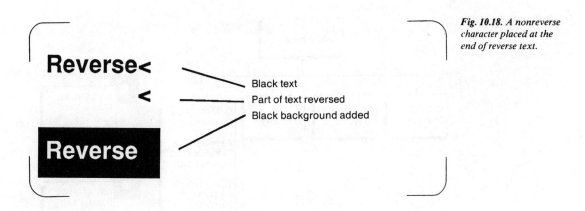

Fig. 10.18. A nonreverse character placed at the end of reverse text.

Disk-File Organization for One-Column Format with Flush-Left Heads

All text and PageMaker files for this document are stored in one subdirectory on the hard disk (see fig. 10.19). When making backups and archiving the final files, you copy all the text files on one floppy disk and all PageMaker files on another floppy disk because the text and publication files together are too large to fit on one floppy disk. The easiest method is to copy files through the MS-DOS Executive Window menus. If you are not running the full version of Windows, use the following procedure to copy files from the DOS prompt:

1. Insert the floppy disk for text files.

2. From the subdirectory on the hard disk, type

   copy *.doc a:

3. Remove the text floppy, insert the PageMaker-file floppy disk, and type

   copy *.pub a:

Example 10.3: A Two-Column Tabular Format with Small Type

The questionnaire in this example is designed to fit the greatest number of questions on a page by using narrow margins and a relatively small point size for the body copy (9-point Helvetica). This same design can be applied to many list formats (see also Chapter 13, "Creating Brochures, Price Lists, and Directories"). This design would not be good for a book or reference manual, however, without considerable revision of the type specifications to make the

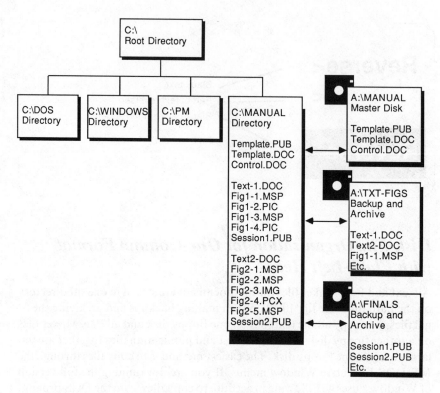

text larger. Books and reports would probably not use changing heads at the top of each column, as this questionnaire does. This example is presented here primarily for its demonstration of working with tabs and small point sizes.

Description of Two-Column Tabular Format

This questionnaire is set up to be exactly 32 pages long, set in 2 columns of 9-point type. All tabs are set in the word-processing program, where all the text is prepared. Figure 10.20 shows the final printouts of two pages.

Design Principles for Two-Column Tabular Format

Many of the design principles that were described at the beginning of this chapter are applied in this report. For example, although the goal is to put a great deal of material on each page, the use of two columns and varying tabs creates white space. The heads are consistent and set in all capital letters to give emphasis and unify the document. Only one principle merits special note here, however.

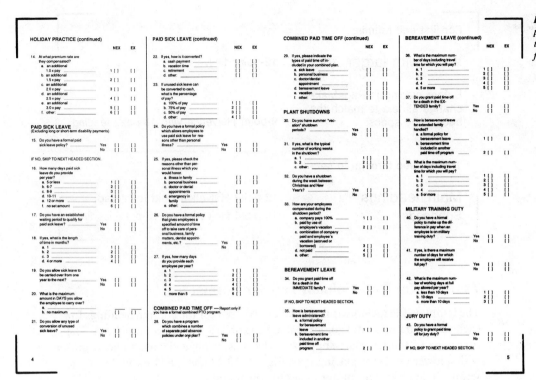

Fig. 10.20. *Printout of pages of questionnaire in two-column tabular format.*

Text on each page should bottom out to the margin. In this case, the overriding rule is to keep the full set of answer choices together with each question, rather than break a series of answers across columns or pages. If the two columns are unequal on a page, leading is added above subhead titles, or the longer column is shortened by moving the last question into the next column.

Production Tricks for Two-Column Tabular Format

Work in large type through the initial text-editing rounds so that the production staff and proofreaders can read the text easily (see fig. 10.21). Convert to a smaller typeface for the last editing rounds. Set tabs in the word-processing program before starting the page-layout process.

Change the default type specification to 9-point Helvetica in the template. This font is used in the questionnaire (except for the column headings and other exceptions noted). After all the text is placed, adjust the leading to make sure that the text fits the prescribed number of pages.

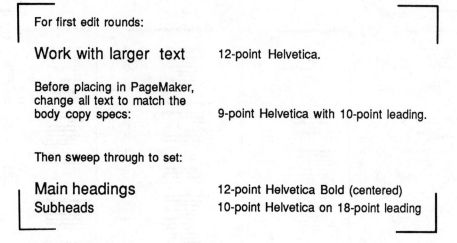

For first edit rounds:

Work with larger text   12-point Helvetica.

Before placing in PageMaker,
change all text to match the
body copy specs: 9-point Helvetica with 10-point leading.

Then sweep through to set:

Main headings   12-point Helvetica Bold (centered)
Subheads   10-point Helvetica on 18-point leading

Template for Two-Column Tabular Format

The template file includes dummy text to be used for the column headings for
each page and horizontal guides to mark the position of the column head. The
first page of the template suppresses the master-page elements and begins
with a lower guide for placing text. Figures 10.22 and 10.23 show the "Page
setup" dialog box and master pages for the template.

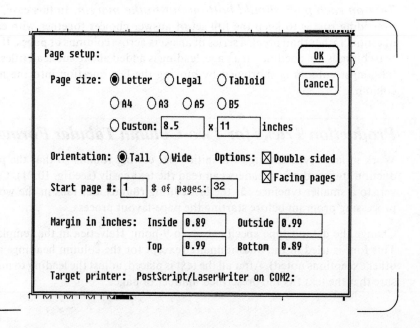

Page setup: OK

Page size: ● Letter   ○ Legal   ○ Tabloid   Cancel

            ○ A4   ○ A3   ○ A5   ○ B5

            ○ Custom: 8.5   x 11   inches

Orientation: ● Tall ○ Wide   Options: ⊠ Double sided
                                        ⊠ Facing pages

Start page #: 1   # of pages: 32

Margin in inches: Inside 0.89   Outside 0.99
            Top 0.99   Bottom 0.89

Target printer: PostScript/LaserWriter on COM2:

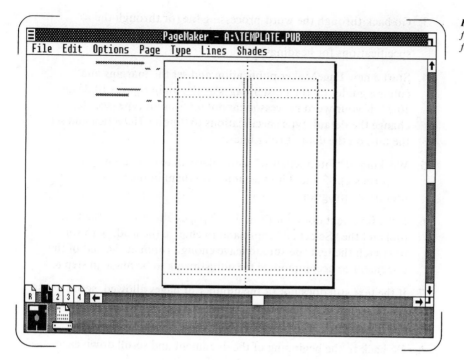

Fig. 10.23. The template for two-column tabular format.

Production Steps for Two-Column Tabular Format

To create this design, follow these steps:

1. Prepare text in a word-processing file. Work in 12-point type through the initial editing rounds. Set tabs far enough apart to show columns correctly in the draft printouts from the word-processing program.

2. As the last step before going into PageMaker—but after all text edits have been entered—select all the text and change it to 9-point type. With all the text still selected, move the tabs to fit the final column width.

   If your word processor cannot set 9-point Helvetica type, save the unformatted text file using the .TXT extension in the file name. You then can perform this step by placing all the text in PageMaker (see step 4). Use the text tool and the "Select all" command to change type specs and tabs. (Initially, the placed text may require more than 32 pages, but the text will shrink to fit when the point size and tabs are changed.)

3. Go back through the word-processing file (or through the PageMaker text, as the alternative in step 2) and set the type specifications for headings.

4. Start a new PageMaker publication and set the margins and column guides on the master pages as shown in figures 10.22 and 10.23. If your word processor cannot set 9-point type (see step 2), change the default type specifications to 9-point Helvetica and set the tabs on the default ruler lines.

5. Working in "Fit in window" view, place all text on all pages. Perform steps 2 and 3 if you cannot do them in the word-processing program.

6. If the final text does not fit in the 32 pages allowed, use the text tool and the "Select all" command to change the leading to shrink or stretch the text. Be sure to leave enough room at the end of the document to accommodate the adjustments to be made in step 8.

7. If the text still does not fit the number of pages allowed, scroll through the file in "Actual size" and selectively change the spacing around each heading or between questions.

8. Go back to the beginning of the document and scroll down each column in "Actual size" view. You then must

   • Force subheads and orphaned or widowed lines into the preceding or next column.

   • Use the "Copy" and "Paste" commands for headings at the tops of consecutive columns, adding the word *(continued)* if needed (see fig. 10.24).

Efficiency Tip

Changing the Spacing around Headings

To change the spacing around section headings throughout a document, first copy a blank line of the desired spacing to the Clipboard; then sweep through the document and at each break:

1. Triple-click the text tool to select the blank line.

2. Press the Ins key to replace the selected line with the blank line stored in the Clipboard.

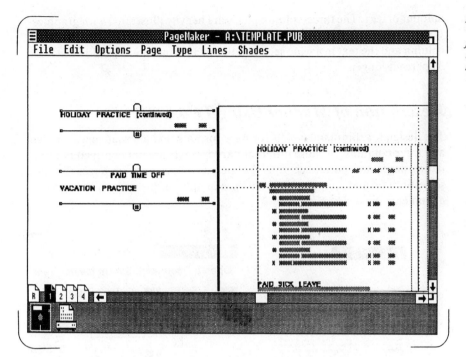

Fig. 10.24. Text for the word continued *is copied from the pasteboard of the template when needed.*

Disk-File Organization for Two-Column Tabular Format

Because this document is composed of one text file (QUESTION.DOC) and one PageMaker file (QUESTION.PUB), both files can be stored in the main directory and backed up on one floppy disk with one command:

    copy QUESTION.* a:

Example 10.4: One Template Used To Switch between Two Grids

The training manual in this example has a format that alternates between two different page designs: one with a narrow left column and a wide right column, the other with three columns. These two layouts are used throughout the publication. This design is rather tricky to work with, and it can be a production headache if you don't set up procedures like those described here.

The same production tips offered here can be modified as appropriate and applied to any publication that uses two or more page layouts within each file. In this case, the two-column pages usually have few graphics compared to the amount of text. The three-column pages are heavily illustrated with graphics. If these pages were laid out as two-column pages with the graphics in the first column and the text in a wide second column, the final book would be at least 30 percent longer.

Description of Manual Using Two Grids

The design for this manual calls for page formats that alternate between two and three columns. Because different page formats are not confined to alternating pages or separate sections, the trick is to devise master pages that can serve both formats. Figure 10.25 shows examples of printed pages from this document.

Fig. 10.25. Printout of manual using two grids.

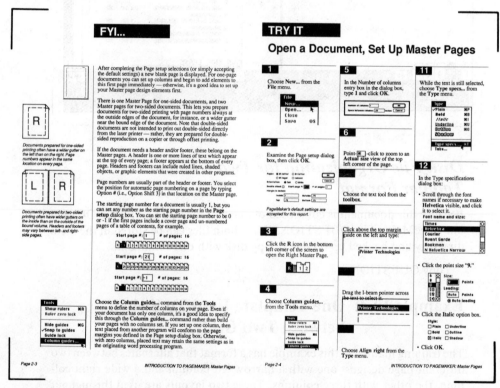

Design Principles for Manual Using Two Grids

Many of the design principles described at the beginning of this chapter are applied in this training manual. The use and spacing of graphic elements is especially important in this publication, as well as the inclusion of ample white space. Note how the following principles particularly enhance the final publication.

Let the same graphic elements carry the theme throughout the document. The common graphic themes are reverse type on black boxes, hairline rules between columns, and horizontal rules between steps. These elements make finding information easy and allow emphasis of the steps.

Don't be afraid of white space. White space occurs primarily on the two-column page layouts where wide spaces are allowed between paragraphs in order to accommodate figures in the narrow column. On three-column pages, the columns are allowed to be ragged at the bottom margin so that a step is not broken across columns. This publication deliberately violates the principle: Text on each page should bottom out to margin.

Use running heads and feet to help readers find topics. The running feet on left-hand pages show the session number; the feet on right-hand pages show specific subtopics. This manual is the only example in this chapter that uses uppercase text as a deliberate design strategy. Because the most common head is "FYI..." ("For Your Information") and all the other heads are short phrases ("OVERVIEW," "TRY IT," "NOTES," and "SUMMARY"), all heads are set in uppercase so that they carry the same visual weight.

Be sure that the space between text and graphics is the same for all figures. Spacing guides are used to position all graphics and captions and to separate one step from the next. Careful spacing gives the page a clean balanced appearance.

Production Tricks for Manual Using Two Grids

All text is formatted in the word-processing file as flush left with no indents. One tab is set at 0.3 inches for bulleted lists and commands. Figure 10.26 shows the six fonts from two typeface families that are used throughout the document.

Template for Manual Using Two Grids

The "Page setup" margins define the limits of the text for both formats (see fig. 10.27). Vertical rules on the master pages fall outside these limits (see fig. 10.28). Two-column guides on the master pages are customized. The default line style is changed to hairline rule.

Fig. 10.26. Type
specifications table for
manual using two grids.

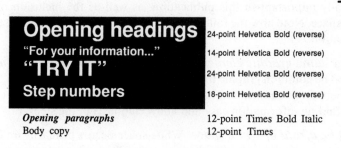

Opening headings	24-point Helvetica Bold (reverse)
"For your information..."	14-point Helvetica Bold (reverse)
"TRY IT"	24-point Helvetica Bold (reverse)
Step numbers	18-point Helvetica Bold (reverse)
Opening paragraphs	12-point Times Bold Italic
Body copy	12-point Times

Fig. 10.27. "Page setup"
dialog box for manual
using two grids.

Page setup: [OK]

Page size: ◉ Letter   ○ Legal   ○ Tabloid   [Cancel]

            ○ A4   ○ A3   ○ A5   ○ B5

            ○ Custom: [8.5] x [11]   inches

Orientation: ◉ Tall ○ Wide   Options: ☒ Double sided
                                        ☒ Facing pages

Start page #: [1]   # of pages: [11]

Margin in inches: Inside [0.89]   Outside [0.99]
                      Top [0.99]   Bottom [0.89]

Target printer: PostScript/LaserWriter on COM2:

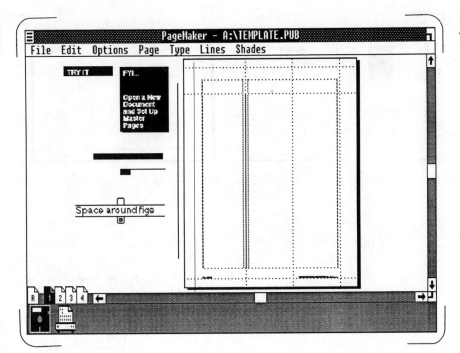

Fig. 10.28. The template
for manual using two
grids.

Efficiency Tip

Use Thumbnail Printouts for Production Notes

When the template for the publication is complex, print thumbnails of
the template and mark them up with instructions to the production team
(see fig. 10.29).

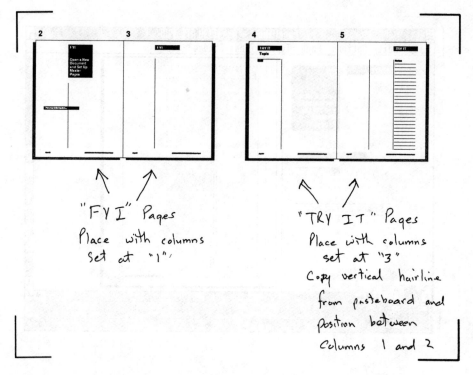

Fig. 10.29. Thumbnails of the template for manual using two grids.

"FYI" Pages
Place with columns
set at "1"

"TRY IT" Pages
Place with columns
set at "3"
Copy vertical hairline
from pasteboard and
position between
Columns 1 and 2

Production Steps for Manual Using Two Grids

To create the publications, take the following steps:

1. Prepare all text files flush left with one tab for bulleted lists.

2. Set up the template with a customized two-column format on the master pages (see fig. 10.30 for this procedure).

3. As you go through the document, note the following:

   - When you need a page in format 1—two columns—keep the master-page elements.

   - When you need a page in three-column format, use the "Column guides..." command to set up three columns, and use the "Copy" and "Paste" commands to move the vertical rule from the pasteboard into the space between columns 2 and 3.

   - The trick to this alternation is that the column width set up automatically by the "Column guides..." command is exactly the same as the first column width of the customized format.

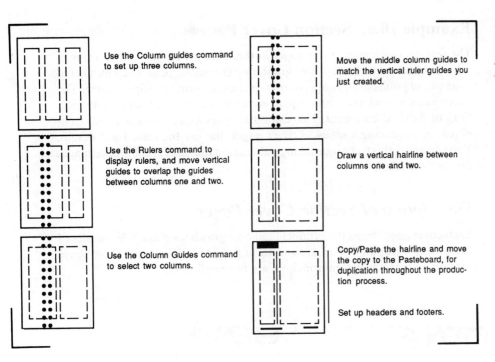

Use the Column guides command to set up three columns.

Use the Rulers command to display rulers, and move vertical guides to overlap the guides between columns one and two.

Use the Column Guides command to select two columns.

Move the middle column guides to match the vertical ruler guides you just created.

Draw a vertical hairline between columns one and two.

Copy/Paste the hairline and move the copy to the Pasteboard, for duplication throughout the production process.

Set up headers and footers.

Disk-File Organization for Manual Using Two Grids

All text files and PageMaker documents for this manual are stored in the same subdirectory (see fig. 10.31).

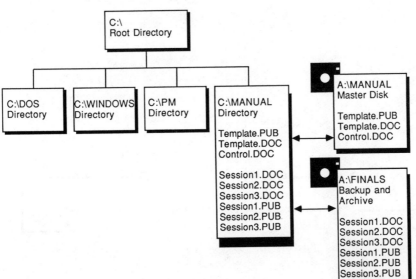

Fig. 10.31. Disk-file organization for manual using two grids.

C:\ Root Directory

C:\DOS Directory

C:\WINDOWS Directory

C:\PM Directory

C:\MANUAL Directory

Template.PUB
Template.DOC
Control.DOC

Session1.DOC
Session2.DOC
Session3.DOC
Session1.PUB
Session2.PUB
Session3.PUB

A:\MANUAL Master Disk

Template.PUB
Template.DOC
Control.DOC

A:\FINALS Backup and Archive

Session1.DOC
Session2.DOC
Session3.DOC
Session1.PUB
Session2.PUB
Session3.PUB

Example 10.5: Section Cover Pages

The section, or chapter, cover pages in this example are created as a single-sided publication with a repeated graphic on the master page. Each numbered page of the publication contains only the new section or chapter name. The cover pages are printed without page numbers and inserted between the sections of the final document. This example is provided to show a simple technique for producing a series of cover pages that use the same basic design. You can apply this technique to any publication that uses graphic cover pages for each section.

Description of Section Cover Pages

Each cover page shows the product logo on a gray background. Examples of pages from this publication are shown in figure 10.32. Because these pages contain no text, the design principles are not applicable.

Fig. 10.32. Final page printout of section cover pages.

Production Tricks for Section Cover Pages

These cover pages are prepared for printing on 8.5-by-11-inch paper, but they are to be part of a document trimmed to 6 by 9 inches. The pages, therefore, can accommodate the bleed from the larger paper and show crop marks as well. If the final pages were to be 8.5 by 11 inches, the page size selected in this dialog box should be even larger in order to accommodate the bleed. (As explained in Chapter 9, *bleed* is the term used in offset printing to describe pages on which the inked area runs to the trimmed edges of the final document.)

This document is set up as single-sided because all the pages are right-hand pages, even though the larger document into which they are inserted is double-sided. The margin settings reflect the limits of the text—not the bleed or the trim. The "Page setup" dialog box settings used for the template are shown in figure 10.33.

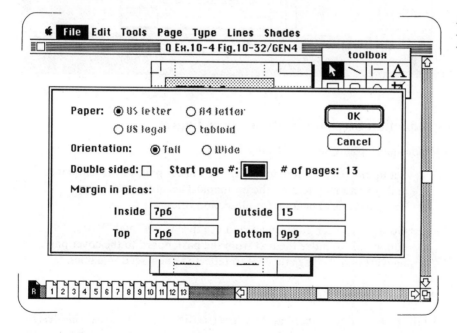

Fig. 10.33. The "Page setup" dialog box for section cover pages.

The master page of the template includes the logo and the gray background, with guides to show the position of the section name (see fig. 10.34). Crop marks on the master page show the printer where to trim the printed covers. The pasteboard includes a skeletal text block that can be moved with the "Copy" and "Paste" commands and modified for each section.

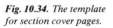

Fig. 10.34. *The template for section cover pages.*

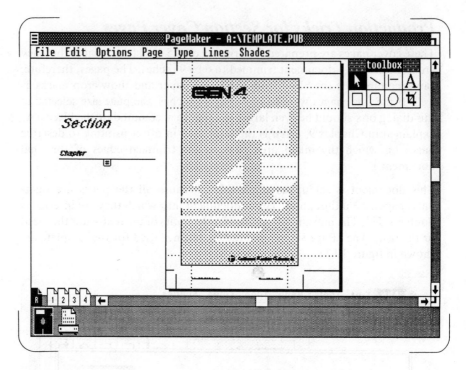

Production Steps for Section Cover Pages

The design steps are short and simple.

1. Set up the background design on the master page of the template and type dummy text on the pasteboard according to the type specifications to be used for all section titles.

2. Go through each cover page, and use the "Copy" and "Paste" commands to move the text from the pasteboard to the cover page background. Change the text to reflect the new section names.

Preparation for Reproduction

All the pages call for a bleed at the edges (see fig. 10.35). Usually, this design means that the color must be printed beyond the trim area. The pages with bleeds, therefore, should be delivered to the offset printer as a set separate from the rest of the document. Include a note stating that the pages call for a bleed. Pages like these are often handled separately because larger paper and more cuts are required than for other pages. Page numbers outside the bleed area indicate where each page will be inserted into the finished document.

Fig. 10.35. Cover page designed for a bleed at the edges.

Summary

This chapter has presented general descriptions and specific applications of the design principles and production tips that apply to long documents, such as books, manuals, and reports. After studying the examples in this chapter, you should be better equipped to design your own long documents, set up the templates, and implement efficient production procedures. If you are still new to PageMaker and long document production, remember to take a small portion of the text through the entire production cycle before you finalize the full cycle of production steps in your project plan.

Finally, beware of setting tight production deadlines—or even trying to predict the completion date—for your first large production project with PageMaker.

Designing and Producing Newsletters and Similar Publications

11

Magazines, newsletters, and newspapers have become so much a part of our daily lives that many readers tend to take these publications for granted. Readers expect the design and layout to be inviting and the information to be presented clearly. Publishers of these documents share an interest in special touches that complicate the production process. These activities include kerning headlines, wrapping text around graphics, and varying page layouts. At the same time, producers of magazines, newsletters, and newspapers face more pressure to meet the deadline than are faced for any other type of publication. Therefore, the demand for efficiency in production techniques is especially important.

Following are four characteristics that distinguish these types of publications:

- The publications use at least two columns, usually more, in the underlying grid. The number of columns can change from page to page.

- The flow of text for a single article or story can jump from one page to a point several pages later.

- The documents are usually produced as a series. A document of the same basic format and length is produced at regular intervals.

- The documents often call for special layouts that may involve kerning headlines, wrapping text around graphics, or pasting display ads from one PageMaker document into another.

Figure 11.1 demonstrates all these characteristics.

Fig. 11.1. Examples of the documents in this chapter.

These and other characteristics involve their own special design and production problems and practices. These special concerns are explained and illustrated in this chapter. Once you understand the underlying principles, you can apply the suggestions in this chapter to other types of documents, too.

Using PageMaker helps you with newsletters and similar publications. Because you can use PageMaker to plan your designs, you save time. Once you have a good design for a newsletter, for example, you can use the master pages for every issue. You do not need to create formats again. As discussed in Parts I and II, PageMaker also eases typesetting chores, such as kerning, wrapping text, and using different typefaces.

Design Principles

The design principles that apply to newsletters derive from the long traditions of newspaper and magazine publishing. Because these publications are relatively short, their design is particularly important. You need to convey information in a limited space and in an uncluttered, attractive format. The principles stressed in this chapter address these needs. The principles range from the number of typefaces and the use of ruled lines to considerations of margins and provision of ample white space.

Some of these principles apply to all types of publications, not just those mentioned in this chapter. This section provides a general description of the application of these principles to newsletters, magazines, and newspapers. With each example, the applicable principles are repeated, accompanied by a description of their specific application to that example.

Use only one or two different typefaces in a document.

Magazines and newsletters often use many more typefaces than the business reports, books, and manuals shown in the preceding chapter, especially when the magazine or newsletter includes display ads. The basic principle of simplicity, however, remains the best guide. Table 11.1 shows some of the typefaces commonly used in magazines and newsletters. In these publications, display ads often contain a wide variety of typefaces, but headlines and body copy use only one or two.

Use variations in the grid to help distinguish different sections of the magazine.

You have probably seen how some newsletters and magazines distinguish sections by giving them different grid structures. Figure 11.2 shows an example. The main feature begins on a facing-page spread. A graphic, the story title, and one column of text fill the lefthand page. The feature continues on the righthand page with three columns of text. Another variation might be to have letters to the editor occupying three columns and the articles, two columns. Example 11.2 uses this technique.

Use ruled lines to help set off the grid of the pages.

In addition to using nonprinting guides to help lay out your pages, you can use PageMaker's ruled lines to enhance the appearance of the pages. For example, designers often drop hairline rules between columns of text. This technique is demonstrated in examples in this chapter (see figs. 11.7 and 11.13).

All columns on all pages should bottom out to the same point.

This rule is much more strictly applied in magazines than in most newsletters, or any other type of document described in this book. As mentioned in the preceding chapter, the problems associated with alignment are compounded when you add subheadings in an article, have strict rules about the spacing around graphics and between paragraphs, and do not allow widows and orphans. You may need to adjust the space around headings and figures in order to force columns to meet the bottom margin.

Table 11.1
Typefaces Used in Magazines and Newsletters
(Y = used; N = not used)

Typefaces	Newsletters	Magazines
ITC American Typewriter	Y	N
ITC Avant Garde	Y	N
ITC Benguiat	Y	Y
ITC Bookman	Y	Y
Courier	N	N
ITC Friz Quadrata	Y	Y
ITC Galliard	Y	Y
ITC Garamond	Y	Y
Glypha	Y	Y
Goudy Old Style	Y	Y
Helvetica	Y	Y
ITC Korinna	Y	N
ITC Lubalin Graph	Y	Y
ITC Machine	N	N
ITC New Baskerville	Y	Y
New Century Schoolbook	Y	Y
Optima	Y	Y
Palatino	Y	Y
ITC Souvenir	Y	Y
Times	Y	Y
Trump Mediaeval	Y	Y
ITC Zapf Chancery	N	N

Fig. 11.2. Varying the grid structure to distinguish sections.

On the other hand, a ragged bottom margin, as illustrated in figure 11.3, allows much more flexibility in copy fitting. The ragged margin is better than an even margin that stops above the bottom of the grid. This strategy is used deliberately in Example 11.1 (see the second page in fig. 11.7). Other examples in this chapter also illustrate bottom alignment and provide production tips for copy fitting.

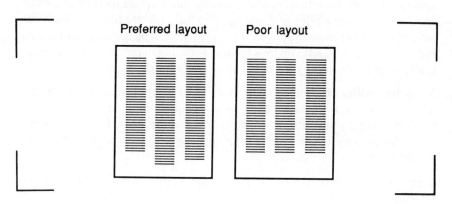

Preferred layout   **Poor layout**

Fig. 11.3. Deliberately making a bottom margin ragged.

Don't be afraid of white space.

Applications of this principle vary greatly. Some magazines—*The New Yorker*, for instance—fill every column completely with small type. This kind of design can be attractive as well as functional; it produces the greatest number of words in the fewest number of pages. Good designers can make designs like this work; but if you are just beginning to learn the ins and outs of page layout, you should follow the rule of allowing some white space on the pages. In the examples in this chapter, you will see that white space occurs primarily around article titles and subheads. This practice is common to newsletters and newspapers in particular.

Provide estimates of the number of characters per column for contributors and editors.

Providing character-count estimates is something that most professional editors do as a matter of course when they make an assignment. These estimates help eliminate the many problems that arise when you begin to lay out the pages. What is involved is planning or estimating the amount of space to be allocated for the text of each article and letting the type specifications for the article determine the number of words that will fit in the space. Chapter 8 describes methods of counting characters and copy casting before placing the text in PageMaker.

Production Tips

In this chapter, the emphasis is on documents that are laid out in several columns and use figures of varying widths. The production tips are particularly applicable to these kinds of publications and cover all stages of production from building the publication to getting it ready to take to a printer. For example, you learn when to use a drawing program to create banners and when and where to place a table of contents. You learn how to handle documents with many illustrations and how to scale figures and pictures to column widths. The tips also tell you how to adjust spacing in multiple-column publications and how to get your publication ready for the printer.

Many tips in this chapter apply to other types of publications, such as the booklets described in Chapter 13. This section describes how the tips are applied generally to newsletters, magazines, and newspapers. In the examples, the pertinent tips are repeated with explanations of their specific applications to that example.

If you need type larger than 127 points, use a draw program to create the banner.

The largest type you can specify directly in PageMaker is 127 points. If your banner calls for larger type, you can create the banner by using a draw program and then place the file in PageMaker and scale the image to a larger size. The banner for the "Update" tabloid was created this way (see fig. 11.12). You can stretch text from a draw file to any size and get good results on a printer that can handle large type sizes. Otherwise, try the technique suggested next.

If your printer cannot handle large type sizes, use a scanned image or a paint figure for the banner.

If you are using a font cartridge that does not have large display type, you can create a banner by scanning large type. You also can create the banner by using large type in a paint file. The scanned image provides the best quality on the printout if the image is saved as a high-resolution image. In either case, you probably need to clean up the image pixel-by-pixel to get smoothed edges. The results always are of lower quality than if you use 127-point type in PageMaker. (For examples of scanned and paint-type graphics, see Chapter 5; for examples of bit-mapped characters, see Chapter 8.)

If your publication includes a list of contents that can vary in length, place or type the list before filling the rest of the page.

Rather than place long articles on the pages first, type or place elements that cannot be jumped to later pages. The list of contents is just one example of this kind of element. You do not need to know the exact page numbers when you first type the table of contents, but you do need to know the number of articles that will appear in the issue and the lengths of the titles.

For example, the calendar of events on page 1 in figure 11.8 must be placed before the rest of the page is laid out. Similarly, the list of contents at the top right corner of page 1 in figure 11.13 must be placed before the rest of the page can be completed.

Use a spacing guide to position text and graphics and to adjust the spaces between articles.

Precise spacing is especially important in newsletters and magazines. See Chapter 9 for a description of spacing guides. You'll see spacing guides on the pasteboard of the template for each example in this chapter (see figs. 11.10 and 11.18).

Scale pictures and figures to precise column widths.

A picture can span more than one column, but all pictures should conform to the grid lines. For example, a picture can be one column, two columns, or three columns wide in a three-column grid design but should not be one and a half columns wide unless your grid is *designed* to accommodate this variation. For example, figure 11.20 shows the layout of a page of figures that range from one-half column wide to two columns wide.

Pages with several figures look best if the figures are aligned with other pictures or headlines.

Figure 11.4 provides examples of various layouts that either follow or violate this guideline. The pages on the left in the example position figures by making one edge of each figure align horizontally or vertically with the edge of another figure on the page. The pages on the right do not follow this rule. As a result, the pages on the right lack balance and look haphazard.

Use black boxes to reserve space for photographs that need halftones dropped in by the printer.

When offset printers prepare plates for pages that require halftones, the preparers usually black out the space on the camera-ready mechanicals so that the camera creates a clear "window" in the negative. You can save the printer this extra step by using PageMaker's black boxes to reserve space for halftones. The camera-ready master pages are printed directly from PageMaker in black images on white paper. The photographic negative is prepared by the offset printer; the print image is transparent on a black background. The plate made from the negative has a raised surface that picks up ink from the roller and lays the ink on the paper. The plate is a mirror image of the final page.

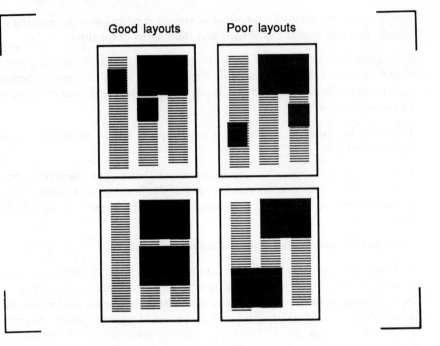

Good layouts   Poor layouts

Efficiency Tip

Talk to Your Printer before Preparing Final Camera-Ready Pages

If you have not dealt with the offset-printing process before, find out what form your printing service prefers for camera-ready pages. Also find out how the printing charges might change if you do more or less of the preparation yourself.

Use white boxes to reserve space for line art that will be pasted in before copy is sent to the printer.

The printer wants to lay halftones on transparent windows in the negative (created by black boxes on the camera-ready page), but the pasteup artist usually wants to paste figures down on a white background. Figure 11.5 shows how you can type the name or number of the figure in the space reserved for each figure. To draw the white box to size, you use PageMaker's square-corner tool. To type the figure number in the box, you use Page-Maker's drag-place feature: you select the text tool and drag the I-beam inside the figure area to define the text's width before you start typing.

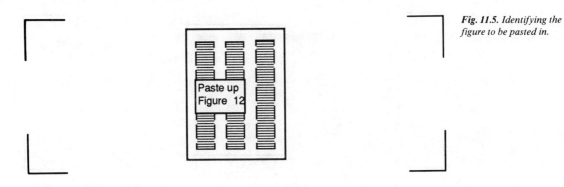

Fig. 11.5. Identifying the figure to be pasted in.

Use a template for all issues.

The template systems for newsletters and magazines can be elaborate compared to those for most other types of documents. In some of the examples that follow, you will see how comprehensive a template can be. Figure 11.18 shows a template for a tabloid with 13 different place holders for type specifications, several spacing guides, and three different page layouts. Chapter 9 provides a fuller discussion of template systems.

Do all character formatting in advance.

This suggestion carries extra weight for magazines and newsletters. When you are working under the pressure of a regular deadline, you need to use the best tools available for each function. As explained in Chapter 3, word processors are more efficient than PageMaker for editing and formatting text. Word processors are faster because they do not need to perform all the additional screen-imaging functions required for WYSIWYG graphics systems.

Use pull-out quotes to extend copy that falls very short of filling the space allowed.

Pull-out quotes are short sentences excerpted from the text, printed in larger type, and set off from the rest of the page by boxes or lines. Magazines and newsletters frequently use pull-out quotes to fill space and to emphasize points from the article. A pull-out quote usually is set four to six points larger than the body copy (see fig. 11.6).

You can expand the text to fill pages by using pull-out quotes. To help estimate the number of lines you need, you use formulas based on your type spec-

Fig. 11.6. Using pull-out quotes to fill space or emphasize specific text.

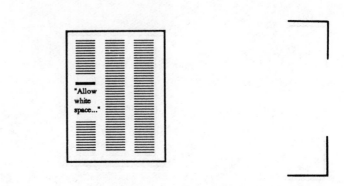

ifications. Following are some examples of formulas based on using 16-point type with 18-point leading and allowing 1/4 inch for a ruled line above the pull-out quote:

Number of Lines in Quote	Number of Inches Added
1	.5
2	.75
3	1.00
4	1.25
5	1.5

Use leading changes to make fine adjustments in copy fitting.

If the final text does not fit in the space allowed, change the leading of the body copy for selected columns, pages, or articles. As mentioned in Chapter 8, leading changes should be made consistently in adjacent columns and on facing pages. The quickest way to make text fit a specific space is to select a whole article and change the leading globally to shrink or stretch the text. You may need to scroll through the columns in "Actual size" to reset the leading on headings and captions and to check for widows and orphans. The alternative is to sweep through adjacent pages and select body copy only, paragraph by paragraph, and change the leading. This technique, however, is slower and involves displaying more dialog boxes.

Try not to let articles span more than 128 pages.

The 128-page limit is enforced by PageMaker, but you may set a much lower limit for your publications, especially if they contain many graphics. Remember that you do not want to build a single publication file too large to be backed up on one floppy disk.

The point is that you want to keep each text file (from the word-processing program) confined to a single PageMaker file, if possible. Otherwise, the text blocks will not be linked between documents; and if the blocks are not linked, problems can arise when the text is edited later.

Examples

This chapter contains two examples of newsletters. The first example is a two-page newsletter, every issue of which contains the same basic elements. The second example is a tabloid newsletter prepared for two-color printing.

11.1. A Two-Page Newsletter with Repeated Basic Elements

11.2. A Tabloid Newsletter Prepared for Two-Color Printing

Example 11.1. A Two-Page Newsletter with Repeated Basic Elements

The two-page newsletter in this example is designed for ease of production by a group of volunteers who have many other, perhaps more pressing, responsibilities. The trick is that the newsletter always contains the same set of features, each of which is always the same size and occupies the same position on the pages. A collection of extra copy and artwork—"house" ads, helpful tips, and interesting quotations—is available for use in a month when a feature is short or missing.

The techniques used here can be applied to any publication that is regularly produced by a group whose primary function is *not* publishing. Such publications include newsletters produced by volunteer staff, house organs produced by administrative staff, and event calendars with descriptions of the offerings produced by educational institutions and seminar agencies.

Description of the Two-Page Newsletter

This two-page newsletter uses a three-column format that routinely presents the calendar of events for a seminar agency. The contents always follow that same basic "formula":

- A calendar of events (varying length), always on page 1

- A feature article about the main event (300–400 words), always on page 1

- An article about secondary events (300–400 words), always on page 1

- An article about a person or agency, usually one of the event leaders or sponsors (200–250 words), which can start on page 1

- An article (300–400 words) offering information on a topic of general interest to the readers, usually written by one of the seminar leaders and usually found on page 2

- No more than three miscellaneous "fillers" such as house ads, special announcements, short tips, and notable quotations

Figure 11.7 shows how these basic elements are laid out in one issue.

Fig. 11.7. Printout of two-page newsletter.

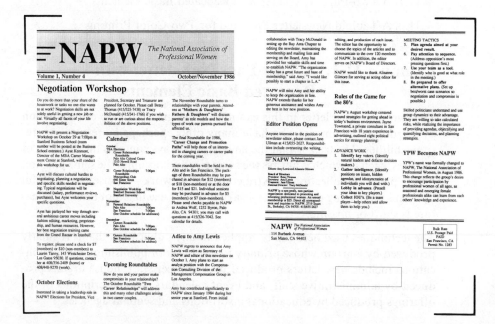

Using the same basic design elements enables each contributor to know exactly how many words to write. And if one contributor fails to meet the deadline for copy, the editor can fill the space with one of the "canned" house ads, tips, or quotations.

A spacing guide is included in the template as a standard for the minimum space allowed between articles, but this space can be increased as needed to make the articles fill the pages. These loose standards make this publication easy to lay out.

Design Principles for the Two-Page Newsletter

The design principles listed at the beginning of this chapter generally have been applied in this newsletter. Four of those principles have been applied in a way that intentionally simplifies the production process. Because the producers of the newsletter are not professional publishers, these principles are especially important.

Use only one or two different typefaces in a document. Only one typeface, Times, is used, in five fonts, as shown in the type specifications table in figure 11.8. This relatively short list of elements helps simplify the production of the newsletter.

Logo

127-point Times

Banner Tag	18-point Times Italic
Volume/Issue ID	14-point Times Bold
Main Article Title	24-point Times Bold
All Other Titles	14-point Times Bold, 24-point leading
Body Copy	10-point Times, auto leading
Calendar text	8-point Times
Masthead	7-point Times

Fig. 11.8. Type specifications table for two-page newsletter.

Use ruled lines to help set off the grid of the pages. Horizontal rules are used to set off standing elements such as the "Calendar" and the masthead information. All rules except one use the double-line option (also called an Oxford rule) from the Lines menu. Figure 11.10 shows that on page 1 of the newsletter, two-column-wide ruled lines are stored for future placement around the calendar text.

Provide estimates of the number of characters per column for contributors and editors. The length of each feature is standard. The total newsletter is 7,500 characters, or about 1,500 words. Before beginning an assignment, a writer knows how long it should be. The editor's primary concern is that the assignment not exceed the expected word count. If an article is too short, the extra space can be filled with a house ad, tip, or short quotation.

All columns on all pages should bottom out to same point. This general rule is not rigidly applied in this case. If a contributor writes too much or too little, columns are left uneven; the text is not edited to change the length, and the leading is not changed.

Production Tricks for the Two-Page Newsletter

The production tips offered here can be applied to any publication for which a primary goal is simplicity in the production process. The tips include ways to deal with material that comes in varied formats and suggestions for setting up the template. You also are led through all the steps of the production process for this kind of publication.

Sources of Data

You can usually expect a wide range of sources for the text in any publication that consists of articles by a number of different authors unless you are producing an in-house newsletter for which all the contributors use the same computer system. Because the newsletter is only two pages long, the editor can type short articles directly into PageMaker if they are not supplied on disk. All text formatting is done in PageMaker.

The Template for the Two-Page Newsletter

Figure 11.9 shows the "Page setup" dialog box for the newsletter. The template is set up with two pages, and the relatively wide margins provide white space that helps balance the wide spacing between articles.

The template, shown in figure 11.10, uses a simple three-column format. The first page contains a standing banner and two ruled lines that will be positioned around the calendar. Page 2 contains the masthead information and mailing label area. A list of production steps is stored on the pasteboard for easy reference.

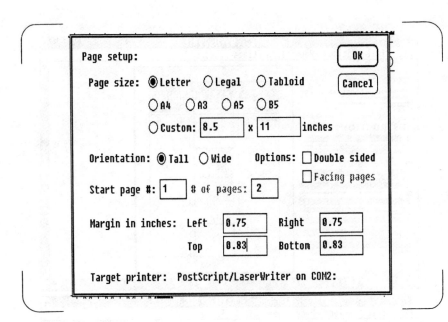

Fig. 11.9. "Page setup" dialog box for two-page newsletter.

Production Steps for the Two-Page Newsletter

As an aid to the producers of this quarterly newsletter, the following steps appear on the pasteboard of the template. These steps apply to this specific newsletter, but you can apply them easily to any publication of this type.

1. Collect all text files, either on disk or paper. The target character count is 7,500 for the entire newsletter, or about 1,500 words, including the "Calendar" but excluding the standing items on the template.

2. Open the template for this newsletter. Save the template, using a new name that includes the issue number, such as VOL1-04.PUB.

3. On page 1, change the issue identification below the banner. (See "Design Principles" for suggestions for creating banners.)

4. Working in "Actual size" or "70% size", type or place each article in the space allowed, formatting text as you go (see fig. 11.8 for fonts).

5. If the final text is too long to fit within the two pages allowed, change the leading to shrink the text. You may need to scroll down each column to check for widows and orphans and to make fine adjustments to the space between articles.

Fig. 11.10. Template for two-page newsletter.

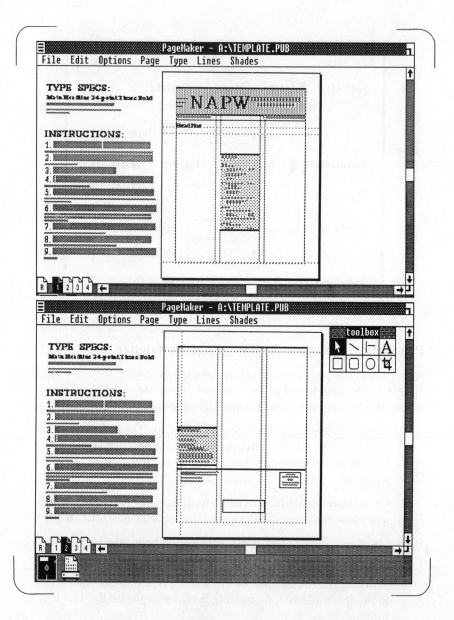

6. If the text is too short to fill the number of pages allowed, add a house ad or a famous quotation from the files. Fill empty space with items from the text files named HOUSEADS.DOC or QUOTES.DOC, or from one of the graphics files named HOUSEAD1.PIC, HOUSEAD2.PIC, and so on. (Names of your files may differ.) You also can increase the spacing between articles.

7. Before printing the final master copy, print the newsletter on a laser printer for proofing. Be sure that the event coordinator (or other director) sees a copy before it is sent to the print shop.

8. Print the newsletter on a laser printer and send the camera-ready pages to the printing company. Specify type, color, and weight of the paper and the number of copies.

9. Copy the PageMaker file for this issue to the archive disk named NEWS (or any name you choose) and delete all text files from the hard disk.

Efficiency Tip

Adding Space around Article Titles

When changing the spacing between sections throughout a document, copy a blank line of the desired spacing into the Clipboard; sweep through the document; and, at each break, do the following:

1. Triple-click to select the blank line.

2. Press Ins to replace the selected line with the blank line stored in the Clipboard.

Disk-File Organization for the Two-Page Newsletter

For all issues of this newsletter, all work is done in one directory (see fig. 11.11). Only the PageMaker version of each issue, along with the template, is saved on the archive disk.

Example 11.2. A Tabloid Newsletter Prepared for Two-Color Printing

The newsletter used in this example is more similar in design and format to a newspaper than to most newsletters. The tabloid-size (11-by-17-inch) pages are printed in tiled pieces on 8.5-by-11-inch paper for the editing reviews, and the final camera-ready pages are printed full size on a Linotronic 300 typesetter.

The design and production tips provided here can be applied to any newsletter or newspaper publication, particularly publications consisting of many different articles, figures, and photographs. The tips that specifically address two-color printing can be applied to any two-color publication; they also can be adapted for three- and four-color jobs.

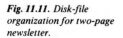

Fig. 11.11. *Disk-file organization for two-page newsletter.*

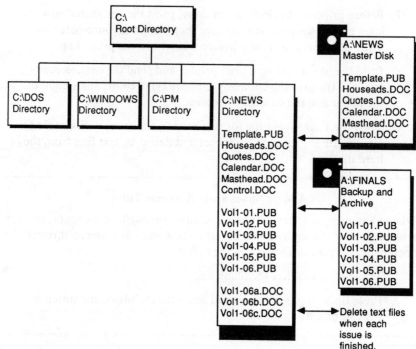

Description of the Tabloid Newsletter

The tabloid-size newsletter shown in figure 11.12 is assembled from text contributed in various forms by many different authors. The production process involves a considerable amount of coordination among contributors, editors, and the production staff. Because the people involved are scattered over a wide geographic area, files are telecommunicated through a modem.

The final telecommunication occurs when the production group sends the finished PageMaker files to the editorial group for the final review. The editors make changes directly to the files and send them back to the production group. Then, the files are printed on a Linotronic typesetter and marked up (on tissue overlays) for two-color (black and red) printing.

Design Principles for the Tabloid Newsletter

All the design principles described at the beginning of this chapter are applied in this report. Some principles, however, are particularly well illustrated. The tabloid makes effective use of ruled lines, white space, and variations in the grid. Estimates of character counts are essential for this kind of production.

Fig. 11.12. Printout of tabloid newsletter.

Use variations in the grid to help distinguish different sections of the newsletter. The three pages shown in figure 11.12 provide good examples of grid variations: the basic grid is four columns; the "President's Report" is two columns wide; and a page of graphs and tables includes tables and graphs that vary from one-half column to two columns wide. These grid variations help differentiate sections and maintain the reader's interest, as well as accommodate a variety of formats.

Use ruled lines to help set off the grid of the pages. This design uses hairline rules between columns and horizontal rules above article titles (see figs. 11.12 and 11.13). These rules help set off different types of material and highlight the variations in the grid.

Provide estimates of the number of characters per column for contributors and editors. The character counts for each article are assigned to the writers initially, but the final count may change when figures are added. The editors expect to do a great deal of editing after they receive the text from various sources.

All columns on all pages should bottom out to same point. This rule is strictly followed in this newsletter, as in most newspapers (the models from which this design is derived). As you can see in figure 11.12, the pages are carefully aligned at the bottom margin of the grid. This alignment produces a neat, clean tabloid newspaper.

Don't be afraid of white space. White space is achieved primarily by leaving a great deal of space above headlines (see fig. 11.13). Otherwise, the page layouts are very dense. Again, this design strategy deliberately imitates most newspaper designs.

Fig. 11.13. White space above the headlines.

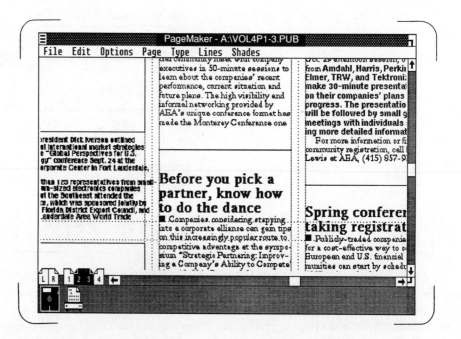

Production Tricks for the Tabloid Newsletter

To produce a tabloid of this size and complexity every month, the production team and editors must use every trick they can to make production as smooth and efficient as possible. The following anecdote helps put this process in perspective.

A tabloid produced by conventional methods had required 200 person-hours for the full production. Expecting to save a great deal of time, the production team switched to desktop publishing. The team members took a one-day class in PageMaker and engaged a designer experienced in PageMaker to build the first template (which took 4 days).

The first issue took more than 400 hours to produce. Much of that time was spent learning how to use PageMaker efficiently and adapting the specifications to PageMaker's options. By the time the team had produced the sixth issue, however, the total production time was reduced to fewer than 40 hours—less than a fourth of the time previously required.

The tips and tricks provided here are not complete "cookbook recipes" for producing this newsletter. Many details have been left out because they were specific to this team's word- processing programs, graphics programs, and editorial standards. The suggestions, however, do provide a good overview of what this type of production entails, and the ideas can be adapted to any large or complex publication project.

Sources of Data

The author's manuscripts come in all forms. Authors in the same building with the editors and production crew deliver the files on disks. Other authors telecommunicate their text through modems. Occasionally, an author submits a manuscript on paper only. The editors work on the files in any word processor available and type the stories that were received on paper. The editors then turn over the files to the production group, along with marked-up thumbnails of the template, indicating where each story should be placed (see fig. 11.14).

If the disk files and telecommunicated files for the text are not already formatted, the production staff members convert the files to their word-processing program and do the formatting. If the files are already formatted in one of the word-processing programs PageMaker supports, the production people place the files in PageMaker. Most word processors cannot handle the wide variety of fonts used in this newsletter (see fig. 11.15), so much formatting is done in PageMaker. In particular, the large initial drop cap used in the opening paragraphs of certain articles must be positioned in PageMaker rather than in the word-processing program.

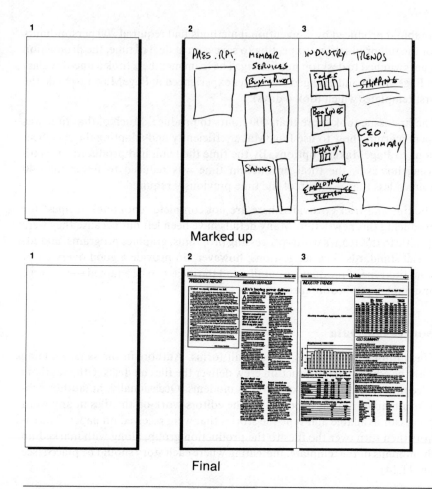

Marked up

Final

Efficiency Tip

When To Request ASCII Text Files

For best and most efficient results, you want the authors to use the same word-processing program that the production team uses. Otherwise, ask the authors to save their files as text-only (ASCII) files and let the production team format the text with a word processor that PageMaker supports.

Logo/banner	Created in Windows Draw and stretched to 160-point Times	
Volume/Isuue ID	14-point Times	

Headlines:

3-col. Headlines   36-point Times Bold, 25-point leading

2-col. Headlines   27-point Times Bold, 24-point leading

1-col. Headlines   18-point Times Bold, auto leading

SUBJECT HEADINGS   24-point Helvetica, all caps

Body Copy   11-point Times, 12-point leading,
Body Copy   3-line initial drop cap,
Body Copy   paragrpahs indented 1 pica
Body Copy

Words highlighted within text   10-point Helvetica Bold, 12-point leading

Large Captions within text   18-point Helvetica Italic, centered,
2-point rule above and below

"INSIDE"   18-point Helvetica Bold Italic, 33-point leading, all caps

Inside text   14-point Helvetica Bold italic, 14-point leading,
extra line between paragraphs
Photo Captions   8-point Helvetica Bold, 9-point leading
Subheads within articles   12-point Times Bold

Fig. 11.15. Type specifications table for tabloid newsletter.

The Template for the Tabloid Newsletter

The "Page setup" dialog box in figure 11.16 shows that this newsletter has a tabloid format. Not all laser printers can handle the narrow inside and outside margins (0.33 inches); some printers force a minimum margin of 0.5 inches. The template is set up initially with three pages; the first page, the second page, and a special page of graphs. Additional pages are added when needed. (As is evident in the production steps, which follow, this 12-page newsletter can be developed as several PageMaker publications so that the production team can distribute the work more equally.)

Fig. 11.16. "*Page setup*"
dialog box for tabloid
newsletter.

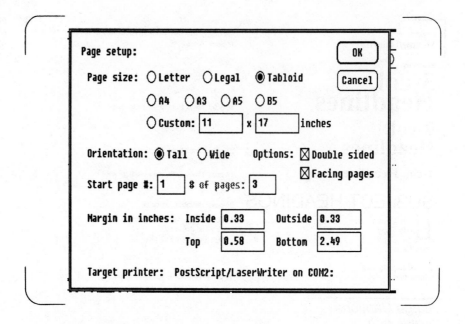

Divide a 12-Page Tabloid into Several PageMaker Files

The template is set up as a three-page document. Each page or series of consecutive pages is started from this template, but a single issue is stored as three or more different PageMaker files (see fig. 11.17). With this arrangement, a group of people can share the production and editing tasks.

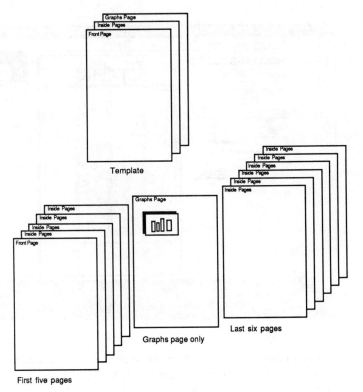

Fig. 11.17. Developing the tabloid newsletter in several files.

The template for this complex document is an essential production aid for each issue (see fig. 11.18). The master pages are set up as 4-column formats with running heads. Standard elements, including ruled lines, 13 different text place holders, and several spacing guides, are stored on the pasteboard. Page 1 of the template includes the banner, a box where the contents are listed, and a ruler guide for starting articles on this page. Page 2 includes the masthead information, and page 3 contains drop-shadow boxes where graphs and tables will be placed.

Building the template requires more than 40 hours. The design is based on specifications that match previous issues done using traditional typesetting and pasteup. This number of hours includes time to test building one page, printing it by using PageMaker's "Tile" feature, and writing up specifications to be followed by the production staff and by the authors and editors—who did not previously participate in the typesetting and formatting.

The editors use thumbnails to mark the locations of articles. To create thumbnails, the editors open the template document and use the "Insert pages..."

Fig. 11.18. Template for tabloid newsletter.

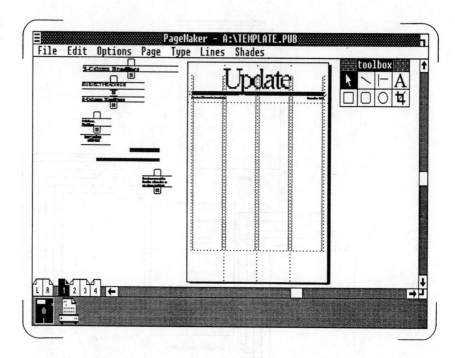

command to create a 12-page empty document. Then they print the empty document with the "Print..." command's "Thumbnails" option (see fig. 11.19).

Fig. 11.19. Thumbnails for tabloid newsletter.

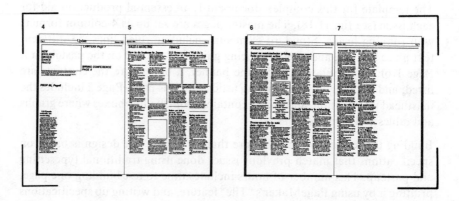

Efficiency Tip

Print Reductions of Each Page Instead of Using Thumbnails

Because the newsletter itself is assembled as several different files and because the tabloid pages are so complex, thumbnails are not practical for viewing finished pages. Using a percentage reduction to print quick miniatures of each finished page produces more helpful results. For example, with PostScript you can print the pages at a 45-percent reduction (using the "Print..." command's "Scaling" option) to fit on one sheet of 8.5-by-11-inch paper. These reductions can be used for control and review purposes but not for detailed proofreading or for final production.

Production Steps for the Tabloid Newsletter

If the production group uses more than one PageMaker file to build the publication, each file (partial publication) must include sequential pages; and the stories must be self-contained within that file. At any given time during the production cycle, the pages or groups of pages may be at different stages in the following sequence of steps. (As mentioned previously, these steps are intended to give you a basis for building your own production techniques.)

1. The staff collects the text files from all contributors.

2. The editorial staff edits each article before passing it to the production group. The editors mark the dummy thumbnails for positioning of articles and graphics.

3. The production staff formats the text if it has not already been formatted.

4. The production staff positions each article and places black boxes where photographs will be printed.

5. A senior editor reviews the first printouts of the composed pages. These pages are printed in pieces on 8.5-by-11-inch paper, using the "Print..." command's "Tile" option. If the copy is too short, the editor adds copy or pull-out quotes to fill space. The editor also makes notes to the production staff if any headlines need to be kerned manually.

6. After each page is laid out and edited so that all columns are aligned, a member of the production group scrolls through each column, measuring all spaces around headings and figures against the spacing guide and adding ruled lines around article titles and pull-out quotes. The standard ruled lines are stored on the pasteboard and placed on the pages with the "Copy" and "Paste" commands. Headlines are kerned manually.

7. The final pages are printed full size on a Linotronic 300 typesetter.

Pages with graphs require special handling:

1. Graphs are created by using a spreadsheet graphing program to create the bars or lines.

2. The graphs are then opened in Freelance® Plus, where additional formatting is performed.

3. The graphs are placed in PageMaker, where drop-shadow borders mark the positions, as shown in figure 11.20.

Fig. 11.20. Using drop-shadow boxes to mark the positions of graphs that appear in every issue.

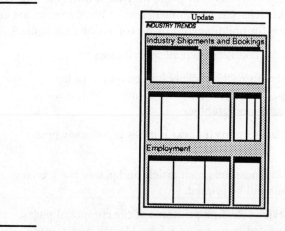

Preparation of Pages for Reproduction

The final full-size typeset pages are marked for the printer. Tissue overlays identify elements that are printed in different colors and show where half-tones must be stripped in (see fig. 11.21). The photographs supplied to the printer may need to be marked for sizing and cropping.

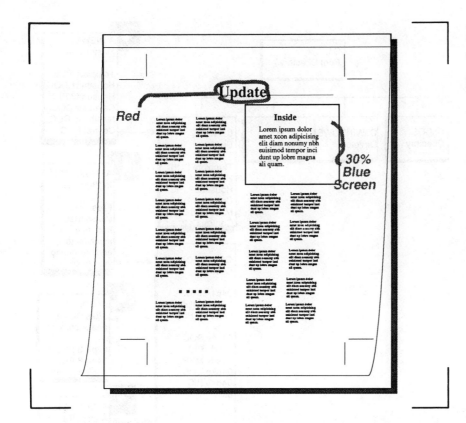

Fig. 11.21. *Using tissue overlays to show the printer how to separate the image for color printing.*

Disk-File Organization for the Tabloid Newsletter

Besides the template, the second factor in making each issue's production run smoothly is a carefully controlled organization of disk files (see fig. 11.22). The team must be able to use the file names to distinguish one article from another within an issue. The team also must be able to distinguish between the latest version of an article and earlier versions that may have been left on disks or archived.

In naming files, the team follows certain conventions:

- All names begin with the issue number. (Volume number is not necessary because it can be deduced from the date of the file.)

- Signed articles are identified with the author's initials (preferably three letters).

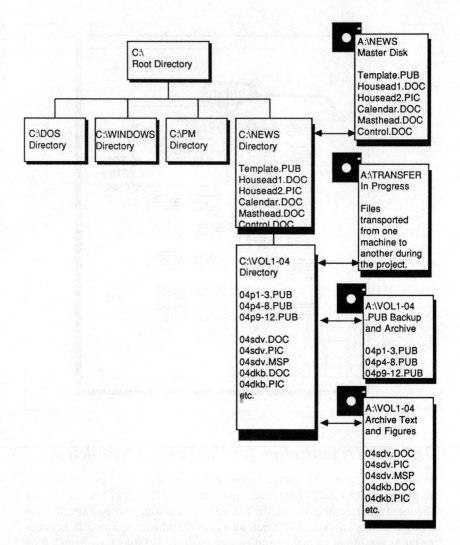

Fig. 11.22. *Disk-file organization for tabloid newsletter.*

- Text and graphics files are distinguished by suffix only. (See Chapter 5 for a list of graphics file suffixes and their meanings.) The PageMaker file names include issue number and page number(s).

The members of the production team keep current versions of their files on their hard disks in separate subdirectories set up for each issue. The staff members remove files from their hard disks whenever they send files to another computer for further changes. Each team member has a floppy disk reserved for each issue and backs up each file before sending it on. The members also keep current the date and time stored in their systems so that questions about the most recent version of a file can be resolved by looking at the date of the file.

After the issue is printed, all current files are copied from all hard disks to one or more floppy disks and stored with other archived data.

Summary

The two examples presented in this chapter illustrate two extremes of production. The short newsletter has a relatively simple format and relaxed standards; the newsletter is easy to produce by a team whose primary function is *not* publishing. The tabloid-size newsletter, on the other hand, involves complex grid variations and strict production standards, which are applied by a team of professionals. The design and production tips provided at the beginning of the chapter and illustrated by the examples give you a good overview of what is involved in producing a newsletter, magazine, or newspaper. You can apply these ideas to your own newsletter production and other publications.

Creating Overhead Transparencies, Slides, and Handouts

12

Desktop publishing usually is associated with books, reports, newsletters, and magazines; but PageMaker is also an excellent tool for creating presentation materials. You can develop tables and graphs in other programs, place them in PageMaker, and then add captions and topic summaries with PageMaker's text tool. To produce overhead transparencies, you can use a laser printer to print the images on clear acetate. If you want 35mm slides for a presentation, you can print the images on paper and then photograph the printed sheets.

Some examples presented in this chapter (see fig. 12.1) are designed specifically for use as overhead transparencies or slides. Other examples are designed as printed handouts, but all examples all share the following characteristics:

- Presentation materials consist of a series of similar parts.

- The items are primarily graphics, and words usually appear in a large type font.

- Each item requires some extra touches in PageMaker that are not possible in the graphics programs that create the graphs and diagrams.

Fig. 12.1. *Examples from the documents in this chapter.*

Example 12.1

Administrative Uses of Personal Computers

Number of Respondents: 30

Including Word Processing Department

Small business
and professionals—100%

Figure 3.2

Example 12.2

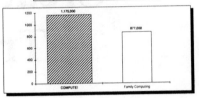

HOME PERSONAL COMPUTERS
Household Owners
SPRING 1986 MRI

	Total%	COMPUTE!	Family Computing
UNWGT	2,480	134	123
(000)	19,958	1175	877
VERT%	11.70	61.91	57.81
HORZ%	100.00	5.89	4.39
INDEX	100	529	494

Graphed by Readership

Example 12.3

Different System Configurations

Hard disk   **Two 800k disk drives**   **One 800k disk drive**

Hard disk:
• *Copy of the PageMaker program*
• *System folder*
• *All text and graphics files*

Internal disk drive:
• *Copy of the PageMaker program*
• *System folder*

External disk drive:
• *All text and graphics files to be placed.*

Disk 1:
• *Copy of the PageMaker program*
• *System folder*
• *PageMaker document*

Swap disk 2:
• *All text and graphics files*

You will always need to have the PageMaker Master disk for verification when you start the program.

Course Objectives

• Place text and graphic objects from other programs into PageMaker

• Use PageMaker's text and graphics tools

• Set up page margins, column guides, and non-printing snap-to guides

• Set up master pages

• Open, save, and print PageMaker documents

• Use PageMaker's menu commands

Example 12.4

HOME/PERSONAL COMPUTERS
SPRING 1986 MRI

		TOTALS	READ BYTE	READ COMPUTE	READ FAMILY COMPUTING	READ PERSONAL COMPUTING
TOTALS	UNWGT	20330	231	218	186	342
	(000)	170699	1466	1898	1517	2655
	VERT%	100.00	100.00	100.00	100.00	100.00
	HORZ%	100.00	0.86	1.11	0.89	1.5
	INDEX	100	100	100	100	100
HOUSEHOLD OWNS	UNWGT	2480	114	134	103	158
	(000)	19958	782	1175	877	1321
	VERT%	11.70	53.34	61.91	57.81	49.76
	HORZ%	100.00	3.92	5.89	4.39	6.62
	INDEX	100	456	529	494	425
APPLE COMPUTER	UNWGT	309	22	17	14	24
	(000)	2471	162	209	141	181
	VERT%	1.45	11.05	11.01	9.29	6.82
	HORZ%	100.00	6.56	8.46	5.71	7.32
	INDEX	100	763	760	642	471
COMMODORE	UNWGT	738	25	63	41	51
	(000)	6206	222	537	376	575
	VERT%	3.64	15.14	28.29	24.79	21.66
	HORZ%	100.00	3.58	8.65	6.06	9.26
	INDEX	100	416	778	681	595
IBM	UNWGT	205	19	5	6	21
	(000)	1557	95	34	50	122
	VERT%	0.91	6.48	1.79	3.30	4.60
	HORZ%	100.00	6.10	2.18	3.21	7.84
	INDEX	100	710	196	361	503

Efficiency Tip

Use Thumbnails To Help Prepare Your Presentation

Use the "Thumbnails" option in the "Print..." command dialog box to print a capsule summary of the topics for reference during the presentation (see fig. 12.2). Make notes on the thumbnails about the points you want to emphasize. (This option is available on PostScript and DDL printers only.)

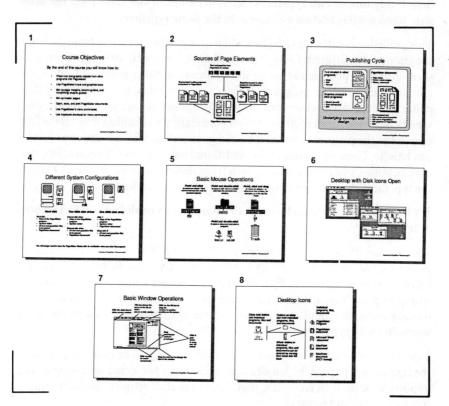

Fig. 12.2. Thumbnails used to help prepare presentation notes.

Design Principles

The design principles that apply to presentation materials are derived from a mix of basic design traditions, advertising guidelines, training theory, and the technology of projecting images for an audience. The principles emphasized in this chapter concern the selection and sizes of typefaces, the amount and content of text, and the sizes of the images themselves.

Several guidelines are dictated by the dimensions of the final product; for instance, slides are usually 35mm by 25mm. Other guidelines are borrowed from the advertising industry because the best presentation materials are similar to billboards and display ads. The application of these principles to presentation materials is described generally in this section. In the "Examples" section, the same principles are repeated and applied to specific examples.

Select only one or two typefaces. Keep headings of the same level the same size. Keep similar text on all images in the same typeface.

This guideline is difficult to follow when graphic images come from different programs with different fonts. The number of fonts available in your spreadsheet-graphing program is probably smaller than the number of fonts available in your drawing program. PageMaker probably has more fonts than either your spreadsheet or your drawing program. Before you make the final specifications for a set of presentation materials, you should know all the font options of the programs you will be using, as well as which fonts your printer can handle. Consult Chapter 9 for additional suggestions for controlling type specifications when images are drawn from several sources. Table 12.1 shows the typefaces that are commonly used in presentation materials.

Try to keep the text on each overhead transparency or slide down to 25 words or fewer.

The number 25 is somewhat arbitrary. You set different limits for different purposes; but, generally, brevity increases effectiveness. Billboard designers follow a rule of not exceeding 7 words if possible—and billboards have a strong impact. You also may have seen the other extreme and had difficulty reading and understanding slides and overhead transparencies with too many words in small type.

You may decide that your limit is 50 words per page—or more, especially if the text is on a page to be handed out rather than projected on a screen. The important point is to recognize that these materials require special attention to word count and point size.

Give graphs descriptive titles.

Your titles should include enough information to be meaningful. The graph title "1987 Income," for example, conveys little information. Use more descriptive titles, like those used in newspapers and magazines. For example, the title "1987 Income Shows Increased Widget Sales Relative to Other Categories" lets viewers understand the purpose of the graph.

Table 12.1
Typefaces Used in Tables, Graphs, and Overhead Transparencies
(Y = used; N = not used)

Typefaces	Tables	Graphs	Overheads/Slides
ITC American Typewriter	Y	Y	Y
ITC Avant Garde	Y	Y	Y
ITC Benguiat	N	N	N
ITC Bookman	N	Y	Y
Courier	Y	N	N
ITC Friz Quadrata	N	N	Y
ITC Galliard	Y	Y	Y
ITC Garamond	Y	Y	Y
Glypha	Y	Y	N
Goudy Old Style	N	N	Y
Helvetica	Y	Y	Y
ITC Korinna	Y	Y	N
ITC Lubalin Graph	Y	Y	Y
ITC Machine	Y	Y	Y
ITC New Baskerville	N	N	N
New Century Schoolbook	Y	Y	Y
Optima	Y	Y	Y
Palatino	Y	Y	Y
ITC Souvenir	N	N	Y
Times	Y	Y	Y
Trump Mediaeval	Y	Y	Y
ITC Zapf Chancery	N	N	Y

For images that will be projected as slides or overhead transparencies, use large point sizes for the text.

For overhead transparencies, one rule of thumb is that the image on the paper (not the projected image) should be easy to read from approximately 10 feet (see fig. 12.3). For most audiences, this rule means that important words should be set no smaller than 36 or 24 points.

For slides, an image on 8.5-by-11-inch paper should be easy to read from 7 feet (see fig. 12.4). This rule means that the text is 18 or 24 points in size, slightly smaller than the text on overhead transparencies.

Transparencies, Slides, and

Fig. 12.3. Printout for overhead transparencies—readable at 10 feet.

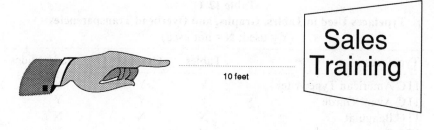

Fig. 12.4. Printout for slides—readable at 7 feet.

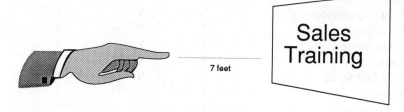

For overhead transparencies, fit all images into a 7-by-9-inch area.

This rule applies particularly to framed overhead transparencies because a transparency frame usually has a 7.5-by-9.5-inch window (see fig. 12.5). You can specify a page size of 7 by 9 inches in the "Page setup" dialog box, or you can simply set the margins of an 8.5-by-11-inch page to confine the text and graphics to a 7-by-9-inch area.

Fig. 12.5. Overhead transparency proportions.

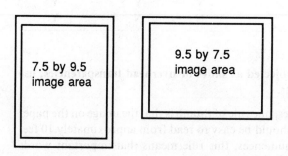

The 7-by-9-inch ratio is a good guide to follow even when the images will not be framed. Viewing conditions may restrict some people in the audience from seeing the edges of the overhead, but the center of the image will be visible to everyone in the room. If you want the option of using the same visual material in both slides and transparencies, these measurements also approximate the

24mm-by-35mm proportions used in slides. Another advantage of these presentation sizes is that your graphic images benefit from being surrounded by white space.

For materials to be made into slides, set all images within an area of approximately 3:2 proportions.

Frames for 35mm slides usually have a 35mm-by-24mm clear window. You should design your graphics—especially slide images with a ruled border—within this 3:2 proportion. If you are not using 35mm film for your slides, you will need to calculate the right proportions based on the final size of your slide window. Use the following formula:

$$\frac{\text{slide width Page}}{\text{slide height}} = \frac{\text{Maker image width}}{\text{PageMaker image height}}$$

For example, if you decide to use a width of seven inches for your images, you can calculate the proportional height by using this formula:

$$\text{PageMaker image height} = \text{PageMaker image width} \times \left(\frac{\text{slide height}}{\text{slide width}} \right)$$

If possible, design all the images in a series to use the same page orientation—choosing either "Tall" or "Wide" in the "Page setup" dialog box.

This consistency makes the production steps easier than mixing "Tall" and "Wide" pages in a series. If the material being presented is not consistent in orientation, you must develop the presentation materials in two or more different PageMaker publications.

Production Tips

The production tips in this chapter are specifically applicable to presentation materials that will be projected on a screen for an audience. The tips tell you ways to produce material easily and to get high-quality results. By observing these tips, you frequently can eliminate one or more steps in the entire production process, thereby increasing efficiency and decreasing time spent in production.

The reasons for applying these tips are described generally in this section. Some of the same tips are repeated with the examples, accompanied by explanations of their specific applications to that example.

Use automatic page numbering to number the set in sequence.

You can use PageMaker's automatic page-numbering feature to number the images used in a presentation. In this way, you can easily find the images in the PageMaker document when you want to update selected materials. If you do not want the numbers to show when you are projecting the images, use a small point size (12 points or less) and place the page numbers at the bottom of the image area (see fig. 12.6). This trick is used in all the examples in this chapter.

If the sequence changes for particular presentations, or if some presentations may be shortened by omitting selected images, you can still use the automatic page-numbering feature to number the master set and print alternate numbers on each page in the same small font.

Fig. 12.6. Automatic page numbering for a set of presentation materials.

If you use a laser printer for the final output, use a gray screen rather than solid black areas for the best projection image.

If your printer's toner cartridge is at its peak performance, you can get solid black areas to print solidly on special laser paper. Even with a good cartridge, however, black areas may print unevenly when you print directly on acetate sheets for transparencies. This unevenness is exaggerated when the image is projected. You can reduce the effects of uneven toner by using gray fill patterns instead of black (see fig. 12.7).

To create overlays, copy the complete image on several pages; then delete portions of the image from each page.

To create a set of overhead transparencies with overlays, first create the whole image on one page. Copy the complete image to subsequent pages—one for each overlay. Then go back to the first page and delete the parts of the image

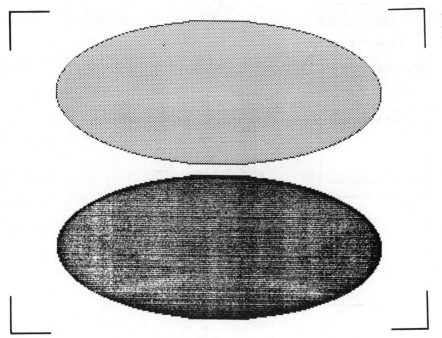

Fig. 12.7. Comparison of printed black and gray areas.

that will appear on the overlays. On each following page, delete all parts of the image except what will appear on that single overlay. One example of a set of overlays is shown in figure 12.8.

You can achieve a similar effect when you prepare slides. Build the full image first; then copy the complete image to subsequent pages. Keep the full version on the last page in the series, and delete selected elements from each page that precedes the full image (see fig. 12.9).

To summarize, pages in a series for overlays of overhead transparencies do not repeat the same elements, but each page in a series of slides repeats elements from the previous pages and adds new elements.

Fig. 12.8. Building a
series of overhead
overlays.

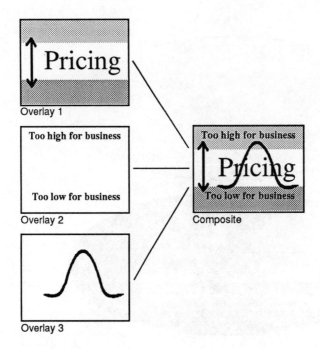

Overlay 1

Overlay 2

Overlay 3

Composite

Fig. 12.9. Building a
series of slides.

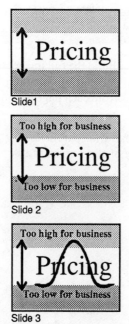

Slide1

Slide 2

Slide 3

Examples

The examples used in this chapter have been selected to demonstrate a variety of formats and to illustrate various applications of the general design principles and production tips discussed in the preceding sections. The four examples presented here are the following:

12.1. A Series of Transparencies of Graphs in the Same Format

12.2. A Handout Showing Tabular Figures and Graphs

12.3. A Series of Transparencies with Varied Formats

12.4. A Handout Showing a Table with Shaded Columns

Example 12.1. A Series of Transparencies of Graphs in the Same Format

This series of pie graphs is designed to report the results of a survey or questionnaire. Each pie graph represents a different question and the responses of a specific set of respondents. The production tips for this example can be applied to many similar situations, such as a series of sales reports on the same list of products (in which each pie represents a different geographical region or a different purchasing group), a series of stock reports (in which each line graph represents a different stock), or a series of profit-and-loss projections for a new company or a new product (in which each graph represents a different set of assumptions about advertising expenses, pricing, and market penetration).

Description of a Series of Transparencies of Graphs in the Same Format

This overhead presentation is composed of a series of pie graphs generated with a spreadsheet graphing program (see fig. 12.10). The percentage labels and part of the legend were retained from the graphing program, but the graph title and legend tags were cropped off when the image was placed in PageMaker. The legend text, graph titles, and captions then were added with PageMaker's text tools.

Fig. 12.10. Printout of
pages of series of graphs
in the same format.

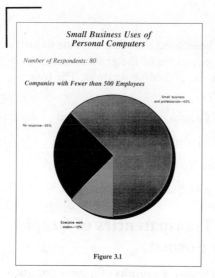

**Small Business Uses of
Personal Computers**

Number of Respondents: 80

Companies with Fewer than 500 Employees

Small business
and professionals—63%

No response—25%

Executive work
station—12%

Figure 3.1

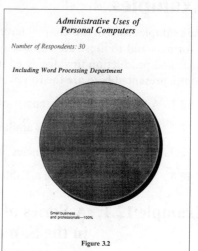

**Administrative Uses of
Personal Computers**

Number of Respondents: 30

Including Word Processing Department

Small business
and professionals—100%

Figure 3.2

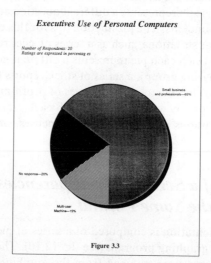

Executives Use of Personal Computers

Number of Respondents: 20
Ratings are expressed in percentages

Small business
and professionals—65%

No response—20%

Multi-user
Machine—15%

Figure 3.3

Design Principles for a Series of Transparencies of Graphs in the Same Format

All the design principles described at the beginning of this chapter are applied in this report. The choice of typefaces and the size of the type are especially important in these transparencies.

Select only one or two typefaces. Keep headings of the same level the same size. Keep similar text on all images in the same typeface. In this example, the choice of fonts in the spreadsheet graphing program is the limiting factor. The percentage labels around each pie graph are preserved from the graphing program because typing and locating the labels in PageMaker would be too time-consuming. The legend text and graph titles are typed in PageMaker in larger type sizes than those available with the graphing program.

For images that will be projected as slides or overhead transparencies, use large point sizes for the text. As already mentioned, the graphing program's titles are not large enough. PageMaker's tools are used to add text in order to get the larger type sizes required for presentations.

Production Tricks for a Series of Transparencies of Graphs in the Same Format

Producing transparencies is easy in PageMaker. The process is the same as producing any publication. Normally, you will use only one template. For the best results, you need to be especially careful about printer settings.

If you use a laser printer for the final output, use a gray screen rather than solid black areas for the best projection image. The drop-shadow around each pie is filled with a 40-percent screen ("40%" on PageMaker's Shades menu). This arrangement eliminates the risk of uneven toner that could occur if the drop-shadow were solid black (see figs. 12.10 and 12.13).

The Template for a Series of Transparencies of Graphs in the Same Format

The "Page setup" dialog box is used to set the margins that show the limits of the image area on each page (see fig. 12.11). The margin settings force an image area of 6 by 8 inches—well within the 7-by-9-inch limits recommended for transparencies.

The master page for this series includes the text of the legend, positioned to match the legend from the graphing program (see fig. 12.12). The graph title on each page is copied from a text block stored on the pasteboard of the template. The drop-shadow circles are created in PageMaker, stored on the pasteboard, and copied to each page.

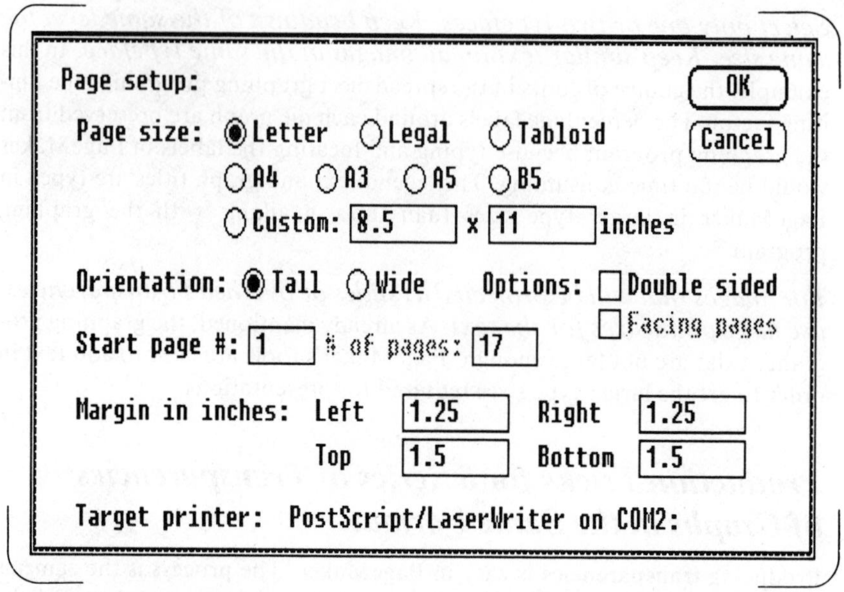

Fig. 12.11. *"Page setup" dialog box for series of graphs in the same format.*

Page setup: (OK)

Page size: ⦿Letter   ○Legal   ○Tabloid   (Cancel)
            ○A4   ○A3   ○A5   ○B5
            ○Custom: [8.5]   x [11]   inches

Orientation: ⦿Tall ○Wide   Options: ☐Double sided
                                         ☐Facing pages

Start page #: [1]   # of pages: [17]

Margin in inches: Left   [1.25]   Right   [1.25]
                    Top   [1.5]   Bottom [1.5]

Target printer: PostScript/LaserWriter on COM2:

Fig. 12.12. *Template for a series of graphs in the same format.*

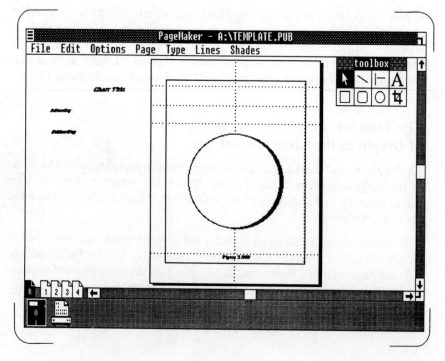

PageMaker - A:\TEMPLATE.PUB
File Edit Options Page Type Lines Shades

toolbox

Production Steps for a Series of Transparencies of Graphs in the Same Format

Creating this series of graphs is not difficult. If you take particular care with the first page, developing the others will be simple. Take the following steps:

1. Determine the content of the presentation.

2. Create one sample graph with the graphing program and place the sample in PageMaker to check the size and position of the image. Based on this test, refine the specifications to be used in the graph program (if your graph program lets you adjust final graph size or font sizes).

3. Begin to build the template for the series by typing the legend text and page numbers on the master page. Draw a border around the image area and set guidelines for positioning the graphs. Type text in the size to be used for each graph title, and place the text on the pasteboard.

4. Create the drop-shadow using PageMaker's circle tool and place the drop-shadow on the page.

5. Place the sample graph (from step 2), and check the position of the legend text and the size of the drop-shadows (see fig. 12.13). Make sure that the longest graph title fits on the page.

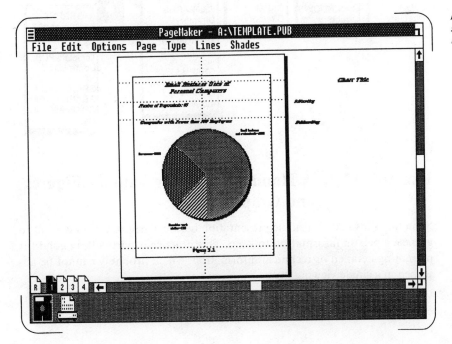

Fig. 12.13. Checking one sample graph against the template.

6. Create all the graphs with a graphing program that can transfer to PageMaker.

7. Place each graph in PageMaker. Copy the title text block from the pasteboard, and type the current graph title before cropping the graph title and legend text from the graphing program.

8. Remember to save the file each time you complete a page.

Disk-File Organization for a Series of Transparencies of Graphs in the Same Format

All graphs are saved under file names that are shown in the proper sequence in the alphabetical listing in the "Place..." command dialog box. This order means using 01, 02, 10, and so on, instead of 1, 2, 10, and on (see fig. 12.14). Otherwise, for example, the file GRAPH11 would precede GRAPH2 in the list of figures in the "Place..." command dialog box.

Fig. 12.14. *Disk-file organization for series of graphs.*

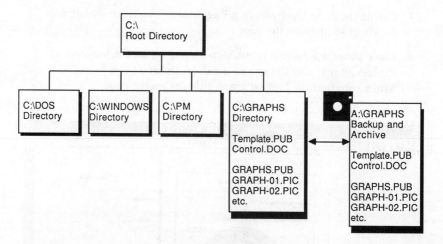

Example 12.2. A Handout Showing Tabular Figures and Graphs

Sometimes instead of a single presentation before a group, you may want to give each person information to keep. This practice is particularly good for presenting detailed or technical information, which probably cannot be absorbed in a single viewing.

Description of Handout with Tabular Figures and Graphs

The images in this example are designed as handouts rather than overhead transparencies or slides. The goal is to show a table of statistics on the same page as a graph of those values (see fig. 12.15)—a combination that is not easy to achieve with a spreadsheet program alone. (In fact, most spreadsheets do not support this feature.)

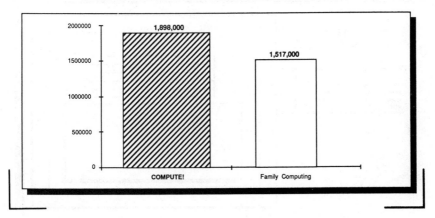

TOTAL ADULTS
Magazine Readership
SPRING 1986 MRI

	Totals	COMPUTE!	Family Computing
UNWGT	20330	218	186
(000)	170599	1898	1517
VERT%	100.00	100.00	100.00
HORZ%	100.00	1.11	.89
INDEX	100	100	100

Fig. 12.15. Printout of page containing a table and graphs.

Design Principles for Handout with Tabular Figures and Graphs

All but one of the design principles given at the beginning of this chapter have been applied to this set of handouts. The exception is that you do not need to keep the text down to 25 words or fewer. In this case, you may have more than 25 words on each image if you count the entries in the tables of numbers. These figures are set in a small point size in order to leave white space on the pages. The small sizes are acceptable because these materials are handouts rather than overheads.

Production Tricks for Handout with Tabular Figures and Graphs

The production tricks used for these handouts are different from those given at the beginning of this chapter. In the description of the template, however, and in the steps for production, you will find valuable instructions and shortcuts.

The Template for Handout with Tabular Figures and Graphs

The template in this case includes a drop-shadowed ruled grid on the master page (for the tabbed text) and a drop-shadow border for the graphs. The numbers themselves are set up as tabbed dummy text stored on the paste-board along with dummy text for the graph titles (see fig. 12.16). Ruler guides on the master page mark the positions of the title and table.

Fig. 12.16. The template for combined table and graph.

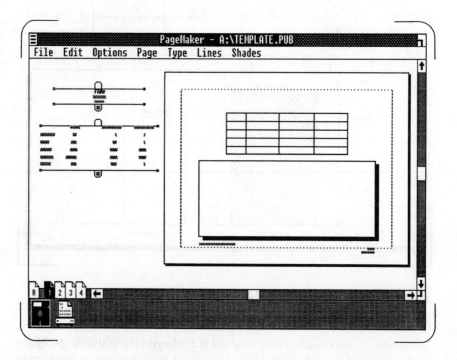

Production Steps for Handout with Tabular Figures and Graphs

Some of the production steps for the series of transparencies also apply to these handouts. Combining tabular material with graphs, however, requires additional steps.

1. Determine the content of the presentation.

2. Begin building the template for the series. Create the drop-shadowed grid using PageMaker's square-corner and perpendicular-line tools. Place the grid on the master page.

3. Type the tabbed numbers as a text block using dummy numbers, and set the tabs to match the grid. Place the tabbed dummy numbers on the pasteboard.

4. Create one sample graph with the drawing program, and place the sample in PageMaker to check the size and position of the image. Based on this test, refine the specifications for the drawing program.

5. Make sure that the longest graph title fits in the area allowed before you specify the type size for the titles.

6. Create all the graphs with the drawing program.

    Because these graphs are all bar graphs and can be created easily in a drawing program that offers a wide range of formatting options, a spreadsheet graph program is not used. A template file is created with the drawing program and copied for each bar graph (see fig. 12.17). The template includes all the basic elements. Only the length of each bar needs to be adjusted.

7. Place each graph in PageMaker. Crop the graph titles entered in the drawing file, and re-create them using the dummy title text from the PageMaker template pasteboard.

8. Copy the tabbed dummy-number text block onto each page; then edit the numbers (see fig. 12.18).

9. Remember to save the file each time you complete a page.

Fig. 12.17. Graph template from the drawing program.

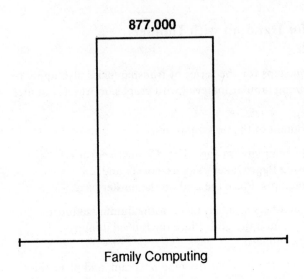

877,000

Family Computing

Fig. 12.18. Tabbed numbers and grid created with PageMaker tools.

	Totals	COMPUTE!	Competitor
UNW GT	75	4	0
(000)	455	45	0
VERT%	0.27	2.37	0.00
HORZ%	100.00	9.89	0.00
INDEX	100	889	0

Disk-File Organization for Handout with Tabular Figures and Graphs

As in Example 12.1, the list of graph-file names in the "Place..." command dialog box is in sequential order (see fig. 12.19). This order means using 01, 02, . . . 10, and so on, rather than 1, 2, . . . 10, and so on. (Otherwise, the file GRAPH11 would precede GRAPH2 in the list of figures in the "Place..." command dialog box.)

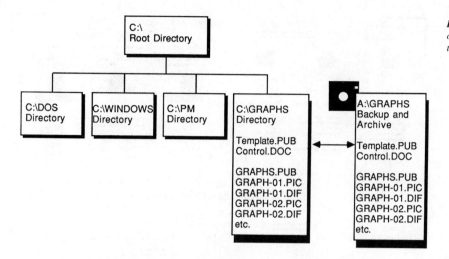

Fig. 12.19. Disk-file organization for series of tables and graphs.

Example 12.3. A Series of Transparencies with Varied Formats

Frequently, you will want to combine different formats in a single presentation. For example, you may need an opening page with a scanned image or a list of points to be presented. Then, you may include graphs, tables of different sizes, and more explanatory material. This example shows you how to combine formats into a unified presentation.

Description of Transparencies with Varied Formats

This set of overheads presents topics and concepts with a variety of formats (see fig. 12.20). The graphics include both figures from a drawing program and bit-mapped screen dumps. The grid has been changed from page to page to accommodate page-wide captions as well as titles and narrow figure labels.

Design Principles for Transparencies with Varied Formats

Most of the design principles listed at the beginning of this chapter are demonstrated in this set of transparencies. Two exceptions, however, merit some discussion because of the nature of this example. As mentioned previously, guidelines are just that: guidelines. At times, you will have valid reasons for exceptions.

Fig. 12.20. Examples of varying formats in a single presentation.

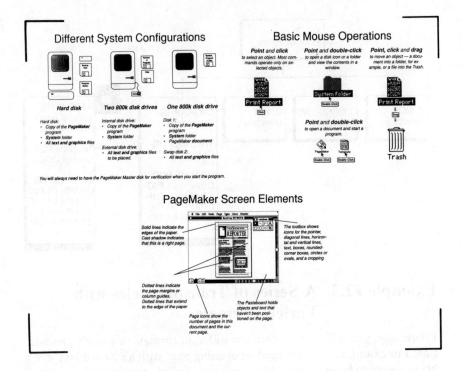

Try to keep the text on each overhead down to 25 words or fewer. The number was extended to 50 words to accommodate some of the detailed bulleted lists and figure captions. This exception to the rule is acceptable in this case because of the classroom setting in which these transparencies are used. Each transparency remains projected on the screen for several minutes as the instructor describes the concepts in detail.

For images that will be projected as slides or overhead transparencies, use large point sizes for the text. The smallest point size used on these transparencies is 16-point (see fig. 12.21). In all these figures, Helvetica is used in four different sizes: 40-, 26-, 20-, and 16-point. The relatively small 16-point captions are still easy to read because Helvetica is a sans serif typeface with individual characters that are actually larger than the same characters in 16-point Times.

Figure Title

40-point Helvetica, centered

Subhead

26-point Helvetica, flush left

Text in bulleted lists

20-point Helvetica, flush left

Captions

16-point Helvetica Italic

Fig. 12.21. Type specifications table for transparency with varied columns.

Production Tricks for Transparencies with Varied Formats

An important trick is using automatic page numbering to number the set (as in every example in this chapter). The other primary production trick is to use the "Column guides..." command to change from one column to four columns as needed for each transparency (see the production steps).

The Template for Transparencies with Varied Formats

The template, shown in figure 12.22, consists of a master page with the basic grid laid out in ruler guides. Dummy text for each type of element is stored on the pasteboard. A spacing guide is provided for positioning text and graphics on a page. The running foot on the master page includes the page numbers.

Production Steps for Transparencies with Varied Formats

The steps for producing this series of transparencies are quite similar to those for developing other transparencies. Before you begin production, create the text blocks you need and store them in the pasteboard. Then proceed to do the following steps:

1. Develop the complete list of figures and decide which ones require placement of files from the drawing program or bit-mapped screen dumps.

2. Determine the maximum size for each figure; draw the figures to size in the drawing program.

3. Make the screen dumps using a screen-dump utility.

Fig. 12.22. *The template for transparencies with varied formats.*

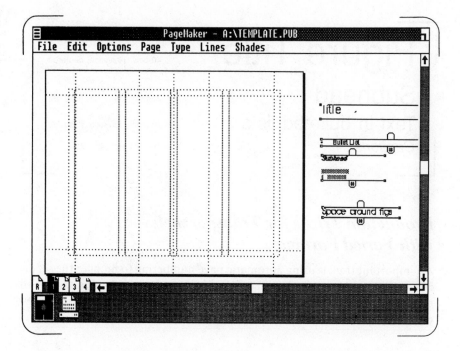

4. Open the PageMaker template and begin building each page. Clone the main-heading text from the pasteboard first.

5. Place figures from other programs on each page before typing the captions; then clone the quarter-page-width text blocks from the pasteboard and type the appropriate text.

6. Make a rough layout of figures with captions to decide how many vertical grid lines are involved; then use the "Column guides..." command to lay out the vertical grid. The column guides help position the figure labels, not define the width of the labels. Figure 12.23 shows different column settings used for positioning figure labels.

7. Determine the final layout of figures with captions and save the file each time you complete a page.

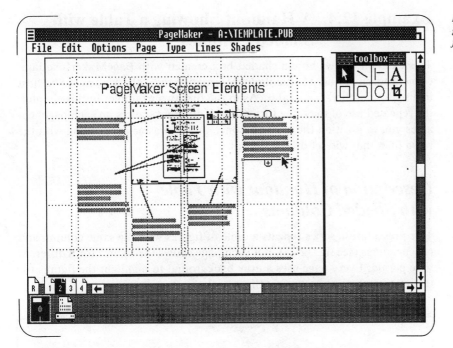

Fig. 12.23. Using column guides to help position figure captions.

Disk-File Organization for Transparencies with Varied Formats

All figures from the drawing program and screen dumps are saved under file names that show in the proper sequence in the alphabetical listing in the "Place..." command dialog box. This order means using 01, 02, . . . 10, and so on, rather than 1, 2, . . . 10, and so on (see fig. 12.24).

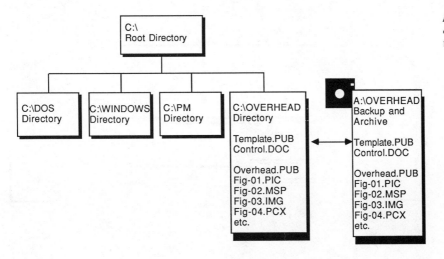

Fig. 12.24. Disk-file organization for series with changing formats.

Example 12.4. A Handout Showing a Table with Shaded Columns

This example shows how a shaded box created with PageMaker's square-corner tool can be used to highlight information that otherwise might be "lost in a sea of numbers" in a table. As in the first two examples in this chapter, the repeated use of the same format (with different figures on each page) enables you to position the gray box once on the master page, along with the ruled lines that will set off the figures.

Description of Handout with Table with Shaded Columns

This presentation series repeats a table of figures with the same column and row headings (see fig. 12.25), but each page shows the figures for a different time period. Every page uses a gray background to highlight the figures for the presenter's product against those of the competitors.

Fig. 12.25. Printout of tables with shaded columns.

HOME/PERSONAL COMPUTERS
SPRING 1986 MRI

		TOTALS	READ BYTE	READ COMPUTE	READ FAMILY COMPUTING	READ PERSONAL COMPUTING
TOTALS						
	UNWGT	20330	231	218	186	342
	(000)	170599	1486	1898	1517	2655
	VERT%	100.00	100.00	100.00	100.00	100.00
	HORIZ%	100.00	0.86	1.11	0.89	1.5
	INDEX	100	100	100	100	100
HOUSEHOLD OWNS						
	UNWGT	2480	114	134	103	156
	(000)	19958	782	1175	877	1321
	VERT%	11.70	52.34	61.91	57.81	49.76
	HORIZ%	100.00	3.92	5.89	4.39	6.62
	INDEX	100	456	529	494	425
APPLE COMPUTER						
	UNWGT	339	22	17	14	24
	(000)	2471	162	209	141	181
	VERT%	1.45	11.05	11.01	9.29	6.82
	HORIZ%	100.00	6.56	8.46	5.71	7.32
	INDEX	100	763	760	642	471
COMMODORE						
	UNWGT	736	25	63	41	51
	(000)	6208	222	537	376	575
	VERT%	3.64	15.14	28.29	24.79	21.66
	HORIZ%	100.00	3.58	8.65	6.06	9.26
	INDEX	100	416	775	681	595
IBM						
	UNWGT	205	19	8	8	21
	(000)	1557	95	34	50	122
	VERT%	0.91	6.48	1.79	3.30	4.60
	HORIZ%	100.00	6.10	2.18	3.21	7.84
	INDEX	100	710	196	361	503

		TOTALS	READ BYTE	READ COMPUTE	READ FAMILY COMPUTING	READ PERSONAL COMPUTING
GRAPHIC TABLET						
	UNWGT	123	6	6	5	8
	(000)	928	30	30	18	39
	VERT%	0.54	2.05	1.58	1.19	1.47
	HORIZ%	100.00	3.23	3.23	1.94	4.20
	INDEX	100	376	291	216	270
PLOTTER						
	UNWGT	58	3	3	1	3
	(000)	411	21	15	2	15
	VERT%	0.24	1.43	0.79	0.13	0.56
	HORIZ%	100.00	5.11	3.65	0.49	3.65
	INDEX	100	595	328	55	235

For more information on how COMPUTE! best serves your advertising needs in reaching the home market of personal computers owners, please call:

1. *New England & Mid-Atlantic*
   Bernard J. Theobald, Jr   212 315-1665
   Tom Link   212 315-1665

2. *Southeast & Foreign including Canada*
   Harry Blair   919 275-9809

3. *Midwest, Southwest, West & British Columbia*
   Jerry Thompson   Chicago   312 726-6047
   Lucille Dennis   Texas   713 731-2605 • Colorado 303 595-9299 • California 415 348-8222

COMPUTE! Publications Inc
825 Seventh Ave, New York, NY 10019

*Source: Spring 1986 MRI

Production Tricks for Handout with Table with Shaded Columns

One production trick in particular is emphasized in this example:

Type titles and column headings with PageMaker's tools, but use a word processor to prepare the rows of data. In this example, this rule is especially important because the table has so many rows and columns of data. Remember that tabs can be repositioned in PageMaker if needed. The time required to produce this set could double if you use PageMaker alone to prepare all the text.

The Template for Handout with Table with Shaded Columns

The template in this case includes the table title, column headings, and slug at the bottom of the page (see fig. 12.26). A ruled line separates the headings from the rest of the text. Ruler guides show the positions of the rows of data and the time-period subhead. Dummy text for the time-period entry is stored on the pasteboard.

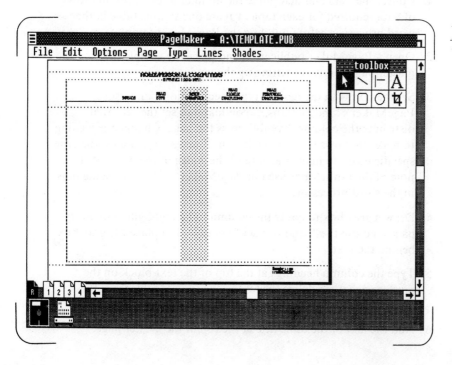

Fig. 12.26. The template for the table with shaded columns.

This design uses Palatino and Helvetica in a limited variety of sizes and styles, as listed in figure 12.27.

Fig. 12.27. Type specifications table for table with shaded columns.

MAIN HEAD	14-point Palatino Bold, 14-point leading, all caps, centered on page
SUBHEAD	12-point Helvetica, all caps, centered on page
COLUMN HEADS	11-point Palatino, all caps, centered in column
Product names	11-point Palatino, 18-point leading, all caps, flush left
Numbers	11-point Helvetica, 12-point leading, flush right in column
Slug at bottom of page	9-point Helvetica, flush left

Production Steps for Handout with Table with Shaded Columns

Because of the columns and the shading, constructing this handout involves more steps than some of the other examples. For good results, work carefully through the following procedure.

1. Collect the data and determine the number of columns and rows of data required for each table. Create one sample table in the word processor before building the PageMaker template.

2. Open a PageMaker publication and place the sample table on the master page for use in setting up the guides.

3. Set the text with the desired type specifications, and use PageMaker's "Indent/tabs..." command to set the tabs that distribute the columns evenly across the page. Change the leading to make the rows fit the page length. If necessary, change the type specifications to make the data fit the width of the page. Make a note of the tab settings used in PageMaker, and set the same tabs in the word processor.

4. Draw a gray box to cover the column to be highlighted on every page, and use the "Send to back" command to place the gray box behind the text.

5. Type the column headings at the top of the text block on the master page; then delete the text of the sample table from the master page.

6. Add the text of the table title at the top of the master page.

7. Type the dummy text for the time period on the pasteboard. Use horizontal ruler lines to mark the positioning of the time-period text and the top of the tabular text on the page.

8. Draw a two-point rule below the column heads. Type the slug at the bottom of the master page.

9. In the spreadsheet, type the data for all pages of the presentation. Save the data as a single file; then save the file as text-only.

10. Format the tabular data with your word processor. Set tabs as noted in step 3. Be sure that the tabs are the same throughout the document.

11. Open the template, and begin placing the tabular data on the first page. If any changes to the tab settings are required, use the text tool to select all the text so that every table is formatted with the same tab settings.

12. Continue placing data on all the pages.

Disk-File Organization for Handout with Table with Shaded Columns

This publication has only five files: the original spreadsheet data, the text-only spreadsheet data, the formatted word-processing file, the PageMaker template, and the finished publication (see fig. 12.28). If this set of materials will be used for this presentation only and not be re-created with different data, the template file can be the final publication, leaving only one PageMaker file in the system.

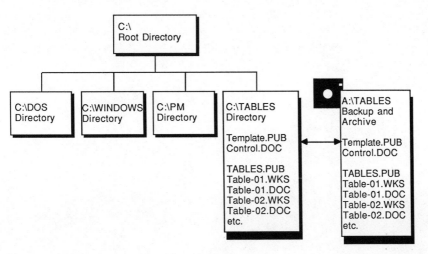

Fig. 12.28. Disk-file organization for handout table with shaded columns.

When archiving the files, you can discard the text-only file. If, however, you expect to change the figures extensively for next year's presentation, save the spreadsheet data. Making new entries down each column to replace the old entries should be easy as long as the row and column headings remain the same. If you expect minor changes, you can update the PageMaker file directly. If you expect to change many entries in scattered rows and columns, save the formatted text file for those changes.

Summary

Transparencies, slides, and handouts are used frequently in almost all business settings. By using PageMaker, you can create effective presentation materials in less time and at less expense than you can using other methods. As demonstrated in the examples in the chapter, you have few limitations as to the formats you can use. You can combine formats in any way that you need. You also can save the files so that you can use the same templates whenever you need to create new transparencies.

Creating Brochures, Price Lists, and Directories

13

This chapter shows you how to use PageMaker to create brochures, price lists, and directories (see fig. 13.1). These documents are described as a group because they all are promotional materials. However, the three types of documents appear in a wide variety of forms.

Brochures are frequently designed to fit on 8.5-by-11-inch paper folded into three panels or as four (or more) 8.5-by-11-inch pages printed on 11-by-17-inch paper and folded in half. These formats are economical because they don't require special cutting and they fit neatly into standard business envelopes. Price lists often are produced in one of these formats unless the lists are very long, in which case they become booklets. In either case, price lists are like brochures in that they usually are mailed in standard business envelopes. Directories and membership lists can be longer than brochures and price lists, and some lists are bound as books rather than stapled as booklets. Regardless of the final trim size, PageMaker easily handles all these formats.

In a PageMaker file, brochures usually are only one or two pages long, although the finished document may be folded into four or more panels, as in Example 13.1. Example 13.2 is four pages long; it is printed on 11-by-17-inch paper and folded in half. Some of the tips in this chapter also can be used to produce longer brochures, such as the booklets in the third and fourth examples in this chapter. (See Chapter 10 for more tips on producing longer documents.)

Price lists can be any number of pages long. The tabbed-list format shown in Example 13.5 can be used for restaurant menus, wine lists, parts lists, inven-

Fig. 13.1. Examples of
documents in this
chapter.

Example 13.1

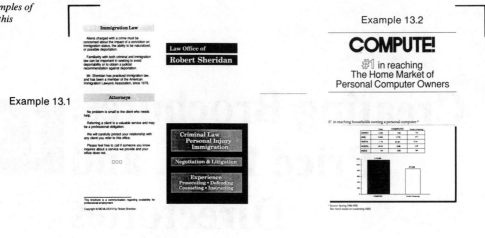

Example 13.2

Example 13.2

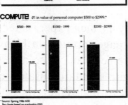

Example 13.3

Example 13.4

Example 13.5

tories, telephone lists, and many other documents. Long price lists, like member lists, can be derived from spreadsheet data or database files. Example 13.3 shows how a database file can be converted to a list.

The longer publications in this category are often a nonstandard size because the final pages may be trimmed and folded. If the directory or price list is more than eight pages, the booklet may be stapled or bound.

Design Principles

Many documents in these categories follow the basic design principles that have been recommended throughout this book (particularly in Chapters 8 through 12), but you will find exceptions to the guides applied to brochures in general (and the publications in Chapter 14). Two design principles merit a full discussion in this chapter: the use of white space and the limit on the number of different typefaces used.

Don't be afraid of white space.

White space is especially important if the publication presents your product or service to your clients and the general public. For example, a price list also may serve as a detailed catalog of your products with illustrations to attract the readers' interest or to explain the value of a special offer. Increased white space can improve the overall effectiveness of the publication as a sales tool.

A reverse effect can occur if you put too many words in a brochure or list of members or services. The final document appears uninviting, and readers may ignore anything written in small type.

When you work with a small format, like many brochures, opening up white space may translate into writing less copy or using fewer illustrations. If you are creating a brochure for your own small business, you probably want to give the readers as much information as possible but, at the same time, save printing and postage costs by holding down the number of pages. If you are writing your own copy, follow the example of professional copy writers, who can get a point across in the number of words specified by the designer. By choosing your words carefully, you can get a few important points across and draw the reader to call for service or come to your store.

Adding pages to your publication design sometimes can be done without significantly increasing the printing or production costs. If you start out with a specific number of pages as a goal and find that this creates a crowded design, you should check into the costs of adding pages.

This guideline is often relaxed in functional reference listings, such as telephone directories for an association, a company, or a department and for long inventory lists or price lists that are used for reference rather than for marketing. If you have a great deal of information in a repetitive format, as in a price list for a large store or warehouse, the reader can find a specific product more easily if the information is compact.

Use only one or two different typefaces in a document.

Table 13.1 shows some of the typefaces used for the types of publications presented in this chapter. Notice that brochures can use almost any typeface, but lists usually are limited to typefaces that are readable in small sizes.

Table 13.1.
Typefaces Used for Brochures, Price Lists, and Directories
(Y = used; N = not used)

Typefaces	Brochures	Price Lists	Directories
ITC American Typewriter	Y	N	N
ITC Avant Garde	Y	Y	Y
ITC Benguiat	Y	N	Y
ITC Bookman	Y	N	N
Courier	N	N	N
ITC Friz Quadrata	Y	N	Y
ITC Galliard	Y	N	Y
ITC Garamond	Y	N	N
Glypha	N	Y	Y
Goudy Old Style	Y	N	N
Helvetica	Y	Y	Y
ITC Korinna	Y	N	N
ITC Lubalin Graph	Y	N	N
ITC Machine	Y	N	N
ITC New Baskerville	Y	Y	N
New Century Schoolbook	N	Y	Y
Optima	Y	N	N
Palatino	Y	Y	Y
ITC Souvenir	Y	N	N
Times	Y	Y	Y
Trump Mediaeval	Y	Y	Y
ITC Zapf Chancery	Y	N	N

The choice of font sets the tone of the piece. Brochures often use decorative or unusual typefaces for the headings and sometimes for the body copy. The typeface you choose can convey a sense of seriousness, elegance, or frivolity. If you are not sure how different typefaces affect the reader, you should stay with the traditional faces rather than experiment with more decorative ones. Traditional typefaces (and their modern adaptations) include American Typewriter, Avant Garde, Bookman, Galliard, Garamond, Goudy, Helvetica, Korinna, Lubalin Graph, New Baskerville, New Century Schoolbook, Optima, Palatino, Times, and Trump Mediaeval. Decorative typefaces include Benguiat, Friz Quadrata, Machine, Souvenir, and Zapf Chancery.

In addition to the preceding principles, also use the following guidelines (discussed in Chapters 10–12) for promotional materials:

Use all capital letters as a deliberate design strategy rather than a method for emphasizing text or showing a heading.

Treat all figures consistently: fonts, line weights, and fill patterns.

Be sure that the space between text and graphics is the same for all figures.

Let the same graphic elements carry the theme throughout the document.

Use ruled lines to help set off the grid of the pages.

All columns on all pages should bottom out to same point.

These principles, and the two discussed in detail in the preceding paragraphs, are repeated with the examples with comments about their applications to the specific examples.

Production Tips

The first production tip has been mentioned repeatedly throughout this book, but the second tip is unique to the list formats in this chapter. The application of these tips to promotional materials is described generally in this section. In the "Examples" section, the same tips are repeated, accompanied by explanations of their applications to the specific examples.

Use templates if you are producing more than one brochure.

If you are designing a series of brochures that describe different products offered by the same company, you can develop one template and clone it for each brochure, as has been recommended throughout this book. On the other hand, if you are a designer with many clients, you may want each brochure you produce to be "unique"; therefore, a template system is not applicable.

Regardless of how the details of the designs change from one brochure to another, you still can create a template for any series of brochures that are the same paper size and have the same number of folds. Figures 13.2 and 13.3 show two different templates for folded brochures. Text typed on each page of the template shows the sequence of the panels when the brochure is folded.

If your laser printer forces a wide margin around large paper sizes, you can solve this problem by using the trick described in Example 13.1. In the template for the four-panel, legal-size brochure, 8.5-by-11-inch paper was used to get around the margins imposed by the laser printer. See "Production Tricks for the Four-Panel Brochure" for an explanation of why this procedure was required.

Fig. 13.2. Templates for three-panel brochures.

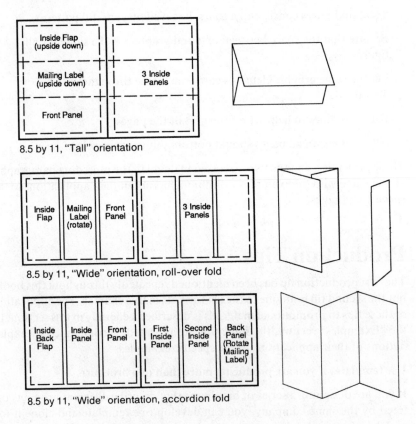

Inside Flap (upside down)

Mailing Label (upside down)

3 Inside Panels

Front Panel

8.5 by 11, "Tall" orientation

Inside Flap | Mailing Label (rotate) | Front Panel | 3 Inside Panels

8.5 by 11, "Wide" orientation, roll-over fold

Inside Back Flap | Inside Panel | Front Panel | First Inside Panel | Second Inside Panel | Back Panel (Rotate Mailing Label)

8.5 by 11, "Wide" orientation, accordion fold

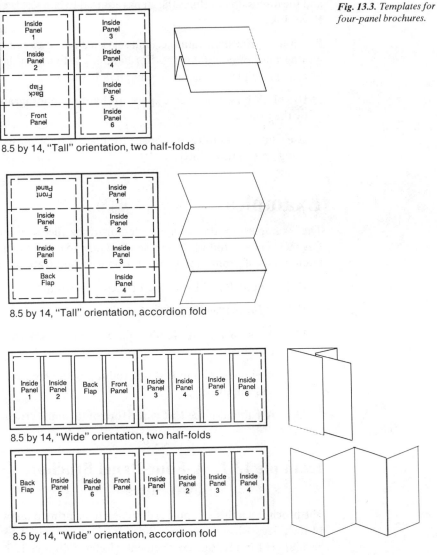

Fig. 13.3. Templates for four-panel brochures.

8.5 by 14, "Tall" orientation, two half-folds

8.5 by 14, "Tall" orientation, accordion fold

8.5 by 14, "Wide" orientation, two half-folds

8.5 by 14, "Wide" orientation, accordion fold

Take a small amount of data from a spreadsheet or database through a test run of the complete production cycle before you complete the specifications for a long list.

If you are converting data from a spreadsheet or a database, you should run a small sample of the data through the production steps before you complete your design specifications. In this way, you can develop a list of specific required steps and learn how many design specifications can or must be handled in the database or spreadsheet. Examples 13.3 and 13.4 used database lists, and the discussion outlines the steps required to convert the data into text for PageMaker.

Brochures, price lists, catalogs, and service directories can be illustrated with photographs or computer art. For handling artwork in these examples, follow the principles presented in Chapters 10 and 11:

Use black boxes to reserve space for halftone photographs dropped in by the printer.

Use white boxes to reserve space for line art to be pasted in before being sent to the printer.

Examples

The examples in this chapter demonstrate the wide range of formats PageMaker can produce. You also learn how to use databases to produce different kinds of promotional and informative publications. The examples are

13.1 A Four-Panel Brochure Printed on Two Sides

13.2. A Four-Page Brochure Consisting of Many Repeated Elements

13.3. A Two-Column Membership Directory Derived from a Database

13.4. A Single-Column List of Products with Descriptions, Prices, and Suppliers

13.5. A Tabloid Price List with Horizontal and Vertical Rules

Example 13.1. A Four-Panel Brochure Printed on Two Sides

The brochure in this example is designed to be printed on two sides of 8.5-by-14-inch (legal-size) paper and folded into four panels. This same design can be adapted for any folded document. (Refer to figures 13.2 and 13.3 and the accompanying discussion to see how templates can be used for folded brochures.)

Description of the Four-Panel Brochure

This brochure may surprise you. Even though the final brochure is printed on 8.5-by-14-inch paper (a size PageMaker supports), the page size is 8.5 by 11 inches. The final printouts are pasted on the 8.5-by-14-inch layout. The screen patterns behind some of the text in the final printed piece are created by a photographic halftoning process (see fig. 13.4). Although PageMaker creates screen patterns, they are used in this example for draft reviews only, not for the final camera-ready printouts. For an explanation of the reasons for these exceptions, see "Production Tricks for the Four-Panel Brochure."

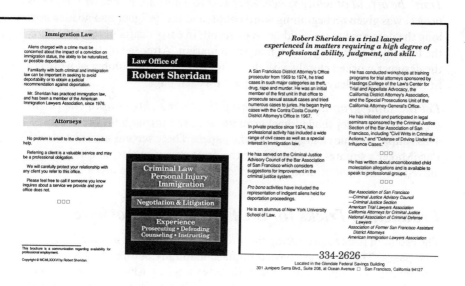

Fig. 13.4. *Printout of pages of four-panel brochure.*

Design Principles for the Four-Panel Brochure

Two design principles merit special mention in this case. The use of white space gives a pleasing uncluttered appearance, and unity is achieved by repeating the graphics.

Don't be afraid of white space. Keep text to a minimum. The writer on this project was given no beginning word count, and the designer had no idea how long the delivered text would be. As a result, in early drafts of this brochure, the text filled every page from margin to margin. After seeing the first draft, the designer worked closely with the writer to reduce the number of words to fit the space and leave more white space on each page.

Let the same graphic elements carry the theme throughout the document. In this case, shaded backgrounds are used throughout the brochure. This simple graphic element unifies the panels. These screens are created with PageMaker's square-corner tool for the draft review cycles, but they are removed for the final printout and added as halftones by the offset printer.

Production Tricks for the Four-Panel Brochure

The essential trick to producing this brochure is to create it as four 8.5-by-11-inch pages. The pages are pasted in place manually before the document is reproduced. You may wonder about the advantage of using an 8.5-by-11-inch page because PageMaker has an option for producing 8.5-by-14-inch pages—the final size for this brochure. The answer is not obvious at first—until you consider the way the different printers work.

This brochure is designed to be printed on a LaserWriter printer, which does not print all the way to the edges of the paper. One edge of the paper is used by the grippers inside the printer. (Offset printers also require 0.25 inch at the edge of the paper for the grippers on the press.) The other three edges of the paper are defined by the PostScript code inside the printer.

Apple's engineers designed the printer this way to conserve memory. The larger the image area, the more memory is used. The Apple engineers, therefore, made the maximum image area for the printer slightly larger than 8 by 10.5 inches—taking about one pica away from the top and bottom of a page, and about 1.5 picas away from the sides. In the printer's terms, this allowance yields a maximum number of pixels per page: 300 pixels per inch, or 90,000 pixels per square inch. When this 90,000-pixel limit is applied to 8.5-by-14-inch pages, the margins around the edge become even wider (see fig. 13.5).

You can test the limits for any printer by opening a PageMaker document, drawing a black or shaded box to cover the entire page, and then printing the page. On an Apple LaserWriter printer, the 8.5-by-11-inch pages have margins of 1 pica at top and bottom and 1.5 picas at the sides. The 8.5-by-14-inch pages have top margins of 3.5 picas and side margins of 5 picas. On a Hewlett-Packard LaserJet printer, these margins are even wider. On a Linotronic typesetter, however, you can print an image larger than 11 by 17 inches without a forced margin around the image.

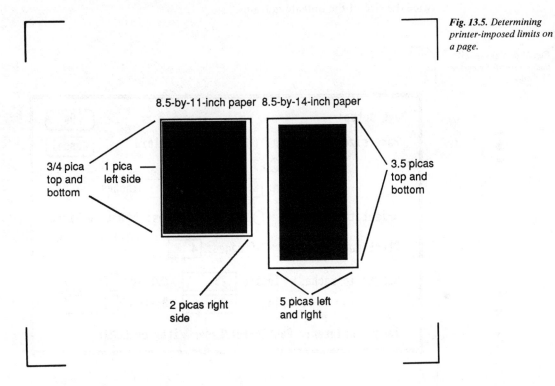

Fig. 13.5. Determining printer-imposed limits on a page.

8.5-by-11-inch paper 8.5-by-14-inch paper

3/4 pica
top and
bottom

1 pica
left side

3.5 picas
top and
bottom

2 picas right
side

5 picas left
and right

These limitations are not a problem for most documents; but when you are designing a small brochure, you want the freedom to come within 0.25 inch of all sides—the same limit that is imposed by the offset printer unless you pay the extra charges for printing bleeds. The problem is eliminated entirely with the Linotronic typesetter, which has no limits and uses 12-inch-wide film.

Figures 13.6 and 13.7 show the dialog box and template for this brochure. Notice that the template uses a page size of 8.5 by 7 inches (half legal size) with "Tall" paper orientation. (If the printer could have handled the full-size page layout, as a Linotronic typesetter can, the template would have been set up with a page size of 8.5 by 14 inches and "Wide" orientation.) So that each panel in the completed folded brochure is centered, the space between columns (entered in the "Column guides..." command dialog box) is specified as twice the size of the outside margins.

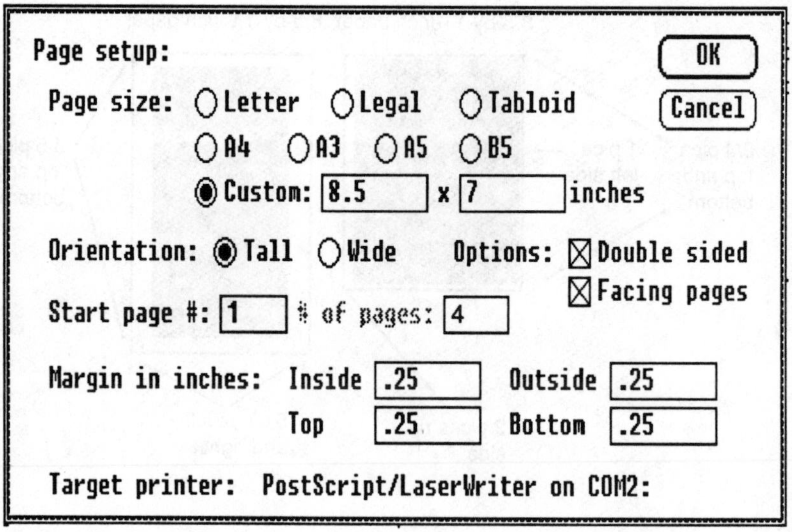

Fig. 13.6. "Page setup" dialog box for four-panel brochure.

Page setup: [OK]

Page size: ◯ Letter   ◯ Legal   ◯ Tabloid   [Cancel]
                ◯ A4   ◯ A3   ◯ A5   ◯ B5
                ⦿ Custom: [8.5]   x [7]   inches

Orientation: ⦿ Tall   ◯ Wide   **Options:** ☒ Double sided
                                                      ☒ Facing pages

Start page #: [1]   # of pages: [4]

Margin in inches: Inside [.25]   Outside [.25]
                          Top [.25]   Bottom [.25]

Target printer: PostScript/LaserWriter on COM2:

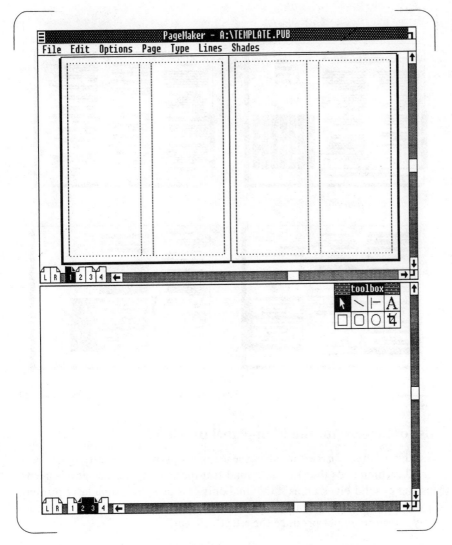

Fig. 13.7. The template for the four-panel brochure.

Efficiency Tip

Bleeding across Paste-Up Lines

When designing pages that will be pasted together for final reproduction, do not cross seamed edges with gray fill patterns: use solid white or black only. Otherwise, when you paste the pages together, you will be able to see the seam where two edges of a gray pattern meet. Figure 13.8 shows thumbnails indicating how the parts of Example 13.1 are printed.

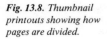

Fig. 13.8. Thumbnail *printouts showing how pages are divided.*

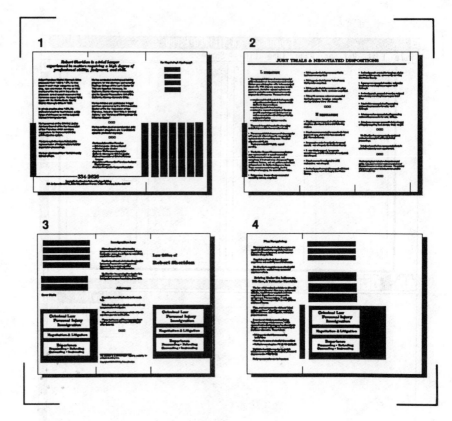

Use of Screens for the Four-Panel Brochure

Another production trick involves the use of gray screens in the design. Chapter 12 recommends that for slides and transparencies, you use gray screens instead of solid black areas if the final output is produced on a laser printer. If you use offset printing to produce a large quantity of brochures, however, gray screens may not produce the effect you want.

If you create gray screens using PageMaker's Shades menu and have your brochure offset printed, either the text or the screen may not print clearly. When the camera is set to pick up a fine screen—a 10-percent fill pattern, for example—the photographic process may darken each character of the text and at the same time blur the edges of characters. On the other hand, if the camera is set to sharpen the text, the 10-percent screen may disappear in the photographed image. In other words, if the image includes very light gray tones or a wide range of gray tones, you will have trouble finding a camera setting that both picks up the 10-percent screens and produces the correct darkness for text and for screens darker than 10 percent.

If your final output will be offset printed, use tissue overlays and let the offset printer's cameraperson make the screens rather than using PageMaker's shading, as done with this brochure (see fig. 13.9). Also with this method, you can produce screens of a higher resolution (more dots per inch) than the 300-dots-per-inch resolution of the laser printer.

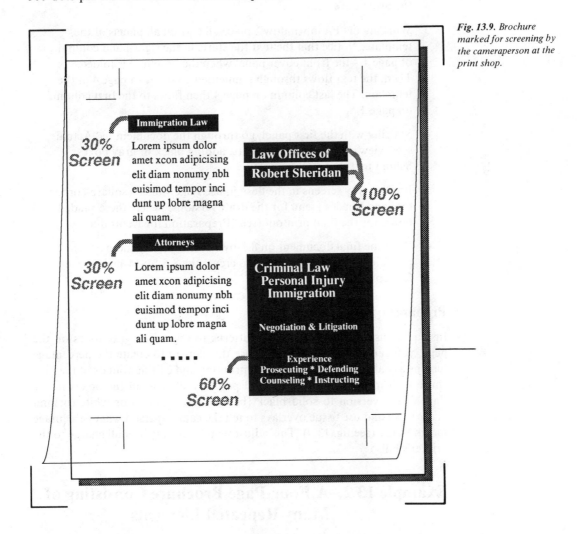

Fig. 13.9. Brochure marked for screening by the cameraperson at the print shop.

Production Steps for the Four-Panel Brochure

The production steps for this brochure follow much the same pattern as those for other publications. You need to pay close attention, however, to the order of the pages so that the text flows in the correct sequence after the layout is pasted up (see step 3).

1. Type and format all text in the word-processing program.

2. Open the template for this brochure and save the template under the brochure's name.

3. Working in "Fit in window", place all text on all panels of the template. Notice that the text file starts in the right-hand column of page 1—the front cover panel when the brochure is folded. Then, the text flows through segmented columns to page 4 of the template. The last column on page 4 then flows to the first column on page 1.

4. Starting with the first panel, go through the document in "Actual size" view and make adjustments, adding black or gray boxes behind text.

5. For the gray screens in the design, use PageMaker's square-corner tool and Shades menu for the draft versions. Delete these shaded boxes for the final printout (see "Preparation for Reproduction").

6. Print the final document on 8.5-by-11-inch paper, and paste the pages in the correct locations to create the 8.5-by-14-inch master for reproduction.

Preparation for Reproduction

Instead of using PageMaker's fill patterns to create the gray tones on the page, you can let the offset printer use the camera to create the percentage screens as halftones. After the initial proofing and editing rounds of the brochure with mixed percentages of fill patterns, change all the boxes in the PageMaker version to solid black (behind reverse type) or white (behind black type) and use tissue overlays to tell the cameraperson what percentage screen to use (see fig. 13.9). This adjustment adds only a small charge to the printer's bill.

Example 13.2. A Four-Page Brochure Consisting of Many Repeated Elements

This 8.5-by-11-inch brochure is printed on 11-by-17-inch paper and folded in half. Because of the many duplicate elements in the brochure, this example illustrates the use of dummy text and graphics stored on the pasteboard of the template. The design and production tips can be applied to any publication that uses the same elements on every page (with changes to the text or content but not to the format).

Description of Four-Page Brochure with Repeated Elements

This four-page brochure is composed of text and graphics created using PageMaker's tools, plus graphs from 1-2-3 (see fig. 13.10). All text was typed directly into PageMaker. The logo— "COMPUTE!"—was kerned manually. The final 8.5-by-11-inch pages are offset printed on 11-by-17-inch sheets, which are folded in half.

Design Principles for Four-Page Brochure with Repeated Elements

Many of the design principles described at the beginning of this chapter and in Chapters 8 through 12 are applied in this publication. The five principles that are especially well illustrated by this example are repeated and described here.

Use all capital letters as a deliberate design strategy rather than a method for emphasizing text or showing a heading. In this case, the word "COMPUTE!" is in uppercase, and the letters are kerned to meet the designer's specifications. This customization of the text creates a unique logo. The logo is kerned once and then duplicated and scaled to various sizes. Whenever this logo is used, the same relative kerning adjustments are applied. The kerning adjustments are preserved when text is sized in PageMaker. (For more information about kerning in PageMaker, see Chapters 4 and 8.)

Treat all figures consistently: fonts, line weights, fill patterns. The same two fill patterns are used in every bar graph. All graphs are scaled to the same size, and all line weights and labels are the same size. This consistency helps highlight the significant differences—the data variations—in the figures.

Be sure that the space between text and graphics is the same for all figures. Spacing guides are used to position all graphics. (See the production tricks and the template in fig. 13.13.) This arrangement ensures consistency in all pages in the brochure.

Let the same graphic elements carry the theme throughout the document. Each graph is framed in a drop-shadow border. This border helps the reader group related information on the page.

Fig. 13.10. *Printouts of pages of four-page brochure with repeated elements.*

COMPUTE!

#1 in reaching
The Home Market of
Personal Computer Owners

#1 in reaching households owning a personal computer.*

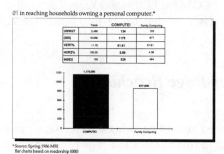

* Source: Spring 1986 MRI
Bar charts based on readership (000)

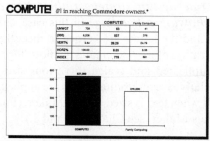

COMPUTE! #1 in reaching Commodore owners.*

COMPUTE! #1 in reaching Apple owners.*

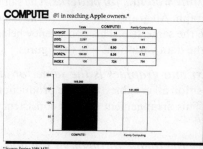

* Source: Spring 1986 MRI
Bar charts based on readership (000)

COMPUTE! #1 in reaching Apple, Commodore & IBM owners.*

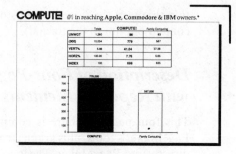

COMPUTE! #1 in value of personal computer $500 to $2999.*

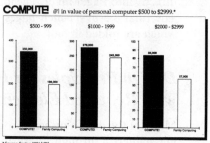

* Source: Spring 1986 MRI
Bar charts based on readership (000)

COMPUTE! #1 in total adults.*

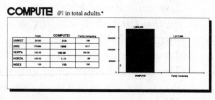

COMPUTE! #1 in reaching households with children under the age of 18.*

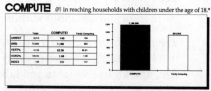

For more information on how **COMPUTE!** best serves your advertising needs in reaching the home market of personal computers owners, please call:

1. *New England & Mid-Atlantic*
    Bernard J. Theobald, Jr   212 315-1665
    Tom Link   212 315-1665

2. *Southeast & Foreign including Canada*
    Harry Blair   919 275-9809

3. *Midwest, Southwest, West & British Columbia*
    Jerry Thompson   Chicago   312 726-6047
    Lucille Dennis   Texas   713 731-2605
                                                            Colorado   303 595-9299
                                                            California   415 348-8222

COMPUTE! Publications Inc
825 Seventh Ave, New York, NY 10019

* Source: Spring 1986 MRI
Bar charts based on readership (000)

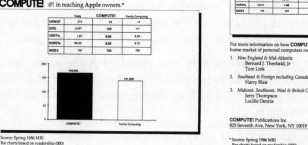

Select only one or two typefaces, and use the same sizes for headings and other text on all images. The brochure uses only two typefaces, a total of seven different fonts altogether (see fig. 13.11). Except for the axis labels on the bar charts, which are generated by 1-2-3, all text is typed directly into PageMaker and "cloned" from the pasteboard elements.

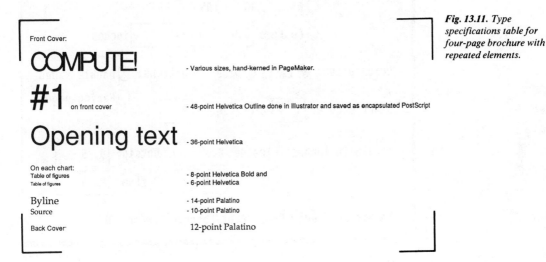

Fig. 13.11. Type specifications table for four-page brochure with repeated elements.

Production Tricks for Four-Page Brochure with Repeated Elements

The graphs are created in 1-2-3. All options for the size of the graphs, size of the axis labels, and fill patterns are specified in advance; and the same specifications are used for every graph. When placed in PageMaker, the graphs are cropped down to the axis labels; the titles and legends are removed. The drop-shadow border and all other text are added in PageMaker.

The Template for Four-Page Brochure with Repeated Elements

The template is set up as a double-sided document, but the "Facing pages" option is not used (see fig. 13.12). This technique leaves a wider pasteboard area for storing the standard drop-shadow box and table of data, which appear on every graph (fig. 13.13). The pasteboard holds dummy text for all text elements that are repeated on every page, including the tabular information, which is framed in ruled lines created with PageMaker's perpendicular-line tool. A spacing guide is provided for positioning the bar graphs within the drop-shadow borders.

Fig. 13.12. "Page setup"
dialog box for brochure
with repeated elements.

Page setup: OK

Page size: ●Letter   ○Legal   ○Tabloid   Cancel

            ○A4   ○A3   ○A5   ○B5

            ○Custom: 8.5   x 11   inches

Orientation: ●Tall ○Wide   Options: ☒Double sided
                                          ☐Facing pages

Start page #: 1   # of pages: 4

Margin in inches: Inside 0.99   Outside 0.75
                    Top 0.75   Bottom 0.75

Target printer: PostScript/LaserWriter on COM2:

Fig. 13.13. "The template
with spacing guides and
drop-shadow boxes on
the pasteboard.

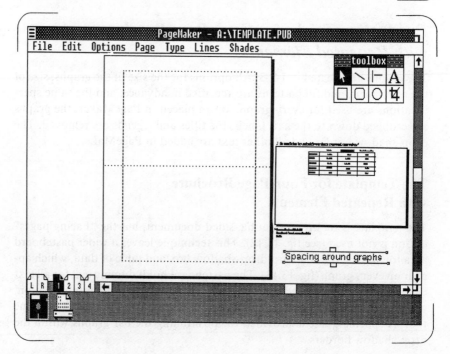

PageMaker - A:\TEMPLATE.PUB

File Edit Options Page Type Lines Shades

toolbox

Spacing around graphs

L R 1 2 3 4

Production Steps for Four-Page Brochure with Repeated Elements

This type of publication uses the pasteboard to great advantage. To produce this brochure, you work through the following steps:

1. Open a new publication to build the template and set up the margins as shown in figure 13.12.

2. Type the logo on the pasteboard in 127-point Helvetica and manually kern the letters to tighten the entire word. Then make two copies of the logo. Change one copy to 14-point and one to 8-point Helvetica. Store all three sizes on the pasteboard.

3. Type the dummy text for the byline and source for the graphs, and place these two text blocks on the pasteboard.

4. Using Pagemaker's text tools and tab settings and dummy data, create the table for the first graph. Draw a box around the text and add horizontal and vertical rules. Place the entire table (text and graph) on the pasteboard (see fig. 13.14).

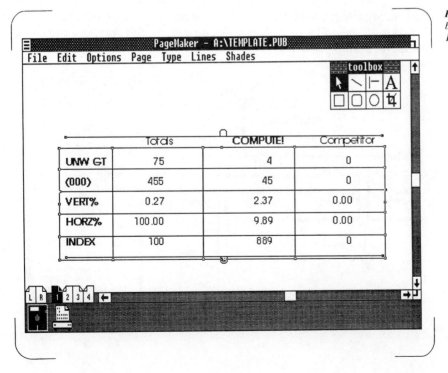

Fig. 13.14. A tabbed block of text framed by PageMaker's ruled lines.

5. Save the template.

6. Go over each page in "Fit in window" view. Copy and paste the drop-shadow box, all its contents, and the title dummy text from the pasteboard to the page and place each graph.

7. Go back to the first page and, working in "Actual size", edit the text as needed to adapt it to each graph.

Preparation for Reproduction

If you can, print the final version of this brochure on a Linotronic typesetter in order to produce solid black drop-shadows. If you use a laser printer for the final output, use a coated paper stock for the best image or spray the final pages with a matte finish to darken the solid black areas before you send the document to the offset printer. You can purchase matte-finish spray in any local art supplies store.

Disk-File Organization for Four-Page Brochure with Repeated Elements

During production, all the 1-2-3 .PIC files are stored on the hard disk in the same subdirectory as the PageMaker document (see fig. 13.15). Later, you can copy all these files to the same backup disk. In this way, you can easily update the graphs periodically and rebuild the brochure quarterly or annually using new data.

Fig. 13.15. Disk-file organization for brochure with graphs.

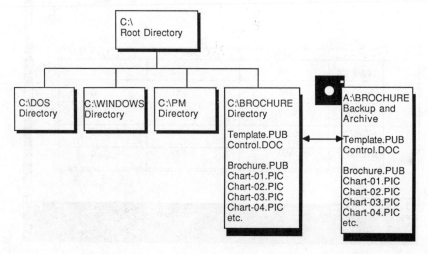

Example 13.3. A Two-Column Membership Directory Derived from a Database

This directory is designed as a two-column layout on narrow pages. The list of names and addresses is converted from a database format into text. The design and production methods used in this example can be applied to any directory, regardless of the page size or number of columns. The conversion steps used for the database information can be adapted for any publication that uses a database or spreadsheet file as a primary source of text.

Description of Two-Column Membership Directory

This 80-page booklet lists the names, addresses, and telephone numbers of more than 1,500 members of a professional association (see fig. 13.16). The information is converted from a database to a word-processing file and formatted before being placed in PageMaker.

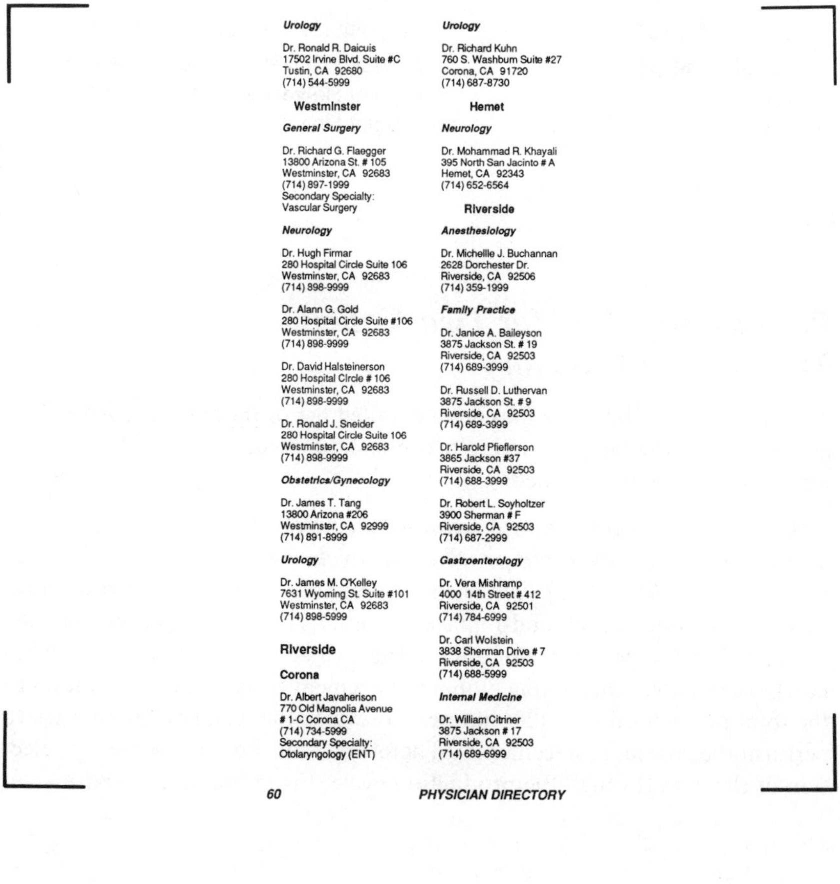

Fig. 13.16. Printout of one page of membership directory.

Urology

Dr. Ronald R. Daicuis
17502 Irvine Blvd. Suite #C
Tustin, CA 92680
(714) 544-5999

Westminster

General Surgery

Dr. Richard G. Flaegger
13800 Arizona St. # 105
Westminster, CA 92683
(714) 897-1999
Secondary Specialty:
Vascular Surgery

Neurology

Dr. Hugh Firmar
280 Hospital Circle Suite 106
Westminster, CA 92683
(714) 898-9999

Dr. Alann G. Gold
280 Hospital Circle Suite #106
Westminster, CA 92683
(714) 898-9999

Dr. David Halsteinerson
280 Hospital Circle # 106
Westminster, CA 92683
(714) 898-9999

Dr. Ronald J. Sneider
280 Hospital Circle Suite 106
Westminster, CA 92683
(714) 898-9999

Obstetrics/Gynecology

Dr. James T. Tang
13800 Arizona #206
Westminster, CA 92999
(714) 891-8999

Urology

Dr. James M. O'Kelley
7631 Wyoming St. Suite #101
Westminster, CA 92683
(714) 898-5999

Riverside

Corona

Dr. Albert Javaherison
770 Old Magnolia Avenue
1-C Corona CA
(714) 734-5999
Secondary Specialty:
Otolaryngology (ENT)

Urology

Dr. Richard Kuhn
760 S. Washburn Suite #27
Corona, CA 91720
(714) 687-8730

Hemet

Neurology

Dr. Mohammad R. Khayali
395 North San Jacinto # A
Hemet, CA 92343
(714) 652-6564

Riverside

Anesthesiology

Dr. Michellie J. Buchannan
2628 Dorchester Dr.
Riverside, CA 92506
(714) 359-1999

Family Practice

Dr. Janice A. Baileyson
3875 Jackson St. # 19
Riverside, CA 92503
(714) 689-3999

Dr. Russell D. Luthervan
3875 Jackson St. # 9
Riverside, CA 92503
(714) 689-3999

Dr. Harold Pfieflerson
3865 Jackson #37
Riverside, CA 92503
(714) 688-3999

Dr. Robert L. Soyholtzer
3900 Sherman # F
Riverside, CA 92503
(714) 687-2999

Gastroenterology

Dr. Vera Mishramp
4000 14th Street # 412
Riverside, CA 92501
(714) 784-6999

Dr. Carl Wolstein
3838 Sherman Drive # 7
Riverside, CA 92503
(714) 688-5999

Internal Medicine

Dr. William Citriner
3875 Jackson # 17
Riverside, CA 92503
(714) 689-6999

60   **PHYSICIAN DIRECTORY**

Design Principles for Two-Column Membership Directory

The design principles given throughout this book are generally followed in this example. Two principles in particular merit comment here.

Don't be afraid of white space. In this document, the white-space guideline is relaxed because the final product is a functional reference list like a telephone directory. Most of the white space is achieved by leaving a wide bottom margin between the lists and the running foot. A blank line (two carriage returns) is left between entries.

Use only one or two different typefaces in a document. The typeface used throughout this list is Helvetica (fig. 13.17). This typeface is clean-looking and easy to read in small point sizes.

Fig. 13.17. Type specifications table for two-column membership list.

Main Title	14-point Helvetica
Level 1 Head	12-point Helvetica Bold, flush left
Level 2 Head	10-point Helvetica Bold, centered
Level 3 Head	8-point Helvetica Bold Italic, flush left
Listings	8-point Helvetica

Production Tricks for Two-Column Membership Directory

The primary trick involves making a detailed list of the steps needed *before* going through the full production process. A tip recommended at the beginning of this chapter is applied:

Take a small amount of data from a spreadsheet or database through a test run of the complete production cycle before you complete the specifications for a long list. The text-preparation steps in this project require many global search-and-replace operations in the word-processing file. Because of the large volume of data in this project, each global search takes nearly 20 minutes. One wrong global replacement adds at least 40 minutes to the total production time (20 minutes to reverse the changes, 20 minutes to perform the correct replacements). Therefore, you should run a short selection of the data through the production cycle. From this run, prepare a detailed list of steps in order to reduce the chances of making a major mistake in text preparation and increasing production time.

Initially, the data is stored in a database format. Converting the data to a spreadsheet format provides a convenient way to switch the order of the information and to add three columns for title, secondary specialty tag, and a comma between city and state (see fig. 13.18). After the data is sorted by the column labeled "Specialty 1", print the data from the spreadsheet program as a reference during production. Then delete the "Specialty 1" column, save the data as text-only, and format it with a word-processing program.

Last Name	First Name	Initial	Building/Suite	Street	City	State	Zip	Phone	Specialty 1	Specialty 2		
Miller	Stuart	L.	Suite 708	12 W. 6th	NewYork	NY	10010	345-123	Cardiollogy	Vascular		

Title	First Name	Initial	Last Name	Building/Suite	Street	City	State	Zip	Phone	Tag	Specialty 2
Dr.	Stuart	L.	Miller	Suite 708	12 6th	NewYork ,	NY	10010	345-12	Secondary Specialty:	Vascular

Fig. 13.18. Changing order and adding columns in a spreadsheet program.

The rather convoluted process demonstrated by this example can be considered a "worst case" scenario in terms of data conversion. Some database programs offer the option of saving data formatted as a mailing list so that the word-processing step is not required, and some programs even have the capability of switching the order of the data and adding new fields without going through a spreadsheet.

The Template for the Two-Column Membership Directory

The template is set up on a 4-by-9-inch page with the inside margin slightly larger than the outside margin (see fig. 13.19). Because the lists have a ragged right margin, the column margins have been shifted by dragging them manually to the right of the page margins on each page. This technique gives a balanced appearance (see fig. 13.20). Otherwise, the text would appear to be left of center.

Page setup:
OK
Cancel
Page size: Letter Legal Tabloid
A4 A3 A5 B5
Custom: 4 x 9 inches
Orientation: Tall Wide
Options: Double sided
Facing pages
Start page #: 1
# of pages: 80
Margin in inches: Inside 0.75 Outside 0.5
Top 0.5 Bottom 0.5
Target printer: PostScript/LaserWriter on COM2:

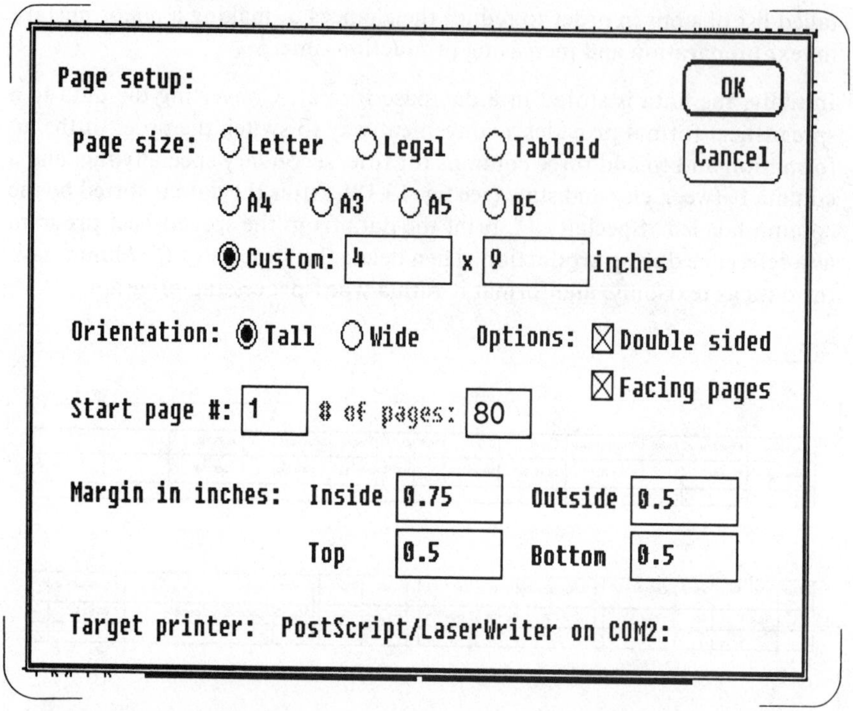

Fig. 13.19. *"Page setup" dialog box for the membership list.*

PageMaker - A:\TEMPLATE.PUB
File Edit Options Page Type Lines Shades
toolbox
Physician Directory
March 1987
L R
1 2 3 4

Fig. 13.20. *The template for the membership list, with column margins manually shifted to the right.*

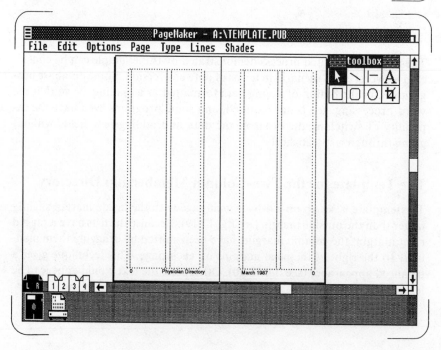

Production Steps for the Two-Column Membership Directory

Producing this two-column list from database material requires more steps and more attention to detail than the other examples given in this chapter. The following steps guide you through the entire process:

1. Select a small portion of your data and take it through the entire process, carefully noting the steps required for full database conversion.

2. Use the small sample of data to estimate the number of pages required for different designs and type specifications. The final design specifications are tempered by considerations of white space, readability, functionality, and printing costs. The final design in this example accommodates about 16 names per page set in 8-point Helvetica (see fig. 13.21).

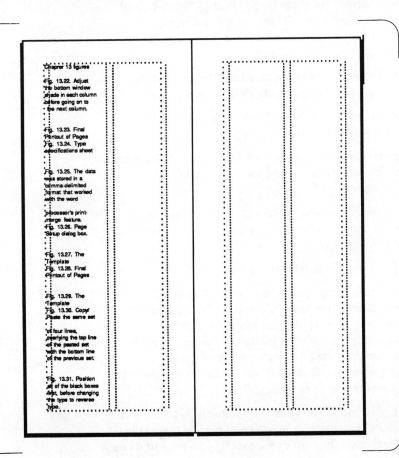

Fig. 13.21. A template using sample data to estimate the full page count.

3. Convert the data to a spreadsheet format (again see fig. 13.18). First, save the data as text-only information. If this conversion results in commas between the items of information, use a word processor and globally change the commas to tab characters. The spreadsheet program interprets each tab as indicating a new column.

4. Open the spreadsheet file and move each first name and initial to precede the last name. Insert three new items (the title *Dr.* before each name, the comma between city and state, and the phrase *Secondary Specialty* where applicable).

5. Sort the data by "Specialty 1" and print the list from the spreadsheet for use as a reference. Save the spreadsheet.

6. Delete the "Specialty 1" column. Before each data column, add a blank column (before "Building/Suite," "City," "Phone," and "Tag"). Each blank column will begin a new line in the final version. Then, under a new file name, save the data from the spreadsheet as text-only information.

7. Perform global changes and detailed edits with the word processor. In this case, four separate global searches are required:

   - To add a blank line after each entry, change all single carriage returns to two carriage returns.

   - To convert the blank columns inserted in step 6 to carriage returns in the word-processed files, change each "(tab)(tab)" to "(carriage return)".

   - In the spreadsheet, you added a column of commas between city and state. Now change each "(tab-comma-tab)" to "(comma-space)".

   - Change all remaining tabs to spaces.

8. Print the word-processing files to be proofread against the spreadsheet printout (from step 5). Use your word processor to edit the file before you place the text in PageMaker. Add subheads to identify the different locations and specialties. You can mark the heads on the printout for entry in the word processor, or you can scroll through the list on-screen and enter the subheads before you print the text file.

9. Open the template and go through the document in the "Fit in window" view, adding pages as needed and placing the text in columns on each page. In most cases, exactly 16 names fit on each

page; but if any entry is broken across columns or across pages, adjust the bottom windowshade to force the whole name and address into the next column or page (see fig. 13.22).

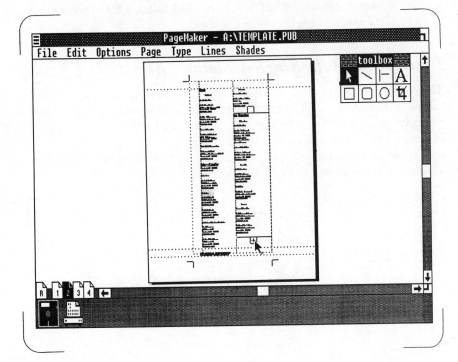

Fig. 13.22. Adjusting the bottom windowshade in each column.

10. Go through the document in "Actual size" view, working from front to back to make any fine adjustments missed during the first sweep.

11. Print all the pages and proofread them for format. In this reading, a quick count verifies that all the names have been printed, but no detailed proofreading of the names and addresses is necessary because this check is done during word processing.

Example 13.4. A Single-Column List of Products with Descriptions, Prices, and Suppliers

The product list in this example is designed as a catalog for a fund-raising auction. This same format can be adapted for any directory that includes sentences or paragraphs of descriptive information in addition to names and addresses, or for a product catalog that includes product descriptions as well as prices and product numbers. The list of products could easily have been a list of people (with descriptions of their achievements or skills), a list of companies (with descriptions of their services or product lines), a list of restaurants (with brief reviews of what they offer), and so on.

Description of the Single-Column List

This 48-page booklet lists more than 100 products to be auctioned in a fund-raising event (see fig. 13.23). The listing for each product includes the product name, list price, a brief description, and the name and address of the supplier or donor. Text is wrapped around the large-type item numbers. The page size is designed to accommodate paid advertisements that are exactly the size of a standard business card (2 by 3.5 inches).

Fig. 13.23. Printout of one page of list of products.

Design Principles for the Single-Column List

Besides the general rules related to consistency in design, two principles deserve special mention here.

Don't be afraid of white space. The white space on these pages is produced by indenting the name and address of the donor for each product. Product descriptions are allowed a maximum of five lines each in order to limit the total number of pages.

Use only one or two different typefaces in a document. The Times typeface is used for text throughout this booklet (fig. 13.24). This consistency helps balance the variety of typefaces in the business cards and display ads supplied by advertisers and pasted up manually on the final printouts.

000   Product numbers, 24-point Helvetica

Product title   10-point Times Bold
Product description   10-point Times Roman
Company name   10-point Times Bold

Fig. 13.24. Type specifications table for single-column product list.

Production Tricks for the Single-Column List

The original data is stored in a comma-delimited file, which is the source file. A word-processing program is used to merge print the data for the product lists into a merge-print file (see fig. 13.25). The trick in this case is that the merge-print file is sent to a disk instead of to the printer. (Note that not all word-processing programs can print to a disk.)

Comma-delimited format

001,Your Next Brochure,"We prepare typeset copy and graphics for ads, brochures, fliers, booklets, reports, and presentations (overhead transparencies or slides). We can incorporate your photographs as half-tones, or as computer-digitized images. Good for 2-sided flier, or $50 off any order.",50,15,Grace Moore,TechArt,3915 24th Street,San Francisco,CA,94114,(415) 550-1110

Fig. 13.25. Data stored in comma-delimited format and the merge-print formatted file.

001

Your Next Brochure
We prepare typeset copy and graphics for ads, brochures, fliers, booklets, reports, and presentations (overhead transparencies or slides). We can incorporate your photographs as half-tones, or as computer-digitized images. Good for 2-sided flier, or $50 off any order.
Value: $50   Minimum bid: $15
Donor: Grace Moore
                   TechArt
                   3915 24th Street
                   San Francisco, CA 94114
                   (415) 550-1110

Merge-print file

Because the data itself has already been edited and corrected, little processing is required. The same data is used to send form letters to the donors to confirm their participation, to send them formal invitations and complimentary tickets to the event, and to send thank-you notes after the event. This data also is used to merge print all the materials used on the night of the auction, such as item tags (produced on mailing labels) and item lists for the auctioneer and the staff members collecting the payments.

The PageMaker template is set up to print three items per page in a small (4.5-by-6.5-inch) booklet format (see figs. 13.26 and 13.27). The 0.5-inch margins result in a column width of exactly 3.5 inches—the width of a standard business card and the size of the ads used throughout the booklet. A ruled line is stored on the pasteboard of the template and placed between the product entries. A 2-by-3.5-inch border is also stored on the pasteboard and used to mark the positions for ads to be pasted in manually.

Production Steps for the Single-Column List

Unlike other examples, this publication requires steps to merge the data before you place it in PageMaker. You may need to adapt these steps to meet the requirements of your own word processor.

1. Enter the data in the merge format used by your word processor.

2. Merge print the formatted data to a disk file, including carriage returns and character formatting specifications (see fig. 13.25).

3. Create the boxes used to mark the positions of the ads. Store these boxes and the necessary rules on the pasteboard.

4. Place the formatted text in the PageMaker template. Break the product number and description into separate text blocks, and use the techniques described in Chapter 6 to wrap the text around each product number (see fig. 13.23).

5. Copy and paste the boxes from the pasteboard to the appropriate pages, in order to reserve space for the advertisers' cards to be pasted in manually.

6. Print all the pages and proofread the results before pasting business cards on the final version.

Preparation for Reproduction

Advertiser's business cards are pasted by hand into the boxes reserved for them. Business cards supplied by advertisers should be white cards with black text and graphics. Cards in colored inks or on colored paper may require photostatting to get a good black-and-white image.

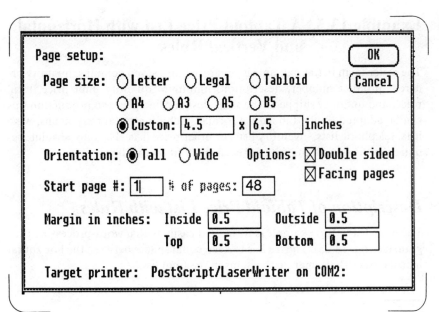

Fig. 13.26. "Page setup" dialog box for the product list.

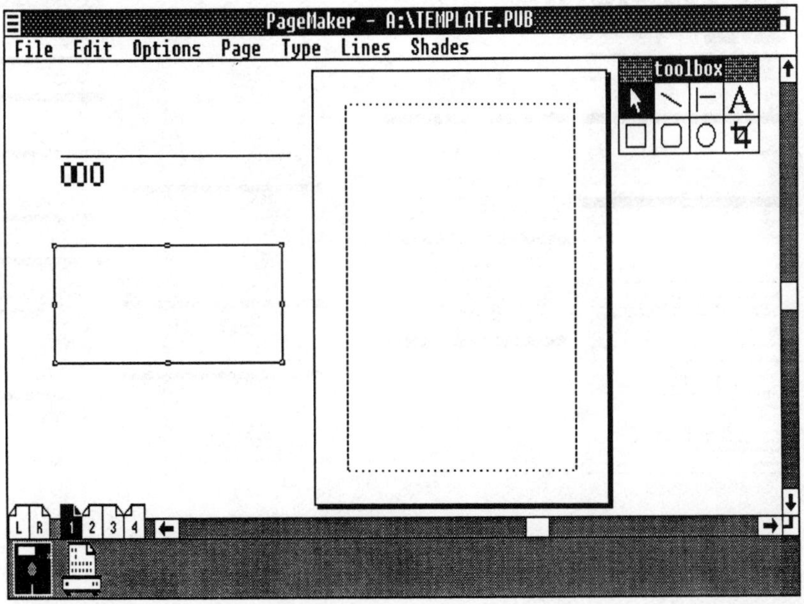

Fig. 13.27. The template for the product list.

Example 13.5. A Tabloid Price List with Horizontal and Vertical Rules

The order form in this example is organized into seven columns: quantity ordered, product number, description, minimum quantity, unit price, total price, and quantity shipped. The same design principles and production tips can be adapted to any tabbed list format, including restaurant menus, wine lists, telephone lists, inventory lists, or other price lists. The only absolute requirement is that all the data for each entry fit on one line.

Description of Tabloid Price List with Rules

The price list in this example is formatted easily with a word-processing program (see fig. 13.28). The trick is to keep equal spaces between the horizontal hairline rules that separate the items in the final list.

Fig. 13.28. Printout of pages of tabloid price list.

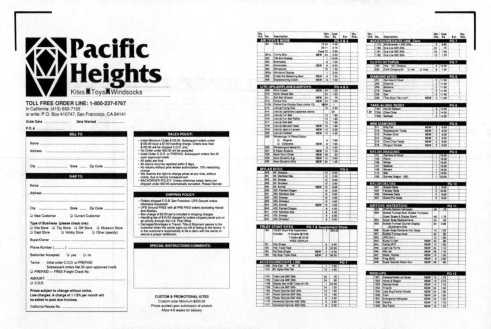

Production Steps for Tabloid Price List with Rules

You must maintain equal spacing between PageMaker's hairline rules. To accomplish this spacing, carefully position the first five lines in a "200% size" of the page. You then copy these five lines to the pasteboard and paste them as a group, moving down each column in the "200% size".

The steps are as follows:

1. Format the text in the word-processing program, setting left, right, center, and decimal tabs as needed. The reverse type is set in PageMaker in a later step.

2. Set up the simple template shown in figure 13.29, and place the text in PageMaker. Scroll down each column in the "Actual size" view to make adjustments as necessary before you reverse the heading type and add the black boxes and hairline rules required by this design.

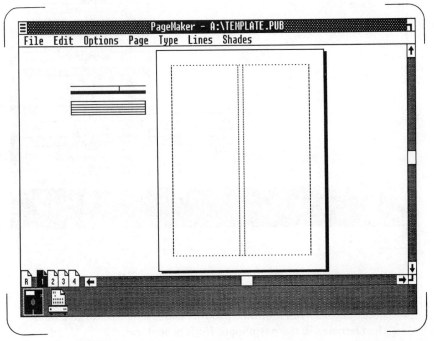

Fig. 13.29. The template for the tabloid price list.

3. Draw a hairline border around one column; then copy and paste the border to the other columns. You can adjust the length of the box to create two different borders in the first column of the price list.

4. Draw one vertical hairline down a column, and copy and paste the same line in the correct position across the column. Then copy and paste this set of lines to all other columns.

5. Change to "200% size" and draw a horizontal hairline rule across one column. Copy and paste this hairline in positions to separate five lines of text. Copy and paste the set of five lines onto the pasteboard.

6. Scroll down each column in "200% size". Paste the same set of five lines, aligning the top line of the pasted set precisely over the bottom line of the preceding set (see fig. 13.30).

Fig. 13.30. Copying and aligning the set of five rules.

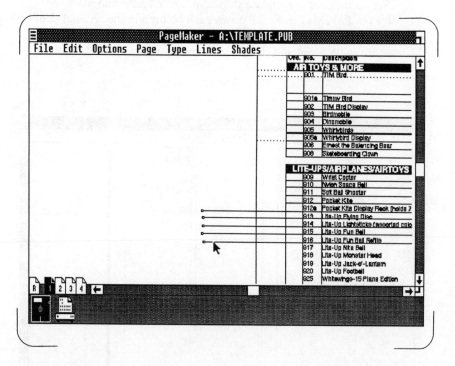

7. As you work, use the "Clear" command to delete lines as necessary between multiline product listings. The set of five lines then remains in the pasteboard for repeated use.

8. After you have positioned all the horizontal hairlines, go back to the beginning and scroll down each column in "200% size", this time deciding where to put the black boxes behind reverse-text headings.

9. Draw one black box the appropriate size and copy the box to the pasteboard. Then paste the box over each heading, and use the "Send to back" command to position the box behind the text. Don't change the text to reverse type until you have positioned all the black boxes (see fig. 13.31).

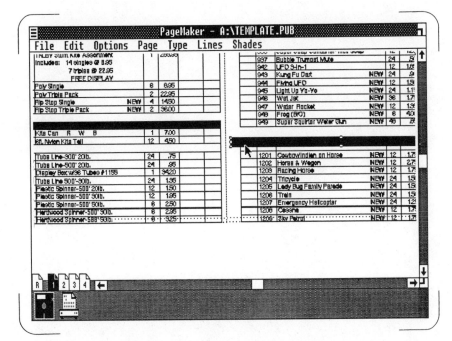

Fig. 13.31. Positioning the black boxes before changing to reverse type.

10. Scroll through the publication once more with the text tool selected. Change each heading, now invisible as black type on black boxes, to reverse type. Triple-click to select the whole line; then select "Reverse type" from the Type menu.

Summary

In this chapter, you have seen examples of publications that use unusual formats: folded brochures, small booklets, and tabloid-size price lists. You have also seen how information stored in a database, spreadsheet, or mail-merge format can be converted to text and placed in PageMaker. The design principles and production tricks illustrated in this chapter can be applied to a wide variety of brochures and lists and adapted to meet your specific needs. By studying these examples, you can make your own designs more effective and your production steps more efficient.

Creating Fliers and Display Ads ██14██

Throughout this book, the focus has been on multiple-page publications that repeat the same basic master-page elements on every page and apply the same type specifications throughout. In this chapter, you learn how PageMaker can be used to produce one-page fliers and display ads (see fig. 14.1). One example demonstrates how a simple resume can be turned into a marketing tool. You will also see how PageMaker can be used to generate a series of different designs for one flier. Finally, you will learn how to create a series of ads for different franchisers who offer the same product. The fliers and display ads discussed in this chapter share two important characteristics:

- The documents are usually only one or two pages long in a PageMaker file.

- Fliers and ads are often a nonstandard size—the final pages may be trimmed and folded.

Design Principles

The design principles in the preceding chapters generally apply to the publications in this chapter, but you are likely to find more exceptions to the rules in this category—fliers and ads—than in any other. Some of the common exceptions are described in this section in order to give you an idea of how and why fliers and ads can "break the rules."

Keep text to a minimum.

Following this guideline can be difficult when you work with small formats. When designing a small ad or flier, most people tend to include as much information as possible about the product or service. Too many words in an ad,

Fig. 14.1. *Examples of fliers and display ads.*

however, can make the final image uninviting. Readers simply may not read text printed in a small point size. By choosing your words carefully, you can get a few important points across and still draw the reader to call or come to the event or store.

Try to follow the rule of thumb that has evolved from the billboard industry: express the message in seven words or fewer. Examples 14.2 and 14.4 apply this principle. Examples 14.1 and 14.3, on the other hand, are exceptions to this rule. In these cases, a small point size is used to fit the large number of words in a small space and still leave white space on the page or in the ad.

The choice of font sets the tone of the piece.

Ads and fliers often use decorative or unusual typefaces for the headings and sometimes for the body copy as well. Different typefaces can convey a sense of seriousness, elegance, or frivolity. If you are not sure how typefaces affect the reader, you should probably stay with traditional typefaces rather than experiment with more decorative ones.

In developing Example 14.2 in this chapter, for example, the designer experimented with several typefaces and finally chose Avant Garde to set the tone in a flier for a hair salon. In contrast, Example 14.3 is a display ad for a law firm that requires the more serious traditional tone of a serifed font like Times.

Use only one or two different typefaces in a document.

Almost any font can be used in a flier or ad, but the same rule applies here as with all other publications: use only one or two typefaces. The use of too many fonts in a small space causes the ad or flier to look "busy" and detracts from the message. The resume in figure 14.2, for example, uses only Helvetica Narrow. Notice that the designer calls attention to headings by using reverse type instead of another typeface.

Don't be afraid of white space.

If you skim through any magazine, you are likely to find several full-page ads that leave most of the page blank. These are extreme examples of this principle, but they usually make their point well.

You may sometime deliberately violate this principle, however. As already mentioned, Examples 14.1 and 14.3 use small point sizes for the type in order to gain white space. Some of the variations in Example 14.2 have absolutely no white space because the scanned image fills the whole page, but the impact of the flier is still strong (see fig. 14.7). The scanned image itself invites the reader's attention, and very few words are required to get the message across.

Use all capital letters as a deliberate design strategy rather than a method for emphasizing text or showing a heading.

You should avoid using all uppercase letters in long blocks of text. Remember that all uppercase text can be difficult to read, especially in sentences.

On the other hand, you can use all capitals instead of a larger point size in order to make a few words stand out on the page. You also can use uppercase rather than changing the typeface for a head. Figure 14.2, for example, uses the combination of uppercase and reverse type to emphasize the headings for each section. Uppercase text has the greatest impact if the words or phrases are short. The appearance of the uppercase text often can be improved by manually kerning the spaces between certain pairs of letters. (Refer to Chapters 4 and 8 for information about kerning.)

Production Tips

Many production tips that improve productivity when you are producing long documents are irrelevant for one-page documents like those illustrated in this chapter. Other production tips are unique to one-page ads and fliers. Some production tips to keep in mind for documents like the resume and ads illustrated in this chapter are listed here.

Compensate for ragged right text by setting unequal right and left margins.

The need for a balanced appearance is evident in these examples. Because of the ragged right text, the right margin may appear to be different from the left. You can compensate for this visual difference by using different margin settings.

Store background boxes on the pasteboard to use behind text. Copy boxes to the page as you need them.

Several examples in the preceding chapters and the resume in this chapter use background boxes. You can create the box only once, store it on the pasteboard, and paste it on the page in as many different locations as you wish.

For ads containing mostly graphics with little text, create your text on the pasteboard and copy text to the page after you have positioned your graphic.

In many ads, the graphic fills most of the available space. As a result, the position of the graphic is the most important factor of the page layout. Text is frequently short and to the point. You can save a great deal of time by positioning the graphic before you place the text. Changing the text to fit the graphic is much easier than trying to change the graphic to fit the text.

If your ad includes a border, remember to set the overall ad size including the border in the "Page setup" dialog box.

If you use a border in your ad, you need to set the page size so that it accommodates both the border and the margin surrounding the border.

If your ad includes a border, set narrower margins inside the border than the margins between the edge of the page and the border.

The border should be an integral part of the entire design. If the margins inside the border are larger than those outside, the final product will not be as attractive or unified as it should be.

Examples

Many readers will find the examples in this chapter the most useful in this book because one-page fliers and ads are used frequently. With PageMaker you can easily produce short fliers and ads and add variations with only a few additional steps. The examples in this chapter range from a resume to a series of one-page ads. Some use scanned images, and others rely entirely on type.

14.1. A Photographer's Resume with a Scanned Photograph

14.2. A One-sided Flier with Several Design Variations

14.3. A Series of Display Ad Designs with Varied Borders

14.4. A Series of Ads in the Same Format for the Same Service

Example 14.1. A Photographer's Resume with a Scanned Photograph

This resume is included under the category of fliers and ads because the creative use of a scanned image and reverse text transforms this list of credentials into a promotional piece. The piece conforms to the 8.5-by-11-inch full page that most employers or interviewers are accustomed to receiving from individuals, but the four-column format and large scanned image in the lower left corner give the resume the impact of a flier or brochure that describes a service. One clear lesson of this example is this: PageMaker can transform any traditional format—resume, memo, agenda, balance sheet—into a marketing tool that will help sell whatever is being presented.

Fig. 14.2. *Printout of*
resume.

Description of Resume

This brochure is a photographer's resume, which has been dressed up with a scanned photograph (see fig. 14.2). The final version was printed on a Linotronic typesetter and then sent to an offset printer for reproduction.

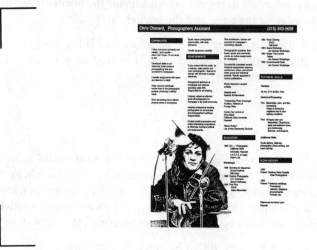

Design Principles for Resume

In this example, one design principle—keep text to a minimum—is stretched somewhat in order to list all the photographer's awards and qualifications. The danger of over-crowding the page is reduced by using a small point size of a narrow typeface: Helvetica Narrow. To compensate for the small size of the section headings, the designer uses all uppercase letters and reverse type. The final effect is a well-balanced composition in a clean, readable typeface with adequate white space.

Don't be afraid of white space. Even though the resume contains a great deal of text, the resume uses white space to distinguish the sections and make reading easy. Notice in figure 14.2 the white space between columns and the four points of leading between each head and following text.

Use only one or two different typefaces in a document. This resume uses Helvetica Narrow throughout (see fig. 14.3). Helvetica Narrow is a compact, clean, readable typeface that helps support the photographer's image as a fine artist and sophisticated technician. Using this typeface also allows the use of more text without creating a crowded effect.

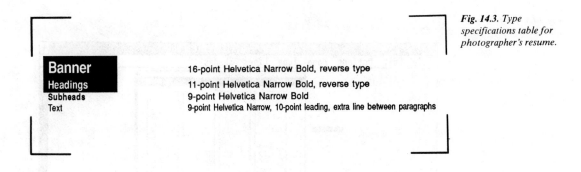

Fig. 14.3. Type
specifications table for
photographer's resume.

Banner	16-point Helvetica Narrow Bold, reverse type
Headings	11-point Helvetica Narrow Bold, reverse type
Subheads	9-point Helvetica Narrow Bold
Text	9-point Helvetica Narrow, 10-point leading, extra line between paragraphs

Production Tricks for Resume

The inside margin is wider than the outside margin, as specified in the "Page setup" dialog box (see figs. 14.4 and 14.5); but both margins appear equal on the page (see fig. 14.2). The unequal margin settings compensate for the effect of ragged-right text. The pasteboard of the template includes a black box that is copied and pasted behind the reverse text of each heading.

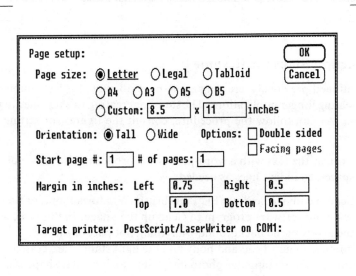

Fig. 14.4. "*Page setup*"
dialog box for resume.

Fig. 14.5. *The template*
for the resume.

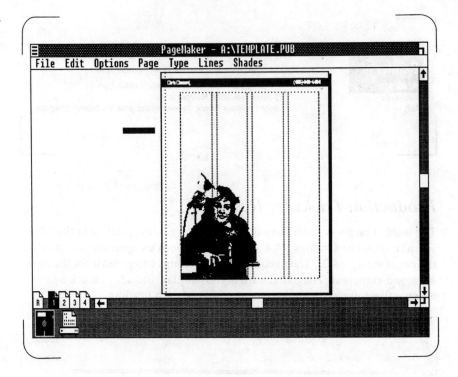

Production Steps for Resume

As mentioned previously, creating a one-page document is less complicated than creating longer publications. The steps for creating this resume are given in detail. As you follow the procedure, consult the figures for settings and positions.

1. Format the text with a word-processing program. Use tabs, not spaces, to indent lines as needed.

2. Scan the image, and use PC Paintbrush, Windows Paint, or the scanning software program to clean up the image. In this case, all the pixels in the background—anything not part of the photographer's head and body and the light stand—are erased to convert the rectangular photo image into an irregular shape that becomes more visually integrated with the text.

3. Open a new PageMaker publication, making the page setup and column settings match those shown in figures 14.4 and 14.5.

4. Working in the "Fit in window" view, place the text in four columns.

5. Still working in the "Fit in window" view, place the scanned image in position on top of the text. Crop and scale the image if necessary.

6. Send the scanned image to the back of the text, using the "Send to back" command. Refer to Chapter 5 for more detailed instructions on this process.

7. Select the text blocks one by one, and roll up the bottom handles to move the text off the image. Continue text to the last column, and adjust all the blocks until the last column reaches the margin.

8. Change to the "Actual size" view, and move down each column changing the headings to reverse type and adding black boxes as backgrounds for the headings. To accomplish this,

   • First, draw a black box around the first heading within a column. Use the "Send to back" command to place the box behind the text, and use the "Copy" command to copy the box to the pasteboard.

   • Move to each heading and paste the black box from the pasteboard. Position the box over the heading and use the "Send to back" command.

   • Go back to the beginning and use the text tool to make the headings reverse type.

9. Print drafts on the laser printer.

10. Print the final copy on the Linotronic typesetter to get crop marks and solid black areas that reach the edge of the paper (see fig. 14.6).

Fig. 14.6. Printed image of resume with crop marks.

Preparation for Reproduction of Resume

The offset printer must be informed that you want part of the image to bleed off the paper. Keep in mind that the bleed adds to the printing charges because of the oversize paper and trimming required. Otherwise, no particular preparation is necessary because the crop marks are printed by the Linotronic.

Efficiency Tip

Printing Black Areas

Even if your laser-printer cartridge is printing black areas poorly so that they appear unevenly gray, the image often blackens when converted to offset printing plates. True grays are retained when you use gray fill patterns composed of black dots. See the warning about using a wide range of gray tones in Example 13.1.

If you are not using a typesetter to produce solid black images, use coated paper stock in the laser printer. You also can darken the image printed on the laser printer by spraying the page with a matte finish (available in any art supply shop). This trick works best with uncoated paper.

Example 14.2. A One-sided Flier with Several Design Variations

The approach used in designing this flier can be applied to any one-page document. The trick is to place all the basic elements on the pasteboard and then copy and paste them onto each page of the design publication, making a different arrangement of elements and testing different type specifications and paragraph formats on each page. The result is a series of design ideas that can be reviewed with your team or client.

Description of Flier with Design Variations

This flier began as a series of eight designs that used the same text but different graphics as backgrounds. In the end, three different designs were selected for reproduction on three different colors of paper (see fig. 14.7). The fliers were mailed to the same mailing list at three-month intervals, using a different flier each month. In this way, the prospective customers were reminded three times of this service, and the variations of the same design helped renew the reader's interest for each mailing.

Fig. 14.7. Printouts of flier with several designs.

Production Tricks for Flier with Design Variations

The few words required for this piece were typed on the pasteboard of the template. Several different scanned images were candidates for use in the final design. The designer placed each of these images on a separate page and then copied and pasted the text from the pasteboard and modified the text to create different design ideas.

You may need to keep track of the series of variations but not want to use page numbers on the ads themselves. You can print thumbnails of the entire design file, as the designer did for this example. The thumbnails show the design on each page of the template with the corresponding page number (see fig. 14.8). The numbers give quick access to any variation both before and after the final design is chosen. In this way, the full-size printouts of the pages are not cluttered with page numbers that are not part of the design.

Fig. 14.8. Thumbnails showing the design on each page.

Production Steps for Flier with Design Variations

The production steps for this example are simple. The greatest attention is needed for placing the different versions of the image and fitting the text with the image.

1. Create a PageMaker publication with the text of the flier on the pasteboard.

2. Go through the document in "Fit in window" view, adding pages as needed. Place a different scanned image on each page or

position the same image in a different location on each page. Some of the scans in this case were deliberately distorted (stretched out of proportion).

During this step, copy and paste the text from the pasteboard into position on each page, but don't change the type specs.

3. Go through the document in the "Actual size" view. You can work from front to back or vice versa. Change the type specs and break the type into different blocks on each page to create unique designs.

4. Print thumbnails of all the designs and choose the one you want.

5. Delete all unwanted variations from the file.

6. Print the variations as you need them.

Example 14.3. A Series of Display Ad Designs with Varied Borders

Like the preceding example, this example demonstrates the use of Page-Maker to produce design variations. The new twist in this case is that the final printout is pasted into a larger publication as a display ad. You can apply the recommendations about using special paper for the final printout to any ad or publication that will be pasted manually on larger pages or boards.

Description of Series of Varied Display Ads

This series of display ad designs is similar to Example 14.2 in at least two ways: all the text is predetermined (a list of associates in a law firm), and the size of the ad is predefined (a full-page ad in a booklet). The designer can make variations in the border style and in the type specs and text layout (see fig. 14.9). For example, the address information is set in different type specifications and the size of the box is varied.

Fig. 14.9. Printouts of series of display ads.

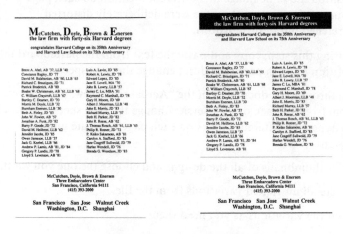

Production Tricks for Series of Varied Display Ads

Use the "Page size" setting in the "Page setup" dialog box to define the size of the ad including the border; set narrow margins inside the border area (see fig. 14.10). Store the text and a box the size of the ad border on the pasteboard in the template (see fig. 14.11). Both the page setup and the template are straightforward. You can follow the settings shown in the figures without complicated procedures.

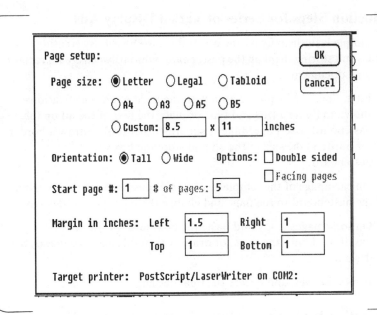

Fig. 14.10. "*Page setup*" *dialog box for series of ads.*

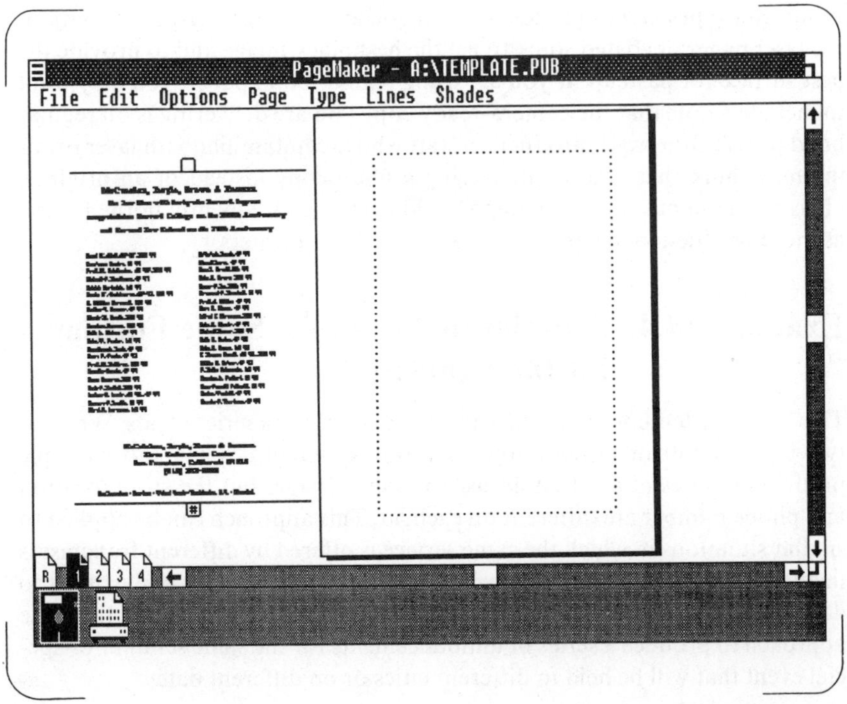

Fig. 14.11. *The template for the series of ads.*

Production Steps for Series of Varied Display Ads

This example leans heavily on the use of the pasteboard. By creating borders and rules and storing them on the pasteboard, you easily can create variations in the final document.

1. First, open a new publication with the page setup specifications shown in figure 14.10 and type or place the text of the ad on the pasteboard. Use PageMaker's square-corner tool to draw a border (or borders) the size of the ad and store the box on the pasteboard.

2. On each page of the template, copy and paste the text block from the pasteboard to the page and change the type specs as desired.

3. On some pages, copy and paste the box border from the pasteboard onto the page, or draw horizontal rules to enhance the design.

4. Print all pages, and decide the final design.

Preparation for Reproduction of Series of Varied Display Ads

Ads to be sent to other publications for insertion should be printed on the Linotronic typesetter or photostatted. If you are sending laser-printer output, use laser paper or coated stock to get the best black image and to provide the best surface for pasteup. If you are using regular bond paper, you may want to include a note that the camera-ready copy you are delivering is on regular bond paper. Otherwise, production staff who are unfamiliar with laser printing may think that you are delivering a photocopy instead of an original. (This common misunderstanding should occur less frequently in the future, as more production departments start using laser printers.)

Example 14.4. A Series of Ads in the Same Format for the Same Service

This example demonstrates a new twist in developing a series of ads. Whereas two preceding examples develop a series of different designs, this example produces a series of ads that all use the same design; but the store location and phone number are different on each ad. This approach can be applied to similar situations in which the same service is offered by different franchisers in different regions. The economy lies in using a central design department to develop ads for dealers in widely separated locations. You can adapt the same approach to produce a series of announcements for the same seminar or special event that will be held in different cities or on different dates.

Description of Ads in the Same Format

The preceding example shows a series of ad designs from which only one is chosen. In this case, a series of ads is created for different stores that offer the same service (see fig. 14.12). The ad is set up on the master page, and a different store address and phone number are entered on each numbered page.

Fig. 14.12. Printouts of pages for series for same service.

Production Tricks for Ads in the Same Format

The trick is to lay out the basic ad design on the master page (see fig. 14.13). On each page in the document, only the store address is changed. As you can see, the template holds the graphic elements and dummy text. Other text is stored on the pasteboard and used as needed.

Fig. 14.13. *The template for series for same service.*

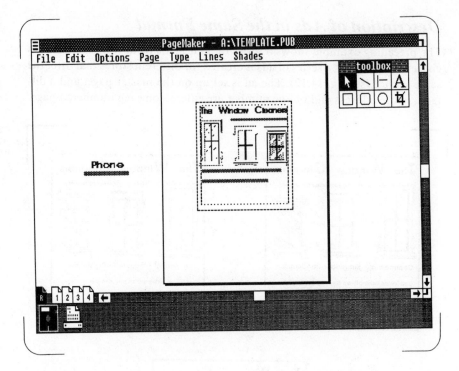

Production Steps for Ads in the Same Format

Because this ad has only one design, only one master page is needed. The variation is achieved with the text.

1. Lay out the ad design on the master page. For the address lines, store dummy text, set in the correct type specifications, on the pasteboard.

2. On each page of the document, copy and paste the store-address lines from the pasteboard to the page, and change the address as appropriate.

Summary

Part III of *Using PageMaker on the IBM* illustrates PageMaker's wide range of uses and helpful features for producing professional documents. No matter what equipment you may be using—dot-matrix printer, laser printer, or typesetter—PageMaker guarantees high-quality output. Whether your publishing projects are large or small, PageMaker has the capabilities to produce high-quality published documents that just a few years ago could be produced only by professional designers and typesetters.

With PageMaker, professional quality is available to individuals, businesses, nonprofit, educational, and government organizations. You may be producing books and manuals or single-page fliers and ads. Part III helps you with each stage—designing, creating, and printing the professional documents you need for your job. We hope that the examples in this section of the book will get you started toward making PageMaker a true publishing tool.

Appendix
Hardware and Software Vendors

This appendix lists, with the vendors, products that are compatible with PageMaker for the IBM. These products include computers, fonts, graphics drawing programs, painting programs, scanners, graphics cards and monitors, input devices, output devices, and word-processing and other software.

Computers

COMPAQ Deskpro 286®, 386®

COMPAQ Computer Corporation
20555 FM 149
Houston, TX 77070

Hewlett-Packard Vectra®

Hewlett-Packard Company
Personal Office Computer Division
974 East Arques, Box 486
Sunnyvale, CA 94086

IBM® Personal Computer AT, Series 30, 50, 60, 80

International Business Machines
1133 Westchester Avenue
White Plains, NY 10604

Tandy® 2000, 3000

Tandy Corporation
1500 One Tandy Center
Fort Worth, TX 76102

VAXmate™

Digital Equipment Corporation
146 Main Street
Maynard, MA 01754

Fonts

Adobe Systems, Inc.
1870 Embarcadero Road
Palo Alto, CA 94303

Bitstream®
215 First Street
Cambridge, MA 02142

Xiphias
13464 Washington Blvd.
Marina Del Rey, CA 90292

Graphics

Drawing Programs

AutoCAD®

Autodesk, Inc.
2320 Marinship Way
Sausalito, CA 94965

In*a*Vision™

Micrografx, Inc.
1820 N. Greenville Avenue
Richardson, TX 75081

Instinct®

Cadlogic Systems Corporation
2635 North First Street, Suite 202
San Jose, CA 95134

Windows Draw™

Micrografx, Inc.
1820 N. Greenville Avenue
Richardson, TX 75081

Painting Programs

HALO DPE™

Media Cybernetics, Inc.
8484 Georgia Avenue
Silver Spring, MD 20910

Microsoft® Windows Paint

Microsoft Corporation
16011 NE 36th Way
Redmond, WA 98073

PC Paint™

Mouse Systems Corporation
2600 San Thomas Expressway
Santa Clara, CA 95051

PC Paintbrush®

ZSoft Corporation
1950 Spectrum Circle, Suite A495
Marietta, GA 30067

PostScript®
Adobe Illustrator™

Adobe Systems, Inc.
1870 Embarcadero Road
Palo Alto, CA 94303

Scanners

Canon® IX-12

Canon U.S.A., Inc.
One Canon Plaza
Lake Success, NY 11042

Datacopy
1215 Terra Bella
Mountain View, CA 94043

Dest
1202 Cadillac Court
Milpitas, CA 95035

Microtek MS-300A

Microtek Lab, Inc.
16901 S. Western Avenue
Gardena, CA 90247

Graphics Cards/Monitors

ConoVision 2800™

Conographic Corporation
17841 Fitch
Irvine, CA 92714

Enhanced Graphics Adapter/Monitor

International Business Machines
1133 Westchester Avenue
White Plains, NY 10604

LaserView™

Sigma Designs, Inc.
46501 Landing Parkway
Fremont, CA 94538

Moniterm Viking I®

Moniterm Corporation
5740 Green Circle Drive
Minnetonka, MN 55343

NEC MultiSync®

NEC Home Electronics, Inc.
Personal Computer Division
1401 Estes Avenue
Elk Grove Village, IL 60007

WY-700™

Wyse Technology, Inc.
3571 First Street
San Jose, CA 95134

Input Devices

LogiMouse®
    (Logitech Mouse)

Logitech, Inc.
805 Veteran's Blvd., Suite 201
Redwood City, CA 94063

Manager Mouse®

The Torrington Company
59 Field Street
Torrington, CT 06790

Microsoft® Mouse

Microsoft Corporation
16011 NE 36th Way
Redmond, WA 98073

PC Mouse™

Mouse Systems Corporation
2600 San Thomas Expressway
Santa Clara, CA 95051

Output Devices

Apple LaserWriter® and LaserWriter Plus®

Apple Computer
20525 Mariani Avenue
Cupertino, CA 95014

AST TurboLaser®

AST Research, Inc.
2121 Alton Avenue
Irvine, CA 92714

Epson FX-80™

EPSON America, Inc.
2780 Lomita Blvd.
Torrance, CA 90505

Hewlett-Packard LaserJet™ and Hewlett-Packard® Series II Laser Printer

Hewlett-Packard Company
8020 Foothills
Roseville, CA 95678

IBM Proprinter™

IBM International Business Machines
1133 Westchester Avenue
White Plains, NY 10604

Linotronic™ 100/300

Allied Corporation
425 Oser Avenue
Hauppauge, NY 11788

Word-Processing Software

IBM DisplayWrite 3™

International Business Machines
1133 Westchester Avenue
White Plains, NY 10604

Microsoft® Windows Write

Microsoft Corporation
16011 NE 36th Way
Redmond, WA 98073

Microsoft® Word

Microsoft Corporation
16011 NE 36th Way
Redmond, WA 98073

MultiMate®

Multimate International
52 Oakland Avenue
East Hartford, CT 06108

Volkswriter®

Lifetree Software, Inc.
411 Pacific Street, Suite 315
Monterey, CA 93940

WordPerfect®

WordPerfect Corporation
288 West Center Street
Orem, UT 84057

WordStar®

MicroPro International
33 San Pablo Avenue
San Rafael, CA 94903

XyWrite III™

XyQuest
P.O. Box 372
Bedford, MA 01730

Other Software

1-2-3® and Symphony®

Lotus Development Corp.
55 Cambridge Pkwy.
Cambridge, MA 02142

Glossary

"Actual size". A command on the Page menu. Shows in the publication window a page approximately the size in which that page will be printed, depending on the screen's characteristics.

Alignment. The positioning of lines of text on a page or in a column: aligned left (flush left, ragged right); centered; aligned right (flush right, ragged left); or justified (flush on both left and right).

Ascender. The part of a lowercase letter that rises above its main body. Technically, only three letters of the alphabet have ascenders: *b, d,* and *h.* Uppercase letters and the lowercase letters *f, k, l,* and *t* also reach the height of the ascenders. See also *Descender.*

ASCII. The form in which text is stored when saved as "Text only", a "Save" command option available for most databases, spreadsheets, and word processors. These files include all the characters of the text itself (including tabs and carriage returns) but not the non-ASCII codes used to indicate character and paragraph formats. See also *Text-only file.*

Bad break. Term referring to page breaks and column breaks that result in widows or orphans or to line breaks that hyphenate words incorrectly or separate two words that should stay together (for example, *Mr. Smith*). See also *Nonbreaking space* and *Orphans/widows.*

Baseline. In a line of text, the lowest point of letters excluding descenders (for example, the lowest point of letters such as *a* and *x,* but not the lower edges of descenders on *p* and *q*).

Bit map. A graphics image or text formed by a pattern of dots. PC Paint, Windows Paint, and PC Paintbrush documents produce bit-mapped graphics as well as scanned or digitized images. Low-resolution images are sometimes called *paint-type* files, and they usually have a lower number of dots per inch (dpi) than high-resolution images.

Bleed. Term used to describe a printed image that extends to the trimmed edge of the sheet or page.

Block. See *Text block.*

Blue lines. A preliminary test printing of a page to check the offset printer's plates. This test printing is done using a photochemical process (rather than printers' inks) that produces a blue image on white paper. See also *Prepress proofs* and *Press proofs*.

Blue pencil/blue line. Traditionally, a guide line drawn with a blue pencil or printed in light blue ink on the boards and used for manually pasting up a page layout. The blue ink is sometimes called *nonrepro blue* because the color is not picked up by the camera when a page is photographed to make plates for offset printing. With PageMaker, you can create nonprinting margins, column guides, and ruler guides on the screen to help you position text and graphics; these lines do not appear when the page is printed.

Board. A sheet of heavyweight paper or card stock onto which typeset text and graphics are pasted manually. See also *Blue pencil/blue line*.

Body copy. The main part of the text of a publication, as distinguished from headings and captions. See also *Body type*.

Body type. The type (font) used for the body copy. Generally, fonts that are used for body copy, as distinguished from display type. See also *Body copy*.

Boilerplate. See *Template*.

Brochure. A folded pamphlet or small booklet.

Call out. In PageMaker, text that points out and identifies parts of an illustration. Also, headings that appear in a narrow margin next to the body copy. See also *Pull-out quote*.

Camera-ready art. The complete pages of a publication assembled with text and graphics and ready for reproduction. Literally refers to pages ready to be photographed as the first step in the process of making plates for offset printing. See also *Mechanicals* and *Offset printing*.

Caps and small caps. Text in which the letters that are usually lowercase are set as uppercase letters smaller than normal capitals. An option in the "Type specs..." dialog box.

Captions. Descriptive text identifying photographs and illustrations. See also *Call out*.

Carriage return. A line break you insert by pressing the carriage return (Return key) at the end of a line or paragraph. Sometimes called a *hard carriage return* to distinguish it from the *soft carriage returns*, which result from wordwrap at the right margin of a page or right edge of a column.

Check box. In a dialog box, the area you click to turn an option on or off.

Cicero. A unit of measure equivalent to 4.55 millimeters, commonly used in Europe for measuring font size. Use the "Preferences..." command on the Edit menu to select ciceros as the unit of measure for the ruler lines and dialog box displays. You also can enter a value in ciceros in any dialog box by inserting a *c* between the number of ciceros and the number of points; for example, *3c2* indicates 3 ciceros and 2 points. See also *Measurement system.*

Click. To press and release a mouse button quickly.

Clipboard. A feature of Microsoft Windows; temporarily stores text or graphics cut or copied by the commands on the Edit menu. The "Paste" command brings the contents of the Clipboard to the page. The "Clipboard" command displays the contents of the Clipboard.

Close. To choose the "Close pub" command from the File menu and stop work on the current publication, or to choose the "Close" command from the System menu and leave PageMaker.

Collated. Printed in numerical order with the first page on top of the stack that comes out of the printer. An option in the "Print..." dialog box. Multiple copies are grouped into whole sets of the publication.

Color separations. In offset printing, separate plates used to lay a different color of ink on a page printed in multiple colors. Using PageMaker, you can create masters for color separations by preparing different pages with the elements to be printed in one color on each page. If the colors do not overlap, you also can use a tissue overlay to specify colors to the offset printer. See also *Overlay.*

Column guides. Dotted vertical nonprinting lines that mark left and right edges of columns created with PageMaker's "Column guides..." command.

Column rules. Vertical lines drawn between columns with PageMaker's perpendicular-line tool.

Command button. A large rectangular area in a dialog box; contains a command such as "OK" or "Cancel". Command buttons surrounded by a thick black line can be activated by pressing the Return key.

Comp. Traditionally, a designer's "comprehensive" sketch of a page design; shows the client what the final page will look like when printed. Usually a full-size likeness of the page, the comp is a few steps closer to the final than a *pencil rough* and can be composed using ink pens, pencils, color markers, color acetate, pressure-sensitive letters, and other tools available at art supply shops. Created with PageMaker, a comp resembles the finished product, with typeset text, ruled lines, and shaded boxes created in PageMaker; the comp can be used as a starting point in building the final document.

Continued line. See *Jump line*.

Continuous-tone image. An illustration or photograph, black-and-white or color; composed of many shades between the lightest and the darkest tones and not broken up into dots. Continuous-tone images usually need to be converted into dots, either by scanning or by halftoning, in order to be printed in ink or on a laser printer. See also *Halftone*.

Control Panel. A Microsoft Windows application program used to add or delete fonts and printers, change printer connections and settings, and adjust mouse and screen settings.

Copy fitting. To determine the amount of copy (text set in a specific font) that will fit in a given area on a page or in a publication. To make copy fit on a page in PageMaker by adjusting the line spacing, word spacing, and letter spacing.

Corner style. See *Rounded-corner tool*.

Crop. To use PageMaker's cropping tool to trim the edges from a graphic to make the image fit in a given space, or to remove unnecessary parts of the image.

Crop marks. Lines printed on a page to indicate where the page will be trimmed when the final document is printed and bound. PageMaker prints these marks if the page size is smaller than the paper size and if the "Crop marks" option is selected in the "Print..." command dialog box.

Cropping tool. Tool used to trim a graphic.

Crossbar. The shape of the pointer when one of PageMaker's tools for drawing lines and shapes has been selected.

Custom. In PageMaker, a word to describe unequal columns, which you can create in PageMaker by dragging column guides into the desired position.

Default. The program initial setting of a value or option. Default settings usually can be changed by the operator.

Descender. The part of a lowercase letter that hangs below the baseline. Five letters of the alphabet have descenders: *g*, *j*, *p*, *q*, and *y*. See also *Ascender* and *Baseline*.

Deselect. In PageMaker, to select another command or option or to click on a blank area of the pasteboard to cancel the current selection.

Desktop. The menu bar and blank area PageMaker displays when no publication is open.

Desktop publishing. Use of personal computers and software applications like PageMaker to produce copy that is ready for reproduction.

Diagonal-line tool. Tool used to draw a straight line in any direction.

Dialog box. A window or full-screen display that appears in response to a command that calls for setting options.

Digitize. To convert an image to a system of dots that can be stored in the computer. See also *Scanned-image files.*

Dingbats. Traditionally, ornamental characters (bullets, stars, flowers) used for decoration or as special characters within text. The laser font Zapf Dingbats includes many traditional symbols and some new ones.

Directory. A named area reserved on the hard disk where a group of related files can be stored together. Each directory can have subdirectories.

Discretionary hyphen. A hyphen inserted when Ctrl-[hyphen] is pressed. Identifies where PageMaker can divide a word to fit text in the specified line length when "Hyphenation" is on (as specified in the "Paragraph..." command dialog box). The hyphen appears on the screen and on the printed page only if the hyphen falls at the end of a line. See also *Hyphenation.*

Display type. Type used for headlines, titles, headings, advertisements, fliers, and so on. Display type is usually a large point size (several sizes larger than body copy) and can be a decorative font.

Dots per inch (dpi). See *Resolution.*

Dot-matrix printer. A printer that creates text and graphics by pressing a matrix of pins through the ribbon onto the paper. These impact printers usually offer lower resolution (dots per inch) than laser printers and are used only for draft printouts from PageMaker.

Double-click. To press and release the main mouse button quickly twice in succession.

Double-headed arrow. The shape of the pointer tool when a handle, ruler guide, or column guide is being dragged.

Double-sided publication. An option in the "Page setup..." dialog box for creating a publication to be reproduced on both sides of the sheets of paper. The front side of a page has an odd-numbered page, and the back side has an even-numbered page. See also *Facing pages*.

Drag. To hold down the main mouse button, move the mouse until the object is where you want it, and release the button.

Drag-place. To drag the mouse diagonally to define the width of a graphic or text as you're placing it and so override the column guides.

Draw-type files. See *Object-oriented files*.

Drop-down menu. A list of commands that appears when you select a menu. In PageMaker, the menu titles appear on the menu bar along the top of the screen, and the menu commands "drop down" in a list below the menu title selected.

Dummy publication. Traditionally, a pencil mock-up of the pages of a publication, folded or stapled into a booklet, which the offset printer uses to verify the correct sequence of pages and positions of photographs. PageMaker's thumbnails can serve the function of a dummy publication. See also *Template* and *Thumbnail*.

Ellipse. A regular-shaped oval. Shape created with PageMaker's oval tool, as distinguished from irregular ovals, which are egg-shaped.

Ellipsis. Series of three dots in text (. . .), used to indicate that some of the text has been deleted (usually from a quotation). A closed ellipsis (without spaces) appears after every PageMaker command that opens a dialog box ("Open..").

Em. Unit of measure equaling the point size of the type; for example, a 12-point em is 12 points wide. The width of an em dash or an em space. See also *En*.

En. One half the width of an em. The width of an en dash or an en space. See also *Em*.

Enter key. Key you press to break a line when the text tool is active or to confirm the selected options in a dialog box. Usually has the same effect as the Return key. See also *Carriage return*.

Facing pages. The two pages that face each other when a book, brochure, etc., is open. Also an option used in double-sided publications. Facing pages have an even-numbered page on the left and an odd-numbered page on the right. See also *Double-sided publication*.

Flow text. To click the mouse button to discharge a loaded text icon and place text on a page.

Flush. Aligned with, even with, coming to the same edge as. See also *Alignment.*

Flush right (or right-justified). Text in which lines end at the same point on the right margin. Opposite of ragged right or left-justified. See also *Alignment.*

Folio. Page number on a printed page, often accompanied by the name of the document and date of publication. See also *Running head* and *Running foot.*

Font. One complete set of characters (including all the letters of the alphabet, punctuation, and symbols) in the same typeface, style, and size. For example, 12-point Times Roman is a different font from 12-point Times Italic, 14-point Times Roman, or 12-point Helvetica. Screen fonts (bit-mapped fonts used to display text accurately on the screen) can differ slightly from printer fonts (outline fonts used to describe fonts to the laser printer) because of the difference in resolution between screens and printers.

Footer. See *Running foot.* See also *Folio.*

Format. Page size, margins, and grid used in a publication. Also the character format (font) and paragraph format (alignment, spacing, and indentation).

Four-headed arrow. Shape of the pointer when used to drag a selected text block or graphic.

Generic font. A screen representation of alphanumeric characters, may not look like the printed characters. See also *Font.*

Grabber hand. A PageMaker icon; appears when you press the Alt key and drag the mouse to move around in the window.

Graphic. A line, box, or circle that you draw with PageMaker; an illustration brought into a PageMaker publication from another application.

Greek text (greeked text). Traditionally, a block of text used to represent the positioning and point size of text in a designer's comp of a design. Standard greeked text used by typesetters actually looks more like Latin: "Lorem ipsum dolor sit amet . . ." See also *Greeking.*

Greeking. The conversion of text to symbolic bars or boxes that show the position of the text on the screen but not the real characters. Text is usually greeked in the "Fit in window" view in PageMaker; small point sizes may be greeked in closer views on some screens. See also *Greek text*.

Grid. The underlying design plan for a page. In PageMaker, the grid consists of nonprinting horizontal and vertical lines (margins, column guides, and ruler guides) that intersect to form a grid.

Guide. A nonprinting line (margin guide, ruler guide, or column guide) created to help align objects on a page. In PageMaker, nonprinting guides look like dotted lines, dashed lines, or blue lines, depending on the screen's resolution and color settings.

Gutter. The inside margins between the facing pages of a document; sometimes describes the space between columns. In some word processors, the gutter measure is entered as the difference between the measures of the inside margin and the outside margin. See also *Margin*.

Hairline. The thinnest rule you can create—usually 0.25 point. (Some laser printers do not support hairline rules.) See also *Rules*.

Halftone. The conversion of continuous-tone artwork (usually a photograph) into a pattern of dots or lines that look like gray tones when printed by an offset printing press. See also *Continuous-tone image*.

Handles. The eight small black rectangles enclosing a selected shape; the two small rectangles at the ends of a selected line; the small black rectangles at the four corners of a selected text block. You can drag the handles to change the size of the selected object.

Hanging indent. A paragraph with the first line extending to the left of the other lines. A hanging-indent format can be used to create headings set to the left of the body copy. See also *Indentation*.

Hard carriage return. See *Carriage return*.

Hard disk. Disk storage that is built into the computer or into a piece of hardware connected to the computer; distinguished from removable floppy disk storage.

Header. See *Running head*. See also *Running foot* and *Folio*.

Headline. The title of an article in a newsletter, newspaper, or magazine.

Hierarchical filing system. A disk storage system in which files can be stored in separate directories, which, in turn, can contain subdirectories. See also *Directory*.

Highlight. To distinguish visually. Usually reverses the normal appearance of selected text, graphic, or option (for example, black text on a white background appears as white on black).

Hyphenation. Hyphenation can be achieved in several ways: (1) PageMaker automatically hyphenates text (based on a built-in dictionary) as text is placed or typed on the page; (2) PageMaker recognizes hyphens inserted by the word-processing program; (3) you can activate prompted hyphenation through the "Paragraph..." command and insert hyphens in words that PageMaker displays in a dialog box as the text is being placed on the page; (4) you can insert *discretionary hyphens* (displayed only when they fall at the end of a line) by pressing Ctrl-[hyphen] within a word. See also *Discretionary hyphen.*

I-beam. The shape of the pointer when the text tool is selected.

Icon. Graphic on-screen representation of a tool, file, or command.

Image area. Area inside the margins of the page; contains most of the text and graphics.

Increment. Distance between tick marks on a ruler. See also *Measurement system.*

Indentation. Positioning the first line of a paragraph (or second and following lines) to the right of the left column guide (to create a left indent), or positioning the right margin of the paragraph to the left of the right column guide (to create a right indent) relative to the other text on the page. In PageMaker, you set indentation through the "Paragraph..." command dialog box or the "Indents/tabs..." command. See also *Hanging indent.*

Insertion point. A blinking vertical bar where text will be typed or pasted.

Inside margin. Margin along the edge of the page that will be bound. In single-sided publications, always the left margin. In double-sided publications, the inside margin is the left margin of a right-hand page or the right margin of a left-hand page. See also *Gutter* and *Margin.*

Italic. Letters that slope toward the right, as distinguished from upright, or Roman, characters.

Invert. See *Reverse.*

Jump line. Text at the end of the text of an article on a page indicating on what page the article is continued. Also, the text at the top of a continued article, indicating from where the article is continued. Also called a *continued line.*

Justified text. Text that is flush at both the left and right edges. See also *Alignment.*

Kern. To adjust the spaces between letters, usually to move letters closer together. See also *Kerning*.

Kerning. Amount of space between letters, especially certain combinations of letters that must be brought closer together in order to create visually consistent spacing around all letters. For example, the uppercase letters *A W* may appear to have a wider gap between them than the letters *M N* unless a special kerning formula is set up for the *A W* combination. In PageMaker, letters larger than the point size specified in the "Paragraph..." command dialog box are kerned against a table of kerning pairs. You also can adjust the space between letters manually with the text tool by pressing Ctrl-Backspace to decrease space or Ctrl-Shift-Backspace to increase space. See also *Kern*.

Landscape printing. The rotation of a page to print text and graphics horizontally across the longer measure of the page or paper (usually 11 inches). In PageMaker, the "Wide" option in the "Print..." command and in "Target printer..." command dialog boxes. See also *Orientation* and *Portrait printing*.

Laser printing. Term used to describe printing with one of the toner-based laser printers. These printers use laser technology—*l*ight *a*mplification by *s*timulated *e*mission of *r*adiation—to project an intense light beam with a very narrow band width (1/300th of an inch in 300-dots-per-inch printers). This light creates on the printer drum a charge that picks up the toner and transfers it to the paper. Some typesetters (such as the Linotronic 100 and 300) also use laser technology with their photochemical processing but are usually referred to as phototypesetters rather than laser printers. See also *Phototypesetting*.

Layout. The process of arranging text and graphics on a page. A sketch or plan for the page. Also the final appearance of the page. In platemaking, a sheet indicating the settings for the step-and-repeat machine.

Layout grid. See *Grid*.

Leaders. Dotted or dashed lines that can be defined for tab settings. PageMaker offers three types of tab leaders, plus a custom leader option, through the "Tabs/indents..." command.

Leading. Historically, the insertion of thin strips of metal (made of a metal alloy that included some lead) between lines of cast type to add space between the lines and to make columns align. In modern typography, the vertical space between the baselines of two lines of text. In PageMaker, leading is actually measured from ascender to ascender between two lines of text and is entered in points in the "Type specs..."

command dialog box. As an example of the terminology, 12-point Times with one point of leading is "one-point leaded" type; 12-point Times with 13-point leading is "12 on 13 Times." Type specs are sometimes written as "12/13 Times."

Letter spacing. Space between letters in a word. The practice of adding space between letters. In PageMaker, unjustified text has fixed letter spacing; justified text has variable letter spacing, which is adjusted within the limits entered in the "Spacing..." command dialog box. See also *Kerning* and *Word spacing*.

Ligatures. Character combinations that are often combined into special characters in a font. For example, some downloadable fonts come with the combinations *fi* and *fl* as special characters.

Line break. The end of a line of text, created by automatic wordwrap and hyphenation. See also *Carriage return*.

Line length. Horizontal measure of a column or a line of text.

Line spacing. See *Leading*.

Line style. Appearance of the border of a shape or a line drawn in Page-Maker; selected through the Lines menu.

List box. Area in a dialog box that displays options.

Lock. In PageMaker, using the "Lock guides" command to anchor column guides and ruler guides on the current page or to anchor the zero point of the rulers. Locked guides cannot be inadvertently moved during the process of laying out text and graphics.

Logo. A company trademark. Also, the banner on the front cover of a magazine or newsletter. See also *Masthead*.

Main mouse button. See *Mouse buttons*.

Margin. Traditionally, the distance from the edge of the page to the edge of the layout area of the page. In PageMaker, page size and margins are defined in the "Page setup" dialog box. The margins in PageMaker should be used to define the limits of text. Running heads, running feet, and column rules should be outside the margins. See also *Gutter* and *Inside margin*.

Margin guides. Dotted nonprinting lines displayed near the borders of the screen page to mark the margins of a page as specified in the "Page setup..." dialog box. See also *Margin*.

Master items. Items on a master page; may include text (running heads), graphics (rules), and nonprinting guides (column guides). See also *Master page.*

Master page. Page containing text, graphics, and guides you want repeated on every page in a publication. Opened by clicking the L or R page icon in the publication window. A single-sided publication has only one master page. A double-sided publication has two master pages: left-hand (even-numbered) and right-hand (odd-numbered). See also *Master items, Double-sided publication*, and *"Single sided".*

Masthead. Section of newsletter or magazine giving its title and details of staff, ownership, advertising, subscription, and so on. Sometimes, the banner or wide title on the front cover of a magazine or the front of a newsletter or newspaper. See also *Logo.*

Measurement system. Units chosen with the "Preferences..." command on the Edit menu: inches, decimal inches, millimeters, picas and points, or ciceros. The chosen units appear on the rulers and in all dialog boxes that display measurements. You can enter a value in any unit of measure in a dialog box—regardless of the current "Preferences..." selection—by typing the abbreviation for the unit in your entry. For example, *3.5i* indicates 3.5 inches, *3p2* specifies 3 picas and 2 points, *3.5m* indicates 3.5 millimeters, and *3c2* specifies 3 ciceros and 2 points. See also *Cicero* and *Pica.*

Mechanicals. Traditionally, the final pages or boards with pasted-up galleys of type and line art, sometimes with acetate or tissue overlays for color separations and notes to the offset printer. See also *Camera-ready art* and *Offset printing.*

Memory. Area in the computer where information is stored temporarily while you're working; also called RAM, or random-access memory. PageMaker automatically saves a publication from the memory onto a disk whenever you turn a page or click a page icon; these saves are called *minisaves.* You also can copy the contents of the memory onto disk by using the "Save" or "Save as..." command.

Menu bar. Area across the top of the publication window, where menu titles are displayed.

Minisave. PageMaker's automatic save of a publication whenever you turn a page or click a page icon. Minisaves create temporary documents on disk and do not overwrite the publication file. Use the "Save" command to overwrite the last saved version of the publication. See also *Memory.*

Moiré pattern. An undesirable grid pattern that may occur when two transparent dot-screen fill patterns are overlaid or when a bit-mapped graphic with gray fill patterns is reduced or enlarged. PageMaker's "magic stretch" feature (you hold down the Ctrl key as you drag) can help eliminate this effect.

Mouse buttons. The main mouse button, or primary mouse button, is used to carry out most PageMaker actions. Use the Control Panel to specify the main button as the left or right button of a two- or three-button mouse. Some PageMaker commands also use the secondary mouse button on a two-button or three-button mouse. See also *Control Panel.*

Negative. A reverse image of a page, produced photographically on a clear sheet of film as an intermediate step in preparing plates from camera-ready mechanicals for offset printing.

Nonbreaking space. A special character inserted between two words so that they are not separated by a line break. See also *Bad break* and *Orphans/widows.*

Nonprinting master items. The ruler guides and column guides on a master page. See also *Margin guides* and *Master page.*

Object-oriented files. Draw-type files consisting of a sequence of drawing commands (stored as mathematical formulas). These commands describe graphics (such as mechanical drawings, schematics, charts, and ad graphics) that you would produce manually with a pencil, straight-edge, and compass. Usually contrasted with paint-type files or bit maps. See also *Bit map.*

Offset printing. Type of printing done using a printing press to reproduce many copies of the original (in PageMaker printed on a laser printer). The press lays ink on a page according to the raised image on a plate created by photographing the camera-ready masters. See also *Camera-ready art*, *Laser printing*, and *Mechanicals.*

Option button. In a dialog box, the round area you click on to select an option.

"Orientation". Page position options: "Tall" or "Wide." In "Tall" orientation, text runs horizontally across the narrower width of the page, and columns run down the longer length of the page. In "Wide" orientation, text runs horizontally across the wider measure of the page. See also *Landscape printing* and *Portrait printing.*

Orphans/widows. The first line of a paragraph is called an *orphan* when separated from the rest of the paragraph by a page break. The last line of a paragraph is called a *widow* when forced to a new page by a page break and separated from the rest of the paragraph. Most publishers generally consider widows and orphans to be bad page breaks (or column breaks). The term *widow* is also used to describe bad line breaks that result in the last line of a paragraph having only one word, especially when it falls at the end of a column or page. See also *Bad break* and *Nonbreaking space*.

Outline font. A printer font in which each letter of the alphabet is stored as a mathematical formula, as distinguished from bit-mapped fonts that are stored as patterns of dots. See also *Bit map* and *Font*.

Outside margin. The unbound edge of a publication. In single-sided publications, the outside margin is the right margin. In double-sided publications, the outside margin is the right margin of a right-hand page or the left margin of a left-hand page. See also *Margin*.

Overhead transparency. An image printed on clear acetate and projected onto a screen for viewing by an audience.

Overlay. A transparent acetate or tissue covering a printed page; contains color specifications and other instructions to the offset printer. Also, an overhead transparency that is intended to be projected on top of another transparency. See also *Color separation*.

Oversize publication. Publication in which page size is larger than paper size. See also *Page size, Paper size*, and *Tile*.

Page icon. An icon displayed in the bottom left corner of the publication window. Icons represent the master page(s) and every regular page. See also *Icon*.

Page number marker. A series of characters (Ctrl+Shift+3) entered on a master page (displayed as 0) or on a regular page (displayed as the current page number); instructs PageMaker to number pages automatically.

Page size. The dimensions of the pages of your publication as set up in the "Page setup..." dialog box. Page size can differ from paper size. See also *Margin* and *Paper size*.

Paintbrush icon. Shape of the pointer when a bit-mapped (or paint-type) file is being placed.

Paint-type file. See *Bit map*.

Paper size. The size of the printer paper. Standard paper sizes are letter (8.5 by 11 inches), legal (8.5 by 14), European A4 (8.27 by 11.69), and European B5 (6.93 by 9.84).

Pasteboard. The on-screen work area surrounding the page(s) on which you are working. You move text and graphics to the pasteboard, where they remain when you turn to another page or close the publication.

Pasteup. See *Mechanicals*.

Pencil icon. Shape of the pointer when an object-oriented (draw-type) file is being placed.

Perpendicular-line tool. Tool used to draw a straight line at any 45-degree increment.

Phototypesetting. Producing a page image on photosensitive paper, as when documents are printed on a Linotronic 100 or 300. This process is sometimes referred to as *cold type* to distinguish it from the older method of casting characters, lines, or whole pages in lead (*hot type* or *hot metal*). See also *Laser printing*.

Pica. A unit of measure equal to approximately 1/6 inch, or 12 points. Use the "Preferences..." command on the Edit menu to select picas and points as the unit of measure for the ruler lines and dialog box displays. You can also enter a value in picas and points in any dialog box by typing a *p* between the number of picas and the number of points: for example, *3p2* specifies 3 picas and 2 points. See also *Measurement system*.

Pixel. The smallest unit on a computer display. Monitors can have different screen resolutions, or pixels per inch, and different sizes (total number of pixels).

"Place". Command used to bring into PageMaker a text or graphics file created in a word processor or graphics program.

Point. To place the mouse pointer on top of an object on the screen.

Point size. The smallest unit of measure in typographic measurement and the standard unit of measure for type; measured roughly from the top of the ascenders to the bottom of the descenders. A pica has 12 points; an inch, approximately 72 points; a point equals 1/12 pica, or 1/72 inch. See also *Cicero*, *Pica*, and *Measurement system*.

Pointer. The on-screen icon that moves when you move the mouse.

Pointer tool. The PageMaker tool used for selecting and manipulating text and graphics. When the pointer tool is selected, the pointer looks like an arrow.

Portrait printing. The normal printing orientation for a page: horizontally across the shorter measurement of the page or paper (usually, 8.5 inches). In PageMaker, the "Tall" option in the "Print..." command and "Target printer..." command dialog boxes. See also *Orientation* and *Landscape printing.*

PostScript. A page-description language developed by Adobe Systems, Inc.; used by the LaserWriter, the IBM Personal PagePrinter, and other high-resolution printers and typesetters.

"Preferences...". A PageMaker command on the Edit menu used to select the unit of measure displayed on ruler lines and in dialog boxes. See also *Measurement system, Cicero,* and *Pica.*

Prepress proofs. Sometimes called *blue lines,* these proofs are made using photographic techniques. See also *Press proofs* and *Blue lines.*

Press proofs. A test run of a color printing job through the printing press to check registration and color. See also *Prepress proofs* and *Blue lines.*

Print area. The area on a piece of paper where the printer reproduces text and graphics; always smaller than the paper size. See also *Margin.*

Print queue. Files in the spooler waiting to be sent to the printer. Files are sent in the order they are received. See also *Spooler.*

Printer font. A bit-mapped or outline font installed in the printer or down-loaded to the printer when a publication is printed. Usually distin-guished from the screen font, which displays the text on the computer screen. See also *Bit map, Font,* and *Outline font.*

Proofread. To read a preliminary printout of a page and check for spelling errors, alignment on the page, and other features that are not related to the technical accuracy of the content.

Proofs. See *Prepress proofs, Press proofs,* and *Blue lines*

Publication. A collection of pages created with PageMaker by integrating text and graphics files created with other applications and with PageMaker.

Publication window. Window appearing when you start PageMaker. Dis-plays a view of one or two pages, pasteboard, page icons, pointer, scroll bars, title bar, menu bar, and toolbox window.

Pull-out quote. Quotation extracted from the text of an article and printed in larger type, often set off by ruled lines.

Ragged right. Text in which lines end at different points near the right margin. Opposite of flush right or justified text. See also *Alignment*.

RAM. See *Memory*.

Release. Letting go of a mouse button.

Resolution. Number of dots per inch used to create an alphanumeric character or a graphics image. High-resolution images have more dots per inch and look smoother than low-resolution images. The resolution of images displayed on the screen is usually lower than that of the final laser printout. Laser printers print 300 dots per inch or more; typesetters print 1,200 dots per inch or more.

Reverse. Text or a graphic on the printed page that appears opposite of normal. Usually, text and graphics are black on a white background; when reversed, they are white on black.

Right-justified. See *Flush right* and *Alignment*.

Roman. Upright text styles, as distinguished from italic. Sometimes used to refer to "Normal" style, as opposed to "Bold" or "Italic", on PageMaker's Type menu.

Roughs. Traditionally, the preliminary page layouts done by the designer using pencil sketches to represent miniature page design ideas. You can use PageMaker's "Thumbnail" option in the "Print..." command dialog box to produce the equivalent of roughs. See also *Thumbnail*.

Rounded-corner tool. PageMaker tool used to draw squares and rectangles with rounded corners. You can adjust the degree of roundness by the "Rounded corners..." command on the Options menu.

Ruler guides. Nonprinting extensions of the tick marks on the rulers, which form horizontal and vertical dotted, dashed, or blue lines on the page; used to align text and graphics on the page. Select the "Rulers" command to display the rulers and then drag the pointer tool from a ruler onto the page in order to create a guide.

Rulers. Electronic rulers displayed one across the top of the publication window and one down the left side. Also, the text ruler displayed by the "Indents/tabs..." command on the Type menu. Rulers show measures in inches, picas, or millimeters. Use the "Rulers" command to display or hide the rulers. Use the "Preferences..." command on the Edit menu to select the unit of measure displayed on the ruler lines and dialog box displays. Increments (tick marks) on the rulers depend on the size and resolution of your screen, as well as on the view ("Actual size", "Fit in window", "200%", and so forth). See also *Measurement system*.

Rules. Black lines added to a page—for example, between columns—to improve the design or increase readability of a publication; created with PageMaker's perpendicular-line or diagonal-line tool. The Lines menu sets the thickness and style of the rules.

Runaround. See *Text wrap*.

Running foot. One or more lines of text appearing at the bottom of every page. In PageMaker, the running foot is entered on the master pages. Also referred to as the footer. See also *Folio*.

Running head. One or more lines of text appearing at the top of every page of a document. In PageMaker, the running head is entered on the master pages. Also referred to as the header. See also *Folio*.

Sans serif. Typefaces without serifs, such as Helvetica and Avant Garde. See also *Serif*.

Scanned-image files. Bit-mapped files created with hardware that digitizes images (converts a two- or three-dimensional image to a collection of dots stored in the computer's memory or on disk). PageMaker reads the scanned-image files directly from disk.

Scanned-image icon. Shape of the pointer when a scanned-image file is being placed.

Screen. Gray tone usually identified as a percentage on PageMaker's Shades menu. A 100-percent screen is solid black; a 10-percent screen is light gray. Also, any of the other line patterns on the Shades menu.

Screen font. See *Font*.

Script fonts. Type designed to look like handwriting or calligraphy, such as Zapf Chancery. See also *Font*.

Scroll bar. Gray bars on right side and bottom of the publication window; moved horizontally or vertically to change the view in the publication window. Scroll bar has a scroll box and scroll arrows at both ends. List boxes also can have scroll bars for viewing long lists of files or options.

Secondary mouse button. On a multiple-button mouse, the left or right button that is not the main button. See also *Mouse buttons*.

Select. To click or drag the mouse to designate the location of the next action.

Selection area. Area of a text block or graphic defined by the handles displayed when you select that text block or graphic. See also *Handles*.

Selection box. A box drawn by dragging the pointer tool to enclose and select more than one graphic or text block at a time. See also *Drag*.

Serif. Line crossing the main stroke of a letter. Typefaces that have serifs include Times, Courier, New Century Schoolbook, Bookman, and Palatino. See also *Sans serif*.

Shade pattern. Pattern selected on the Shades menu to fill an object drawn with PageMaker. See also *Screen*.

Shape. An object drawn with PageMaker: a square, rectangle, circle, or oval.

Signature. In printing and binding, the name given to a printed sheet of (usually) 16 pages after folding.

"Single sided". An option in PageMaker's "Page setup..." dialog box, used to set up a publication with pages to be reproduced on one side only of each sheet of paper. See also *Double-sided publication*.

Size. To make a graphic smaller or larger by dragging the handles. See also *Handles*.

Small caps. See *Caps and small caps*.

Snap-to. The effect of various types of nonprinting guide lines—margin guides, ruler guides, and column guides. These guides exert a "magnetic" pull on the cursor, text, or a graphic that comes close to the guides. Useful for aligning text and graphics accurately.

"Snap-to guides". PageMaker command that, when turned on, causes margin guides, column guides, and ruler guides to exert a "magnetic" pull on the pointer or any text or graphic near the guides.

Soft carriage return. See *Carriage return*.

Spacing guides. A PageMaker object used to help measure and standardize the spaces between text and graphics, between headings and body copy, or between any elements on a page. In PageMaker, spacing guides can be stored on the pasteboard.

Spooler. A Microsoft Windows application for sending files to the printer. PageMaker's "Print..." command sends the publication to the spooler, not directly to the printer. The spooler holds files in the print queue and prints them in the order in which they were received. You can continue working on other files while a file is being printed. See also *Print queue*.

Square-corner tool. PageMaker tool used to create squares and rectangles with square corners.

Stacking order. Order in which overlapping text and graphics are arranged on the page and on-screen.

Story. All the text from one word-processing file: all the text typed or compiled at an insertion point outside existing text blocks. Can be one text block or several text blocks threaded together. See also *Text block*.

Style. One of the variations within a typeface, such as Roman, bold, or italic. See also *Font* and *Typeface*.

System menu. The Microsoft Windows menu listing commands for working with windows, getting PageMaker help, using the Clipboard, and leaving PageMaker.

System menu box. Small square displayed in the upper left corner of the publication window. You click this box to select the System menu.

Target printer. The printer on which you intend to print the final version of your publication. If no target printer is selected, PageMaker uses the default printer chosen when Windows was installed.

Template. A PageMaker publication containing only the layout grid, master pages, estimated number of pages, and boilerplate text and graphics for a periodical or book. Serves as the starting point for creating many similar documents, such as chapters of a book or issues of a newsletter. Variable items—text and graphics that are not common to all chapters or issues—are added to the template document and saved under another name so that the original template document remains unchanged.

Text block. A variable amount of text identified by *handles*, small squares at the four corners of the text block, or by *windowshades*, two horizontal lines, each with a loop, at the top and bottom of the text block.

Text box. In a dialog box, area in which you type text.

Text icon. Shape of the pointer when loaded with text.

Text-only file. Text created with another application and saved without type specifications or other formatting. PageMaker reads text-only files directly from disk. See also *ASCII*.

Text tool. Tool used to select text for editing. When this tool is selected, the pointer looks like an I-beam.

Text wrap. Automatic line breaks at the right edge of a column or at the right margin of a page. Also, the ability to wrap text around a graphic on a page layout. In PageMaker, you can wrap text around a graphic by changing the width of a text block (dragging the text handles) or by using the drag-place feature. See also *Carriage return.*

Threaded text. Blocks of text that are connected across the columns on a page and across pages from the beginning to end of the article. PageMaker threads all words in a file you place or text you type inside an existing text block. When you edit threaded or chained text, PageMaker moves lines across columns or pages to adjust to the new text length. Text typed outside existing text blocks becomes part of a new text block, and all words in that new text block are threaded together.

Thumbnail. A miniature version of a page created with the "Thumbnails" option in the "Print..." command dialog box; used to preview publications. PageMaker prints up to 64 thumbnails on a page. Available on printers with a page-description language, such as PostScript or DDL. See also *Roughs.*

Tick marks. Marks on the rulers showing increments of measure. See also *Measurement system.*

Tile. Used in oversize publications. A part of a page printed on a single sheet of paper. For a complete page, the tiles are assembled and pasted together. See also *Oversize publication.*

Time-out error. Printer stops because it has not received information for a while. Occurs when you are printing complex pages and printer takes a long time to image a large bit-mapped image. Saving before printing helps reduce chances of loss of data.

Toggle switch. An on/off switch, command, or option. Used to describe cases in which the same command is invoked to turn a feature on and off. On PageMaker menus, these commands display a check mark when they are on.

Tones. The shades of a photograph or illustration that is printed as a series of dots. Tones are percentages of black, with smaller percentages producing lighter tones.

Toolbox window. Window overlapping the publication window and containing icons for the tools you use to work with text and graphics.

Transparency. See *Overhead transparency* and *Overlay.*

Triple-click. To press and release the main mouse button quickly three times in succession.

Typeface. A single type family of one design of type in all sizes and styles. For example, Times and Helvetica are two different typefaces. Each typeface has many fonts (sizes and styles). Sometimes the terms *typeface* and *font* are used interchangeably. See also *Font* and *Style*.

Uppercase. See *Caps and small caps*.

Vector graphics. See *Object-oriented files*.

Vertical justification. Dragging the bottom windowshade to adjust the length of a text block, or adjusting the spaces between lines of text (leading) in fine increments in order to make columns and pages end at the same point.

View. The size of the pasteboard and page as displayed in the publication window. View is determined by selections on the Page menu. The smallest view ("Fit in window") shows either a complete page or two pages (for a double-sided publication with facing pages). The largest view ("200%") shows text and graphics in twice the size in which they will be printed.

White space. Empty space on a page, not used for text or graphics.

Widow. See *Orphans/widows*.

Window. On-screen area where you are running a Windows application. Each window has a title bar, menu bar, and scroll bars.

Windowshade. Horizontal lines, each with a loop, that span the top and bottom of a text block. See also *Handles*.

Word spacing. The space between words in a line or a paragraph. In PageMaker, nonjustified text has fixed word spacing; and justified text has variable word spacing, which is adjusted within the limits entered in the "Spacing..." command dialog box. See also *Kerning* and *Letter spacing*.

Wordwrap. The automatic adjustment of the number of words on a line of text according to the margin settings. The carriage returns that result from automatic wordwrap are called *soft carriage returns* to distinguish them from *hard carriage returns*, which are entered when the Return key is pressed to force a new line. See also *Text wrap* and *Carriage return*.

Wrap. See *Text wrap* and *Wordwrap*.

WYSIWYG. "What You See Is What You Get" (or "wizzy-wig"). Term describes systems like PageMaker, which display full pages on the screen with text and graphics. Some systems are more WYSIWYG than others in the accuracy of the display.

X-height. A distinguishing characteristic of a font. The height of lowercase letters without ascenders or descenders, such as *x*, *a*, and *c*. Also called the body of the type.

Zero point. The intersection of the two PageMaker rulers at 0. The default zero point is at the intersection of the left and top margins but can be moved.

Zoom. When you have two or more windows open, use the "Zoom" command on the System menu to enlarge one window to fill the screen. Use "Zoom" to make a window full-size and again to return the window to its previous size.

Tips Index

INDEX

U-V

W-Z

More Computer Knowledge from Que

MORE COMPUTER KNOWLEDGE FROM QUE

Using 1-2-3, 2nd Edition
by Geoffrey LeBlond and Douglas Cobb

Nationally acclaimed, *Using 1-2-3* is "the book" for every 1-2-3 user. Whether you are using Release 1A or 2, you will find *Using 1-2-3,* 2nd Edition, your most valuable source of information. Spreadsheet, database, graphics, and macro capabilities common to both Releases 1A and 2 or new to Release 2 are all covered in depth. Notations in the text and a tear-out command chart help you locate quickly the differences between Releases 1A and 2. Like over a half-million other 1-2-3 users, you will consider this book indispensable.

> *This title must be one of the greats when it comes to good books on 1-2-3.*
> —Computer Shopper

Using WordPerfect, 3rd Edition
by Walton Beacham and Deborah Beacham

The 3rd Edition of this consistent best-seller features a totally new design and over 150 additional pages covering the many features of 4.2. Reorganized to follow the way the WordPerfect user learns this top-selling word-processing package, *Using WordPerfect,* 3rd Edition, has a progressive, new modular design to guide you easily through the book and to serve as a handy reference book later. New "Quick Start" exercises provide immediate application of the concepts and information presented. A 2-color tear-out keyboard reference offers hands-on assistance.

Using PC DOS
by Chris DeVoney

In the lucid, easy-to-understand style that made him a best-selling author, Chis DeVoney describes both the common and not-so-common operations of PC DOS. DeVoney guides users—both novice and intermediate—through basic and advanced DOS commands. A Command Reference defines every DOS command, gives examples, and tells how to handle common problems. *Using PC DOS* is two books in one—a concise tutorial and a valuable reference you will refer to over and over again.

> *This is the best DOS book I know of. It covers everything and has lots of examples.*
> —Jerry Pournelle, BYTE Magazine

Managing Your Hard Disk
by Don Berliner

Because more and more hard disks are being sold, Que's *Managing Your Hard Disk* introduces innovative techniques to bring the hard disk to peak performance. Storing and retrieving "libraries" of information is simple when you follow the book's easy-to-understand instructions. Learning how to use programs that usually won't run on a hard disk, activating "menu programs," and backing up data also are included in this information-packed book. *Managing Your Hard Disk* may well be the best thing that's happened to hard disk convertees. Keep your copy close by for handy reference.

Mail to: Que Corporation • P. O. Box 50507 • Indianapolis, IN 46250

Item	Title	Price	Quantity	Extension
130	Using 1-2-3, 2nd Edition	$21.95		
98	Using WordPerfect, 3rd Edition	$19.95		
180	Using PC DOS	$21.95		
67	Managing Your Hard Disk	$19.95		
		Book Subtotal		
	Shipping & Handling ($2.50 per item)			
	Indiana Residents Add 5% Sales Tax			
	GRAND TOTAL			

Method of Payment:

☐ Check   ☐ VISA   ☐ MasterCard   ☐ American Express

Card Number _____ Exp. Date _____

Cardholder's Name _____

Ship to _____

Address _____

City _____ State _____ ZIP _____

If you can't wait, call **1-800-428-5331** and order TODAY.

All prices subject to change without notice.

FOLD HERE

_____

_____

_____

_____

Place
Stamp
Here

Que Corporation
P. O. Box 50507
Indianapolis, IN 46250

REGISTER YOUR COPY OF
USING PAGEMAKER ON THE IBM

Register your copy of *Using PageMaker on the IBM* and receive information about Que's newest products. Complete this registration card and return it to Que Corporation, P.O. Box 50507, Indianapolis, IN 46250.

Name _____

Company _____ Title _____

Address _____

City _____ State _____ ZIP _____

Phone _____

Where did you buy your copy of *Using PageMaker on the IBM*?

_____

How do you plan to use this book?

_____

_____

_____

What other kinds of microcomputer publications would you be interested in?

_____

_____

_____

_____

Which operating system do you use? _____

_____

Do you have any other comments or suggestions? _____

_____

_____

THANK YOU!

FOLD HERE

_____

_____

_____

_____

Que Corporation
P. O. Box 50507
Indianapolis, IN 46250